Nation and Migration

Nation and Migration
Past and Future

Edited by David G. Gutiérrez and
Pierrette Hondagneu-Sotelo

The Johns Hopkins University Press, Baltimore

The Johns Hopkins University Press
2715 North Charles Street
Baltimore, Maryland 21218-4363
www.press.jhu.edu

ISBN 13: 978-0-8018-9281-3
ISBN 10: 0-8018-9281-3

Library of Congress Control Number: 20088936303

A catalog record for this book is available from the British Library.

These articles were originally published in the September 2008 issue of *American Quarterly*.

Cover design: Bill Longhauser. Front and back cover: *Sleep Dealer* (2008), directed by Alex Rivera, courtesy of Maya Releasing.

Special discounts are available for bulk purchases of this book. For more information, please contact Special Sales at 410-516-6936 or specialsales@press.jhu.edu.

The Johns Hopkins University Press uses environmentally friendly book materials, including recycled text paper that is composed of at least 30 percent post-consumer waste, whenever possible. All of our book papers are acid-free, and our jackets and covers are printed on paper with recycled content.

Contents

Writing Migration

Event Review

Preface

The images on the front and back covers of this book from *American Quarterly, Nation and Migration: Past and Future*, are from Alex Rivera's *The Sleep Dealer* (2008), a near-future science fiction film set in Mexico that reflects on the political economy of migration through the eyes of a would-be migrant worker. We are grateful to Alex and to Maya Entertainment, his distributor, for permission to reproduce them. As the director explains, the film

> basically uses the genre of science fiction to flash forward five minutes or five years to look at the politics between the United States (and Mexico) if they keep going the way they're going today. I guess science fiction is always looking at political and economic realities shot into the future, but this is from a perspective we haven't seen before: the U.S. from the outside . . . [I]n this future, the border is closed. Instead of physically coming to the United States, workers go to cities in Mexico and work in giant factories or sweatshops where they connect their bodies to high-speed, network-controlled robots that do their labor. So their pure labor crosses the border, but their bodies stay in Mexico. It's kind of a sick and twisted spin on the American dream.[1]

The Sleep Dealer develops a scenario Rivera first presented in *Why Cybraceros?* (1997), a short film in which a fictional corporation promises to use new computer technology to solve the "immigration problem." A satiric response to the "Internet utopianism" of the late 1990s, it incorporated footage from the 1959 agribusiness-made short called *Why Braceros?*, which attempted to dispel nativist opposition and promote the Bracero guest worker program by framing it as a temporary measure that would be unnecessary in the future, when agriculture would be largely automated.[2] Such agribusiness self-representations have long been haunted by science fiction fantasies of replacing migrant workers with machines. Though largely based in contemporary concerns, *The Sleep Dealer's* vision of the near future resonates with a longer history.

Ernesto Galarza's important study *Farm Workers and Agri-Business in California, 1947–1960* presents a history of mechanization and migrant farm labor that in some ways anticipates Rivera's near-future dystopia. Published in 1977, Galarza's work tells the story of how corporate agriculture effectively sought to discipline farmworkers and destroy their unions (including the local of the National Farm Workers Union that Galarza helped to organize after

World War II in California's San Joaquin Valley) by mechanizing production. During the late 1940s and early 1950s, according to Galarza, automatic machines "were taking over" in the orchards and fields, using electronic "brains" and "eyes" to plant, tend, harvest, and sort produce. Agribusiness machinery "became awesome, like the motorized cotton picker; graceful, like the spidery walnut pruner; delicate, like the electronic lemon sorter; or spectral, like the eighty-foot land leveler moving through clouds of its own dust." Particularly striking for Galarza was the automated cotton harvester that, along with its "mechanical partners" the cotton "planter-cultivator" and "the scrapper that salvaged un-harvested bolls . . . could move in formation sweeping through hundreds of acres of cotton fluff like a rumbling herd of trunkless elephants" or "an assembly out of science fiction."[3]

But while the dream of mechanization was "to eliminate people from production," that goal could never be completely realized.[4] Rather than totally eliminate migrant workers, mechanization enabled agribusiness to reduce its labor force but also to restructure and discipline the remaining workers. The introduction of new automatic sorters, for instance, served to deskill certain jobs. "As packing operations moved from town sheds to movable assemblies on wheels they were reclassified as field work with lower rates of pay."[5] At the same time women were substituted for men on the moving harvesting rigs and were paid less. More dramatically, mechanization in the fields was meshed with the Bracero Program. As part of an agreement between the United States and Mexico, between 1942 and 1964 the Bracero Program brought millions of Mexican contract workers to the United States. In *Farm Workers and Agri-Business*, Galarza noted that the program was molded by corporate lobbyists and reflected "the vertical integration of government with private interests" in California agriculture.[6] In an earlier work called *Strangers in Our Fields* (1956), he analyzed the imperial dimensions of the Bracero Program's mass militarization of migrant labor. As part of his research for the book, Galarza visited and photographed a variety of institutional spaces where braceros were housed, including a massive cattle corral with open privies in Yuba City as well as a barbwired military base and a county fair cattle pavilion in Stockton. (I was reminded of these images recently when it was revealed that the migrant workers from Mexico and Guatemala arrested at an Iowa meatpacking plant as part of the largest single-site federal immigration raid in U.S. history were detained at the livestock pavilion of a local fairground.)[7] Galarza thus analyzed a situation in which agribusiness technology was fetishized in ways that partly obscured or distracted attention from the industry's ongoing dependence on migrant farm labor.

These different historical visions of the future of migration suggest that migration is not a marginal, episodic, or temporary feature of life in the United States but rather a central and permanent part of it—and hence a topic of ongoing interest for scholars in and around American studies. The juxtaposition of these very different moments further reveals continuities in their ideologies and fantasies about migration that simultaneously undermine linear narratives of progress while potentially bringing into even sharper relief the relative distinctiveness of each moment. A similar yet much more expansive perspective on such continuities among differences is well represented by individual essays and this special issue as a whole. Indeed, the volume is complexly comparative in terms of different histories, diasporas, and national and regional contexts. Contributors engage the topic from a variety of disciplinary and interdisciplinary perspectives, including ethnic studies, history, sociology, anthropology, literary studies, and politics and international relations. And finally, recalling the migrant eye's view of Rivera's film, a number of authors critically and self-reflexively research and analyze the concrete experiences of migrants themselves.

Many people working together have made this book possible, starting with its guest editors, David G. Gutiérrez and Pierrette Hondagneu-Sotelo, whose keen and generous intellects shaped the project at every turn. I would also like to thank the members of the *American Quarterly* managing editorial board who read and commented on the final group of essays, including Grace Hong, Lisa Lowe, Laura Pulido, and Dylan Rodríguez. Orlando Serrano and Jeb Middlebrook, *American Quarterly*'s excellent outgoing and incoming managing editors, have contributed greatly to the project, as have editorial assistants Kristen Fuhs, Karen Alonzo, Jaclyn Mahoney, Sara Rogers, and Paul Saiedi. Stacey Lynn copyedited the volume with great care and skill, and Bill Longhauser designed the striking cover.

We are also grateful to the Department of American Studies and Ethnicity, the College of Arts and Science, the Critical Studies Department, and the School of Cinematic Arts at the University of Southern California, whose support enabled us to complete this project.

Curtis Marez
Editor
American Quarterly

Notes

1. Interview with Alex Rivera, *The Reeler*, January 23, 2008, http://www.thereeler.com/sundance_features/alex_rivera_sleep_dealer.php (accessed June 19, 2008).
2. Both films can be viewed online. For *Why Cybraceros?* see the director's Web site, http://www.invisibleamerica.com/movies.html (accessed June 19, 2008). For *Why Braceros?* see the Internet Archive, http://www.archive.org/details/WhyBrace1959 (accessed June 19, 2008).
3. All quotations in this paragraph are from Ernesto Galarza, *Farm Workers and Agri-Business in California, 1947–1960* (Notre Dame: University of Notre Dame Press, 1977), 66–69.
4. Ibid., 71.
5. Ibid.
6. Ibid., 86.
7. *Des Moines Register*, May 12, 2008. http://www.desmoinesregister.com/apps/pbcs.dll/article?AID=/20080512/NEWS/80512012/1001 (accessed on June 16, 2008).

Nation and Migration

Introduction
Nation and Migration

David G. Gutiérrez and Pierrette Hondagneu-Sotelo

It is not an exaggeration to argue that much of the terrain in American studies—and in the humanities and social sciences more generally—has been transformed in recent years by a fundamental reconsideration of the relationship between capitalism, the nation-state, and human migration spurred by the so-called transnational turn. Born of the historical conjuncture of the global economic crisis of the early 1970s, the worldwide decline of Fordism and the gradual ascendance of neoliberal economic philosophy, and the movement of ever increasing numbers of economically displaced populations from less developed regions of the world to established metropoles and developing regions, a growing number of scholars and social critics have shifted their vantage points away from analyses that were formerly rooted largely or exclusively in single nation-states to new perspectives that are much more attentive to transnational social fields created through the ongoing interactions between the world system of nations, the expansions and contractions of global capitalism, and the movement of human populations.

Although the linked notions of globalization and transnationalism have only recently come into wide usage as conceptual tools, a small number of perceptive social critics and scholars had begun to explore these phenomena much earlier. Indeed, as early as the first decades of the twentieth century, during the height of what might be termed the first era of intensive economic globalization, forward thinking social critics such as Randolph Bourne, as well as migration scholars such as William I. Thomas and Florian Znaniecki, Paul Schuster Taylor, and a few others had begun to explore what they recognized to be systemic linkages between capitalist development, state policing of labor migration, and the emergence of an increasingly integrated global economic system. These important interpreters of the early twentieth century brought very different points of view to bear on the profound changes they saw unfolding around them. But together, Bourne's ruminations on the possible emergence of a cosmopolitan "trans-national" America (1916), Thomas and Znaniecki's innovative exploration of the complex social and economic networks linking Polish peasants in Europe to new communities of settlement in the United States (1918–1920), and Taylor's prescient analysis of the accelerating integration of the Mexican and American economies and labor markets (1928–1932) can all be seen as early examples of an experimental transnational scholarship.[1]

It was not until nearly a half-century later, however, that scholars and social critics began to explore more comprehensively some of the insights first suggested by these pathbreaking social analysts. Although forms of what are now recognizable as the notions of "transnationalism" and the "transnational" were articulated in a different context as early as the early 1970s,[2] it was not until the late 1980s and into the 1990s that these ideas began to gain currency and wider discussion. A special number of the *Annals of the American Academy of Political and Social Science* published in 1986, devoted to "transnational migration and the emergence of new minorities," signaled a strong shift in this direction.[3] In the 1990s, another quantum leap occurred with the publication of a number of important studies that explicated a multifarious transnational project.[4] Again, while each of these important authors brought a unique emphasis to his or her research, together, the publication of these works signaled a sea change in the conceptualization of the nexus between economic restructuring, population movement, cultural production and reproduction, and the future of the nation-state. Attempting to move beyond the conceptual constraints imposed by the shaping force of "methodological nationalism"[5]—and the teleological assumptions about immigrant incorporation that stem from it—revisionist thinkers sought to explore what the anthropologist Roger Rouse has called the "alternative cartography of social space" of transnational migratory circuits.[6] Defined by proponents as the interstitial social spaces traversed and occupied by migrants in their sojourns between places of origin and places of destination, transnational spaces are envisioned as multisited "imagined communities" whose boundaries stretch across the borders of two or more nation-states.

Space limitations preclude a full review of the contributions made by scholars and critics who employed transnational perspectives in their work, but several clear trends have emerged since the mid-1980s. On the most fundamental level, this kind of work forced gradual recognition of the extent to which the emergence of transnational social fields (of more or less historical durability depending on local circumstance) had long been a common corollary of the use of foreign labor by developed and developing countries—and that this phenomena appears to have intensified with the current spate of global economic restructurings. Innovation and expansion in transportation and communication technology also facilitated the frequency of transnational contacts and connections.

These insights have led to a tremendous transformation of historical scholarship in recent years as historians, historical sociologists, and others set out to explore how both the permanent settlement and the more or less permanent *circulation* of migrants and immigrants have been central dynamics of capitalist expansion since at least the late eighteenth century.[7] Growing awareness of the permanence of both population settlement *and* population circulation stimulated by the expansion of capitalism led historians and other critical scholars to reconsider definitions of local "community"—and to point to the notion of the "translocal" as another way to conceive of human migration and demographic change. This is perhaps the most crucial single conceptual leap transnational scholars have contributed to debates over the trajectory of modernity. By shifting conception of human migration away from notions of a linear progression of people moving from one place to another to a model of an innovative social formation "that links transmigrants, the localities to which they migrate, and their locality of origin," transnational scholarship has emphasized the historical ubiquity of transnational circuits characterized by reciprocal social relations at each terminus as central components in the evolution of global capitalism.[8]

Transnational life and translocal communities take multiple forms today, reflecting the diversity of class composition and national origins of contemporary migrants. During the late twentieth century, and into the first decade of the current one, we have witnessed an upsurge in the migration of elites. Unlike the classic narrative of labor migration that begins with entry at the bottom echelons of national social and economic hierarchies, elites begin by entering at the top. These processes are tightly bound to the development of global capitalism, as business and professional elites associated with sectors of finance, import-export, and post-Fordist hi-tech industry have now joined labor migrants in movements around the globe.[9] Many of these elite migrants, particularly those from China and South Asia, begin their U.S. sojourns in American universities, clustering in the fields of science, engineering, and computers, leading Aihwa Ong to conclude that universities in the United States are increasingly becoming "an extension of world trade."[10] In the process, Ong argues, what were once national institutions of higher learning are transforming into transnational institutions, and perhaps tilting the educational focus from political liberalism, humanities, and multiculturalism toward producing neoliberal "borderless entrepreneurial subjects abroad."[11]

The upsurge in the transnational migration of elites, in tandem with other processes, has also prompted new citizenship arrangements. Not only the United States but also Canada, Mexico, Asian nations, and the European Union are adopting neoliberal forms of citizenship based on market calculations, bringing about new forms of "flexible citizenship"[12] as well as new forms of exclusion.[13] When people hold multiple passports allowing them to do business in multiple nations, and when nations offer millionaire investors fast tracks to legal status and citizenship while denying the same rights to those who have lived and worked for decades within the national territory, then our old familiar way of thinking about citizenship as the rights of those who "belong" to a particular nation-state seem anachronistic, almost quaint.

Yet the project of disarticulating citizenship rights from belonging to a particular national territory is far from complete. Not only is it uneven but globalization and transnationalism are also accompanied by new intensive expressions of nationalism, even as they promote what Sassen has called new "assemblages of territory, authority, and rights."[14] Partial inclusions and exclusions are now the norm.[15]

Acknowledgment of these social and political processes has provoked new conceptual trends. For example, by challenging state-centered hagiographic descriptive and prescriptive accounts of the existence of homogeneous national cultures and the inevitable "assimilation" of various émigré populations into those presumed dominant cultures, such insights also raised important questions about the notion of national citizenship and other institutional features of the nation-state. While the institution of national citizenship has long been broadly accepted as an emancipatory institutional feature of liberal democracies,[16] recent scholarship has raised a number of serious questions about this premise. Some critics have pointed to the institution's fundamentally exclusionary nature and dependence on the negative referent of noncitizens to give it meaning.[17] Others have noted how easily the institution has been manipulated to effect internal discrimination, produce "illegality," and maintain various types of hierarchies within the nation despite claims of the inherent and universal equality of citizens.[18] Still others have noted the complex ways noncitizens themselves decided to engage—or chose *not* to engage—local politics of citizenship.[19]

Indeed, in one of the most compelling recent trends in this kind of critical research, a growing number of scholars have begun to explore the ways in which national citizenship has often been deployed in contradictory ways by different subaltern players. At one end of the spectrum, some analysts have demonstrated how contact between differentially racialized populations in certain contexts sometimes results in the emergence of panethnicity or other forms of coalition building that use citizenship as a jumping-off point for political organization and mobilization.[20] At the other end of the spectrum, however, scholars have explored the ways in which certain groups of "native minorities" and transmigrants often utilized their own claims to formal national membership as a tool to reproduce various types of social hierarchies and asymmetries of power. This has been particularly apparent in contexts in which recent immigrants and migrants are thrown into close contact with other racialized groups. Under such pressurized social situations, contact between racialized "domestic minorities" and émigré groups can stimulate intergroup competition and conflict even among populations that are otherwise nearly identical in their material circumstances and social positioning vis-à-vis the "host" society. In such cases, citizenship status was—and often is—used as a cudgel against groups perceived as threats, as in the recent case study by De Genova and Ramos-Zayas of the relationship between Puerto Rican and Mexican immigrant residents of Chicago.[21]

Nevertheless, neither casual observers nor scholars can afford to ignore the recent emergence of a full-blown immigrant rights movement in the United States, the demands around which it organized, and the challenges this poses to thinking about nation, migration, and citizenship. This movement developed in response to nationalist restrictionist measures, and it was strategically nurtured over time with support from various sectors, including organized labor and religion, and with organizers using new communications technologies such as nationally disseminated Spanish language radio, conference calls, and the Internet.[22] The spring 2006 marches were the largest show of immigrant rights support ever witnessed in the United States, but here's the rub: although globalization and transnationalism characterize the present moment, the resurgent immigrant rights movement in the United States has paradoxically focused squarely on claims to rights located at a national level, namely legalization and citizenship. The meanings of acquiring a particular national citizenship are certainly changing, as increasingly people seek U.S. citizenship for protection from deportation and for the pursuit of economic opportunity,[23] but it is nonetheless striking that at this particular historical moment, immigrant rights claims are still made on the nation, not on transnational, supranational, or global institutions. Moreover, "integration"—social, economic, and political—is emerging as the strategic operative framework in nearly all postindustrial societies of immigration.[24]

Transnational scholarship has also brought into sharper relief the ubiquity of both historical and contemporary examples of the process of cultural hybridization and bricolage that mass population movements have inevitably caused. Heightened awareness of the process of cultural melding and cultural innovation has led, in turn, to a number of other important conceptual trends. For example, scholars of transnationalism and citizenship have turned increasing attention to indigenous migrants from Mexico, Central America, and the Andean region who grapple with the many ambiguities involved in the establishment of their own transnational circuits. Members of these populations, who often speak Spanish as a second language (if at all) and are racialized in specific ways within their own nations of origin, are compelled to negotiate entirely different systems of racial, cultural, national, and class hierarchies when they migrate. This process of negotiation often results in the formation of new subjectivities and panethnic senses of collective political identity that reflect their unique social positioning in a shifting borderlands matrix among competing national societies.[25]

Scholars exploring gender and transnational networks and circuits among labor migrants have exposed similar contradictions, shedding light on both the micro and macro sociological levels. At the macro level, observers have noted a shift in gendered patterns of transnational labor recruitment. Migrant men were once recruited to do "men's work" in building industrial infrastructure, with Chinese, Filipino, Japanese, Irish, Italian, and Mexican men taking turns in systems of subordinated labor regimes in nineteenth and twentieth century America. The Bracero Program, which issued nearly 5 million temporary labor contracts to Mexican agricultural workers (and smaller numbers of workers originating in the Caribbean) in the United States between 1942 and 1964, and various guest worker programs in postwar Europe, which recruited Turkish, Algerian, and Italian men to rebuild cities and stoke factories in postwar Western Europe, are exemplars of these modern systems. These systems depended on state-enforced circular migration and gave rise simultaneously to both transnational communities of men who were denied full membership and family life in the societies where they worked *and* to the development of permanent settlement and major demographic transitions.

Today, with the decline of Fordist manufacturing and the expansion of service sectors in postindustrial societies, new state systems and informal mechanisms facilitate the recruitment and absorption of women into service and social reproductive jobs such as nursing, care work, and cleaning jobs of all sorts around the globe.[26] New regional and transnational circuits have emerged, and different state apparatus accompany these changes. Many of the newly industrializing Asian nations, such as Taiwan, Hong Kong, and Singapore, as well as oil-rich Middle Eastern nations rely on state projects to recruit and control migrant domestic workers.[27] These systems allow women into intimate domestic spaces, yet deny their full integration and belonging in society, keeping them "perpetual foreigners."[28] Meanwhile, the nations from which they originate seek to capture remittances, and hence they collaborate on contract labor programs that mandate the submission of transnational workers. Consequently, nations such as the Philippines, Indonesia, Sri Lanka, and Thailand actively promote transnational migration of women. In the Philippines, both the state and the media encourage "hero" veneration of the women who work abroad and the notion of the Philippines as "home," thereby ensuring the migrant women's participation in nation-building economic projects and discouraging new claims on the societies in which they work.[29]

This scholarship is a good reminder that gender is implicated in migration processes not only at the level of family and households but also in the state and political economy. In fact, in hindsight we can see that earlier scholarship on migration and gender focused almost exclusively on gender renegotiations in families and households, with debates centering on the relative empowerment of women and relative disenfranchisement of men and patriarchy brought about through migration.[30] These debates continue,[31] but feminist scholarship of migration now recognizes other institutions and sites—jobs, workplaces, citizenship, public opinion, immigration law, and the media to name a few—as important locations of inquiry into the intersections of gender and transnationalism.[32] This scholarship on gender and transnationalism calls attention to the ways in which gender constructions inform new transnational occupations, such as cross-border couriers;[33] the nature of transnational family forms, such as transnational motherhood, fatherhood, and childhood;[34] the disciplining of female sexuality through transnational imaginaries;[35] and the ways in which new transnational hometown migrant associations can serve as spaces for "masculine gendered projects," allowing migrant men to recapture lost social status.[36] Clearly, transnationalism has helped propel inquiries of gender and migration beyond the confines of family and households.

Of course, a paradigm shift of the magnitude that has occurred with the emergence of transnational scholarship has inevitably stimulated a critical backlash among observers who have questioned some of the larger claims made at the height of the first wave of this kind of scholarship and social critique. One of the earliest critics of the transnational turn was the social historian

Peter Kivisto, who cast a critical eye on the utility of transnationalism as a novel conceptual tool.[37] One of his main criticisms—and one that has since been articulated by others[38]—centered on what he argued is the ahistoricism of early proponents of the concept. While acknowledging that rapid technological advances in communication, transportation, and relations of production have greatly facilitated potential migrants' ability to move between nations, Kivisto and critics like him insist that regional and transnational circuits had been a common feature of capitalist restructuring from the dawn of the industrial age. He thus tends to dismiss most of the claims of novelty made by the first wave of transnational scholarship in the late 1980s and early 1990s. Beyond this, Kivisto advances the case that although its initial proponents intended the model of transnationalism as a replacement for what they considered to be outmoded models of assimilation and cultural pluralism, he finds that the older models not only remain applicable to earlier periods of immigration history, but that they remain serviceable in providing convincing explanatory frameworks for contemporary patterns of migration and immigrant incorporation.[39] Moreover, Kivisto questions whether the manifestations of transnationalism that *are* observable (remittances, hometown associations, émigré political activity) are not simply common first-generation activities that are destined to wane with subsequent generations.

Other observers have been even more scathing in their criticism. Of this group, the most strident is probably UCLA sociologist Roger Waldinger. In a series of single- and coauthored articles,[40] Waldinger and his colleagues have gone so far as to dismiss the transnational turn in the social sciences as little more than an "intellectual fashion."[41] As with many critics of transnational frames of reference, Waldinger and his colleagues level particularly harsh criticism at those who either implicitly or explicitly see transnational phenomena as evidence of a weakening of the state, its institutions, and its functions in the modern world. To the contrary, they insist, virtually any action occurring transnationally a priori and necessarily "involves the *interaction* of migrants with states and civil society actors in both sending and receiving countries."[42] More recently, Waldinger has amplified his earlier critique. Noting the inconsistencies and vagueness among transnational scholars in defining both transnationalism as a social process and "transmigrants" as social actors, he reviews recent polling data among immigrants of different duration of residence to assess the empirical basis for such claims. Based on this review, Waldinger argues that over time, the coercive forces of state regulation of movement, combined with the forces of integration experienced by long-term immigrants, makes transnationalism an ephemeral phenomenon actively practiced by only a small minority. In a ringing indictment of the assumptions he sees as undergirding transnational scholarship, he concludes: "given these myriad, contradictory pressures, many international migrants may engage in trans-state social action of one form or another, but 'transnationalism' is a relatively rare condition of being. . . . Likewise, 'transmigrants,' understood as a 'class of persons' generally do not exist."[43]

The fourteen essays in this special number of *American Quarterly* make important interventions in a number of the ongoing debates discussed above. We begin with a section on the state and citizenship. State power is seen most clearly in the restriction and disciplining of migrant subjects, so it is no accident that the essays gathered in this first section, Citizenship and State Power, examine the contemporary mechanisms through which immigrants' exclusions and partial inclusions are regulated by agents and institutions of the state. In the first essay, Rachel Ida Buff analyzes the recent wave of deportation raids in the United States as part of a long legacy of racialized social control, one with strong echoes of deportation practices used against Mexicans and others during the height of the McCarthy era in the mid-twentieth century. Buff argues that while ostensibly designed in the post-9/11 era to regulate the threat of terrorist "others," these new mechanisms employed by the aptly Orwellian named Homeland Security and ICE (the Bureau of Immigrant and Customs Enforcement) depend on the mobilization of terror through the threat and practice of deportation and forcible removal. Here, Buff encourages us to see deportation not as an exception, but rather "a social process constitutive of the nation across different periods."

In the current period, we have also witnessed discontinuities in forms of restrictionism and exclusions. Here, Philip Kretsedemas provides an important examination of a relatively recent phenomenon in the United States, the rise of state and municipal efforts to control, restrict, and regulate migration. U.S. immigration law has always emphasized selective and racialized restrictionism, starting with the Page Law of 1875 and the Chinese Exclusion Act of 1882 (although it should be noted that regulation of immigration remained largely adjudicated by state and local officials up until this time). But these laws, and subsequent legislation, held immigration to be a federal matter handled at the national level. Now, something new is happening: local municipalities and states are trying to retake immigration control into their own hands. One of the earliest and perhaps the most infamous instances of this is California's Proposition 187, an initiative passed by California voters in 1994 to deny undocumented immigrants and their children access to education and health services. In 2007, at least 180 immigration control measures were passed by local government entities. Kretsedemas argues that these measures signal a new neoliberal governing strategy, one based on a type of nationalism that paradoxically ruptures the nation-state and traditional ways of thinking about national citizenship and sovereignty.

The current era of globalization and the consolidation of the European Union (EU) have allowed nations such as Ireland, Italy, and Spain to transform in a few decades from being nations of labor emigration to sites of labor immigration. These rapid transformations have prompted realignments in citizenship policies, and in their essay, authors JoAnne Mancini and Graham Finlay examine the Irish 2004 referendum to deny territorial birthright citizenship to newcomers. This revocation of jus soli, the authors argue, represents an unambiguously nondemocratic approach to citizenship, a model that should be consciously resisted in the United States and elsewhere. In fact, it replicates the old story of ambivalent migrant welcome—the recruitment and welcome of workers but not members of the nation.

If, on one level, access to citizenship is about empowering oneself and one's community in a particular environment, then it is important to examine the agency and meanings with which migrant subjects approach the processes of naturalization. In his contribution, Adrián Félix conducts a political ethnography of a Southern California citizenship class. While Mexicans historically have had the lowest rates of naturalization in the United States, in recent years, rising rates of naturalization have prompted debates about what this trend signifies. Does it suggest assimilation and the adoption of American patriotism or, conversely, a certain defensiveness and strategy of self-protection in a hostile climate? While there are many motives for naturalization, Félix argues that a "reactive naturalization," one that is rooted in both a hostile context of reception *and*, importantly, in a positive, proactive stance toward political enfranchisement, best characterizes contemporary processes. While naturalization is often thought of in individualistic fashion, the empirical work here draws attention to the collective effervescence, solidarity, and emotional work that is involved in this political project. Félix predicts that the acquisition of U.S. citizenship will foster immigrant political engagement on both sides of the border.

The next section brings different views to bear on the increasingly controversial and debated phenomenon of transnationalism. Indeed, the section's first article by Laura Briggs, Gladys McCormick, and J. T. Way grapples with some of the central areas of debate we have touched upon earlier in this introduction. On one level a rumination on the uses and abuses of the concept of transnationalism, this piece is also an effort to take stock of the extremely unsettled historical moment scholars of transnational phenomena currently face. Seeking to develop what they unabashedly call a "politically left intellectual tradition," the authors survey a variety of critical historiographical and theoretical interventions in this direction. In developing this alternative cartography, Briggs, McCormick, and Way juxtapose and link a number of recent intellectual trends that are often not explicitly compared. This is particularly true of their insightful discussion of "Third World" feminisms. They illustrate the many ways that critical interventions by feminist scholars of color have served as a tonic against some of the totalizing and often imperial tendencies of "white feminism," while at the same time pointing to similar tendencies among certain contemporary transnational scholars. Turning finally to the sites of their own specific areas of research, the individual authors begin to map new ways to critique nationalism and the constantly morphing nation-state, while simultaneously helping to point to some potentially fruitful ways that thoughtful and disciplined transnational approaches might improve social, cultural, and political analysis.

Cultural critic Fatima El-Tayeb turns a similarly keen eye on the phenomenon of transnationalism, in this case by exploring the contradictions exposed by the consolidation of the EU. A meditation on what she sees as the intentional elisions involved in the emergence of this particular form of supranational political reorganization, El-Tayeb's contribution shines a bright light on the EU's consistent refusal to deal honestly with the permanent presence and significance of its racialized immigrant and "domestic minority" populations. She notes that just as the borders and passport controls between member states were relaxed within the boundaries of the EU, another comprehensive system of informal controls and limitations to social membership were erected, most visibly against Europe's African and Muslim residents—and crucially, against their European-born children as well. Indeed, drawing obvious comparisons to the ways that many Asian and Latin American populations in the United States are inscribed with a kind of perpetual foreignness—regardless of the length of their actual residence in the country—El-Tayeb demonstrates the ways that the status of "migrant" has been an inherited label applied to the children born and raised in Europe and the grandchildren of people who had migrated to the continent many years before. In El-Tayeb's analysis, this has led to the current impasse in the European Union: while touted as a model of postnational cosmopolitan political organization, the EU is actually a site in which powerful and increasingly sophisticated new technologies of differentiation, ascription, and what she calls "externalization" are being applied to proscribed minorities. Thus, in her view, many of the mechanisms of social sorting and social control that had previously been perfected and imposed at the level of the nation-state are now being reproduced in powerful new forms on a supranational level.

Kornel Chang takes another critical tack on the history of transnationalism by examining the joint efforts by the governments of Canada and the United States to develop new regimes of immigration control in the Pacific Northwest in an era that previously had been characterized by more or less free-flowing labor migration. His careful case study of the steady hardening of the U.S.-Canadian border in the aftermath of passage of the first Chinese exclusion laws illustrates the ways in which competing interests—including labor recruiters, self-described "native" American and Canadian workers, South and East Asian migrants, and agents of both states—collided in the early years of the twentieth century. Based on close analysis of a wide range of primary sources, Chang's study explicates the manner in which binational immigration policy, when combined with mutually increased border surveillance and enforcement efforts, transformed patterns of regional labor migration informally regulated by human agency and local markets into an early version of modern strategies for comprehensive state management, rationalization, and control of these processes.

How do migrant subjects and communities experience their liminal positions and the multiple forms of exclusion and partial inclusions? This next section, Migrant Experiences, addresses precisely this question. In the opening essay in the section, Sunaina Maira focuses on a group of South Asian Muslims that does not usually receive much public or scholarly attention: youth. Based on qualitative research conducted with South Asian Muslim teens in New England, Maira examines their experiences of displacement and belonging. In the post-9/11 climate of intensified hostility and scrutiny, these teens sought solace and strength by crafting deliberately transnational identities. Cultural citizenship, as expressed particularly through popular culture found in Bollywood films, South Asian television programs, and Hindi Web sites was important to them, as was a kind of "aspirational citizenship" as expressed through the desire for higher education and economic mobility.

In her contribution, Elaine A. Peña examines the aesthetic and political dimensions of transnational religiosity. Here, the focus is on the creation of a transnational sacred space, where devotional performances of prayer, pilgrim-age, dance, and hymns allow Mexican labor migrants from central Mexico to create a sense of "home" in Chicago, and yet simultaneously incorporate other Latino immigrants in their alternative religious spaces. Guadalupanos (worshippers of the Virgin of Guadalupe) create a Second Tepayac in Chicago, and in the process they construct new spaces that are at once transnational, multiethnic, spiritually powerful, and politically empowering.

Racial exclusions of migrants are widely acknowledged as a major promoter of transnationalism, but in the next essay in this section, historian Julie Weise examines Mexicans in the South during the early twentieth century and offers some surprising findings and analysis. Weise skillfully traces the ways Mexico's racial politics—particularly the postrevolutionary ideology of *mestizaje* and cultural whitening—melded with New Orleans' own complex racial traditions in the era of Jim Crow. She shows that in New Orleans and the Mis-sissippi Delta, the black-white binary created incentives and opportunities for Mexicans to embrace a European-like white ethnic identity. Bolstered by class resources, Mexican migrants imported their own racial categorization and rhetoric of national homogeneity from Mexico, laying claim to white privilege, yet in the process, they appear to have dampened transnational ties and connections.

The final essay in this section focuses on the creation, maintenance, and legacies of illegal immigrant status. Here, Claudia Sadowski-Smith brings a much needed historical perspective to the phenomenon of unauthorized migration associated with economic globalization. She points out that al-though unsanctioned entry into the United States has long been coded as "Mexican," the issue of illegality has antecedents that lie much earlier in the history of the Industrial Revolution and the worldwide economic restructuring that accompanied it. Like other recent historians of migration,[44] Sadowski-Smith perceptively notes that the passage of nearly any kind of law almost inevitably produces outlaws—and that this is particularly true in the case of immigration law and national border enforcement. She traces the process of the ever-widening net of criminalization to the first years of the twentieth century, noting how successive groups of transmigrants were sanctioned or outlawed in turn. Sadowski-Smith's historical analysis of what she calls "the spiral of illegality" provides an important contextual backdrop that adds to our understanding of what increasingly appears to be the capricious and arbitrary policing of national borders in an era of intensifying globalization.

In the final section of this special issue of the journal, Writing Migration, Asha Nadkarni and Sarika Chandra delve into different dimensions of literary representations of the entwined processes of imperialism, globalization, and transnational migration.

In her subtle and insightful essay, Asha Nadkarni provides a close critical reading of Katherine Mayo's inflammatory polemic *Mother India* to analyze what the book and its author reveal about the relationship between Anglo-American imperialism, immigration, and projected anxieties about women's sexuality in the first decades of the last century. Nadkarni carefully maps an extremely complex historical juncture in which growing opposition to British imperial rule in India among certain Progressive-era Americans uneasily coexisted with an even more powerful movement to exclude Indians—and all other potential Asian immigrants—both from entry into the United States and access to U.S. citizenship. Against this contradictory historical backdrop, Nadkarni explores the ingenious manner in which Mayo combined Progressive-era ideas about science, hygiene, and public health—as well as reactionary notions about the role of women and mothers in the reproduction of the nation—to build an argument that simultaneously advocated the continuation of stern imperial (remote) control over the Indian subcontinent as part of a larger policy of cultural containment that included shoring up U.S. borders against Indian (and pan-Asian) contagion. Reminiscent of contemporary American imperial discourses that seek to influence political, economic, moral, and environmental issues abroad to the advantage of vested U.S. interests, Nadkarni concludes that Mayo was well ahead of her time in redefining empire as a strategy to "extend a strong arm overseas as a[nother] means of policing the boundaries of the nation at home."

In her contribution, Chandra sets out to wrestle with the complex positioning of "American literature" (or more accurately, "U.S. literature") within a global frame. Chandra draws on some of the critical insights generated both by scholarship on transnationalism and the history of citizenship to cast a skeptical eye on the shifting intellectual and ideological contexts of the production of "American" literatures. Beyond this, she is centrally focused on the different ways discourses on "American ethnic identity" and "multiculturalism" have covertly helped to reproduce traditional U.S. "nationalist paradigms." To do this, she revisits Julia Alvarez's widely read *How the García Girls Lost Their Accent*. Chandra, while noting that Alvarez's novel—and similar semi-autobiographical examples of this kind of ethnic literature—has often been portrayed as speaking against the grain of the presumed canon of American literature by allowing alternative voices to be heard, carefully demonstrates how this work, and the larger genre of which it is a part, often helps to reproduce the same kind of positivist/nationalist narrative it supposedly critiques. Adding her own critical reading to other thematic treatments of the novel, Chandra calls for a new level of criticism that takes into account the ways a long and continuing history of American imperialism and cultural domination of far distant lands colonize regional consciousness and often help to shape and subvert, if not completely predetermine, expressions of cultural difference and dissent both at "home" and "abroad."

In the final contribution, Sasha Costanza-Chock calls our attention to the use of new technologies in the contemporary immigrant rights mobilizations. Reflecting on the backlash and the violence incurred at Los Angeles' Macarthur Park during the one-year anniversary of the immigrant rights marches, where police brutality extended to journalists and was captured on popular videos and Internet sites, Costanza-Chock forces us to think about how the democratization of new technologies can serve as tools against repression. Although MySpace, YouTube, and text messaging were all widely envisioned as potential democratic communication breakthroughs, Costanza-Chock's essay cautions community and scholar-activists to be aware not only of how such media are being "monetized" but also how they can be used as tools of surveillance and political control. The trick, he suggests, is to utilize new communications technologies while remaining vigilant about the different uses to which they can be put. As the essays gathered in this volume suggest, there are many borders to cross in the new scholarship on migration and nation, and sometimes unexpected sites, like these new technologies, hold the promise of progressive transformation.

Notes
1. Randolph Bourne, "Trans-National America," *Atlantic Monthly*, July 1916, 86–97; William I. Thomas and Florian Znaniecki, *The Polish Peasant in Europe and America: Monograph of an Immigrant Group*, 5 vols. (Chicago: University of Chicago Press, 1918–1920); Paul S. Taylor, *Mexican Labor in the United States*, 4 vols. (Berkeley: University of California Press, 1928–1932).
2. Joseph Nye and Robert O. Keohane, "Transnational Relations and World Politics: An Introduction," *International Organization* 25.3 (Summer 1971): 329–49.
3. Martin O. Heisler and Barbara Schmitter Heisler, eds., "From Foreign Workers to Settlers? Transnational Migration and the Emergence of New Minorities," special issue of *Annals of the American Academy of Political and Social Science* 485 (May 1986).
4. See, for example, Arjun Appadurai, *Modernity at Large: Cultural Dimensions of Globalization* (Minneapolis: University of Minnesota Press, 1996); Linda Basch, Nina Glick Schiller, and Cristina Blanc-Szanton, *Nations Unbound: Transnational Projects, Postcolonial Predicaments, and Deterritorialized Nation-States* (New York: Gordon and Breach, 1994); Thomas Faist, "Transnationalization in International Migration: Implications for the Study of Citizenship and Culture," *Ethnic and Racial Studies* 23.2 (2000): 189–222; Ulf Hannerz, *Transnational Connections: Culture, People, Places* (Lon-

don: Routledge, 1996); Michael Kearney, "Borders and Boundaries of State and Self at the End of Empire," *Journal of Historical Sociology* 4.1 (1991): 52–74; Peggy Levitt, *The Transnational Villagers* (Berkeley: University of California Press, 2001); Alejandro Portes, Luis Guarnizo, and Patricia Landolt, "The Study of Transnationalism: Pitfalls and Promise of an Emergent Research Field," *Ethnic and Racial Studies* 22.2 (1999): 217–37; Roger Rouse, "Mexican Migration and the Social Space of Postmodernism," *Diaspora* 1.1 (1991): 8–23; Saskia Sassen, *Losing Control? Sovereignty in an Age of Globalization* (New York: Columbia University Press, 1996); Michael Peter Smith and Luis Guarnizo, eds., *Transnationalism from Below* (New York: Transaction, 1998); and Stephen Vertovec, "Conceiving and Researching Transnationalism," *Ethnic and Racial Studies* 22.2 (1999): 447–62. For an excellent review of the development of the field, see Peggy Levitt and B. Nadya Jaworsky, "Transnational Migration Studies: Past Development and Future Trends," *Annual Review of Sociology* 33 (2007): 129–56.

5. See Andreas Wimmer and Nina Glick Schiller, "Methodological Nationalism, the Social Sciences, and the Study of Migration: An Essay in Historical Epistemology," *International Migration Review* 37.3 (2003): 576–610.

6. Rouse, "Mexican Migration," 12. See also Avtar Brah, *Cartographies of Diaspora: Contesting Identities* (London: Routledge, 1996).

7. Adam McKeown, "Global Migration, 1846–1940," *Journal of World History* 15. 2 (2004): 155–89, and "Periodizing Globalization," *History Workshop Journal* 63 (Spring 2007): 218–30.

8. Michael Peter Smith and Luis Guarnizo, "The Locations of Transnationalism," in *Transnationalism from Below*, ed. Smith and Guarnizo, 13.

9. See Alejandro Portes and Rubén Rumbaut, *Immigrant America: A Portrait*, 3rd ed. (Berkeley: University of California Press, 2006).

10. Aihwa Ong, *Neoliberalism as Exception: Mutations in Citizenship and Sovereignty* (Durham, N.C.: Duke University Press, 2006): 140.

11. Ibid.

12. Aihwa Ong, *Flexible Citizenship: The Cultural Logics of Transnationality* (Durham, N.C.: Duke University Press, 1999).

13. See Stephen Castles and Alastair Davidson, *Citizenship and Migration: Globalization and the Politics of Belonging* (New York: Routledge, 2000).

14. Saskia Sassen, *Territory, Authority, and Rights: From Medieval to Global Assemblages* (Princeton, N.J.: Princeton University Press, 2006).

15. See Castles and Davidson, *Citizenship and Migration*.

16. See, for example, the classic statement on this issue: T. H. Marshall, *Citizenship and Social Development* (Chicago: University of Chicago Press, 1964). See also Will Kymlicka and Wayne Norman, "Return of the Citizen: A Survey of Recent Work on Citizenship Theory," *Ethics* 104 (1994): 352–81.

17. See, for example, Linda Bosniak, *The Citizen and the Alien: Dilemmas of Contemporary Membership* (Princeton, N.J.: Princeton University Press, 2006); Phillip Cole, *Philosophies of Exclusion: Liberal Political Theory and Immigration* (Edinburgh: Edinburgh University Press, 2000); Susan B. Coutin, "Contesting Criminality: Illegal Immigration and the Spatialization of Legality," *Theoretical Criminality* 9.10 (2005): 5–333; Nicholas De Genova, "The Legal Production of Mexican/Migrant 'Illegality,'" *Latino Studies* 2 (2004): 160–85, De Genova, "Migrant 'Illegality' and Deportability in Everyday Life," *Annual Review of Anthropology* 31 (2002): 419–47; Thomas Hammar, *Democracy and the Nation-State: Aliens, Denizens, and Citizens in a World of International Migration* (Aldershot, U.K.: Gower, 1990); Bonnie Honig, *Democracy and the Foreigner* (Princeton, N.J.: Princeton University Press, 2003); Engin Isin, *Being Political: Genealogies of Citizenship* (Minneapolis: University of Minnesota Press, 2002); Victor C. Romero, *Alienated: Immigrant Rights, the Constitution, and Equality in America* (New York: New York University Press, 2005); and Monica M. Varsanyi, "The Paradox of Contemporary Immigrant Political Mobilization: Organized Labor, Undocumented Migrants, and Electoral Participation in Los Angeles," *Antipode* 37.4 (September 2005): 775–95, and "Interrogating 'Urban Citizenship' vis-à-vis Undocumented Migration," *Citizenship Studies* 10 (2006): 229–49.

18. Ali Behdad, *A Forgetful Nation: On Immigration and Cultural Identity in the United States* (Durham, N.C.: Duke University Press, 2005); Neil Gotanda, "A Critique of Our Constitution Is Colorblind," *Stanford Law Review* 44.1 (1991): 23–36, and "The Nullification of Citizenship: The Impossibility of Asian American Politics," in *Asian Americans and Politics: Perspectives, Experiences, Prospects*, ed. Gordon Chang, 79–101 (Washington, D.C.: Woodrow Wilson International Center Press, 2001);

Lisa Lowe, *Immigrant Acts: On Asian American Cultural Politics* (Durham, N.C.: Duke University Press, 1996); Mae Ngai, *Impossible Subjects: Illegal Aliens and the Making of America* (Princeton, N.J.: Princeton University Press, 2004); Michael Omi and Howard Winant, *Racial Formation in the United States: From the 1960s to the 1990s*, 2d ed. (New York: Routledge, 1994); and Rogers Smith, *Civic Ideals: Conflicting Visions of Citizenship in U.S. History* (New Haven, Conn.: Yale University Press, 1997).

19. See, for example, Susan Bibler Coutin, *Legalizing Moves: Salvadoran Immigrants' Struggle for U.S. Residency* (Ann Arbor: University of Michigan Press, 2000); David G. Gutiérrez, "The Politics of the Interstices: Reflections on Citizenship and Non-Citizenship at the Turn of the Twentieth Century," *Race/Ethnicity* 1.1 (Autumn 2007): 89–120, and "Citizens, Non-Citizens, and the Shell Game of Immigration Policy Reform: A Response to Dan Tichenor," *Labor: Studies in Working-Class History of the Americas* 5.2 (Summer 2008): 71–76; Patricia Landolt, "The Transnational Geographies of Immigrant Politics: Insights from a Comparative Study of Grassroots Organizing," *Sociological Quarterly* 49.1 (Winter 2008): 53–77; A. McNevin, "Irregular Migrants, Neoliberal Geographies and the Spatial Frontiers of the 'Political'," *Review of International Studies* 33.4 (October 2007): 655–74; and Cecilia Menjívar, "Liminal Legality: Salvadoran and Guatemalan Immigrants' Lives in the United States," *American Journal of Sociology* 111.4 (2006): 999–1037.

20. Yen Le Espiritu, *Asian American Pan-Ethnicity: Bridging Institutions and Identities* (Philadelphia: Temple University Press, 1992); Suzanne Oboler, *Ethnic Labels, Latino Lives: Identity and the Politics of (Re)Presentation in the United States* (Minneapolis: University of Minnesota Press, 1995); and Felix Padilla, *Latino Ethnic Consciousness: The Case of Mexican Americans and Puerto Ricans in Chicago* (Notre Dame, Ind.: University of Notre Dame Press, 1985).

21. Nicholas De Genova and Ana Ramos-Zayas, *Latino Crossings: Mexicans, Puerto Ricans and the Politics of Race and Citizenship* (New York: Routledge, 2003). For other recent examples exploring the dynamics of intergroup conflict and competition over issues of citizenship and differential racialization, see Gabriela Arredondo, *Mexican Chicago: Race, Identity, and Nation, 1916–39* (Durham, N.C.: Duke University Press, 2008); Neil Foley, "Becoming Hispanic: Mexican Americans and the Faustian Pact with Whiteness, in *Reflexiones 1997: New Directions in Mexican American History*, ed. Neil Foley, 53–70 (Austin: Center for Mexican American Studies, University of Texas, 1998); David G. Gutiérrez, *Walls and Mirrors: Mexican Americans, Mexican Immigrants, and the Politics of Ethnicity* (Berkeley: University of California Press, 1995), and "Globalization, Labor Migration, and the Demographic Revolution: Ethnic Mexicans in the Late Twentieth Century," in *The Columbia History of Latinos in the United States since 1960*, ed. David G. Gutiérrez, 43–86 (New York: Columbia University Press, 2004); Gilda Ochoa, *Becoming Neighbors in a Mexican American Community: Power, Conflict and Solidarity* (Austin: University of Texas Press, 2004); and Robert C. Smith, *Mexican New York: Transnational Lives of New Immigrants* (Berkeley: University of California Press, 2006).

22. See Costanza-Chock, "Police Riot on the Net," this volume; Pierrette Hondagneu-Sotelo, *God's Heart Has No Borders: How Religious Activists Are Working for Immigrant Rights* (Berkeley: University of California Press, 2008); and Pierrette Hondagneu-Sotelo and Angelica Salas, "What Explains the Immigrant Rights Marches of 2006? Organizers, Xenophobia, and Democracy Technology," in *Immigrant Rights in the Shadow of United States Citizenship*, ed. Rachel Ida Buff (New York: New York University Press, 2008).

23. See, for example, Irene Bloemraad, *Becoming a Citizen: Incorporating Immigrants and Refugees in the United States and Canada* (Berkeley: University of California Press, 2006); Félix, "New Americans or Diasporic Nationalists?" this volume; Ong, *Flexible Citizenship*; and Romero, *Alienated*.

24. For a more skeptical view of this, see El-Tayeb, "The Birth of a European Public," this volume.

25. See, for example, Leon Fink, *The Maya of Morgantown: Work and Community in the New Nuevo South* (Chapel Hill: University of North Carolina Press, 2003); Jonathan Fox, "Reframing Mexican Migration as a Multi-Ethnic Process," *Latino Studies* 4 (2006): 39–61; Michael Kearney, "Transnational Oaxacan Indigenous Identity: The Case of Mixtecs and Zapotecs," *Identities* 7.2 (2000): 173–95; Carole Nagengast and Michael Kearney, "Mixtec Ethnicity: Social Identity, Political Consciousness, and Political Activism," *Latin American Research Review* 25.2 (1989): 61–91; Gaspar Rivera-Salgado, Mixtec Activism in Oaxacalifornia: Transborder Grassroots Political Strategies," *American Behavioral Scientist* 47.2 (1999): 1439–58; and Lynn Stephen, *Transborder Lives: Indigenous Oaxacans in Mexico, California, and Oregon* (Durham, N.C.: Duke University Press, 2007), and *Zapotec Women: Gender, Class, and Ethnicity in Globalized Oaxaca*, rev. ed. (Durham, N.C.: Duke University Press, 2005).

26. See Pierrette Hondagneu-Sotelo, *Doméstica: Immigrant Workers Cleaning and Caring in the Shadows of Affluence* (Berkeley: University of California Press, 2001); Pei-Chia Lan, *Global Cinderallas: Migrant Domestic Workers and Newly Rich Employers in Taiwan* (Durham, N.C.: Duke University Press, 2006); and Helma Lutz, ed., *Migration and Domestic Work: A European Perspective on a Global Theme* (Aldershot, U.K.: Ashgate, 2008).

27. See Nichole Constable, *Maid to Order in Hong Kong: Stories of Filipina Workers* (Ithaca, N.Y.: Cornell University Press, 1997); Lan, *Global Cinderellas*; Nana Oishi, *Women in Motion: Globalization, State Policies, and Labor Migration in Asia* (Stanford, Calif.: Stanford University Press, 2005); and Rachel Salazar Parreñas, *Servants of Globalization: Women, Migration, and Domestic Work* (Stanford, Calif.: Stanford University Press, 2001).

28. Parreñas, *Servants of Globalization*.

29. Ibid.

30. See, for example, Sherri Grasmuck and Patricia Pessar, *Between Two Islands: Dominican International Migration* (Berkeley: University of California Press, 1991); Jennifer Hirsch, *Courtship after Marriage: Sexuality and Love in Mexican Transnational Families* (Berkeley: University of California Press, 2003); Pierrette Hondagneu-Sotelo, *Gendered Transitions: Mexican Experiences of Immigration* (Berkeley: University of California Press, 1994); and Patricia Pessar, "Engendering Migration Studies: The Case of New Immigrants in the United States," *American Behavioral Scientist* 42 (1999): 577–600.

31. See M. B. Castellanos and D. A. Boehm, eds., "Engendering Mexican Migration—Articulating Gender, Region, Circuits," special issue of *Latin American Perspectives* 35.1 (January 2008).

32. See, for example, Kitty Calavita, "Gender, Migration and Law: Crossing Borders and Bridging Disciplines," *International Migration Review* 40.1 (2006): 104–32; Katherine M. Donato et al., "A Glass Half Full? Gender in Migration Studies," *International Migration Review* 40.1 (2006): 3–26; Gloria González-López, *Erotic Journeys: Mexican Immigrants and their Sex Lives* (Berkeley: University of California Press, 2005); E. Luibheid, *Entry Denied: Controlling Sexuality at the Border* (Minneapolis: University of Minnesota Press, 2002); E. Luibheid and Lionel Cantú, eds., *Queer Migrations: Sexuality, U.S. Citizenship, and Border Crossings* (Minneapolis: University of Minnesota Press, 2005); and Cecilia Menjívar, "The Intersection of Work and Gender: Central American Immigrant Women and Employment in California," in *Gender and U.S. Immigration: Contemporary Trends*, ed. Pierrette Hondagneu-Sotelo, 101–26 (Berkeley: University of California Press, 2003).

33. See Sarah Mahler, "Engendering Transnational Migration: A Case Study of Salvadorans," in *Gender and U.S. Immigration*, ed. Hondagneu-Sotelo, 287–316.

34. See, for example, Loretta Baldassar, "Transnational Families and Provision of Moral and Emotional Support: The Relationship between Truth and Distance," *Identities: Global Studies in Culture and Power* 14 (2007): 385–409; Deborah A. Boehm, "'Now I Am a Man and a Woman': Gendered Moves and Migrations in a Transnational Mexican Community," *Latin American Perspectives* 35.1 (January 2008): 16–30; Mary Chamberlin and Selma Leyderdorff, eds., "Transnational Families: Memories and Narratives," special issue of *Global Networks: A Journal of Transnational Affairs* 3 (July 2004); J. Dreby, "Honor and Virtue—Mexican Parenting in a Transnational Context," *Gender and Society* 20.1 (February 2006): 32–59; Pierrette Hondagneu-Sotelo and Ernestine Avila, "'I'm Here, but I'm There': The Meanings of Latina Transnational Motherhood 4," *Gender and Society* 11 (1997): 317–40; and Barrie Thorne et al., "Raising Children and Growing Up across National Borders: Comparative Perspectives on Age, Gender and Migration," in *Gender and U.S. Immigration*, ed. Hondagneu-Sotelo, 241–62.

35. See, for example, Yen Le Espiritu, "'We Don't Sleep Around Like White Girls Do': Family, Culture, and Gender in Filipina American Lives," *Signs* 26.2 (2001): 415–40.

36. See Luin Goldring, "Gender, Status, and the State in Transnational Spaces: The Gendering of Political Participation in Mexican Hometown Associations," in *Gender and U.S. Immigration*, ed. Hondagneu-Sotelo, 341–58.

37. See Peter Kivisto, "Theorizing Transnational Migration: A Critical Review of Current Efforts," *Ethnic and Racial Studies* 24.40 (2001): 549–77.

38. See, for example, David Fitzgerald, "Towards a Theoretical Ethnography of Migration," *Qualitative Sociology* 29.1 (2006): 1–24; and Nancy Foner, *From Ellis Island to JFK: New York's Two Great Waves of Immigration* (New Haven, Conn.: Yale University Press, and New York: Russell Sage Foundation, 2000).

39. For similar examples, see Richard Alba and Victor Nee, "Rethinking Assimilation Theory for a New Era of Migration," *International Migration Review* 31 (Winter 1997): 826–74; Jonathan Kazal, "The Lost World of Pennsylvania Pluralism: Immigrants, Regions, and the Early Origins of Pluralist Ideologies in America," *Journal of American Ethnic History* 27.3 (Spring 2008): 7–42; and Ewa Morawska, "In Defense of the Assimilation Model," *Journal of American Ethnic History* 13.2 (1994): 76–87.

40. See Roger Waldinger and David Fitzgerald, "Transnationalism in Question," *American Journal of Sociology* 109 (2004): 1177–95, and Roger Waldinger, "Between 'Here' and 'There': Immigrant Cross-Border Activities and Loyalties," *International Migration Review* 42.1 (March 2008): 3–29.

41. Waldinger and Fitzgerald, "Transnationalism in Question," 1176.

42. Ibid., 1179; emphasis in original.

43. Waldinger, "Between 'Here' and 'There,'" 9.

44. See, for example, Erika Lee, *At America's Gates: Chinese Immigration during the Exclusion Era, 1882–1943* (Berkeley: University of California Press, 2003); Ngai, *Impossible Subjects*; and Paul Spickard, *Almost All Aliens: Immigration, Race, and Colonialism in American History and Identity* (New York: Routledge, 2007).

The Deportation Terror

Rachel Ida Buff

The title of this chapter is taken from Abner Green's 1950 pamphlet: "The Deportation Terror: A Weapon to Gag America."[1] In it, Green, the director of the American Committee for the Protection of the Foreign Born from 1942 through his death in 1958, outlined the assault then taking place against foreign-born progressive leaders. The kinds of connections Green made in this publication were characteristic of much of the work of the committee during the long cold war period in linking political repression, domestic militarism, and racism:

> The deportation drive and the hysteria against the foreign born are an essential part of the concentrated drive on the rights of all minorities in the United States and a general assault on the liberties of the American.
>
> Lynching of Negro people in the South . . . the loyalty program for government workers . . . the Hollywood 10 . . . increased police brutality against the Negro people in industrial centers and against Mexican-Americans in the Southwest.[2]

Such connections resound in the contemporary context of domestic and international militarization against the disembodied presence of Terror. Homeland Security, as cultural refrain and federal entity, brings together the previously disparate governmental endeavors of Border and Transportation Security, Emergency Preparedness and Response, Information Analysis and Infrastructure Protection, Science and Technology, the Coast Guard and the Secret Service (see figure 1).[3] In this way, contemporary U.S. discourses of homeland security appear to be something new: a postmodern melding of the functions of government. But as legal scholar Daniel Kanstroom argues, deportation law has always had two facets: control of the borders, and what he calls "post-entry social control." Kanstroom traces the antecedents of deportation of the foreign-born, ranging widely to examine colonial warnings out of people marginal to the social order, the series of removals so crucial to the subsequent legal status of Indian nations, and fugitive slave laws. He writes: "Once deportation law is conceived, even in part, as a system of social control largely deployed against people of color, then its relationship to slavery law becomes easier to see."[4]

Department of Homeland Security

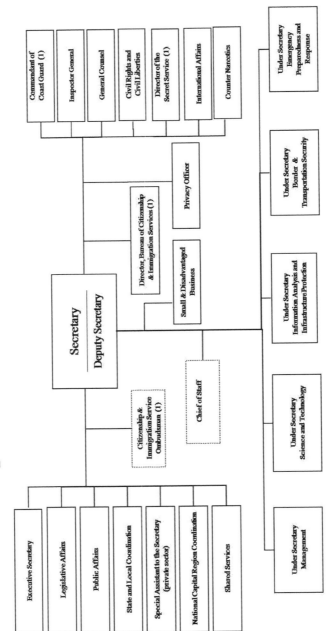

Note (1): Effective March 1st, 2003

The Terror of Homeland Security

In this essay, I work to locate the recent wave of deportation raids carried out since 2005 by the Bureau of Immigration and Customs Enforcement (ICE) in their historical context as a racialized system of social control. I argue that the deportation terror imposed on immigrant communities by these raids is a crucial technology of the state. The creation of statelessness is an ongoing enterprise central to the political coherence of national identity. Deportation, or forcible removal, has long been used to secure and enhance borders, and to extend the gatekeeping work performed at the border deep into the interior.[5]

Currently, immigrants are the central focus of deportation. But Kanstroom's important work allows us to see the parallels to misbehaving and racially marginalized people, particularly women, in the colonial period; Indians; and African Americans, during slavery and the Jim Crow period. Part of the business of maintaining a nation, then, is instilling terror in people potentially subject to forcible removal by the state. This is not a new insight. I present it here, however, to encourage the reclaiming by cultural studies scholars of this most dangerous and politically laden word: terror. In the current historical moment, this word has been almost entirely defined by the homeland security state. A historical and comparative perspective on the experience of terror at the hands of this and other state formations now becomes particularly crucial.

Figure 1.
Depart of Homeland Security. Source:
http://www.dhs.gov/xlibrary/assets/
DHS_Org_Chart-2003.ppt

My central comparison in this essay links the deportations of the early cold war period, 1945–1960, with the current moment, characterized by the detention and deportation of foreign-born people, predominantly men, from the Middle East, North and East Africa, South and Southeast Asia after 9/11, and the immigration raids that have constituted a direct governmental response to the immigrant rights mobilizations of 2006–07. In both periods the mass deportations of primarily Mexican laborers accompany constitutionally questionable detention and deportation of the foreign born for reasons defined by the state as "political." But defining what is political and what is not constitutes ideological practice, after all. Many political deportations target community leaders who represent foreign-born workers. These deportations render workers more vulnerable to exploitative work conditions and unconstitutional practices. In turn, the large sweeps focusing on immigrant workers have often been retribution for political organizing. The notion that these larger sweeps are market driven, rather than political, functions to define and divide foreign-born communities.

A critical aspect of the cultural work of cold war immigration policy was the enduring enshrining of an ideological distinction between political and economic migration: the notion that those arriving from Communist regimes seek freedom and deserve refuge, while migrants from U.S.-backed regimes in places such as Haiti or post-Sandinista Nicaragua move only for economic necessity. But scrutinizing deportation practices yields a more complex picture. It transfers some of our attention away from who is allowed to enter through the mythical "golden door" toward who is ushered out through a much less publicized, indeed, partially hidden, back door.

The deportation of particular foreign-born individuals for reasons of their ideology during the early cold war, or in the case of the "Special Registration" Program implemented in 2002, their birth place or religion, is a component of a racial regime governing entrance and exit. This racial regime includes the deportation of foreign-born workers and their families as well as, in some cases, citizens who are members of racialized communities. So, while public discussion of immigration policy since the cold war has reified the racialized distinction between the figures of the noble political refugee and the craven economic migrant (the latter is almost never figured alone, but moves in waves or hordes), both deportation and immigration policy have been crafted out of the continuities between these two groups. Refugee and immigration policy purportedly act to shelter those fleeing totalitarianism over those motivated solely by economic gain. This cold war distinction has long functioned to underwrite U.S. foreign policy, so that, after World War II, displaced persons fleeing the Iron Curtain were preemptively viewed as seeking freedom, just as the 2 million Iraqis currently petitioning for refugee status must be denied to bolster the illusion of progress there.[6] Similarly, by operating through a rhetoric of threat, whether posed by the foreign-born Communist or Islamic terrorist, deportation policy obscures the relationship between activists and communities. Many of the political deportation cases of the 1940s and 1950s targeted foreign-born labor leaders on charges of communist affiliation. Their roles as labor leaders in immigrant communities were much less publicized. Like the workers swept into custody by ICE raids, all of the Muslim and Middle Eastern post-9/11 deportees have been found guilty only of infractions of immigration law, not of conspiracy to commit acts of terror. Discourses of subversion and terror, then, mask the operation of racialized state terror.

Kanstroom discusses the centrality of the notion of sovereignty defined in Chinese Exclusion-era cases such as *Chae Chan Ping v. U.S.* (1889) and *Fong Yue Ting v. U.S.* (1893), in which the Supreme Court defined "plenary powers" that superseded the individual rights of Chinese plaintiffs.[7] Similarly, Moustafa Bayomi writes of the way in which the Special Registration Program drew on the plenary power doctrine and the laws that grew out of it: "Special registration creates a vast, new legal geography of suspicion for the United States government, a geography that in some way mirrors the 'Asiatic barred zone' of the 1917 Immigration Act."[8]

A historiographic chasm has separated various incidents of deportation in the twentieth and twenty-first centuries. Scholars of immigration have tended to focus on the "golden door" without attending to exits, clearly marked or otherwise. The national frame is still powerful enough to preclude consideration of the transnational process of deportation. By looking at Mexican and U.S. archival sources, Kelly Lytle Hernandez challenges an accepted chronology, suggesting that the summer of 1954 was the culmination of eleven years of Operation Wetback rather than its central staging period. By viewing deportation as a transnational practice, Hernandez's work shifts the chronology of Operation Wetback and points to its broader significance in post–World War II period.

There is a small literature on the repatriation of Mexican Americans during the 1930s,[9] another literature on the deportation of foreign-born radicals in the red scares of the 1920s and 1950s.[10] Recently, legal scholars have written important works seeking to understand the contemporary period in historical perspective, giving consideration to deportation and removal throughout the history of the American state.[11] By suggesting connections among the historical experiences of divergent "impossible subjects," Mae Ngai's magisterial work has done much to bridge this chasm. And both Kanstroom and Bayoumi point, importantly, to the long sweep of continuity in deportation practices. Their work illustrates parallels between forms of racial terror deployed at different moments by the Fugitive Slave Law and detention of Haitian " 'fugees," and between the geographies proposed by the Asiatic Barred Zone and the State Department's contemporary list of state sponsors of terror. (Bayoumi perceptively notes the absence of a special registration program for Cuban Americans, even though Cuba is on that list.)[12] In our current moment, such connections are crucial. In general, though, deportation continues to be thought of as an exception to the rule, rather than a social process constitutive of the nation across different periods, and definitive for immigrant communities.

The historical comparison posed by this essay offers a genealogy of a specific form of state power, the creation of subjectivities, and the conditions of possibility for resistance. As Ngai argues, the numerical restriction implemented by the Johnson-Reid Act of 1924 created the category "illegal alien."[13] While the restrictions of this law were aimed at immigrants from Asia and Europe, quota laws combined with the creation of the border patrol in 1924 and the ensuing criminalization of undocumented crossing in 1929 came to constitute, in her words, "a racialized Mexican identity."[14] In turn, the emergence of the racialized category of the illegal alien—an eminently deportable subject—transformed already existing deportable categories, including anarchists and other groups deemed politically subversive.

The U.S.-Mexico border has been continually militarized since the creation of the border patrol in 1924. Donald Pease argues that the annexation of Mexican territory in the Treaty of Guadalupe Hidalgo represents a founding violence.[15] Wars on, variously, undocumented crossing, illegal drugs, Central American insurgencies, and terrorism have intensified the racialized terror at the border.[16] As Natsu Taylor Saito writes,

> the border now also connotes the imaginary line between safe and unsafe associated with the prevention of terrorism and, as a result, has moved onto the bodies not only of persons presumed to be undocumented but also those who look like potential terrorists, regardless of their legal status. For the latter group, this can mean special registration procedures, prolonged questioning, detention, deportation, or even rendition to a third country for interrogation.[17]

These transformations take place in a broader context of an institutionalized U.S. imperial presence around the world and the growth of transnational capital after World War II. In this context, the emergence of National and, later, Homeland Security regimes have been dependent on the continuous construction of enemies within to justify the human and financial expenses of ongoing global militarization.

During the cold war, the deportation of foreign-born radicals, labor leaders in particular, was anchored by legislation designed in the 1930s to expedite the removal of Mexican American workers from the U.S. economy during the Great Depression. The Spolansky, or Michigan Alien Registration, Act of 1931, for example, targeted communist influence in the Detroit Mexican American community, and was a precedent for the federal Smith Act of 1940, which compelled the registration of noncitizens and provided for the deportation of anyone who had ever belonged to an organization advocating the violent overthrow of the government. The Spolansky Act was mostly used to deport Mexican Americans, many of whom were actually American citizens, from the Detroit area.[18] Labor practices transform categories of identity, as Jeffrey Melnick and Rachel Rubin explain regarding the implementation of the Bracero Program in 1942: "Not only did these labor programs bring hundreds of thousands of Mexican people to the United States, but they established powerful narratives concerning the status and entitlement of these individuals once they entered United States society."[19]

Similarly, in the current period, the deportation terror levied against undocumented laborers shelters under the broad rubric of the "war against terror." Tram Nguyen illuminates the connections made in national security rhetoric between undocumented people, refugees, and potential terrorists as "clandestine transnational actors."[20] Just as laws delimiting the activities of Mexican Americans in Detroit in the 1930s came to apply to political activists of diverse national origins after World War II, heightened surveillance of Muslim and Middle Eastern communities leads to increased ideological and financial support for deporting migrant workers in the current period.[21]

Lisa Flores has described the ways in which racialized portrayals of immigrants have led, historically, to anti-immigrant sentiment and federal deportation programs. She traces a "uniformity in the public vocabulary surrounding immigration and criminality. Whether invoked directly or indirectly, the figure of the 'illegal alien' is hauntingly consistent, as is the quick turn to deportation."[22]

What is crucial about Flores's argument is that the deportation terror, in addition to being a technology of the state, is an ongoing rhetorical practice. As such, this rhetoric takes on particular meanings at different times. Flores illuminates a 1920s mass media discourse in which Mexican American laborers appear as docile "peons," offering cheap labor and little threat, while these same migrants turn up in the 1930s as a dangerous criminal element, threatening to upset the economic and social order. This floating rhetoric can target different populations, as is evident in the transition from the Spolansky Act, later declared unconstitutional because of popular protest, to the Smith Act, used widely against foreign-born people, including but not limited to Mexican Americans, during the cold war.[23] Criminalization, in this case, migrates from supposed communist influences in the Mexican American community to the general community of the foreign-born.

Such rhetoric endures, to powerful effect. Scott Michaelsen writes of the continuities between the jurisprudence justifying the internment of Japanese

Americans during the 1940s, and the USA PATRIOT Act passed by a nearly unanimous congress in 2001. For Michaelsen, the ongoing militarization of the borderlands between the United States and Mexico has enabled what he calls "'the permanent state of racial emergency' or 'the permanent state of legal racial exception.'" Policing the borders against the continuously racialized threat of undocumented migration requires an escalating discourse of exception to notions of due process and equality. This escalated discourse then becomes grounds for spectacular trespasses against civil liberties, such as the internment of Japanese Americans or the detention without cause of legal immigrants from places or of faiths associated with a particular mapping of terrorism.[24]

Sweeping immigration reform seems to have been lost in the current political moment. The raids and resulting deportations carried out by the Bureau of Customs and Immigration Enforcement (ICE) serve as a de facto immigration policy in a political climate characterized by fractious and inconclusive discourse on questions of immigration and national identity at the political level, and accompanied by racialized vigilante terror at the borders. Under the rubric of Homeland Security, congressional appropriations bills have continually funded customs and border protection. These appropriations have included monies for the construction of detention facilities for deportees, as well as for the Bureau of Immigration and Custom Enforcement to hire more agents.[25] According to DHS, ICE is "responsible for locating and removing aliens who are in the U.S. illegally and protecting the jobs of those who are legally eligible for them by inspecting places of employment for undocumented workers."[26] Homeland Security rhetoric echoes the criminalization of immigrants traced by Flores in the 1930s: "A key element of the ICE mission is to remove illegal aliens from the United States, with a focus on criminal aliens."[27] This is Michaelsen's "permanent state of racial emergency."

In order to fulfill its mission, ICE has deployed the previously underutilized employer sanctions contained in the Immigration Reform and Control Act of 1986 to conduct raids on employers utilizing undocumented labor. These employers face penalties of fines and sometimes jail time; undocumented workers face deportation proceedings. And, since identity theft has also become a concern of the Homeland Security state, workers who utilize false social security numbers can be charged with civil crimes. This authorizes local law enforcement personnel to pursue what are essentially immigration, and hence federal, cases.[28] Particularly in the absence of strong political leadership on the immigration issue, except on the radical nativist right, federal funding for deportation and detention replaces a democratically debated immigration policy.[29] Consequently, the current practice of rule by agency regulation responds to the discourse of criminalization identified by Flores, also enshrining a masculinist, militarized rhetoric within ICE and the sheriff's departments with whom they cooperate on raids.

While it is importantly connected to the discourse of criminalization, this masculinist rhetoric emerges from a mass cultural genealogy traceable from late cold war productions such as Rambo to the strange career of Arnold Schwarzenegger. For example, the "Protecting the Homeland" video available at the Border Patrol Web site of the Homeland Security Department Web page commences with a shot of a humvee driving through mountainous, arid country to strains of Wagnerian brass and a martial snare drum.[30] Uniformed officers on horses and all-terrain vehicles are prominently featured in the opening montage. The video hearkens back to images of Texas Rangers patrolling the border before 1924 and locates the founding of the Border Patrol as a continuation of that tradition. With a masculine voice-over, the video exhibits two or three young women of color in uniform. But the figures and context are overwhelmingly male, an archive of an enduring and gendered social imaginary of the frontier.

It makes little difference to those subject to the deportation terror whether they are separated from work, family, and community because of a bill both parties in Congress were able to agree on, or whether their deportation is part of a funded mandate under the powerful but vague rubric of homeland security. For immigrants, the deportation terror creates a culture of fear, which in turn, constitutes de facto immigration policy. Just as Labor Department officials drew on and encouraged the mass media criminalization of Mexicans to convince Mexican Americans, many of them born in the United States, to "return home" in the 1930s,[31] the terror caused by raids and deportations in foreign-born communities in the present day constitutes not-so-gentle persuasion to those lucky enough to escape the sweep, this time.[32] The deportation terror combines with a spate of local initiatives designed to limit the already truncated rights of the undocumented in towns like Hazleton, Pennsylvania; Green Bay and Arcadia, Wisconsin; Smithfield, North Carolina; and Carpentersville, Illinois.[33] Alex Kotlowitz refers to such policies, and the toll they take on immigrant communities throughout the country as "deportation by attrition."[34]

New Bedford, Massachusetts organizer Corinn Williams described the effects of the raid at the Bianco leather plant in March 2007 as making the large Central American community there quieter. In the raid, 361 workers were detained, of whom 200 were quickly sent to new detention facilities in Texas. On the one hand, she said, a core infrastructure of local leadership mobilized in response to the raid. But on the other, she described a transformed city: "For a long time people just didn't go out, they stayed home. We noticed conditions in other workplaces getting worse. . . . I guess on an economic level there have been whole households of people renting apartments that have disappeared."[35]

The deportation terror, then, shapes the landscape of immigrant communities as well as federal and local law enforcement procedures. While fear and "deportation by attrition" are some of the contemporary effects of the deportation terror, immigrants have also mobilized in record numbers during the springs of 2006 and 2007 to demand more just national policy. Mainstream news commentators noticed what flags were flying, and spoke about the presence of these colors as indication of the loyalties of the foreign born. But they were much less likely to point to the fact that, for some of those marching, their public presence constituted personal risk in light of the deportation terror. As Monisha Das Gupta argues, the demands of immigrant rights groups often challenge assumptions about national citizenship and individual rights.[36] The demands described by Das Gupta reflect an evolving grassroots internationalism presaged by advocates for the foreign-born during the cold war.

Abner Green was the son of working-class Jewish immigrants, born in Brooklyn in 1913. He trained as a pharmacist's assistant, and went to work in a "waterfront pharmacy" in Manhattan during the Depression. Establishments of this kind stocked goods utilized by sailors from around the world, many of whom faced deportation and statelessness.[37] It is possible that the stories told by patrons of the pharmacy, along with those Green would have listened to in the immigrant enclaves of Brooklyn, influenced him to become involved in the American Committee for the Protection of the Foreign Born after it was founded by Roger Baldwin of the ACLU in 1933. And sailors would be among the foreign-born needing protection in the early cold war era.

More than ten thousand foreign-born sailors came to serve in the American merchant marine during World War II. After the war, these sailors remained ineligible for citizenship, not having served for five years or more. For example: thirty-six Pakistani sailors were held at Ellis Island in 1949 as deportable aliens.[38] Added to this was the fact that, during the cold war, many maritime workers' unions were suspected in the United States of having communist influences. Members risked deportation (see figure 3).

the
legacy
of
ABNER GREEN
a memorial journal

ISSUED BY THE AMERICAN COMMITTEE FOR THE PROTECTION OF THE FOREIGN BORN, FOR THE 27th NATIONAL CONFERENCE, DEC. 19-20, 1959

Figure 2.
Abner Green, director of the American Committee for the Protection of the Foreign Born, 1942–1958. From "The Legacy of Abner Green: A Memorial Journal," American Committee for the Protection of the Foreign Born Collection, Tamiment Library, New York University. Used with permission.

Greek sailors such as Paul Paschalides, secretary of the New York Branch of the Federation of Greek Maritime Workers, participated during World War II in shipping U.S.-produced materials to European allies. They did this at great risk, not only at sea, where two thousand lost their lives, but in Greece, which was occupied by the Axis powers during the war.[39] After the war, Paschalides faced deportation. Ten Federation of Greek Maritime Union members had been sentenced to death by the U.S.-backed right wing regime in Greece in late 1940s. But the Special Inquiry Office of the Immigration Service found that "despite the applicant's contention, we cannot close our eyes to the fact that Greece is a democratic country."[40] Granted asylum by Poland, Paschalides was deported.

The history of statelessness is, of necessity, a transnational history. It involves voluntary and less than voluntary migration—sometimes, as Hernandez has shown in the case of Operation Wetback, the collaboration of different governments in determining the geographic fate of the deported.[41] The story

Figure 3.
The American Committee for the Protection of the Foreign Born dramatized the position of foreign-born sailors such as Paul Paschalides, valorizing their service at a moment of ascendant anticommunist nativism. "Is This the Way to Treat Heroes?" is from "Foreign Seamen on Our Ships," *New York Times*, July 22, 1945, excerpted on pamphlet. American Committee for the Protection of the Foreign Born Collection, Tamiment Library, New York University Press. Used with permission.

of one deportation, as in the story of Paul Paschalides, leads from New York to Greece to Poland, not to mention the many places he traversed as a maritime worker. As sociologist Steve McKay, whose own work is deeply engaged with the transnational culture of Filipino seamen, pointed out, when asked what the contemporary equivalent of *Moby Dick* for American studies might be: "It's not the whale anymore. It's the ocean."[42] Understanding the deportation terror leads us, as American studies scholars, in pursuit not of the tale of Moby Dick, but of the story of the ocean surrounding the whale: the sailors, those on shore, those on small boats and rafts just outside the frame of the novel.

Ethnic studies scholars George Sánchez and Jeffrey M. Garcilazo have considered the relationship between Mexican American communities and the issue of deportation.[43] Both focus on the Los Angeles Committee for the Protection of the Foreign Born, which worked on deportation cases of political leaders, as well as "average Mexican Americans who found themselves victimized by the new immigration and internal security legislation represented by the McCarran-Walter Act," including children whose parents faced deportation.[44] Garcilazo argues that the defense of high-profile political deportation cases may have seemed outside the mainstream to much of the Mexican American community in Los Angeles during this period. However, Operation Wetback's apprehension of half a million undocumented workers each year between 1947 and 1954 did not.[45]

The connection between the deportations of Operation Wetback and those of Latina labor leaders like Guatemalan Luisa Moreno indicates the consolidation of a particular regime during the cold war period. The vigorous clampdown on labor after WWII represented by the Taft-Hartley bill involved the purging of communists from unions, but also truncated the power of organized labor. The consolidation of a particular cold war political economy took place in national and transnational contexts. As a component of immigration policy, deportation is an aspect of both.

The commissioner of the Immigration and Naturalization Service presiding over Operation Wetback was Lieutenant General Joseph May Swing. Appointed by Eisenhower in 1954, Swing had served with General John Pershing during the occupation of Mexico from 1916 to 1917. More recently, he had been a commanding general during the Sixth Army's occupation of Korea after the Korean War. As INS commissioner, Swing's pursuit of both immigrant workers and political dissidents points to connections between the militarization of domestic and international life and the racialization of citizenship during the cold war.

In addition to Operation Wetback, Swing actively pursued the deportation of foreign born Koreans such as Diamond Kimm, and Chungsoon and Choon Cha Kwak. These émigré Koreans had worked against Japanese domination of Korea during the war. Arriving in the United States as a student in 1936, Diamond Kimm served in the Office of Strategic Services during the war. He also edited the newspaper *Korean Independence*, a bilingual publication attempting to muster Korean support for allied victory. After the war, Kimm continued to edit the paper, often criticizing what he felt were the undemocratic actions of U.S.-allied Syngman Rhee.[46]

Similarly, Chungsoon and Choon Cha Kwak, student activists against the Japanese occupation in Korea, left in 1935 and came to study music in the United States. Active in the Korean American community, both also served in the Korean unit of the Information and Education Division of the U.S. Army during the war, directing the compilation, editing, and publishing of Korean language materials. Chungsoon was a correspondent for *Korean Independence*.[47] Deportation orders were issued on various technical grounds for all three of these activists in 1950, just as all the deportations of Muslim and Middle Eastern men detained after 9/11 have been violations of immigration status. These cases persisted through the mid-1950s, with Swing, recently returned from supporting the Rhee regime in Korea, actively pursuing deportation. The timing of the deportation efforts in the late 1950s corresponds with social upheavals in South Korea that Rhee and his U.S. allies attempted to quell in the name of democracy.[48] And the parallel to contemporary practices suggests the utility of the deportation terror to particular regimes.

A career military man now in charge of the INS, Swing's actions at the border and within the nation on behalf of the alliance he was involved in cementing with South Korea illuminate what Bayoumi terms a "legal geography of suspicion," to which racialized foreign-born workers and intellectuals were subject. This legal geography of suspicion provides us with a racialized map of empire and the sovereign powers that allowed for the deportation of the foreign-born.

With Eisenhower's support, Swing executed Operation Wetback largely outside of congressional or judicial jurisdiction, much like the current ICE raids. Viewed this way, it appears that rights for the foreign-born are often the casualties of particular racial regimes. Three stories about deportation and statelessness in New Bedford, Massachusetts, over a 150-year period illustrate this point.

Three Stories about New Bedford

The history of American repression is strewn with the bodies of the foreign-born.
—Ellen Schrecker[49]

1. Stateless on Board

"It was a form of passport."
—Joseph Ramos, Cape Verdean American whaler interviewed by Dan Georgianna

The whaling industry provided an important source of wealth and economic development in New England that accompanied and enabled early nineteenth century textile-based industrialization. Ships would dock in foreign ports to sign on crews for the difficult and perilous work of whaling. The Cape Verdean islands became an important source of whaling labors after the Civil War.[50] Many Cape Verdeans signed onto ships with the full intent of abandoning them after arrival in an American port. These maritime laborers would have been coming to the East Coast at about the same time the Chinese were arriving in California, precipitating the first alien registration laws in the country.[51] But in a contemporary sense, these were undocumented workers. Former whaler Joseph Ramos, interviewed by economist Dan Georgianna, remembered: "Under the Portuguese flag, they would never let people from the islands immigrate over here. That's why so many people from the islands went whaling. It was a form of passport."[52]

Whaling workers either lived at sea or jumped ship and joined the communities at New England's margins and became difficult to count. Because of this elusive population, New Bedford in this period ranked as the second richest city in Massachusetts, and had one of the highest per capita incomes in the world.[53] Statelessness and wealth were intricately linked in the political economy of whaling in nineteenth century New Bedford.

2. From Terror to Terror

> I had tried to get citizenship before, but when I applied for citizenship, they said, "You're a criminal, we can't give you citizenship." "Why?" "Because you have a crime record." "What do you mean I have a crime record?" "Well, you were arrested a number of times." I said, "Sure, during the strike." And he said, "That's against you as a criminal."
>
> —Eulália Mendes[54]

The history of deportation in the twentieth century maps connections between economic restrictionism, political repression, and racialized nativism. This history is also important because it gives us a sense of the global sweep of migration. Many of the deported arrive in the United States fleeing political, cultural, or religious repression in their home nations, only to become subject to the deportation terror in this country. And, when they are deported, they often migrate to a third location.[55] The story of labor organizer Eulália Mendes traces the migration of one individual from fascist terror to anticommunist terror to comparative shelter in Stalin-era Poland.

Born in Portugal in 1911, Eulália Mendes immigrated with her family to Massachusetts in 1921. Anarcho-syndicalists, the family left Portugal during the instability preceding the emergence of the military dictatorship that would eventually lead to the rise of the right-wing New State led by António Oliveira Salazar until 1974.[56] The family eventually moved to New Bedford, where, like many other young immigrants from Portugal, the British Isles,

French Canada, Poland, and Cape Verde, Eulália joined native-born workers in the textile industry at the age of fourteen. In the mills, she worked forty-four hours a week, including Saturdays, attending school for four hours each week until she reached the age of sixteen.[57]

As a young woman, Mendes became involved with the communist-led Textile Mill Committee's organizing of workers across race, national origins, and craft in response to the wage cut announced at the New Bedford mills in 1928. She told Dan Georgianna:

> We wanted a union that would take in all of the textile workers. We called for an industrial type of union instead of a craft union, and that was quite progressive at that time because most of the unions in the United States at that time were craft unions. The whole idea was to get all of the textile workers in one mill to belong to one union, and all of the textile workers to belong to a single textile union.[58]

This aspiration is characteristic of the evolution of the labor movement in the mid-twentieth century. It would eventually be ratified by passage of the National Labor Relations Act in 1935, and by the consolidation of the Congress of Industrial Workers, so crucial in holding out the possibility of Americanization for foreign-born workers and their children.[59] But not all of the foreign-born workers who participated in these struggles were included in the limited benefits that eventually accrued to organized labor.

The textile strike in New Bedford was broken over the course of six months of confrontations between organizers and police; of dissent between the communist-led Textile Mill Committee and the English and native-born dominated craft union; and of privation on the part of the strikers. In an observation strikingly parallel to Corinne Williams's reflections on New Bedford in 2007, contemporary observer Moshe Nadir wrote: "Many tenement houses stand vacant. The windows are plastered with old newspapers. A city for rent."[60]

Though acquitted in New Bedford Superior Court of charges associated with the strike, Portuguese-born organizer Augusto Pinto was deported to Lisbon by the Immigration Service in 1931. Pinto once commented: "There is no liberty in this country, just a statue."[61] Condemned to prison in Tarrafal, Cape Verde, by the Salazar regime, Pinto died en route.

Emerging from the strike convinced of the compatibility of communist organizations in the United States with her anarcho-syndicalist politics, Mendes married a Portuguese-American communist, Joseph Figueiredo. She went on to become an organizer in Boston and New York for the International Ladies' Garment Workers' Union.[62] In 1950, under the Smith Act, she was arrested for membership in the Communist Party. Offered asylum by Poland, she took voluntary departure in 1953. She said:

> I was deported because I was not a citizen. Picking on foreign-born people was used during the McCarthy days as a pressure against people in general. Even though everybody thought I was an American citizen, my arrest had the effect of creating a lot of fear amongst a lot of the Portuguese people who were not citizens. Most of those people who were deported had to go to countries they had not seen, had not lived in, and most of them had been brought to the United States when they were children.[63]

Mendes arrived in Poland at the age of forty-three and became involved in the International Short Wave Radio project there. She requested permission to return to the United States to visit family, but her requests were denied. She died in Poland in 2005.[64]

In the midcentury United States, Eulália Mendes's organizing activities were criminalized. Like Paschalides, she could not return home to a right-wing regime allied with the United States. Nor could she disappear into the margins of society, as Cape Verdean whalers who jumped ship were able to do. By the mid-twentieth century, a "gatekeeper nation," as Erika Lee calls it, had emerged to keep track of immigrants by counting them at the gates and scrutinizing their behavior after their entrance into the nation.[65] Mendes's deportation, like those of political radicals and Mexican Americans alike during the cold war, was a component of an evolving national identity, and a way in which the state managed conflict under industrial capitalism. At the same time, the forced migration of people like Mendes, Paul Paschalides, and Luisa Moreno under this regime connects the deportation terror to other kinds of political terror gripping places such as Portugal and Greece, dominated by right-wing dictators; Guatemala, which by the mid-1950s was swept into civil war;[66] and Stalin-era Poland. The transnational activities of the deportees illuminate historical connections that might otherwise be difficult to see.

3. A Militarized Hemisphere

> We believe that it is no crime to be undocumented and to work honorably, especially when we were doing it for the Armed Forces of the United States. That is why we ask, "Why don't they take us back to New Bedford?"
> —Elba Patricia Aguilar, Karla Moreno Ochoa, Rosa Sarmiento Santos, Maria Dolores Arrita Guerra, Ruth Carbajal, Josefina Roos, Suely Schnieder, Leonete S. Fernandes, Nafalise Silva, Maria Hernandez G., Maria Hernandez Cruz, Evelyn Pacheco Chinalan, Balvina Lopez Lopez, Hipolita Castro Chaco[67]

In some of the very same mills that the New Bedford strikers of 1928 walked out of, today workers from Portugal, Guatemala, Honduras, Brazil, El Salvador, and Mexico, many of them undocumented, many of them women, work in textiles. On March 6, 2007, ICE raided the factory of defense contractor Michael Bianco, Inc., which produced backpacks and other items for use in the military. ICE apprehended 361 workers. Descriptions of the ordeal by those apprehended include strip searches, isolation, deprivation, and being handcuffed and put aboard planes to uncertain destinations. About a third of those arrested were immediately transported to deportation centers in Texas. Others were detained in Massachusetts and Rhode Island. Inevitably, families were separated, including mothers from nursing children. Between one hundred and two hundred children were separated from one or both parents a result of the raid (figure 4). Community organizers as well as Senators Ted Kennedy and John Kerry and Congressmen Barney Frank and William Delahunt have worked to petition ICE to allow for at least temporary reunification of the families. The raids had been carried out in such a way as to maximize the terror among those apprehended, as well as the broader migrant community in the region.[68]

Central American women, the majority of the undocumented workers apprehended in the raid, have come to the United States as a result of the political turmoil and terror in their homelands. Between 8 percent and 20 percent of El Salvadorans have immigrated to the United States as a result of the political instability of the 1980s; some of these migrants have been afforded Temporary Protected Status (TPS), which means they cannot be relocated in case of a raid. Guatemalans, also displaced by the long civil war in their country, are eligible neither for refugee status nor for the limited amnesty granted by IRCA in 1986.[69] Nicaraguans and Hondurans are in a similar position with respect to immigration and refugee status.

Like Eulália Mendes, these Central American women arrive in New Bedford in the late twentieth and early twenty-first centuries fleeing the terrors of state repression and civil war. But they enter a different political economy. Much of the production done in the early twentieth century by the textile mills of southeastern Massachusetts has been outsourced, first to states in the south, and later to factories in Latin America and Asia. Enterprise zones in countries such as Nicaragua and Cambodia now account for much of the manufacturing of textiles used in producing clothing and home furnishing. Workers at Michael Bianco, Inc., labor for one of the few growth industries in the early twentieth-first century: the military.

Figure 4.
This photo of a young girl dramatizes the separation of families that has so often resulted from recent ICE raids and the resulting detentions and deportations. Separation from family and community was a concern among deportees during the 1940s and 1950s, as well. Photo by Fatima Lopez. Used with permission of MIRA, the Massachusetts Immigrant and Refugee Advocacy Coalition.

Just as cold war alliances mapped the arrivals and deportations of the foreign-born after World War II, the status of contemporary migrant workers is crucially determined by a continuous militarization of the hemisphere. Presidents from Eisenhower through George Bush sent money and troops to stabilize the hemisphere against leftist influences in El Salvador, Nicaragua, and Guatemala. Their efforts paved the way for U.S.-led "free trade" efforts such as the Central American Free Trade Agreement, signed by El Salvador, Honduras, Nicaragua and Guatemala in 2006, and the Dominican Republic in 2007. The regime of free trade drives down wages and working conditions in factories at the same time it discourages and in some places prohibits labor organizing. The combination of these factors drives immigrants to seek opportunities in the United States, where wages remain comparatively high. These immigrants enter a postindustrial economy, where their options include service work, sweatshop labor in places like Bianco, or the military itself.[70]

Endgame

> Oh I am willing to believe they suffer as much as such creatures can suffer. But does that mean their sufferings equal mine? No doubt.
>
> —Samuel Beckett, *Endgame*

Released in 2003, *Endgame* is the name of the ICE Detention and Removal Office "multiyear strategic enforcement plan."[71] Replete with the confident language of bureaucratic mission statement–speak, this *Endgame* advertises such feats as "a hundred percent removal rate for all removable aliens."[72] Predictably, in defining the "unique population" to be removed, the document commingles potential deportees: "The DRO detained population includes illegal economic migrants, aliens who have committed criminal acts, asylum seekers (required to be detained by law) or potential terrorists." While the document encourages the safe and humane treatment of deportees, it is difficult to envision terrorists and committed felons being treated in a manner "strictly administrative in nature, not punitive."[73] And if these putative enemies of the state do not receive human treatment, it is likely that the state of permanent racial exclusion might dictate similar treatment to all of this "unique population."

This document cries out for interdisciplinary analysis. Nowhere is the eponymous term "endgame" explained, even in a glossary that goes to lengths to define words such as *fugitive* and *detention*. To any savvy twelve year old, "endgame" means the end of the video game, and the need for another quarter. Can it be a coincidence that this document was being written right after George W. Bush's famous victory proclamation on board the *USS Abraham Lincoln* in May 2003?

Ghost Towns in the Neoliberal Order and the Emergence of "New Narrative Voices"

> Eulália Mendes never became a naturalized American, which better underscored her internationalized condition and clearly showed that the immigrants' fight was one that would never end.
>
> —Terras da Beira[74]

In the course of writing and researching this article, I traversed some of the places in which raids have taken place in New England and the Midwest over the past two years: Whitewater, Wisconsin; New Bedford, Massachusetts; South Bend, Indiana; Baltimore, Maryland; New Haven, Connecticut. These are postindustrial cities, much of whose industry has fled, and what we might call postagrarian small towns, where small industries such as Star Packaging in Whitewater and the dairy farms in the surrounding counties of "America's Dairyland" alike depend on transnational labor supplies to maintain their operations. Sometimes postindustrial places seem like ghosts of their former selves, with silenced downtowns and decaying civic infrastructure, Wal-Marts perched like vultures on the strips outside once flourishing small towns. But these ghost towns are being repopulated by new immigrants. As parts of an emerging neoliberal economic order, urban and rural places in the United States are in the midst of social and economic transition.

Often, anxieties about this transition take the form of nativism, and support for the deportation terror. As Saskia Sassen has argued, another response to economic globalization is a redefinition of discourses of citizenship and identity.[75] Although Eulália Mendes, when she was interviewed in 1985 by Dan Georgianna, described her inability to become a U.S. citizen as a component of the criminalization of foreign-born laborers, a contemporary left-leaning Web site in Portugal celebrates Eulália as a citizen of the world, a visionary internationalist, for never naturalizing. In this way, migrants redefine the meaning of citizenship at this moment of geopolitical transformation. Das Gupta documents the ways that immigrant political organizing opens up "new narrative possibilities" that provoked her to "tell a different tale."[76]

One effect of the deportation terror is the creation of fear, and the resulting silencing of migrant populations. People go further underground, move to other cities, or leave the country altogether. In June of 2007, for example, the city of New Haven, Connecticut, passed a local ordinance creating a municipal ID available to everyone living in the city. These municipal IDs would have allowed the undocumented to register their children for school, start bank and electrical accounts, and generally conduct the business of daily life. Two days later, ICE staged an unusual neighborhood-based raid in local Fair Haven, arresting migrants from Guatemala, Mexico, Ecuador, and Guinea. ICE claimed that the migrants were arrested on previous deportation orders, but only four of the thirty migrants arrested had such paperwork on file.[77] The fear disseminated by such a raid is very much an intended outcome of policy: the endgame is to win the battle by intimidating opponents. But it is not the only outcome of the deportation terror.

Responding to the deportation terror, the foreign and native-born are developing new coalitions. Allen Petrie, owner of Star Packaging in Whitewater, is currently charged with identity theft in the wake of the 2006 raids at his plant.[78] Along with other small business owners in the area, he has begun to appear at immigrant rights venues, decrying the current system. Dairy farmer John Rosenow, along with high school Spanish teacher Shaun Judge Duval and University of Wisconsin-Extension agent Carl Duley have founded Puentes, a program that supports cooperation between native-born farmers and their increasingly Latina/o employees. Puentes provides Spanish instruction for the dairy farmers, and English instruction for the workers. Farmers and extension students have traveled to Mexico to learn language and culture. In addition, Puentes has developed a certificate course for workers so they can exhibit skills learned on the job.[79] While these alliances do not redress all the inequities operative between native-born farmers and their immigrant employees, the coalition provided by Puentes enables political cooperation and cultural understanding, and undermine the possibilities for white rural nativism. Rosenow, the descendant of Swiss and German immigrants to Wisconsin, expressed an early, public critique of the new social security no-match regulations released in August 2007.[80]

In places such as New Bedford and Whitewater, new migrant political organizations are emerging. New leaders among Mayan, Honduran, Salvadoran, and Brazilian women in Massachusetts have stepped forward to demand the reunification of families and justice for those detained and deported.[81] In New Orleans, where the population of undocumented and H2B migrant contract workers has soared as the city is being rebuilt, workers from Bolivia, Mexico, Peru, and dozens of other countries have organized the Alliance for Guestworkers for Dignity. In Whitewater, Sigma America, founded in 2003 as an immigrant cultural organization, has become a center for political organizing around the raid.[82] Young immigrants, politicized by the effects of the raids on their communities, have become involved in the immigrant rights movement more broadly. A group of high school students from Whitewater chartered a bus to attend hearings on a bill to allow undocumented students to attend Wisconsin public universities at in-state tuition rates; an entire contingent marched in the May 1, 2007, rally in Milwaukee. It is perhaps in part due to the deportation terror in Wisconsin that they were among seventy thousand people to attend this second annual "Day without Latinos."

In North Carolina, as elsewhere in the nation, new immigrants are transforming both the demography of the workforce and ongoing struggles over the rights of workers.[83] In Robeson County, migrants from Mexico and Central America, many of them undocumented, have joined African American, white and Lumbee Indian workers in the struggle to organize the Smithfield meat packaging plant. The company has encouraged labor migration, and has also, reportedly, fostered racialized divisions among the workforce.[84]

Robeson County has long been the site of conflict between the forces of white supremacy and racialized black and Indian communities. In 1958, two years after the federal government recognized that the Lumbee were, in fact, an Indian people but denied them legal recognition as an Indian nation, several hundred Lumbee turned back a rally organized against them by the local Ku Klux Klan in the Battle of Hayes Pond.[85] In neighboring Monroe County in the same period, NAACP president Robert F. Williams coordinated an armed self-defense network to protect the African American community from KKK activities.[86] Violence has also marked the long drive to organize Smithfield Foods. The plant has its own private police force, which has been convicted on charges of violating the 1871 Ku Klux Klan Act by beating, harassing, and intimidating workers.[87]

In the past five years, the workforce at Smithfield Foods has become pre-dominantly newly arrived Latino/as. A recent estimate has the plant at 55 percent foreign-born workers from Mexico and Central America, 30 to 35 percent African Americans, and the rest split between whites and Indians.[88] The United Food and Commercial Workers has hired experienced organizers and set up a workers' center in Red Springs, NC, offering classes in English and basic rights. Like the black and Indian workers at Smithfield, many of the new workers have experience with political organizing and a tradition of marking international holidays such as May Day. Additionally, their status as the most vulnerable workers in an exploitative industry gave immigrants added political momentum. As David Bacon writes, "immigration status itself became an issue for collective action."[89] Hundreds of Latino/a Smithfield workers skipped work to attend the first immigrant rights demonstrations in April and May of 2006.[90]

The racialized violence that has marked Robeson County, and Smithfield Foods in particular, has continued during the current organizing drive. But, just as the KKK opposed the emergence of African American and Indian politi-cal organizing in the 1950s, Homeland Security measures deploy a particular racial terror against immigrant workers. In the wake of the mobilizations of 2006, Smithfield enrolled in the Immigration Customs Enforcement Mutual Agreement between Government and Employers (IMAGE) Program. This program allows ICE access to human resource records of the company, and allows the company to cooperate with ICE in the implementation of raids targeting undocumented workers at the plant.[91] An April 2007 statement submitted to Congress by the UFCW argues that the

> raids were designed and executed as political theater . . . It is not a coincidence that Smithfield has used the IMAGE program as cover to begin firing workers for no-match social security issues at the same time when workers in the plant are gaining momentum in their efforts to secure safer working conditions, better pay, and benefits through union representation.[92]

Deportation has been a crucial technology of the state, as Kanstroom argues, since well before the American Revolution. Municipal governments warned out unruly and racially suspect women during the colonial period; states such as Georgia deported denizens of Indian nations; enslaved Africans could be remanded back to slavery even when living as free persons in nonslave territories; political dissidents and "enemy aliens" could be removed from the nation at times of war and suspicion. Because deportation operates at particular moments as political theater responding to mass mediated fear, American studies scholars are uniquely positioned to understand it. Our historic interdisciplinarity and recent focus on transnationalism are important resources in understanding the evolution of this ongoing terror.

It has been my contention in this article that the emergence of the U.S.-Mexico border as a contested and racialized zone across which migrants and racialized U.S. citizens have been deported en masse at particular moments marks the emergence of a new technology: the deportation terror. The deportation terror draws on the power of the Border Patrol, as it emerged after 1924 and subsequently evolved into the Immigration and Naturalization Service, now subsumed into the Department of Homeland Security. These agencies have implemented mass deportations in the 1930s and again during Operation Wetback and the current ICE raids. The deportation terror draws on these agencies to operate as political theater, responding to mass mediated expressions of fears of violent subversion. The detention and deportation of the foreign-born for political reasons since 1924 is part of the operation of the deportation terror.

Notes

My thanks to Wendy Kozol for her characteristically insightful reading of a prior draft of this piece; to Christine Neumann-Ortiz for telling me to look into what is going on in Smithfield, N.C.; and to the *American Quarterly* editorial board for their thoughtful revision suggestions. "Orange Mike" Lowrey, in a paper for my graduate seminar on immigration history in 2006, first alerted me to the lacunae in the literature on deportation.

1. "The Deportation Terror," issued by the American Committee for the Protection of the Foreign Born for the 27th National Conference, New York, 1959. Pamphlet is held in the Fromkin Memorial Collection of the University of Wisconsin, Milwaukee, library.
2. "The Deportation Terror," 17.
3. See the DHS Web site at http://www.dhs.gov/xabout/history/editorial_0133.shtm.
4. Daniel Kanstroom, *Deportation Nation: Outsiders in American History* (Cambridge, Mass.: Harvard University Press, 2007), 74.
5. The genealogy of these insights includes Hannah Arendt and Giorgio Agamben. See Judith Butler, "I merely belong to them," *Left Review of Books* 29.9 (May 10, 2007), at http://www.lrb.co.uk/v29/n09/brtl02_.html (accessed May 14, 2008) for a discussion of Hannah Arendt's position on nationalism, deportation, and statelessness; Giorgio Agamben, *Homo Sacer: Sovereign Power and Bare Life* (Stanford, Calif.: Stanford University Press, 1995), esp. 166–80; also Linda K. Kerber, "Toward a History of Statelessness in America," *American Quarterly* 57.3 (September 2005): 727–49.
6. "Iraq Refugees Knocking: U.S. to Let in 7,000," Associated Press, May 30, 2007, http://www.msnbc.com/id/18944557/ (accessed May 14, 2008).

7. Kanstroom, Deportation Nation, 16–17.
8. Moustafa Bayoumi, "Racing Religion," *CR: The New Centennial Review* 6.2 (2006): 267–93, quote on 276.
9. Camille Guérin-Gonzales, *Mexican Workers and American Dreams: Immigration, Repatriation, and California Farm Labor, 1900–1939* (New Brunswick, N.J.: Rutgers University Press, 1996); and Lisa Flores, "Crafting Rhetorical Borders: Peons, Illegal Aliens, and Competing Narratives of Immigration," *Critical Studies in Media Communication* 20 (2003): 362–87. See also Abraham Hoffman, *Unwanted Mexicans in the Great Depression* (Tucson: University of Arizona Press, 1974).
10. Arleen DeVera, "Without Parallel: The Local 7 Deportation Cases, 1949–1955," *Amerasia Journal* 20.2 (1994): 1–25; Ellen Schrecker, "Immigration and Internal Security: Political Deportation during the McCarthy Era, Science and Society 60.4 (Winter 1996–1997): 393–426. I am indebted to Michael J. Lowrey, who first brought some of these sources to my attention in an annotated bibliography completed for a graduate seminar I taught in spring 2006.
11. Kanstroom, *Deportation Nation*; David Cole, *Enemy Aliens: Double Standards and Constitutional Freedoms in the War on Terrorism* (New York: New Press, 2003); Kevin Johnson, *The "Huddled Masses" Myth: Immigration and Civil Rights* (Philadelphia: Temple University Press, 2004); Victor C. Romero, *Alienated: Immigrant Rights, the Constitution, and Equality in America* (New York: New York University Press, 2005).
12. Bayoumi, "Racing Religion," 273.
13. Mae Ngai, *Impossible Subjects: Illegal Aliens and the Making of Modern America* (Princeton, N.J.: Princeton University Press, 2004), 57–58.
14. Ngai, *Impossible Subjects*, 58.
15. Donald Pease, "The Mexican-American War and Whitman's 'Song of Myself': A Foundational Borderline Fantasy," in *Immigrant Rights in the Shadow of Citizenship*, edited by Rachel Ida Buff (New York: New York University Press, 2008).
16. Timothy Dunn's 1995 *The Militarization of the U.S.-Mexico Border, 1978–1992* (Austin: University of Texas Press) remains indispensable for an account of the confluence of these sources of militarization.
17. Natsu Taylor Saito, "Reflections on Homeland and Security," *CR: The New Centennial Review* 6.2 (2006): 239–67, quote on 246–47.
18. Kanstroom, *Deportation Nation*, 195; also "Deportation Special: Who's Who in Deportations: Brief Biographies of Workers Held for Deportation," American Committee for the Protection of the Foreign Born, September 1935, Tamiment Library, American Committee for the Protection of the Foreign Born Collection, Box 1, File, "1935–1945"; also see "Selected Immigration Laws" at http://www.lib.umich.edu/socwork/rescue/archive/sw652.html.
19. Rachel Rubin and Jeffrey Melnick, *Immigration and American Popular Culture: An Introduction* (New York: New York University Press, 2007), 53.
20. Tram Nguyen, *We Are All Suspects Now: Untold Stories from Immigrant Communities after 9/11* (Boston: Beacon Press: 2005), xiv.
21. Nguyen writes: "National security concerns have been used as a justification for increased discrimination in arenas of long-standing concern to civil rights activists, including employment, housing and criminal justice." Ibid., xx.
22. Lisa Flores, "Constructing Rhetorical Borders: Peons, Illegal Aliens, and Competing Narratives of Immigration," *Critical Studies in Media Communication* 20.4 (December 2003): 363.
23. "Deportation Special," American Committee for the Protection of the Foreign Born, Tamiment Library, Box 1, New York University.
24. Scott Michaelsen, "Between Japanese Internment and the USA PATRIOT Act: The Borderlands and the Permanent State of Racial Exception," *Aztlán* 30.2 (Fall 2005).
25. The 2004 budget for the Department of Homeland Security (DHS), for example, included $18 billion, double the funding of the 2002 budget to "increase border and transportation security." Department of Homeland Security, Budget in Brief, 2004, 1. The budget for ICE increased by 10% in 2005. Department of Homeland Security, Budget in Brief, 2005, 13; 13.5% in 2006. The 2007 budget alone contained $400 million for the building of detention facilities. These budgets accessed at the DHS Web site, August 9, 2007.
26. DHS Budget in Brief, 2004, 6.

27. DHS Budget in Brief, 2005, 29. For an example of the ways a discourse criminalizes a targeted immigrant population: an in-class debate I staged in the late spring of 2006 on the question of undocumented immigration was won, hands down, by the anti-immigrant side when it cited a study by the Atlanta Violent Crimes Institute proclaiming that there are 240,000 undocumented sex offenders in the United States, and 93 sex offenders and 12 serial sex offenders crossing the border each day (George Putnam, "One Reporter's Opinion," June 16, 2006, newsmax.com). On further research, we found that the Violent Crimes Institute consists of one person, Dr. Deborah Shurman-Kauflin, who holds a PhD of her own design from an online institution. However, the location of her institute in Atlanta and the spectacular nature of her claims, based as they turned out to be on a sample study of 1,500 prison inmates, has led to CNN fame, not to mention speaking and training work around the country. Most recently, her work has been featured on a House report on—what else?—border security. See http://www.drdsk.com.

28. This is already taking place by local fiat in many places, in lieu, again, of federal action to pass the proposed CLEAR Act to facilitate the enforcement of immigration law by local agents.

29. At this writing during the late summer of 2007, for example, DHS has implemented new regulations governing the "social security no-match" letters received by many workers, including undocumented ones, and their employers. These new regulations construe the receipt of no-match letters as evidence that the employer has "constructive knowledge" of employing workers illegally, and therefore justifies potential raids on such employers. See "Why DHS's Final Social Security 'No Match' Letter Rule Is Bad for Workers, Employers and the Economy," National Immigration Law Center, August 10, 2007, http://www.nilc.org (accessed August 16, 2007).

30. Available at http://www.cbp.gov/xp/cgov/careers/customs_careers/border_careers/bp_agent/videos/ (accessed May 14, 2008).

31. Camille Guerin-Gonzales, *Mexican Workers and American Dreams: Immigration, Repatriation, and California Farm Labor, 1900–1939* (New Brunswick, N.J.: Rutgers University Press, 1996), esp. 77–96.

32. I am grateful to Erich Straub, immigration attorney, for laying this out for me in a language I could understand. Interview with the author, July 10, 2007.

33. See Victor Romero, "Who Should Manage Immigration—Congress or the States: An Introduction to Constitutional Immigration Law," in *Immigrant Rights in the Shadow of U.S. Citizenship*, ed. Rachel Ida Buff (New York: New York University Press, 2008); Alex Kotlowitz, "Our Town," *New York Times Magazine*, August 5, 2007.

34. Kotlowitz, "Our Town," 33.

35. Corinn Williams, executive director, Community Economic Development Center, New Bedford; interview with the author, July 26, 2007.

36. Monisha Das Gupta, *Unruly Immigrants: Rights, Activism, and Transnational South Asian Politics in the United States* (Durham, N.C.: Duke University Press, 2006).

37. "The Legacy of Abner Green: A Memorial Journal," issued by the American Committee for the Protection of the Foreign Born for the 27th National Conference, December 19–20, 1959. Held at the Tamiment Library, New York University, ACFPFB Collection, Box 2, Folder 4. On waterfront pharmacies: correspondence with Dr. Greg Higby of the American Institute for Pharmacy History, Madison, Wisconsin, July 2007. According to John W. Sherman, Green also attended City College, where he became involved in the Communist Party. Sherman's book, *A Communist Front at Mid-Century: The American Committee for the Protection of the Foreign Born, 1933–1959* (Westport: Praeger, 2001) is the only recent study of the organization. As is perhaps illustrated by the title, Sherman is centrally concerned with the circumstances of the ACPFB's alliances with the Communist Party.

38. "Foreign Seamen on Our Ships," *New York Times*, July 22, 1945, excerpted on pamphlet; Tamiment Library, ACFPFB, Box 1; also Abner Green, "Excerpts from Report," given at the National Conference Against Deportation, held in Detroit, Michigan, December 1949, ACFPB papers, Box 1, Folder "1935–1949."

39. "Merchant Marine Minister Meets with U.S. Ambassador, Last Liberty Ship to be Donated to Greece," *Hellenic News of America*, October 27, 2006, http://hellenicnews.com/readnews.html?newsid=5797 (accessed August 2, 2007).

40. *National Guardian*, July 9, 1956, found at Tamiment Library, ACFPFB Archives, Box 2, Folder 4.

41. Kelly Lytle Hernandez, "The Crimes and Consequences of Illegal Immigration: A Cross-Border Examination of Operation Wetback, 1943–1954," *Western Historical Quarterly* 37 (Winter 2006): 421–44.

42. At panel on "The Pacific Rim as Geographic Imaginary and Colonial Horizon," American Studies Association Conference, Oakland, California, October 2006. See also Steve C. McKay, "Men at Sea: Migration and the Performance of Masculinity," presented at the American Sociology Association, Montreal, Canada, August 2006.

43. George J. Sánchez, " 'What's Good for Boyle Heights Is Good for the Jews': Creating Multiracialism on the Eastside during the 1950s," *American Quarterly* 56.3 (September 2004): 653–61; Jeffrey M. Garcilazo, "McCarthyism, Mexican Americans, and the Los Angeles Committee for the Protection of the Foreign-Born, 1950–1954," *Western Historical Quarterly* 32.3 (2001): 273–95.

44. Garcilazo, "McCarthyism," 289–90.

45. David R. Gutiérrez, *Walls and Mirrors*, 142, quoted in Garcilazo, "McCarthyism."

46. "The Diamond Kimm Case Has Reached a Critical Stage Requiring Immediate Action to Save His Life," poster, ACPFB, Box 2, Folder 9.

47. "Fact Sheet," 1955, Papers of the International League for the Rights of Man, Social Ethnic Pamphlet Collection (RG 73), Yale Divinity School Library. Courtesy of Joan Duffy, archivist.

48. Quee Young-Kim, "From Protest to Change of Regime: The 4-19 Revolt and the Fall of the Rhee Regime in South Korea," *Social Forces* 74.4 (1996), esp. 1185–88.

49. "Immigration and Internal Security: Political Deportations During the McCarthy Era," *Science & Society* 60.4 (Winter 1996–97): 393.

50. Dan Georgianna and Roberta Hazen Aronson, *The Strike of '28* (New Bedford: Spinner Publications, 1993), 13.

51. See Erika Lee, *At America's Gates: Chinese Immigration During the Exclusion Period* (Chapel Hill: University of North Carolina Press, 2007).

52. Quoted in Georgianna and Aronson, *Strike of '28*, 15.

53. Ibid., 13.

54. Quoted in Georgianna and Aronson, *Strike of '28*, 144. This subtitle echoes the ingenious, resonant, and grim working title of Harvey Amani Whitfield's work on black loyalist emigrants to Canada before the Civil War, *From Slavery to Slavery* (forthcoming).

55. Under the McCarran-Walter Act, for example, the Justice Department created a category called Supervisory Parole for noncitizens who were not yet deported or whose countries of origin no longer existed. "Two Years of the Walter-McCarran Act," ACFPFB Papers, Box 1, Folder "1951–1954."

56. "Stop Her Deportation: Save Her from Death in Portugal," ACFPFB Papers, Box 1, Folder "1951–1954." One source indicates that the Mendes family may also have been Sephardic Jews; I am working to document this. On the emergence of the New State, see Manuel Baoia, "The Political History of Twentieth Century Portugal," *E-journal of Portuguese History* 1.2 (Winter 2003), http://www.brown.edu/Departments/Portuguese_Brazilian_Studies/ejph/ (accessed May 14, 2008); also Filipe Ribeiro de Meneses, "The Origins and Nature of Authoritarian Rule in Portugal, 1919–1945," *Contemporary European History* 2.1 (2002): 152–62.

57. "Stop Her Deportation," pamphlet.

58. Quoted in Georgianna and Aronson, *Strike of '28*, 83.

59. See Lizabeth Cohen, *Making a New Deal: Industrial Workers in Chicago, 1919–1939* (New York: Cambridge University Press, 1991).

60. Quoted in Georgianna and Aronson, *Strike of '28*, 124.

61. Ibid., 118.

62. "Stop Her Deportation." At this writing, I am in the process of obtaining Eulália Mendes's immigration files under the Freedom of Information Act.

63. Quoted in Georgianna and Aronson, *Strike of '28*, 144.

64. "Eulália Mendes: A grande lutador," *Terras da Beira*, April 5, 2001, http://www.freipedro.pt/tb/050401/soc6.htm (accessed July 7, 2007).

65. Lee, *At America's Gates*.

66. Garcilazo, "McCarthyism," 278–79.

67. Letter from detention in Port Isabel, Los Frenos, Texas, April 10, 2007; at http://www.miracoalition.org/home/new-bedford-immigration-raids (accessed August 16, 2007).

48 | Rachel Ida Buff

68. MIRA Web page: http://www.miracoalition.org/home/new-bedford-immigration-raids (accessed August 21, 2007).
69. Cecilia Menjvar, "The Intersection of Work and Gender; Central American Women and Employment in California," in *Gender and U.S. Immigration: Contemporary Trends*, ed. Pierrette Hondagneu-Sotelo, 101–7 (Berkeley: University of California Press, 2003).
70. One of the first U.S. casualties was undocumented Guatemalan-born Jose Gutierrez. Deborah Davis, "Illegal Immigrants: Uncle Sam Wants You," *In These Times*, July 25, 2007; see also Lisa Marie Cacho, "Alien Others: Asian and Latina/o Relational Racializations in Discourses of Immigration," American Studies Association, Atlanta, November 13, 2004, unpublished paper in possession of author.
71. *ENDGAME: Office of Detention and Removal Strategic Plan, 2003–2012: Detention and Removal for a Secure Homeland*, DHS, August 15, 2003, ii.
72. Ibid., 2–9.
73. Ibid., 2–11.
74. April 5, 2001, at: http://www.freipedro.pt/tb/050401/sociedade.htm (accessed August 16, 2007). My thanks to Julie Kline of the Center for Latin American and Caribbean Studies at UWM for the translation.
75. Saskia Sassen, "The Repositioning of Citizenship: Emergent Subjects and Spaces for Politics," *CR: The New Centennial Review* 3.2 (2003): 41–66.
76. Das Gupta, *Unruly Immigrants*, 21.
77. "*Feds Arrest Dozens of Illegal Immigrants in New Haven Raids,*" *Yale Daily News*, June 6, 2007; "ICE Raids Spark Protests in Portland, New Haven," *World War Four*, http://www.ww4report.com/node/4084 (accessed August 16, 2007).
78. Carla McCann, "Whitewater Still Healing Long After Raid," *Janesville Gazette*, July 26, 2007.
79. Georgia Pabst, "Immigration Cultivation: Farmers Gain Insight on New Work Force through Program," *Milwaukee Journal Sentinel*, June 6, 2006, http://www.jsonline.com/story/index.aspx?id=432659 (accessed August 21, 2007).
80. Georgia Pabst, "Immigrant Measures Stir Hiring Concerns: Some Say Federal Moves Are Overdue," *Milwaukee Journal Sentinel*, August 13, 2007, http://www.jsonline.com/story/index.aspx?id=646205 (accessed August 21, 2007).
81. Williams interview, July 26, 2007.
82. Jorge Islas, Sigma America, interview with the author, August 13, 2007.
83. According to the Center for Immigration Studies' *Immigrants at Mid-Decade: A Snapshot of America's Foreign-Born Population in 2005*, North Carolina's immigrant population (both legal and illegal) increased threefold between 1995 and 2005 (170,000 to 590,000). North Carolina, South Carolina, and Georgia accounted for only 575,000 immigrants in 1995, or roughly 2% of the 24 million immigrants in the United States. These three states accounted for 1.5 million immigrants in 2005, or roughly 4% of the 35 million immigrants in the United States. Growth during the past five years has been even more rapid. North Carolina's immigrant population has increased by 58.1% between 2000 and 2005 (373,000 to 590,000). North Carolina is also experiencing rapid growth of illegal immigrants. According to the Pew Hispanic Center's *Estimates of the Size and Characteristics of the Undocumented Population*, North Carolina's undocumented population is 300,000. This makes North Carolina home to the nation's eighth largest population of undocumented migrants. The study claims that undocumented migration is the principal reason for the rapid growth of foreign-born populations in nontraditional settlement areas such as North Carolina, Georgia, Tennessee, and South Carolina. Source: Congressional Representative Sue Myrick's Web page, at http://myrick.house.gov/NC ImmigrationCourtFactSheet.shtml, (accessed March 30, 2008).
84. "The Case Against Smithfield: Human and Civil Rights Violations in Tar Heel, North Carolina," at http://www.ufcw.org/working_america/case_against_smithfield (accessed March 17, 2008); also Mike Ely and Linda Flores, "Strike at Smithfield: Workers under a Changing Sky," *Revolution* 76, January 14, 2007, at http://rwor.org/a/076/Smithfield-en.html (accessed March 17, 2008).
85. "Victory over the Ku Klux Klan," at the Museum of the Native American Resource Center, University of North Carolina at Pembroke, http://www.uncp.edu/nativemuseum/collections/victory/index.html (accessed March 17, 2008).
86. Timothy Tyson, "Robert F. Williams, 'Black Power,' and the Roots of the African American Freedom Struggle," *Journal of American History* 85.2 (September 1998): 540–70, 552.

87. "Smithfield Packing: A Timeline" at http://www.ufcw.org/Smithfield_justice/timeline_of_events/index.cfm (accessed March 17, 2008).
88. "The Case Against Smithfield."
89. David Bacon, "Feds Crack Down on Immigrant Labor Organizers," *The American Prospect*, May 10, 2007, http://www.prospect.org/cs/archive/web_archives_by_month?month=5&year=2007 (accessed March 30, 2008).
90. Ibid.
91. Ibid.
92. "Testimony on Behalf of the United Food and Commercial Workers International Union (UFCW) Submitted in Writing to the House Subcommittee on Immigration, Citizenship, Refugees, Border Security and International Law," April 24, 2007, http://www.ufcw.org/issues/immigration/ufcw_political_involvement (accessed March 17, 2008).

Immigration Enforcement and the Complication of National Sovereignty: Understanding Local Enforcement as an Exercise in Neoliberal Governance

Philip Kretsedemas

Over the past several years, a growing number of local governments have enacted laws that require police, other government workers, and even private citizens to verify the legal status of local residents. Approximately 300 such laws have been enacted over the past four years and more than 180 of them, spanning forty-three states, were enacted in 2007 alone.[1] The primary aim of these laws (often referred to as "illegal immigrant" or local enforcement laws) is to allow local authorities to apprehend unauthorized migrants. Broadly described, the laws appeal to a territorial paradigm of national sovereignty that equates the integrity of the nation with the ability to control its borders. From this perspective, the unauthorized migrant is not just a potential "economic burden" or a "security risk," but an affront to conventional notions of citizenship, which equate political, social, and civil rights with the criterion of legal residence. Hence local enforcement laws are often viewed by their supporters as efforts to restore the rights and privileges of the citizenry by ensuring that unauthorized migrants are unable to vote in local elections, access publicly funded services and resources, or compete for jobs that could be filled by citizens and other legal residents.[2]

Popular and official conceptions of the unauthorized migrant have also tended to focus on racialized populations. In the early twentieth century, enforcement practices targeting illegal aliens disproportionately focused on Latino (Mexican) and Asian (Chinese and Filipino) migrants, despite the fact that the overwhelming majority of immigrants during this period were European.[3] An early precursor to present-day local enforcement laws was the *Fong Yue Ting v. U.S. et al.* (1893) Supreme Court decision, which granted U.S. citizens the authority to check the legal papers of any Chinese worker and to make a citizen's arrest of individuals who were unable to present these papers.[4] In the 1950s, local law enforcement cooperated with federal immigration agents to deport hundreds of thousands of Mexican nationals (under the auspices of Operation Wetback).[5] During this same period of time, administrative procedures that allowed illegal aliens to adjust their status (including persons with criminal convictions) disproportionately benefited European-origin migrants.[6]

The current discourse on the "immigration problem" also blurs the lines between legal status, "race," and culture, where concerns about illegal immigration are conflated with the cultural and demographic changes resulting from immigration in general.[7] In addition, local police often develop racial-ethnic profiles of "illegals" that are based on broad generalizations of how the typical immigrant looks, acts, and sounds. For example, although it is true that most unauthorized migrants are of Mexican origin, national data on local enforcement practices show that Mexicans tended to be apprehended by local police for unlawful entry (and related violations) at a rate that is much higher than the Mexican presence in the undocumented population.[8]

Similar to the controversies surrounding black racial profiling, these trends draw attention to the problem of selective enforcement. However, there is another kind of disparity that has been intensified by local enforcement laws that has not received as much attention, but is no less significant. This disparity concerns the extremely wide variation in the way these laws have been implemented across the United States. As I explain in this essay, this variation is one of the most significant qualities that distinguishes present-day local enforcement laws from earlier versions of local enforcement.

One reason for this variation is the diversity of the concerns of local coalitions that have put these laws into effect. An even more important factor is the influence of the executive branch of the federal government, which opened the door for these diverse concerns by affirming that local governments have the "inherent authority" to enact their own immigration enforcement laws. As I will explain, however, the priorities of the executive branch are not exactly the same as those of local advocates who have pushed for "illegal immigrant" laws. Advocates for local enforcement laws tend to support an immigration control agenda that is grounded in a territorial paradigm of sovereignty. In contrast, the policy agenda of the federal government has been influenced by a free market (or neoliberal) perspective that tends to promote a looser connection among rights, legal status, and territoriality.

In the next section, I provide a more detailed review of discontinuities in the way that local enforcement laws are being implemented today and explain how they differ from earlier enforcement practices that were used to accomplish similar objectives. This is followed by a discussion of the paradigm of national sovereignty reflected in the federal government's policy priorities. Here I draw on the writing of Aihwa Ong to explain how the imperatives of economic expansionism and national security can be combined to produce a "graduated sovereignty" that makes finer distinctions between the rights and privileges of different segments of the national population. I also draw on the work of Giorgio Agamben to explain why this kind of sovereignty becomes increasingly reliant on governing practices that create exceptions to the law.

Finally, I explain how the current wave of local enforcement laws were made possible by executive decisions that overrode prior legal precedent. The practical, short-term outcome of these decisions has been the expansion of local laws that serve an immigration control agenda. But I also illustrate how, instead of using get-tough enforcement to reduce immigration flows, this immigration reform agenda tends to support the expansion of immigration enforcement as a precondition for expanding the supply of noncitizen labor. As a consequence, the mission of immigration enforcement is defined as much by the imperative of labor market regulation as by the imperative of border control.

A Fragmented Terrain: The Expansion of Local Enforcement Laws, 2004–2007

The recent expansion of local enforcement laws has occurred almost entirely during the space of the past four years. The first significant increase occurred in 2004, and the pace of local enforcement legislation has increased precipitously since this time.[9] However, the expansion of these laws also draws attention to their discontinuities. Although more than three hundred city, state, and municipal governments have adopted some version of local enforcement, approximately two hundred local governments have adopted ordinances that are explicitly opposed to local enforcement.[10] Furthermore, many local law enforcement agencies, including many of the police departments that serve urban immigration centers, have taken a decidedly neutral stance on the matter—acknowledging that local police have some authority to enforce immigration laws, but that this should not distract from criminal law enforcement.[11]

The erratic nature of these enforcement practices is illustrated by the immigration raids that were carried out in the Massachusetts town of New Bedford in March 2007.[12] Authorities were successful in apprehending unauthorized migrants at their place of work (which was receiving federal monies to produce vestments for the U.S. military), but the raids also highlighted discrepancies between the priorities of federal enforcement and local police. The raids were carried out as part of a national immigration dragnet that was intended to send a stern warning to employers who hire unauthorized migrants. The New Bedford police department, however, did not see the enforcement of immigration laws as something that fell under their authority.[13] Their position was also supported by Massachusetts governor Deval Patrick, who was openly critical of the New Bedford raids and, several weeks prior, had revoked a Memorandum of Agreement with the Department of Homeland Security that allowed local police to work more closely with federal immigration agents.[14]

Meanwhile, police departments in other parts of New England have gone out of their way to find rationales for enforcing federal immigration laws. A police department in New Hampshire attempted to use local vagrancy laws as a rationale for arresting people who were suspected of being undocumented.[15] This practice was eventually struck down by the local courts, but largely because of the unusual rationale that was being used by the police, who detained unauthorized migrants for trespassing on U.S. national territory. As I will explain later, the vast majority of local enforcement laws use a very different rationale, which is based on the "inherent authority" of local governments to enforce immigration laws. This rationale has also been successfully challenged in a few instances, and these challenges may set the stage for a challenge at the level of the Supreme Court that could lead to the revocation of all local enforcement laws that have used this "inherent authority" argument.[16] At the present time, however, the vast majority of local enforcement laws remain in effect.

Another defining, but seldom acknowledged, feature of recent local enforcement laws is that they are not exclusively focused on the role of local police. In fact, of the 182 local immigration laws that were enacted in 2007, only 12 dealt with law enforcement.[17] The remaining 170 laws authorized a diverse array of government workers and private citizens to screen individuals for legal status. This includes ordinances that require landlords to verify the legal status of their tenants, employers to verify the legal status of their employees, gun shop owners to verify the legal status of their customers, hospital workers to verify the legal status of emergency room patients, educators and social workers to identify unauthorized migrants within their client populations, and electoral workers to verify the legal status of voters (among other examples).

It is likely that forthcoming local enforcement laws will continue to focus on these sorts of nonpolice actors. One reason is that there are already a number of policies that allow local police to enforce immigration laws without requiring a local ordinance. In 2001, for example, the Department of Justice (DoJ) authorized the entry of data concerning immigration violations into the National Crime Information Center database and made this database available to police departments across the United States.[18] As a result, it is now possible for local police to check whether any individual stopped for questioning has an outstanding order of deportation or any other kind of immigration or security-related notice that has been recorded. State governments also have the option of entering into Memorandums of Agreement (MOAs) that allow local police to cooperate with federal immigration agents. The governors of Rhode Island, New Mexico, Florida, North Carolina, and Alabama have all issued executive orders that have established these sorts of partnerships, which vary widely in their scope and provenance.[19] These options, which were authorized by the 1996 Illegal Immigration Reform and Immigrant Responsibility Act, also allow local governments to request training from federal immigration enforcement to assist them in enforcing immigration laws.

Current local enforcement laws differ from these practices because they allow local governments to develop immigration screening practices that do not require the establishment of a formal partnership between local and federal authorities. Localities are still prohibited from writing their own comprehensive immigration laws, but they now have greater authority in determining how existing immigration laws can be enforced. As a result, state and local ordinances can now authorize a range of local actors to proactively screen individuals for legal status according to criteria that are wholly determined by local lawmakers.

Although these laws are motivated by similar concerns as earlier mass deportation strategies, they have taken a very different form. The involvement of local actors in Operation Wetback, for example, operated under a framework that was similar to current state-federal MOAs (although current MOAs give state governments much more leeway in determining how they will partner with federal authorities). On the other hand, the *Fong Yue Ting* decision, which authorized the citizen's arrest of Chinese "illegals," was national in scope. In contrast, present-day local enforcement practices vary by city, county, and state and many of these laws target different aspects of public life.

Such laws reinforce immigrant fears of being targeted by law enforcement, regardless of whether they are legal residents or undocumented persons. Some local enforcement laws have driven large cross-sections of the Latino population out of cities and townships.[20] Because there is no way of tracking these individuals, and especially because many of them are legal immigrants, it is not clear that they have actually left the United States. Instead, it is likely that many of these individuals have moved to other cities and towns that have not enacted local enforcement laws.

These outcomes point toward a very different kind of national sovereignty than what is typically championed by immigration control advocates. Instead of uniformly removing unauthorized migrants from the national territory, current local enforcement laws appear to be pushing unauthorized migrants out of some localities and into others. It also bears noting that fewer than 10 percent of unauthorized migrants are apprehended on an annual basis,[21] and even though formal removals have experienced a moderate increase in recent years (approximately 12 percent, 2000 to 2005) the total number of people apprehended for immigrant violations has remained level for the past three years (2004 through 2006).[22]

At the very least, these data indicate that it is too early to assess local enforcement's impact on national trends in unauthorized migration. The evidence also indicates that it is not possible to make definite statements about the impact of local enforcement outside of the particular localities in which these laws have been enacted, and in even these areas most of the information on outcomes is derived from the anecdotal accounts of local officials. Again, this draws attention to the piecemeal approach toward immigration enforcement that has been set in motion by the recent expansion of local enforcement laws.

In contrast, there is a much clearer connection between local enforcement laws and other policy trends that have created new distinctions between the rights of immigrants and the native born. Local enforcement laws (targeting unauthorized migrants) and recent federal immigration policies (restricting the rights of legal immigrants) operate within a similar paradigm, which has been described by Aihwa Ong as "graduated sovereignty."[23] Although the U.S. form of graduated sovereignty has been shaped by get-tough immigration laws, it is not anti-immigrant or restrictionist in the way these terms are conventionally defined. It has not protected the native-born citizenry by restricting immigration levels, but it has created a policy climate in which legal status plays a more prominent role in widening inequalities between different segments of the national population.

Immigration, Graduated Sovereignty, and the State of Exception

Over the past twelve years, U.S. immigration laws have ushered in a tiered system of legal rights for citizens and noncitizens that is unprecedented in

U.S. history. The 2005 REAL ID Act, for example, is the first piece of U.S. legislation that permanently revoked the writ of habeas corpus for an entire category of noncitizens.[24] Earlier pieces of legislation, dating from the 1996 Immigration and Welfare Reform laws on, have limited immigrant access to social services and given federal enforcement more leeway to monitor and detain noncitizens without regard to normal due process rights.[25]

Although these policies have sent chilling signals to new immigrants, they have also occurred during an immigration boom that began in the early 1990s and continues to this day. The immigration peaks of this boom period equal that of the last major wave of European migration (1870s–1920s), but even more significant has been the growth of the nonimmigrant or temporary visitor population. Whereas annual immigration levels (for persons granted legal permanent residence) have peaked at 1.2 million in recent years, the annual flow of noncitizens has exceeded 33 million (conservatively estimated) and has exceeded 230 million per annum if counting all temporary arrivals.[26]

If the objectives of get-tough immigration policies can be deduced from their outcomes, it is apparent that they are not being used to discourage immigration. Over the past two decades, spending on immigration enforcement has expanded in tandem with the growth of the noncitizen population.[27] It is somewhat misleading, however, to insist that these developments have weakened "immigrant rights" since the people who are most severely affected are not legally defined as "immigrants." Immigrants (or persons granted legal permanent residence) are currently at a much greater risk of being deported for crimes that would merit a relatively minor prison or jail sentence if committed by a native-born person. Depending on when they arrived in the United States, most immigrants also have more limited access to federally subsidized assistance than U.S. citizens do. But upon naturalizing, these foreign-born persons attain legal and social rights that are virtually identical to those of native-born citizens. Nonimmigrants, in contrast, are admitted to the United States under a temporary legal status, with limited social and legal rights, virtually no political rights, and no guaranteed option for naturalization. Every year, small numbers of this population manage to have their status adjusted to that of legal permanent resident (with the option to apply for citizenship), but the vast majority of these persons remain nonimmigrants, and the size of this population is being continually replenished by migration flows that are much larger than the annual inflow of "regular" immigrants.[28] Of course, unauthorized migrants are in an even more precarious legal situation than nonimmigrants. Some legal and human rights for unauthorized migrants have been recognized by the federal courts, but it is also widely acknowledged that unauthorized migrants seldom assert their rights due to fears of deportation.

Despite their differentiated access to legal, social, and political rights, all of these categories of noncitizens have found a niche in the U.S. workforce. Immigration and labor market policies have also tended to reinforce distinctions between these populations. Recent immigration reform proposals, for example, have called for an expansion of temporary workers to fill labor market demands for low-income migrant labor, while providing no guarantees that these individuals will be given preferential treatment if they decide to apply for permanent residence.[29] Meanwhile, proposals for "legalizing" unauthorized migrants have called for the creation of a new kind of temporary legal status (the Z visa) that would be subjected to more stringent guidelines than those applied to other guest workers.[30]

These developments are indicative of a kind of sovereignty that is characterized by a loosening relationship between rights, legal status, and territoriality. Under this framework, the national population is decomposed into an assemblage of different legal categories that are not on the same pathway to citizenship. And conversely, the citizenry becomes just one population among many that resides in the national territory alongside other populations of noncitizens. According to Aihwa Ong, these are also the defining characteristics of graduated sovereignty, which she describes as

> a more dispersed strategy that does not treat the national territory as a uniform political space. Market-driven logic induces the coordination of political policies with the corporate interests, so that developmental decisions favor the fragmentation of the national space into various noncontiguous zones, and promote the differential regulation of populations who can be connected to or disconnected from global circuits of capital.[31]

Ong's discussion of graduated sovereignty has been influenced by, and contributes to, critical investigations into neoliberal governmentality by a variety of Foucauldian scholars.[32]

In the most basic of terms, neoliberalism can be equated with a free market agenda that is oriented toward the expansion of trade and minimal regulation of private corporations (this policy agenda is sometimes referred to as "neoconservatism" in U.S. policy discourse).[33] According to many Foucauldian scholars, however, neoliberalism is not merely an economic platform that weakens government controls, but comprises an array of strategies and techniques that are used to actively create new kinds of political and economic subjects. This process does not merely "shrink the state"; it transforms the organizational form of the state, limiting its authority in some ways and radically expanding its authority in other ways. And this transformation of the state corresponds with another more complex process of transforming the social and economic terrain that had been presided over by the "old state."

It should be noted that this analysis is not unique to Foucauldian scholars. Saskia Sassen, for example, has explained how economic globalization has been made possible by a new, positive kind of regulation that has denationalized many of the functions of the state but without necessarily decreasing its power and influence.[34] Sassen's observations carry implications for an analysis of power, but they are also more focused on explaining globalization as a sequence of objectively existing, structural transformations that include, but are not limited to, neoliberal governing strategies. Nevertheless, it is possible to see how the strategies and technologies that are being used to guide the process of economic globalization (as discussed by Sassen) have been shaped by the imperatives of neoliberalism.

The relatively new forms of stratification that have been produced by neoliberal reforms also set the stage for new governing strategies. Ong explains how, under graduated sovereignty, different populations are managed by the state in different ways.[35] Some segments of the citizenry, regardless of their socioeconomic status, can be subjected to a "pastoral mode of care" that positions the individual as the member of a population that should be nurtured and protected from the destabilizing effects of globalization. Other categories of persons (including immigrants and nonimmigrants) can be subjected to disciplinary techniques designed to stimulate maximum productivity, but with much less concern for the welfare of the individual. There are also categories of persons that may be only partly exposed to these managerial techniques (for example, highly skilled temporary workers who are not nurtured to become corporate or political leaders but who are also not subjected to the same disciplinary measures as lower skilled guest workers).

In this context, it is possible to see how neoliberal governmental priorities can dovetail with the agenda of some immigration restrictionists. Although neoliberal reformers may not share the same policy objectives as restrictionists, they may still share a similar desire to insulate the native-born population from the cultural and economic aftershocks of immigration. It bears emphasizing, however, that neoliberal strategies are more focused on managing an ongoing process of economic growth than they are on preserving the national culture for its own sake. Hence, it becomes important to cultivate skills and capacities in the citizenry that will allow them to occupy leadership positions in a "new economy" that is also being fueled by flows of noncitizen labor.

This emphasis on economic transformation also sets the stage for Ong's discussion of neoliberalism and the state of exception. Unlike Keynesian-era social policy, neoliberalism tends to create zones of decision-making authority made possible by the law, but which also grant its beneficiaries an unprecedented degree of freedom from binding legalities (in other words, "deregulation").

Ong notes that neoliberalism tends to position itself as an exception to other regulatory paradigms, as well as granting itself the prerogative to create exceptions to its own edicts and guidelines. In any event, the primary utility of the exception is that it allows the state to adapt prior laws and practices to new contingencies. This kind of power leads to a sovereignty that is somewhat distinct from the law. Rather than positioning itself as the will of a sovereign people that is expressed through the law (in the vein of modern republicanism) this kind of sovereignty requires the cultivation of an authority that guides or intervenes in the law. As a result, sovereignty becomes a kind of authority that is wielded over the law rather than being coextensive with it.

In describing this aspect of sovereignty, Ong turns to the writing of Giorgio Agamben, who has produced some of the most detailed investigations into the origin and recent permutations of the state of exception. Ong takes issue with some of Agamben's assumptions about the absolute forms of power that follow from this kind of sovereign authority.[36] Even so, Agamben's observations are useful because of the insights they provide into rationales for interpreting (and radically transforming) the law that are consistent with Ong's discussion of neoliberal governance. Perhaps the most relevant aspect of Agamben's theory, in this regard, is his discussion of the manner in which modern governments routinely suspend the law or create exceptions to normal, legal procedures.

In *State of Exception*, Agamben provides a contemporary history of exceptional measures (from the late eighteenth century on).[37] In contrast to Ong, Agamben does not assert that there is a special relationship between the state of exception and neoliberalism. Instead, he argues that the use of exceptional measures tends to increase along with the centralization of power in the executive office of the government (which dominates the courts and legislative branch). And he notes that, ironically, some of the earliest manifestations of this kind of power in the modern era occurred under the "radical" Republican governments of postrevolutionary France (under Robespierre) and, in the United States, under the Lincoln administration.[38]

The classic form of the state of exception occurs under martial law. In this case, the executive office temporarily suspends the law in order to accomplish objectives that are deemed to be in the "higher interest" of the nation. Historically, these exceptional measures have been invoked during times of dire emergency, the post-9/11 War on Terror being a recent example. But Agamben also argues that modern governments tend to craft and expand the definition of "emergency" to suit their political interests. As a consequence, exceptional measures have become an increasingly regular feature of modern governance that are loosely articulated with the rule of law.

Consider the 2001 USA PATRIOT Act, which gave federal enforcement agencies the ability to search the premises of all U.S. residents without a warrant and allowed virtually no restrictions on electronic surveillance.[39] In many respects, the PATRIOT Act created an enforcement climate that was similar to a formal state of emergency. In this case, however, an effect similar to a state of emergency was created by the law, rather than through a suspension of the law. In a similar vein, neoliberal strategies for privatizing and deregulating public sector industries have used new laws to weaken or eliminate the rights and guidelines that were introduced by prior laws. And although these new laws are enacted by legislative bodies, they are often driven by a policy agenda coordinated by the executive office. As a consequence, it becomes increasingly difficult to make a clear distinction between the rule of law and rulings that are used to create exceptions to the law. In any event, the end result is a policy climate that allows the law to be applied in very different ways under different conditions, and where the people charged with the responsibility of implementing these laws are granted more discretionary authority to interpret their meaning. Under these conditions, the exceptional measure is no longer being used to merely suspend the law. Instead, it becomes a tool for making and shaping laws.

Local Enforcement and the Sovereign Decision

The sequence of events that prepared the way for the recent expansion of local enforcement laws provides a very good example of the form of sovereign authority that I have just described. Agamben often describes this kind of sovereignty as being manifest in the form of a decision—a discretionary privilege that allows the executive to reinterpret or suspend the law. On one hand, this kind of authority appears completely antithetical to the role that the law is supposed to play in a liberal, democratic republic. Agamben argues, however, that this kind of authority is usually not articulated in explicit opposition to the law. Instead, it tends to justify its rulings by asserting that they are consistent with intentions that are implicit within the law, despite the fact that they might be out of keeping with legal precedent.

In 2002, for example, the White House and the DoJ issued statements that affirmed the "inherent authority" of local governments to enforce immigration laws.[40] These statements reversed over twenty years of legal precedent on the role of local police in enforcing immigration laws. It is also significant that these statements were initially issued as secret memos that were made public only by a Freedom of Information Act lawsuit that was filed by a coalition of immigrant rights and civil liberties organizations.[41]

Prior to this time, the DoJ had affirmed prior legal precedent, asserting that immigration enforcement was beyond the purview of local police, except where it was relevant to an ongoing criminal investigation.[42] And when the secret memos on local enforcement were made public, a number of local law enforcement agencies criticized the DoJ for departing from a legal precedent that it had affirmed only a few years earlier.[43] During this same period of time, efforts were under way to enact local enforcement laws in Congress (two of the primary vehicles being the Homeland Security and Enforcement Act and the Clear Law Enforcement for Criminal Alien Removal Act).[44] These proposals required all local and state police departments to enforce federal immigration laws and contained measures for sanctioning local police departments that failed to comply (but with very little increase in training and funding to help local police carry out this mandate). This is one reason why these federal proposals drew widespread criticism from local police departments as well as immigrant rights activists and civil libertarians who were opposed to the creation of a "national police force."[45]

In contrast to these failed legislative efforts, the 2002 policy statements of the White House and DoJ completely circumvented the Congress. In the process, they avoided any debate about legal precedent by forcing the decision through executive channels; and the first locally enacted "illegal immigrant" laws began appearing approximately two years later. The "inherent authority" rationale adopted by these policy statements drew on arguments from immigration control advocates asserting that local and state governments had always had the authority to enforce immigration laws.[46]

Immigrant rights advocates have begun to challenge these arguments on the basis of their departure from legal precedent.[47] But what these challenges do not directly acknowledge is how the sovereign decision tends to convert deviations from the law into an alternative paradigm for interpreting legal precedent.[48] Agamben notes, for example, that arguments for the use of exceptional measures tend to be grounded in a legal-philosophical discourse of "necessity."[49] Whereas legal precedent arguments are premised on an unbroken continuity with prior rulings, "necessity" arguments focus on how the law should best be used to regulate unanticipated contingencies. This rational undermines the significance of legal precedent (but without entirely eliminating it). Instead of holding the law accountable to its own precedent, the law is held accountable to the challenges arising from emergent, extralegal phenomena.

In this light, deviations from the law appear as such only because the law has encountered conditions that were never anticipated by its creators. In this context, the exception or deviation can actually be justified as an effort to repair the law, to realign its original intent with "present-day realities." And the executive is the agent who bears the ultimate responsibility for making these adjustments. This is the point at which exceptions to prior legal precedent can be justified as being in the spirit of the very laws they are being used to override. Furthermore, because the necessity that prompted these changes is a matter of dire emergency, it also becomes necessary to expedite these changes with an executive order rather than channeling it through legislative deliberations.

One of the necessities often evoked by immigration control advocates to justify local enforcement laws is the recent growth of the unauthorized migrant population and the challenges it poses to effective border control.[50] According to these arguments, the inherent authority of local governments to enforce immigration laws has always existed, but there was never a need, prior to present-day migration trends, to evoke this authority in the way it is currently being used.

In contrast, the federal government's support for local enforcement seems to have been informed by a different kind of necessity. As I have already noted, over the past several decades the U.S. executive office (including the 2001–2008 Bush administration) has facilitated the expansion of immigrant labor markets, the liberalization of the U.S. economy, and the globalization of trade. So although the Bush administration and the DoJ (which is headed by appointees of the executive office) issued policy statements that allowed for the expansion of local enforcement, there is little evidence that the immigration priorities of the executive office are the same as those of the immigration control movement. But the executive office did have an interest in curbing the influence of immigration control activists who were fomenting divisions within the Republican Party and blocking congressional movement on a new immigration reform bill.

Even after the White House and the DoJ issued statements in support of local enforcement, President Bush and other White House officials publicly chastised the vigilante border control efforts of the Minutemen and threw their support behind a guest worker program that has been vigorously opposed by the immigration control movement.[51] During this same period of time, the White House introduced a guest worker proposal that contained no additional provisions for immigration enforcement.[52] Over the next few years, however, the White House guest worker plan began to include more get-tough enforcement measures, and President Bush began to make public statements that explicitly endorsed the need for local enforcement.[53]

Given the timing of these developments, it would appear that the Bush White House was adapting its stance on immigration to the demands of the anti-immigrant right, even though it continued to distinguish its position from hard-line immigration control advocates.[54] Meanwhile, the Bush administration continued to draw criticism from immigration control advocates for supporting immigration reform proposals that would expand the guest worker program. A typical example is the Senate immigration bill (S. 1639) that was endorsed by President Bush and Senator Kennedy and put before the Congress in summer 2007. Like its recent predecessors, this immigration reform bill was rejected by Congress. It is also significant that it was rejected by the anti-immigrant right along with immigrant rights activists who could not tolerate the enforcement and surveillance measures that had been incorporated as a precondition for expanding visa options for migrant workers.[55] This get-tough emphasis was a product of the past several years of policy deliberations, in which pro-immigration lawmakers agreed to incorporate stronger enforcement measures to ward off criticism that they were "soft" on illegal immigration and immigrant law breakers.[56]

As I noted earlier, this is a pro-immigration/pro-enforcement perspective that is guided by neoliberal concerns for crafting immigrant labor markets.[57] In this context, tougher enforcement measures (including tolerance for some forms of local enforcement) become a feature of the controlled expansion of the migrant workforce, rather than a strategy for restricting immigration levels.

Conclusion

There has been little discussion in U.S. policy or academic circles about the kind of sovereign authority that I have discussed in this essay. One possible reason for this silence is that, unlike some Western democracies, the United

States has never developed a formal, juridical rationale for determining how this kind of authority should be used.[58] Nevertheless, there is a long history of U.S. government administrations using this kind of authority to make landmark policy decisions that can be traced from the antebellum period to the New Deal and the current War on Terror. Historically, the United States has also suspended habeas corpus for different classes and races of people, notably including fugitive slaves, immigrant "radicals" during the early 1900s, and Japanese internees during World War II.

The lack of open discussion on these matters may reflect the interest of U.S. scholars and lawmakers in safeguarding the integrity of constitutional law. As a consequence, laws and policies that have been enacted through executive decisions tend to be assessed only in terms of legal precedent arguments; but this also leaves the workings of the sovereign decision effectively unregulated. And because of the stigma that is often attached to "legal activism," there is a pronounced disinclination to explore the role that executive discretionary authority has played in shaping the law, and how these interventions have become intertwined with the historical development of the law itself.

This essay has attempted to describe how the sovereign decision has been used to shape only one aspect of immigration policy: local enforcement. But it also highlights the need for a more intensive explanation of the dynamics of this kind of sovereign authority. It is also important to consider how constructions of "necessity" can be used to justify departures from legal precedent. Immigration policy has certainly been one of the terrains that has been subjected to these sorts of anxious constructions wherein concerns about unauthorized migration, the cultural difference of immigrant populations, and national security tend to merge indiscriminately into one another.

It is important not to lose sight of the role that these anti-immigrant anxieties have played in shaping local enforcement laws. But I have also tried to show that these laws are not necessarily what they appear to be. On the face of it, local enforcement laws appear to serve an immigration control agenda, but the expansion of these laws was also facilitated by executive officials who support the expansion of immigrant labor markets. In some respects, the willingness of the executive office to cater to restrictionist sentiments is the most incidental feature of the role it played in helping to expand local enforcement laws. More significant is the way that executive decisions were used to intervene in prior legal precedent in light of immediate political contingencies, and as I have argued, these priorities resonate much more strongly with a form of governmentality guiding the process of economic globalization.

This is one reason immigration scholars and advocates need to come to terms with the likelihood that neoliberal priorities will become the driving force behind future local enforcement (and immigration enforcement more generally). Under these priorities, local enforcement becomes a strategy for weeding out "undesirable" noncitizens from an expanding noncitizen workforce rather than being a long-term strategy for the mass deportation of unauthorized migrants. For example, the National Crime Information Center (NCIC) database allows local police to increase their apprehension of noncitizens with criminal records, but it has no bearing for the vast majority of noncitizens (and unauthorized migrants) who do not have a violation on record with the Department of Justice. Restrictions on immigrant use of social services have also given rise to a variety of local screening practices that encourage welfare caseworkers and in some cases educators and health-care workers to check the legal status of their clients. The 1996 Welfare Reform laws introduced a number of these restrictions, which were intended to reduce "welfare dependency" and increase the workforce attachment of immigrants.

In fall 2007, the tragic death of a U.S. citizen child, Edgar Casterno, redirected public attention to immigrant fears of these sorts of screening practices. Edgar died because his undocumented parents were fearful about taking the infant to a local hospital that they thought would ask questions about their legal status.[59] Edgar's tragic death occurred shortly before Oklahoma was about to adopt a statewide local enforcement law. Defenders of the law pointed out that the infant's death had nothing to do with the law, since it had not yet been enacted. But Edgar's death also drew attention to the fact that, even in the absence of "illegal immigrant" laws, there are screening practices that can have a significant impact on the way that noncitizens structure their lives.

The screening practices that Edgar's parents were trying to avoid were not informed by the territorial paradigm of national sovereignty that I referenced at the beginning of this essay. So long as Edgar's undocumented parents avoided the use of all publicly funded services, it is unlikely that these sorts of screening practices would ever have revealed their legal status. But the cost of this aversion—as Edgar's death tragically illustrates—is living a life under the shadow of the law, devoid of even the barest safety net protections, such as access to emergency room care. These sorts of risks are indicative of the forms of graduated sovereignty that have been intensified by the past two decades of immigration policy, in which U.S. residents who live and work alongside each other are being held subject to very different legal-juridical criteria and enforcement practices.

It bears emphasizing that this graduated sovereignty does not stand in opposition to a territorial paradigm of sovereignty; instead it has absorbed this territorial paradigm, plugging it into a much more complex and variegated terrain. Consistent with the pastoral mode of care referenced earlier, local enforcement has given local citizenries a special form of discretionary authority that allows them to protect their communities from the more "undesirable" outcomes of immigration. But these laws are also proliferating in a laissez faire manner that decomposes the national territory into a discontinuous array of enforcement zones. In this regard, recent trends in local enforcement are best characterized as a reorganization of state sovereignty, which, as Saskia Sassen has observed, leads to "a denationalizing of particular components of state authority which nonetheless remain inside the state rather than shifting to the private or global institutional terrains."[60] And once again, it is very likely that this reorganization of state authority will continue apace, and permeate other aspects of immigration policy, irrespective of what happens with the current wave of local enforcement laws. This is why it is important to connect any analysis of local enforcement, and all other aspects of immigration enforcement, to this more diffuse process whereby state authority is used to define, shape, and respond to the political and economic contingencies of globalization.

Notes

1. See National Conference of State Legislators, "2007 Enacted State Legislation Related to Immigrants and Immigration," http://www.ncsl.org/programs/immig/2007/Immigration831.htm (accessed February 15, 2008); National Conference of State Legislators, "2006 Enacted State Legislation Related to Immigrants and Immigration," www.ncsl.org/programs/immig/06ImmigEnactedLegis.htm (accessed February 15, 2008).

2. News coverage has provided some of the best documentation of how these sorts of concerns have led to the enactment of local enforcement laws. See Summer Harlow, "Small Towns Play Big Role on Immigration. Fear of Persecution Forces Many to Move," *News Journal*, October 15, 2006; Michael Rubinkam, "Illegal Immigrant Laws Face Setbacks," Associated Press, January 20, 2007.

3. Mae Ngai, *Impossible Subjects: Illegal Aliens and the Making of Modern America* (Princeton, N.J.: Princeton University Press, 2005).

4. It bears noting that although the *Fong Yue Ting* decision can be regarded as an outmoded form of immigration enforcement, it has never been overturned. It therefore still stands as valid legal precedent. *Fong Yue Ting v. U.S. et al.*, 149 U.S. 698 (1893).

5. Ngai, *Impossible Subjects*, 155–56.

6. Ibid., 75–90.

7. For a typical example of how these themes play out in anti-immigrant discourse, see Patrick Buchanan's latest best-selling book, *State of Emergency: The Third World Invasion and Conquest of America* (New York: St. Martins Griffin, 2007).

8. Mexican persons are little more than 7 percent of the total U.S. population and approximately 56 percent of the unauthorized migrant population. See Jeffrey Passel, "Size and Characteristics of the Unauthorized Migrant Population in the U.S. Estimates Based on the March 2005 Current Population Survey," Pew Hispanic Center, 2006, http://pewhispanic.org/files/reports/61.pdf (accessed May 6, 2008). However, between 2002 and 2004 they composed 71 percent of all individuals who were identified as immigration violators by police departments nationwide that were using the NCIC database. See Hannah Gladstein, Annie Lai, Jennifer Wagner, and Michael Wishnie, "Blurring the Lines: A Profile of State and Local Police Enforcement of Immigration Law Using the National Crime Information Center Database, 2002–2004" (Washington, D.C.: Migration Policy Institute, 2005, http://www.migrationpolicy.rrg/pubs/MPI_report_Blurring_the_Lines_120805.pdf (accessed February 15, 2008).
9. Harlow, "Small Towns Play Big Role"; National Conference of State Legislators, "2007 Enacted State Legislation."
10. National Immigration Forum, Organizations Opposed to Local Enforcement, 2004, http://immigrationforum.org/documents/TheDebate/EnforcementLocalPolice/OppositiontoSLenforcement.pdf (accessed February 15, 2008).
11. Major Cities Chiefs Immigration Committee, "Recommendations for Enforcement of Immigration Laws by Local Police Agencies," 2006, http://www.houstontx.gov/police/pdfs/mcc_position.pdf (accessed April 25, 2008).
12. Alexandra Marks and Christian Lupsa, "After New Bedford Immigration Raid Voices Call for Mercy and Justice," *Christian Science Monitor*, March 16, 2007, http://www.csmonitor.com/2007/0316/p01s02-ussc.html (accessed June 26, 2008).
13. Ray Henry, "Federal Raid Leaves Mass. Town a Mess," *Associated Press*, March 8, 2007.
14. Jonathan Saltzman, "Governor Rescinds Immigration Order: Frees Police from Arrest Pact," *Boston Globe*, January 12, 2007, http://www.miracoalition.org/press/mira-in-the-news/governor-rescinds-immigration-order-frees-state-police-from-arrest-pact (accessed June 26, 2008).
15. Pam Belluck, "Town Loses Tool Against Illegal Immigrants," *New York Times*, August 13, 2005, http://www.nytimes.com/2005/08/13/national/13immig.html?ex=1281585600&en=c91010dd80 4c4102&ei=5090&partner=rssuserland&emc=rss (accessed June 26, 2008).
16. Michael Olivas, "Immigration Related State Statutes and Local Ordinances: Preemption, Prejudice, and the Proper Role for Enforcement," University of Chicago Legal Forum, 2007, http://ssrn.com/abstract=1069121 (accessed February 15, 2008).
17. National Conference of State Legislators, "2007 Enacted State Legislation."
18. Appleseed Foundation, "Forcing Our Blues into Gray Areas: Local Police and Federal Immigration Enforcement," 2007, http://appleseeds.net/servlet/GetArticleFile?articleFileId=177 (accessed February 15, 2008) 15–16.
19. Even within this framework there is a great deal of leeway for expanding the role of local enforcement. Some state-federal MOAs have created a special task force that authorizes a limited number of local police officers (or specific local police departments) to collaborate with federal immigration agents. But there are also MOAs (such as the ones currently in effect in Florida and Rhode Island) that authorize all local police, statewide, to collaborate with federal immigration agents as needed to apprehend immigration violators. Furthermore, the Rhode Island MOA goes a step further than the Florida MOA by requiring all state police to verify the legal status of all civilians they question or detain in the course of routine police duties. See "Immigrations and Customs Enforcement," Department of Homeland Security, Factsheet: Section 287 (g) Immigration and Nationality Act, August 28, 2008, http://www.ice.gov/partners/287g/Section287_g.htm (accessed May 7, 2008); Kathleen Staudt, "Bordering the Other in the U.S. Southwest: El Pasoans Confront the Local Sheriff," in *Keeping Out the Other: A Critical Introduction to Immigration Enforcement Today*, ed. D. Brotherton and P. Kretsedemas, 399–432 (New York: Columbia University Press); Rhode Island Government Online, "Carcieri Signs Executive Order to Address Illegal Immigration in Rhode Island," March 27, 2008, http://www.ri.gov/gress/view.php?id=6114 (accessed May 7, 2008).
20. Harlow, "Small Towns Play Big Role."
21. Recent estimates place the size of the unauthorized migrant population at slightly over 12 million. See Passel, "Size and Characteristics of the Unauthorized Migrant Population." Meanwhile, the total sum of annual removals for noncitizens in recent years (2003–2005) ranges between 1 million and 1.2 million. See Department of Homeland Security, "Table 34: Deportable Aliens Located, Fiscal

Years 1925–2006," 2006 Yearbook of Immigration Statistics, http://www.dhs.gov/xlibrary/assets/statistics/yearbook/2006/OIS_2006_Yearbook.pdf (accessed April 25, 2008). Even though unauthorized entry is by far the largest category among these removals (accounting for approximately 80 percent of annual removals), these figures also include tens of thousands of cases involving lawful entrants who have been removed for other criminal and noncriminal violations. Taking this into account, the number of unauthorized migrants removed each year is probably little more than 6 or 7 percent of the total number residing in the United States.

22. See Department of Homeland Security, "Table 34: Deportable Aliens Located"; Also see Department of Homeland Security, "Table 40: Aliens Removed for Administrative Reasons," 2005 Yearbook of Immigration Statistics, http://www.dhs.gov/xlibrary/assets/statistcs/yearbook/table40.xls (accessed April 25, 2008).

23. Aihwa Ong, *Neoliberalism as Exception: Mutations in Citizenship and Sovereignty* (Durham, N.C.: Duke University Press, 2006).

24. The writ of habeas corpus is a legal safeguard that has been part of the Western legal canon for hundreds of years (predating the Magna Carta). Once issued, it requires the court to investigate and explain why an individual's liberty is being restrained. Habeas corpus reviews are often used to investigate whether an individual is being held under questionable conditions. The 2005 REAL ID Act eliminated habeas corpus review for all noncitizens who have been issued a final order of removal, deportation, and exclusion. See American Immigration Law Foundation, "Judicial Review Provisions of the REAL ID Act, Practice Advisory," 2005, http://www.ailf.org/lac/realid6705.pdf (accessed February 15, 2008); Ira Kurzban, "Democracy and Immigration," in *Keeping Out the Other*, ed. Brotherton and Kretsedemas, 87–110.

25. For several case studies of how these laws affected immigrant communities, see Philip Kretsedemas and Ana Aparicio, eds., *Immigrants, Welfare Reform, and the Poverty of Policy* (Westport, Conn.: Greenwood-Praeger, 2004).

26. See Department of Homeland Security, "Table 26: Nonimmigrant Admissions (I-94 Only) by Class of Admission: Fiscal Years 1998–2006," 2006 Year Book of Immigration Statistics, http://www.dhs.gov/slibrary/assets/statistics/yearbook/2006/OIS_2006_Yearbook.pdf (accessed February 15, 2008); "Table 7: Persons Obtaining Legal Permanent Resident Status by Type and Detailed Class of Admission Fiscal Year 2006," 2006 Yearbook of Immigration Statistics, http://www.dhs.gov/xlibrary/assets/statistics/yearbook/2006/table07d.xls (accessed February 15, 2008).

27. Between 1985 and 2002, spending on immigration enforcement more than quadrupled from 1 billion dollars to 4.9 billion dollars. See Migration Policy Institute, "Immigration Enforcement Spending since IRCA," 2005, http://www.migrationpolicy.org/ITFIAF/FactSheet_Spending.pdf (accessed May 6, 2008). During the same time the annual inflow of immigrants grew by more than 40 percent and the inflow of "nonimmigrants" (or temporary workers/visitors) increased by more than 400 percent. These statistics on nonimmigrants are derived from summaries of annual entries for students and workers admitted with temporary visas (along with children and spouses) reported in the 2000 Yearbook of Immigration Statistics. See Department of Homeland Security, "Table 37: Nonimmigrant Admissions by Class of Admission: Selected Fiscal Years 1981–2000," 2000 Yearbook of Immigration Statistics, http://www.dhs.gov/xlibrary/assets/statistics/hearbook/2000/Table37.slx (accessed February 15, 2008). The observation on the 40 percent increase in legal immigrant admissions (1981–2000) is derived from a comparison of data found in the 2000 Yearbook of Immigration Statistics and the 1997 Statistical Yearbook. See Department of Homeland Security, "Table 5: Immigrants Admitted by Type and Class of Admission Fiscal Year 2000," 2000 Yearbook of Immigration Statistics. http://www.dhs.gov/xlibrary/assets/statistcs/yearbook (accessed February 15, 2008); "Chart C: Immigrants Admitted Fiscal Years 1900–97," 1997 Statistical Yearbook, http://www.dhs.gov/xlibrary/assets/statistics/yearbook/1997YB.pdf (accessed February 15, 2008).

28. At present, the vast majority of individuals who are counted among the annual immigrant flow are not actually new arrivals, but persons already living and working in the United States whose legal status was adjusted (from that of a nonresident to a legal permanent resident). In 2006, people whose status was adjusted accounted for more than two-thirds of the annual immigrant flow (over 800,000 people) compared to half that number (slightly over 400,000) who were recorded as "new arrivals." Furthermore, the flow of people admitted to the United States with temporary legal status is far larger than the flow of immigrants (who are granted legal permanent residence). In 2006, for example, the

number of people admitted to the United States either under student visas or temporary work visas was more than twice the number of the "regular" immigrant intake (over 2.8 million temporary visas for these categories, compared to 1.2 million immigrants). See Department of Homeland Security, "Table 26: Nonimmigrant Admissions"; "Table 7: Persons Obtaining Legal Permanent Resident Status."

29. Eliot Turner and. Marc Rosenblum, "Solving the Unauthorized Migrant Problem: Proposed Legislation in the U.S. Migration Policy Institute, September 2005, http://www.migrationinformation.org/Feature/display.cfm?ID=333 (accessed February 16, 2008).

30. As proposed in Senate Bill 1639. For a critical overview of the Z visa, see National Immigration Law Center, "NILC Opposes Current Senate Bill Because It Would Preclude Real Reform," June 25, 2007, http://www.nilc.org/immlawpolicy/CIR/cir026.htm (accessed February 16, 2008).

31. Ong, *Neoliberalism as Exception*, 77.

32. For several examples, see Andrew Barry, Thomas Osborne, and Nikolas Rose, eds., *Foucault and Political Reason: Liberalism, Neoliberalism, and Rationalities of Government* (Chicago: University of Chicago Press, 1996).

33. It may seem oxymoronic to equate "neoliberalism" with "neoconservativism." This equivalence, however, is historically accurate in the case of the United States (and the United Kingdom), where neoliberal policies were first expanded by the conservative (Reagan/Bush) administrations of the 1980s. In this case, "neoliberal" tends to refer to a laissez faire economic platform, while "neoconservative" refers to a more comprehensive political and cultural agenda that includes neoliberal economics as one of its components. Nevertheless, since neoliberal economic policies have been associated with conservative administrations for the past 30 years of U.S. history (with the exception of the 1992–2000 interlude of the Clinton administration), it becomes possible to connect them to a neoconservative governing ethos.

34. See Saskia Sassen, *A Sociology of Globalization* (New York: W. W. Norton, 2007), and *The Global City: New York London Tokyo* (Princeton, N.J.: Princeton University Press, 1996).

35. Ong, *Neoliberalism as Exception*, 75–80.

36. Ong asserts that there is always room for resistance to the forms of sovereign power described by Agamben—as illustrated by the numerous immigrant rights mobilizations that have taken shape on the global stage (as well as the massive groundswell of support for the U.S. immigrant protests of 2006 and the resistance to "illegal immigrant" laws among many U.S. towns, cities, and states). Agamben provides a useful explanation of the defining tendencies and components of a particular kind of sovereign power, but this is best understood as an ideal-type theorization and not a literal account of how relations between the sovereign and subjected always play out in "reality."

37. Giorgio Agamben, *State of Exception* (Chicago: University of Chicago Press, 2006).

38. Ibid., 11–21.

39. For a thorough critical overview, see Amitai Etzioni, *How Patriotic Is the Patriot Act? Freedom versus Security in the Age of Terrorism* (New York: Routledge, 2004).

40. Appleseed Foundation, "Forcing Our Blues into Gray Areas," 10–12.

41. The lawsuit was *National Council of La Raza et al. v. Department of Justice. For a brief overview, see* New York Civil Liberties Association, "Secret Immigration Enforcement Memo Exposed," 2005, www.nyclu.org/node/127 (accessed April 25, 2008). *For a summary from the official record, also see* Department of Justice, Office of Information and Privacy, "FOIA Post New Decisions, January–March 2005," http://www.usdoj.gov/oip/foiapost/2005foiapost9.htm (accessed April 25, 2008).

42. The 1983 *Gonzales v. City of Peoria* decision, 722 F.2d 468, 475 (9th Cir. Ct. 1983) has been widely credited with establishing this legal precedent. See Appleseed Foundation, "Forcing Our Blues into Gray Areas," 7–9.

43. For one example see the critical comments of the International Association of Chiefs of Police concerning the 2001 decision of the DoJ to include immigration violations in the NCIC database and the implications of this decision for existing legal precedent on the involvement of local police in immigration enforcement. International Association of Chiefs of Police, "Enforcing Immigration Law: The Role of State, Tribal and Local Enforcement," http://www.theiacp.org/documents/pdf/Publications/ImmigrationEnforcementconf.pdf (accessed April 25, 2008), 3.

44. For the original language of these proposed bills, see 108th Congress, 1st sess., Clear Law Enforcement for Criminal Alien Removal (CLEAR) Act, http://frwebgate.access.gpo.gov/cgi-bin/getdoc.cgi?dbname=108_cong_bills&docid=f:h2671ih.txt.pdf (accessed April 30, 2008); Homeland Security Enhancement Act (HSEA, *S.1906*), http://frwebgate.access.gpo.gov/cgi-bin/getdoc.cgi?dbname=108_cong_bills&docidf:s1906is.txt.pdf (accessed April 30, 2008).

45. For an example of this argument, see National Immigration Forum, "Conservatives and Cops Agree: The CLEAR Act and Its Senate Companion Are Bad Public Policy," April 2004, http://www. immigrationforum.org/DesktopDefault.aspx?tabid=587 (accessed April 30, 2008).

46. Kris Kobach, "State and Local Authority to Enforce Immigration Law: A Unified Approach for Stopping Terrorists," Center for Immigration Studies, 2004, http://ssrn.corn/abstract=1097543 (accessed May 5, 2008).

47. American Immigration Law Foundation, "Challenges to State and Local Enforcement Efforts," 2007, www.ailf.org/lac/clearinghouse_120706.shtml (accessed February 17, 2008).

48. In the context of this discussion, *the sovereign decision* refers specifically to neoliberal models of sovereignty, but it bears noting that Agamben's discussion of the rationale for the sovereign decision (and in particular the evocation of "necessity") refers to governing practices that span almost two centuries.

49. Agamben, *State of Exception*, 24–31.

50. For an excellent example, see Michael Olivas's review of the arguments of Kris Kobach and Peter Spiro, who have supported local enforcement and, more generally, the right of states to create and enforce their own immigration laws. Olivas, "Immigration Related State Statutes."

51. Carla Marinucci and Mark Martin, "Governor Endorses Minutemen on Border: Schwarzenegger Parts with Bush on Group of Armed Volunteers That Stops Immigrants," *San Francisco Chronicle*, April 29, 2005, http://www.sfgate.com/cgi-bin/article.cgi?file=/c/a/2005/04/29/GUV.TMP (accessed June 26, 2008).

52. White House Office of the Press Secretary, "President Bush Proposes New Temporary Worker Program," January 7, 2004, http://www.whitehouse.gov/news/releases/2004/01/20040107-3.html (accessed February 15, 2008).

53. White House Office of the Press Secretary, "President Bush Addresses the Nation on Immigration Reform," May 15, 2006, http://www.whitehouse.gov/news/releases/2006/05/20060515-8.html (accessed February 15, 2008).

54. Peter Baker, "Bush Takes Aim at GOP Critics of Immigration Deal, Says Conservatives Use Scare Tactics, 'Haven't Read Bill,'" *Boston Globe*, May 30, 2007, http://www.boston.com/news/nation/articles/2007/05/30/bush_takes_aim_at_gop_critics_of_immigration_deal/ (June 26, 2008).

55. Federation for American Immigration Reform, "Sixteen Reasons to Oppose Bush-Kennedy Amnesty Bill (S. 1639)," 2007, http://www.fairus.org/site/DocServer/factsheet_s1639.pdf?dicID=1501 (accessed February 16, 2008); National Immigration Law Center, "NILC Opposes Current Senate Bill Because It Would Preclude Real Reform," June 25, 2007, http://www.nilc.org/immlawpolicy/CIR/cir026.htm (accessed February 16, 2008).

56. For example, the immigration reform bill (Senate Bill 1639) that was proposed in fall 2007 was rejected by immigrant rights activists because of its enforcement provisions and the restrictions on the temporary legal status it extended to unauthorized migrants (see note 53). These measures, which had originally been introduced to appease the concerns of immigration control advocates, were more stringent than what had been included in the STRIVE Act and the Kennedy-McCain immigration reform bill. See Office of Representative Jeff Flake, "Summary of the Strive Act," 2007, http://flake. house.gov/UploadedFiles/STRIVE%20Summary.pdf (accessed February 16, 2008); Eliot Turner and Marc Rosenblum, "Solving the Unauthorized Migrant Problem: Proposed Legislation in the U.S. Migration Policy Institute," September 2005, http://www.migrationinformation.org/Feature/display. cfm?ID=333 (accessed February 16, 2008).

57. This concern for regulating labor markets is one of the many exceptions that neoliberalism tends to make to its own deregulatory agenda. David Harvey, *A Brief History of Neoliberalism* (Oxford: Oxford University Press, 2007), has observed, for example, that neoliberals tend to be against regulation except when it comes to labor. And as Saskia Sassen, in *A Sociology of Globalization* (New York: W. W. Norton, 2007), has explained, the idea that neoliberalism equates with "deregulation" is very misleading—since neoliberalism is better described as a different paradigm of state regulation, rather than an "anti-regulatory" paradigm. For example, the expansion of global trade in the post–cold war era was not made possible simply by the removal of protectionist measures, but by a variety of proactive policy interventions and disciplinary criteria that were imposed on former Third World and Communist bloc nations by the likes of the International Monetary Fund and the World Bank.

58. Agamben, *State of Exception*, 19–23.

59. "Immigrant Advocates Point to Boys Death," Associated Press, January 25, 2008.

60. Sassen, *A Sociology of Globalization*, 49.

"Citizenship Matters": Lessons from the Irish Citizenship Referendum

J. M. Mancini and Graham Finlay

In 1916, armed insurrectionists revolted against the chief ally of the United States. The rebels surrendered quickly, but were punished severely: 15 were executed, and 3,500 faced imprisonment. Curiously, the British government spared one of the rebel leaders, propelling him to take a central role in an ongoing and ultimately successful campaign to subvert British rule. Even more curiously, nearly fifty years later, in 1964, President Lyndon B. Johnson welcomed this aging insurrectionist—who had abandoned his belief in the use of force against the British only a few years before—to the White House on a state visit. Johnson's greeting to Eamon de Valera, by then the president of the Republic of Ireland, immediately suggests why he was spared: "This is the country of your birth, Mr. President . . . this will always be your home."[1] Although de Valera, the American-born son of an Irish mother and a Spanish father, lived in the United States for fewer than three years, both the British courts and Johnson after them understood de Valera to be an American citizen—despite his expatriation, despite his participation in armed political struggle, and despite his ascent to the leadership of a foreign government.

Until recently, the notion that the country of one's birth determines one's citizenship had as powerful a hold in Ireland—where it was encoded in the 1922 Constitution of the Irish Free State, the Irish Nationality and Citizenship Acts of 1935 and 1956, and from 1998 to 2004 in Article 2 of the Irish Constitution—as it has in the United States, where it is protected by the Fourteenth Amendment.[2] Nonetheless, in 2004, a referendum was called—and passed with a nearly 80 percent majority[3]—removing the constitutional provision of territorial birthright citizenship for the children of noncitizens.[4] This monumental change in the citizenship regime of the newly prosperous Ireland of the "Celtic Tiger" marked a radical departure from the shared history, embodied in de Valera's personal story, that joined Ireland to the United States. At the same time, the citizenship referendum also highlighted both continued and new interconnections between the two nations. In the debates leading up to the referendum, both the American legal example and the historical experience of legal and illegal Irish immigrants in the United States figured prominently. And both the revocation of jus soli and the circumstances leading to its revocation underscored the fact that Ireland's sudden exposure to the complicated political pressures resulting from globalization, including new inward migration from Africa, Asia, and the accession states of the European Union, made its political landscape more like that of the United States than it had been.

In this article, we discuss both the importance of American practice for the normative discussions surrounding the removal of jus soli as an automatic qualification for citizenship in Ireland and the importance of the Irish debates as an example for the historical and normative investigation of the foundations of citizenship in the United States, especially in the field of American studies. In an increasingly interconnected world in which people, and not just goods and capital, are on the move, we argue that the elimination of jus soli as a basis for citizenship was unjustified in the Irish case, despite the popular pressures on Irish politicians, and that the pressure being placed on U.S. politicians to undermine jus soli should be consciously resisted. Changes in the basis of citizenship are not simply about the moral composition of the civic public, but have important economic and social consequences—chiefly, the creation of a docile class of laborers who can be dismissed and deported at will, and who have almost no rights to seek redress for the exploitive aspects of their condition. We believe that it is a lack of attention to these consequences that allowed the Irish government to succeed in removing unrestricted jus soli from the Irish Constitution, leading the debates to be solely carried on in terms of the intensity of immigrants' connections to the Irish state and in terms of Ireland's emigrant past. At a time when politicians from across the political spectrum in the United States propose the replacement of permanent immigrants by guest workers, a similar neglect of the moral, cultural, and economic importance of jus soli threatens to impoverish contemporary debates surrounding immigration in the United States.

Migration and Citizenship in Comparative Perspective: Proscription without Exclusion

One of the key contributions to the understanding of American migration in recent years has been Mae M. Ngai's persuasive articulation of the direct relationship between restrictive naturalization laws and more direct forms of immigration restriction that developed in the late nineteenth and early twentieth century United States. As Ngai argues, "the system of quotas based on national origin was the first major pillar of the Immigration Act of 1924. The second was the exclusion of persons ineligible to citizenship."[5] Both the persuasiveness of Ngai's argument and the significance of historical campaigns for immigration restriction in the United States might tempt observers to conclude that there is a dependent relationship between immigration restriction and citizenship proscription, and that the hidden purpose of the latter is always to bolster the former.

But what if we move beyond this notorious period of immigration restriction, and beyond the historical United States? The consideration of alternative contexts immediately shows that the relationship between immigration restriction and citizenship proscription is not fixed, either in theory or in practice. In theory, it is possible for states to place onerous restrictions on immigration, yet to grant citizenship freely to the small numbers of migrants who are permitted to enter, or, inversely, to accept and even encourage immigration, but to curtail access severely to citizenship for immigrants and their children.

In practice, many European states embody this second scenario. Far from simply excluding foreigners, "Fortress Europe" has millions of non-European Union (EU) nationals living and working within its borders, many of whom are legally resident in Europe and many of whom were encouraged to immigrate by their host countries. In Ireland, the government deliberately promoted immigration on the basis of work permits during the early period of its economic boom, steadily increasing the number of work permits issued to non-European Economic Area (EEA) citizens from 5,750 in 1999 to 40,504 in 2002.[6] These work-permit holders far outnumbered the uninvited migrants who were the target of the government's campaign during the referendum, exceeding seekers of asylum by approximately 4 to 1 in 2002.[7] And, in 2004, Ireland was one of only three states in the newly enlarged EU to allow the entry of unrestricted numbers of workers from the new accession states, leading to a sudden rise in immigration from eastern European and Baltic states,[8] so that by March 2006, "over 160,000" PPS numbers (the social security number needed to work in Ireland) had been issued to citizens of accession countries.[9]

While immigration has been encouraged in recent decades by Ireland and by certain other European states, this encouragement has not necessarily been matched by the liberalization of citizenship laws. Quite the contrary: in all of the three states that permitted unrestricted immigration from the accession states (Ireland, Sweden, and the United Kingdom), recent years have seen the tightening of access to citizenship. In Ireland, it was the very same government that expanded the recruitment of foreign workers that initiated the citizenship referendum, and that also successfully argued in the Supreme Court in 2003 that it had constitutional sanction to deport the noncitizen parents of a citizen child.[10]

The Irish referendum is of particular consequence in Europe, because since the revocation of unrestricted jus soli in Ireland, there is no longer a single nation in Europe that grants unrestricted territorial birthright citizenship to people born within its borders. It should be admitted that Germany introduced important reforms tending toward jus soli in 1999, notably a right to citizenship for second-generation immigrants at birth, provided one parent has been legally resident in Germany for eight years,[11] and, as Christian Joppke has emphasized, that the Netherlands, Belgium, and other countries have added restricted jus soli provisions to their previous jus sanguinis traditions.[12] Nonetheless, Germany's reforms do not reflect a general European trend. Austria, which also has a large population of longtime alien residents, has not changed its citizenship law and has no jus soli component.[13] And some European countries, notably Italy and Malta, have increased restrictions on access to citizenship through territorial naturalization or birth even as they have expanded access to citizenship via jus sanguinis.[14] Moreover, there is a very important difference between unrestricted and restricted forms of territorial birthright citizenship such as "double jus soli," which grants automatic citizenship to the third generation, in that "double jus soli" substantially excludes the same people as a jus sanguinis rule would for at least two generations.

Beyond Europe, the Irish referendum also marks part of a long trend of successful agitation against unrestricted birthright citizenship in countries governed by the common law tradition with which jus soli is traditionally associated. Australia removed unrestricted birthright citizenship in 1986[15] and India in 1987.[16] South Africa required that one parent be either a citizen or permanent resident in the South African Citizenship Act of 1995,[17] and New Zealand removed unrestricted jus soli as of January 1, 2006, for much the same reasons cited in the case of the Irish Citizenship Referendum.[18]

Similar pressures to remove unrestricted jus soli abound in the United States. Over the past ten years, every Congress has seen the introduction of amendments proposing citizenship proscription for the children of some immigrants.[19] FAIR, the Federation for American Immigration Reform, appeals to the example of the Irish Citizenship Referendum and the work of Peter Schuck and Rogers M. Smith, discussed below, in its campaign to reinterpret the Fourteenth Amendment to exclude the children of illegal aliens.[20] Significantly, FAIR's position deploys arguments made during the

Irish campaign, including the costs of births to "illegal alien mothers" and the threat of disease.[21] Taking a different approach, Friends of Immigration Law Enforcement (FILE) argue that territorial birthright citizenship is a threat to national security, citing the case of Yaser Esam Hamdi. FILE, the Center for American Unity, and a number of members of the House of Representatives filed an amicus curiae brief urging an understanding of the Fourteenth Amendment that would deny birthright citizenship to children of individuals, like Hamdi's parents, in the United States on work permits.[22] This brief has been used by print and broadcast commentator Michelle Malkin to call for a reinterpretation of the Fourteenth Amendment that would prevent the creation of "accidental Americans."[23] Access to citizenship has also been the target of proposed state legislation. Leo Berman, a Texas state representative, has put forward a bill that would deny state benefits to the children of undocumented immigrants as "illegal aliens," in an explicit attempt to alter the current interpretation of the Fourteenth Amendment.[24] Thus, while the United States has so far resisted campaigns to restrict territorial birthright citizenship, such campaigns are on the rise.

The Irish Citizenship Referendum: From Jus Soli to Jus Sanguinis

In Ireland, the successful campaign to overturn jus soli was brief and dramatic. Before the 2004 referendum, Article 2 of the Irish Constitution, enacted by referendum in accordance with the Good Friday Agreement in 1998 with a vote of more than 94 percent, determined the citizenship of all children born in Ireland.[25] Based on a straightforward provision of jus soli, Article 2 stated, in terms very similar to the Fourteenth Amendment:

> It is the entitlement and birthright of every person born in the island of Ireland, which includes its islands and seas, to be part of the Irish Nation. That is also the entitlement of all persons otherwise qualified in accordance with law to be citizens of Ireland.[26]

The referendum proposed by the government in 2004, in contrast, trumped the authority of Article 2 via the insertion of an amendment to Article 9 that explicitly distinguishes between the children of citizens and the children of noncitizens. It reads:

> Notwithstanding any other provision of this Constitution, a person born in the island of Ireland, which includes its islands and seas, who does not have, at the time of his or her birth, at least one parent who is an Irish citizen or entitled to be an Irish citizen is not entitled to Irish citizenship or nationality, unless otherwise provided for by law.

While the passage of the referendum did nothing to alter Irish *immigration* law, then, it immediately and radically transformed the legal boundaries surrounding *citizenship*.

The long-term implications of the referendum are difficult to gauge, but two significant changes may be noted. First, the amendment to Article 9 removed the provision of citizenship to the Irish-born children of noncitizens from its protected place within the Constitution to the more uncertain sphere of legislation. At its enactment, sitting elected officials obtained the power to determine not only the terms under which immigrants could become *naturalized* citizens, but also the conditions under which the children of foreigners were eligible for *birthright* citizenship.[27] During previous periods when birthright citizenship was determined by legislation rather than constitutional principle, the designation of citizenship as a legislative matter had no practical effect, as politicians never challenged jus soli. But the 2004 referendum was accompanied by the Irish Nationality and Citizenship Act of 2004, which limited access to citizenship to those children whose parents had resided legally in the state for three of the four years previous to the birth.[28] The government also specified that time spent on student visas or in the asylum process would not count as residence, even retroactively. Thus, the resulting act guaranteed that there would be a class of children, born in Ireland to legal residents, who had access to citizenship solely through the naturalization process. Moreover, the removal of citizenship to the legislative realm also presented the possibility that future governments might propose more onerous citizenship barriers, a scenario that has become increasingly likely with the introduction of legislation in 2006 (reintroduced in a modified form in 2008) that proposed a number of restrictions on immigrants with implications for citizenship—including the proposed requirement that non-EEA nationals seek ministerial approval to marry an Irish national.[29]

Second, the amendment to Article 9 represented a fundamental philosophical shift in Irish law from the principle of citizenship based on birth within the territory to citizenship based on blood descent from the citizenry.[30] Prior to the amendment, Irish law did employ jus sanguinis as a device for recognizing the citizenship of persons born *beyond* its borders: due to its emigrant history, Ireland (unlike the United States) grants citizenship to the foreign-born grandchildren of citizens, and under certain circumstances even to subsequent generations.[31] However, until 2004 Irish law had never used parentage as a basis for the civic exclusion of persons born *inside* Ireland. The passage of the referendum marked a sharp break from both this tradition and the universalism it entails. By imposing a barrier to citizenship that must be crossed only by persons who are not the descendants of citizens, as Oran Doyle argues, the new Article 9 gave constitutional sanction to the granting of legal privilege on the basis of pedigree.[32] By tying the future citizenry more firmly to the citizenry at the time of the referendum, moreover, the amendment also worked to limit temporal and ethnic change in the composition of "the Irish Nation."

There are important parallels, then, between the Irish citizenship referendum and historical efforts to restrict immigration and proscribe citizenship in the United States. Like the fixing of national immigration quotas in the 1920s to the 1910 and 1890 censuses in the United States (and accompanying bars to naturalization for excluded nationalities), the referendum can be seen to work toward "freezing" the nation in time by curtailing the access of "new" ethnic and racial groups. As Brook Thomas suggests, this impulse is more than merely xenophobic, but also represents a central limitation of classical republicanism: the tendency to define "the sovereign people . . . as those who founded the republic, a definition making it impossible to redefine 'the people' in light of changing circumstances."[33] In Ireland, where independence is much more recent than in the United States and lineal descent from the founders of the republic is still the source of great political and social capital, this "republican limitation" is felt even more acutely. Indeed, the politician most associated with the referendum, the then minister for Justice, Equality, and Law Reform Michael McDowell, emphasized that he was the grandson of Eoin MacNeill, who had founded the Irish Volunteers and served as Finance minister after independence.

In contrast to the 1920s United States, however, the Irish government campaign for citizenship restriction was made, as we have suggested, in the *absence* of overt border closures: the government never proposed reductions to overall immigration—or even remotely suggested limitations on immigration based on race or national origin. Nor did it propose more than minimal steps toward tightening Ireland's borders, even though various commentators suggested that the enforcement of airline regulations barring the travel of heavily pregnant women or other small changes would cut entry numbers. Rather, the government insisted throughout the referendum campaign that it was not opposed to immigration, insisting that immigration had "enriched" Ireland's economy and culture.[34] And even within the government, the strongest impulse toward both policies—looser immigration and tighter citizenship—came from one party within the ruling coalition, the minority Progressive Democrats, whose two leading figures were McDowell and Mary Harney, then head of the department that issued the work permits that brought in the majority of Ireland's foreign workforce, the Department of Enterprise, Trade and Employment.

The government's official position was explicitly to distinguish between immigration and citizenship, and to insist that the referendum's purpose was not to keep out immigrants, but to reform citizenship law. Its argument was that Article 2's exclusive intended remit had been to provide constitutional entitlement to Irish citizenship for the children of those caught in quite another border dispute—the partition of Ireland—and that its passage had created an unintended constitutional "loophole" regarding citizenship. Although it is difficult to accept this argument at face value, the government's expressed concerns about citizenship may not have been entirely disingenuous. A number of the arguments presented in favor of the referendum did derive in part from republican theories of citizenship, most prominently notions of duty and fear of corruption. Progressive Democrat TD (Teachta Dála) Fiona O'Malley, for example, drew upon Article 9 of the Constitution, which requires "[f]idelity to the nation and loyalty to the State," to bolster the argument that non-nationals needed to "prove" their connection to the nation by a term of residence before their children could "earn" the right to citizenship.[35] Similarly, the Taoiseach (prime minister) argued that Article 2—and Ireland's status at the time as Europe's only nation fully to recognize unrestricted jus soli—encouraged fraud among non-EU nationals who might have Irish citizen babies *not* so that they could immigrate to Ireland, but so that they could obtain residence in *other* EU states.[36] Particularly after the European Court of Justice offered a preliminary opinion establishing the right to residence in Great Britain of Man Levette Chen,[37] a Chinese woman who traveled to Belfast specifically to have an Irish-born child, the government seized on this possibility as an affront to the duties of citizenship (and to Ireland's EU neighbors).[38]

Nonetheless, it would be naive to think that immigration—and negative feelings toward immigrants within the electorate—did not play a role in the politics of the referendum. The government proposed the referendum at a time when polls showed significant gains for opposition parties, including Sinn Féin (who subsequently opposed the referendum). Although the government denied it, it was widely reported that it had received polling data showing that immigration was a lightning-rod issue for voter discontent.[39] Furthermore, the government scheduled the referendum for the same day as European and local elections, leading opposition parties such as Labour to charge that the government was "facilitating anyone who wanted to play the race card." Even some members of Fine Gael, which ultimately supported the referendum, criticized its timing on the same grounds.[40] Nonetheless, Fine Gael's Dublin candidate for the EU parliament, Gay Mitchell, openly admitted that hostility toward immigrants within the electorate had motivated his party's decision not to campaign against the referendum, but instead to give it passive support.[41] Noting a high degree of anger among voters, and that voters tended to blame all their misfortunes on immigrants, he somewhat paradoxically argued that the making of public arguments against the referendum was *more* likely to fan the flames of racism than the quiet passage of an amendment restricting immigrants' rights to citizenship.[42]

Whatever the effects of Mitchell's passive strategy, the government clearly employed racist and xenophobic tropes to link the presence of immigrants to a pressing contemporary political issue: the crisis in the health-care system. In making its initial case for the need for a referendum, the government alleged that foreign women had overwhelmed the Dublin maternity hospitals, provoking the hospitals' masters (administrators) to demand the change. Although this charge was subsequently discredited,[43] it served to divert attention from the government's extremely unpopular pursuit of maternity and emergency closures within regional hospitals, which erupted into a political crisis in 2002 when a premature baby died after her mother was refused admittance to Monaghan General Hospital.[44] Furthermore, the government's association of migrants with health risks facilitated the spread of a medicalized language of immigrant danger that Alan Kraut has described in the U.S. context as the "double helix of health and fear."[45] Indeed, this link was seized upon by the "Stormfront White Nationalist Community," whose Web site recounted the "minutes of a meeting between Michael McDowell and two of the masters [in which] 'Dr Geary said the high rate of infectious diseases among these groups has huge cost implications for the maternity hospitals [and that] it was surprising that there had not been a major catastrophe within the maternity services as yet.'"[46] Seen in this context, claims by the Health minister Micheál Martin and the Progressive Democrats that citizenship proscription would prevent infant and maternal mortalities took on a clear political aspect.[47]

This, and the fact that Ireland has seen an increase in racist incidents,[48] has led a number of scholars, most notably Ronit Lentin, to apply contemporary critical theories of race to the Irish situation.[49] Lentin and others argue that the referendum was the culminating moment of a process of converting the Irish nation into a racial group. This is a powerful argument, and explains certain seeming anomalies, most obviously efforts by some officials to lobby for a special deal for Irish illegals in the United States—who, as members of Ireland's diaspora are seen as having more of a connection to the Irish state than do actual immigrant residents—even while the government deports people illegally resident in Ireland. Nonetheless, while the government certainly employed developing Irish racism to promote a "yes" vote through hostile appeals to "citizenship tourists" and "bogus asylum seekers" that clearly coded such people as ethnically and racially different—"people from Nigeria [and] Moldovia [*sic*]," as the Taoiseach put it—the purpose of this was not, as Lentin suggests, to separate the different and separate "undeserving" from "deserving" immigrants who contribute to the economy.[50] Rather, we argue that it was precisely to mask the fact that the largest group of people affected by the citizenship referendum was not the asylum seekers from Africa that were the chief target of Irish racism, but the less visible and less politically contentious population of immigrant work permit holders of various races and ethnicities that vastly outnumbered them.[51]

Immigration as Insourcing: Differential Citizenship and the Dual Workforce

Cynical as the Irish government's appeal to anti-immigrant sentiment may have been, it did not amount to a call for immigration restriction. What, then, might the government have hoped to gain from maintaining (and even lowering) legal barriers to entry while simultaneously raising legal obstacles to citizenship? To answer this question, it is first necessary to examine what kind of immigration was facilitated by the government's policy on the eve of the referendum, not least because it contrasts in many respects with much American immigration. First, it was largely an immigration of temporary workers. Unlike in the United States, the vast majority of non-EEA immigrant workers admitted at the time were (and continue to be) work permit holders and students. The latter may work twenty hours per week ("full-time during the university holidays") and themselves represent a significant workforce. Second, this sector of Irish immigration was (and is) dominated by contract labor: unlike American green cards, Irish work permits are issued to employers, rather than directly to immigrants, and do not permit workers to change jobs without first securing a new work permit. For non-EEA citizens, there was and is no legal framework for permanent economic immigration to Ireland, and no equivalent to the "visa lottery."[52] Prospective immigrants from outside the EEA thus faced three choices: get a temporary work permit and hope that it would be renewed, marry an Irish or EEA national, or claim asylum (and be banned from paid employment or third-level education until the resolution of a long and extremely uncertain legal process required to achieve refugee status).[53] In effect, the status of the vast majority of Ireland's non-EEA immigrant workforce was, and continues to be, more akin to that of migrant agricultural laborers in the U.S. H-2 Guest Worker Program than to that of permanent resident aliens in the United States.[54]

The different legal framework surrounding immigration in Ireland thus requires a reassessment not only of the relationship between citizenship proscription and immigration restriction, but also of the economic dimensions of that relationship. In the American context, citizenship proscription and immigration restriction have both primarily been conceived and analyzed in protectionist terms—as a means of preventing competition from immigrants by keeping them out and by limiting their access to economic resources and activities. Yet protectionism is only one potential economic goal of citizenship proscription. As an adjunct to increased migration, citizenship proscription has another possible motive: *increased* competition for jobs and wages. Additionally, in combination with *increased* migration, citizenship proscription has the capacity not just to increase competition, but also to distort it by undermining the regulatory framework and institutions that are designed to ensure its fairness. The joint rise of the temporary work permit/student visa system in Ireland *in conjunction with* citizenship proscription has the potential, thus, to facilitate the emergence of two workforces: one composed of workers who enjoy the full economic benefits of citizenship, including social welfare benefits, and one of "insourced" immigrants who have only minimal recourse even to basic employment protections such as the right to change jobs.

This reading of the current circumstances is lent plausibility on several fronts. The first is that the rights of noncitizens are not equal to those of citizens. Although, as sociologist Yasemin Soysal argues, "international conventions and charters . . . oblige nation-states not to make distinctions on the grounds of nationality in granting civil, social, and political rights,"[55] the Irish Constitution (like many other national constitutions) does restrict certain rights and protections to citizens.[56] Both work permit holders and European workers from the new accession states are excluded from social welfare benefits, which has led to a marked incidence in homelessness and other forms of deprivation among eastern European migrants.[57] In terms of politics, foreign nationals residing in Ireland can vote and run for office at the local level, but they cannot vote in national elections or referenda. Similarly, there is evidence that noncitizens are less likely to feel represented by or to join political parties, particularly mainstream parties[58] and unions.[59] This places noncitizens at an economic disadvantage in, for example, representation at pay negotiations and access to redress for discrimination or wrongful dismissal.[60] Further, Ireland has not ratified the International Convention on the Protection of the Rights of All Migrant Workers and Members of Their Families and has blocked or opted out of European Union directives, such as the 2002 Temporary Agency Workers Directive, that would give migrant workers hired from other countries greater parity with Irish workers in terms of workplace rights.[61]

Second, the outcome suggested above accorded with the stated ideology of prominent members of the government, and with policy goals such as checking inflation (which gained Ireland the censure of the EU in the late 1990s) and maintaining low levels of taxation. McDowell unapologetically embraced the economic benefits of an extreme form of competition and even inequality itself, arguing in an interview with the *Irish Catholic* that "a dynamic liberal economy like ours . . . demands flexibility and inequality in some respects to function."[62] Presumably wage inflation was one of the chief issues in McDowell's mind, as protracted, expensive demands for pay increases had become a commonplace in Ireland by this time. Migrant labor addressed this issue: the recruitment of five thousand Filipino nurses, for example, averted a near-catastrophic labor shortage that threatened to cripple the health service and did so, more importantly, while limiting expansionary or inflationary alternatives such as further increases in outlay for the pay, training, and recruitment of Irish or EU nurses.

Finally, it is instructive to turn to the government's insistence that the referendum, in the words of then minister for Health, Micheál Martin "isn't about migrant workers,"[63] and to reflect upon the children born in Ireland to such workers. With these children in mind, it might reasonably be suggested that Martin's angry refusal to assess how the referendum would affect migrant workers speaks to a very different purpose than the preservation of "loyalty." Rather, it speaks to the urge to make the temporary workforce *more temporary* by severing one of the emotional and legal ties—the birth of a citizen child—that might make temporary workers feel a "connection" to Ireland.[64] Certainly other members of Martin's party had trouble envisioning immigrant workers as anything other than permanently foreign. When pressed on the referendum's impact on the children of Filipino nurses, Martin's Fianna Fáil colleague and candidate for the European Parliament, Jim McDaid, declared that "they are Filipino citizens, protected by Filipino law."[65]

If there is a primary economic lesson from American history that does apply here, we would suggest that it is not the lesson of protectionism offered by immigration restriction. Rather, it is the evidence offered by African American and Native American history that shows how differential citizenship provision can contribute to economic inequality by coercing certain groups into undesirable occupations and working conditions,[66] and by historical immigration policies, notably the Bracero Program, that show how the use of temporary workers ineligible for permanent residence or citizenship served not to prevent "aliens" from working, but to create and maintain a dual and subjugated workforce. As Aristide Zolberg notes, this is a "common solution" to two conflicting demands on "industrial societies—to maximize the labor supply and to protect cultural integrity." In this scenario, migrants are not excluded from the physical borders of the nation but, once admitted are "confine[d] strictly to their economic role by reinforcing the barrier against citizenship, a legal device which can be translated sociologically as the erection of a boundary within the territorial confines of the receiving society to offset the consequences of physical entry."[67]

Indeed, as migration theorist Robin Cohen has argued, the differentiated system of citizenship required by global capitalism has created a world utterly different than that faced by the many early twentieth century migrants who "threw off their poverty and feudal bondage to enter the American dream as equal citizens."[68] The status of today's unskilled workers from poor countries, in contrast, is increasingly that of a "helot" whose origin is an "indelible stigmata, determining a set of life chances, access to a particular kind of employment or any employment and other indicators of privilege and good fortune."[69]

Thus even in partial form, the scenario posed by immigrant "insourcing" raises a central global ethical question: whether or not it is acceptable for wealthy nations to impose policies and conditions upon the people of poor countries that they would not normally impose upon their own citizens.[70] Immigration may not solve the problem of global inequality, but if, as citizens of nations that have benefited from globalization, we are to rely on immigrant labour, we must make sure that that labor is not coerced. One of the ways that we can do that is to give immigrants full access to the protections of citizenship.

Jus Soli: A "Dead Zone" in American Studies

A comparative analysis of the repeal of unrestricted jus soli in Ireland reveals a curious fact about the study of jus soli in the United States: that is, the almost complete absence of research in American studies specifically devoted to this subject, with the important exception of work by Brook Thomas and, more recently, Ngai.[71] This absence is set into relief by the mountain of scholarship on the Fourteenth Amendment that relates to *Plessy v. Ferguson* (1896, 163 U.S. 537) versus the virtually nonexistent literature on *U.S. v. Wong Kim Ark* (1898, 169 U.S. 649), and by the lack even of a keyword entry for jus soli within ABC-Clio's *America: History and Life*.

It is perhaps too much to ask the humanities to take on a cheerleading role for jus soli. Yet, it is to be expected that, within the hundreds of articles and books written each year on virtually every conceivable aspect of immigrant history and life, at least some would specifically analyze how the provision of territorial birthright citizenship has affected the economic, social, political, and cultural life of the native-born children of immigrants and their parents; how jus soli has affected relations between immigrant families and their longer-established counterparts; how its establishment has influenced immigration law, such as the prioritization of family unification; or how the provision of jus soli in the United States has affected the legal and political construction of immigration and citizenship in other countries. Moreover, the lack of such studies arguably has contributed to two problematic results: first, an apparent misunderstanding about what it actually entails, and second, the rise of an interpretation of jus soli in American political studies that we believe to be pernicious.

The first can be seen in the noted historian Linda Kerber's analysis of *Nguyen v. INS* (2001, 533 U.S. 53). In this case, the Supreme Court decided that the adult, resident alien, foreign-born son (Tuan Anh Nguyen) of a U.S. citizen father (Joseph Boulais) and a Vietnamese mother could be deported from the United States for a felony sexual assault conviction.[72] As Kerber notes, if Nguyen's mother had been American, or his parents had been married, his citizenship would have been "automatically" conferred at birth—but as his father failed to meet the requirements for declaring Nguyen's U.S. citizenship before the age of majority, he never obtained it. Kerber argues that the court's decision undermined the Fourteenth Amendment's birthright citizenship clause because it refused to overturn provisions that require American men with foreign-born children to meet a higher burden of proof than women must to obtain citizenship for their children.

We would not defend *Nguyen*'s apparent sanctioning of the differential treatment of men and women, or the ensuing denial of "equal protection of the laws" identified by Kerber. But we would also emphasize that the case does not necessarily infringe upon the Fourteenth Amendment's provisions for the *conferring* of citizenship. This is because the Fourteenth Amendment does not actually protect the "rights of citizenship to the foreign-born descendants of native-born citizens"—or any other forms of citizenship based on heredity.[73] That is a matter for legislation, which has protected it, but only in limited circumstances, since 1790, and which may yet grant citizenship equally to the children of expatriate fathers.[74] The source of this confusion is Kerber's use of the term "birthright citizenship," which does not distinguish between jus soli and jus sanguinis, and which thus implies that all forms of citizenship by birth are equal, equally protected, and equally desirable. This is problematic, because *Nguyen* is clearly a case about jus sanguinis, and as such presents different analytical questions than jus soli. Moreover, these two categories of "birthright citizenship" are radically different, and to defend one or the other is to support radically different principles. Indeed, while there might be legitimate arguments on behalf of jus sanguinis for the children of emigrants, it also could be argued that it is a good thing, from the perspective of equality, that the Fourteenth Amendment does *not* recognize hereditary privilege in the granting of citizenship. On this point, we must concur with legal scholar Gerald Neuman that "U.S. citizenship isn't racial," and suggest that this point is not incidental, but fundamental to understanding the case.[75]

An even graver consequence of the lack of attention to jus soli is the second problematic result we have identified: the fact that it has allowed Smith and Schuck's analysis to have attained disproportionate weight. In his highly influential *Civic Ideals*, Smith characterizes jus soli as an "ascriptive anomaly in America's titularly consensual laws of membership" that, like other "inegalitarian ascriptive principles," assigns "people to places in hereditary hierarchical orders."[76] Smith proposes abandoning this outmoded, "feudal" route to citizenship for one based on consent. His argument there follows upon his earlier argument, outlined in his collaborative work with Peter Schuck, that the Fourteenth Amendment should correctly be interpreted as protecting the birthright citizenship of only those persons whose parents met the criterion of mutual consent between the individual and the state—and not the children of illegal aliens.[77] Emphasizing the purported absence of immigration restriction before the 1870s, Smith and Schuck argued that the drafters of the Fourteenth Amendment could not have envisioned a world in which people obtained citizenship due to their parents' illegal entry into the United States, or they would have placed limitations on citizenship obtained in this way.

Smith and Schuck's argument for citizenship by consent—one might call it *jus consensus*—has provoked a robust critical response from legal scholars, most notably Neuman.[78] Neuman convincingly undermines Smith and Schuck's position on historical and policy grounds. He shows that, before Reconstruction, the United States did not have "open borders": state and federal law restricted the immigration of paupers, the physically infirm, convicts, and, after 1808, illegally imported slaves. Nonetheless, the framers of the Fourteenth Amendment did not seek to exclude from citizenship anyone who descended from these "illegal" entrants. Furthermore, Neuman argues, the adoption of Smith and Schuck's interpretation—and the resulting denial of citizenship to the children of undocumented aliens—would entail great costs. These "include the blighting of the children's lives and the harm to U.S. society and values that would result from the creation of a hereditary undocumented caste;" and the possible emergence of a calculated

> two-track immigration regime, under which some immigrants would be admitted as lawful permanent residents on a naturalization track and others would be induced to reside unlawfully and threatened with a sufficient risk of deportation to render them docile and to avoid the applicability of the amended citizenship clause.

"In a global environment of overpopulation and Third World underdevelopment," Neuman concludes, such developments "could transform the United States into precisely the sort of society that the Fourteenth Amendment sought to prevent."[79]

Without recounting Neuman's prescient argument in full, we would like to make a few additional observations. The first is that Smith's emphasis on the feudal and ascriptive origins of jus soli overlooks its revolutionary adaptation within American law: while British law in the eighteenth century recognized both jus soli and jus sanguinis for the children and grandchildren of subjects, in the United States jus soli was immediately stripped of this tie to heredity in favor of a strict territorial requirement in the Naturalization Act of 1790. The main purpose of this, as Supreme Court Chief Justice William Howard Taft later suggested, was to prevent the descendants of loyalist absconders from claiming American citizenship.[80] There are certainly repressive aspects at work here, as the act deliberately excluded those singled out for proscription by the revolutionary authorities—just as Sections 2 and 3 of the Fourteenth Amendment prohibited from office holding, and excluded from the calculation of "the basis of representation," citizens who had "engaged in insurrection or rebellion." Nonetheless, the repression entailed within this construction of jus soli is of a revolutionary, rather than a feudal, sort and aims to diminish hereditary privileges even as it recognizes rights of birth.

Our second objection to Smith's reading of jus soli is that, although it appeals to the history of international jurisprudence, it fails properly to recognize how citizenship is regulated in national contexts outside of the United States. As a radical utopian possibility, the consensus ideal Smith proposes in *Civic Ideals* has some appeal. Nonetheless, the primary citizenship laws of all nations are based not on consent, but birth: on jus soli, jus sanguinis, or—the most common case—a combination of the two.[81] The only exception is the Vatican. With this in mind, it is necessary to revisit the question of what is constituted by an "ascriptive inegalitarian principle," and to ask whether jus soli is ascriptive and inegalitarian, or merely ascriptive. As the authors of the

1790 Act realized, all birthright entitlements do not have the same implications vis-à-vis equality. What makes ascription inegalitarian is not that entitlements are granted at birth, but that they are granted unequally: in other words, when the circumstances of birth are used to distinguish between those who possess rights and those who do not. Moreover, some forms of ascriptive distinction are more pernicious than others: distinctions based on pedigree, for example, are arguably more harmful than distinctions based on the accidental circumstances of birth (for example, time or place). A policy providing that "all children born after 2004 have the right to free health care" would discriminate against persons born before that date, but it would be less pernicious than a policy limiting health care to persons whose parents are literate or who are members of a particular racial group.

It might be objected that jus soli is inegalitarian insofar as it excludes and treats differently those born outside a particular national jurisdiction. But this problem extends well beyond the question of how citizenship is regulated to the question of citizenship per se. As anyone who has tried to get a Vatican passport can verify, the conversion to a consensual model of citizenship would not solve the problem of exclusion—only the abolition of national citizenship would do that. And jus soli does not necessarily have to be limited to persons born within a state's borders. Indeed, as the Irish example demonstrates, this is not just a theoretical possibility: Article 2 grants birthright territorial nationality not just to every person born in the Republic, but to "every person born in the island of Ireland." As this wording suggests, this entitlement is based on a utopian notion of the Irish nation that, until superseded by Article 9, derived not from heredity but territory.[82] It might also be objected that jus soli contributes to the inferior and repressive treatment of naturalized citizens, such as the constitutional limitation of presidential election to native-born citizens. But this repression does not necessarily derive from jus soli, but from the strength or weakness of the laws governing the rights of naturalized citizens—the Fourteenth Amendment itself requires the equal treatment of "natural" and "naturalized" citizens.[83] As a corollary, it should be noted that jus soli nations other than the United States have not always prohibited the foreign-born from holding high office (such as the first prime minister of Canada, Sir John A. MacDonald). As Rainer Bauböck argues in *Transnational Citizenship*, the territorial principle "minimizes the potential incongruities between the population over which territorial sovereignty can be rightfully exercised and the collective of those formally recognised as citizens."[84] In other words, jus soli is a more inclusive principle of democratic self-government.

Smith's characterization of jus soli as an ascriptive, inegalitarian principle must be re-evaluated both from the practicalities of what is feasible, given the constitutional history of the countries under discussion, and the abstract normative principles we use to evaluate practical policy. Even if a consensual model of citizenship would have the best effects—which given the way that states have employed citizenship law, is unlikely—we may have to settle for a solution that is second best: in this case a constitutionally protected right to full citizenship based on something other than blood or lineage. The removal of unrestricted jus soli as a determination of citizenship and the introduction of some principle of jus sanguinis in reality removes rights and benefits from the children of those most likely to be in the worst off position in society and removes from those children's noncitizen families one of their best chances of bettering their own condition by eventually becoming full citizens. Furthermore, as Jules L. Coleman and Sarah K. Harding have noted, assuming the legitimacy of borders and then arguing that questions of equality apply only to those within those borders begs the question that is at issue in debates over immigration or (as here) over access to citizenship.[85] Such a begging of the question may be occurring both in our argument for the benefits of jus soli to migrant workers—documented and undocumented—and in Smith's arguments for consensual citizenship. On the other hand, the other perspective that Harding and Coleman offer, a cosmopolitan perspective that applies considerations of equality to every individual on earth, makes the justification of borders or limited communities of citizenship quite problematic in themselves.[86] As Coleman and Harding note, these restricted entities are justified only if they further the project of cosmopolitan equality. If Cohen is right, however, about the international division of labor, then the "helots" who occupy the lowest rung of the hierarchy of workers more approximate the globally worst off than the candidates for Smith's consensual citizenship. They are also the individuals we can most easily help, however imperfectly, through a conception of citizenship that affords them a greater real chance of gaining an equal share of the world's wealth and a greater exercise of their rights.

Why Jus Soli Matters

Why, then, should we reinvigorate the study and defense of unrestricted jus soli? The first answer is that the need for an ethical response to globalization demands it. The movement of capital and persons and the dynamics of international labor markets mean that we must take an interest not just in migrations across the American border, but in migrations across all borders—particularly the borders of nations like Ireland with a high degree of economic and political interdependence with the United States. In so doing, we must be sure to understand how citizenship, like immigration policy, creates borders between the global haves and the global have-nots. Just as the trade policies and farm subsidies of the European Union are relevant for an understanding of the ethical dimensions of U.S. trade policy, so the citizenship regulations of European Union states are relevant for the ethical consideration of U.S. citizenship regulation. This means stepping "outside the frame" of American studies, which treats jus soli as an invisible, inevitable right, and recognizing that it is neither inevitable nor without tangible implications. If nothing else, more comprehensive research on jus soli's historical role in American life will provide comparative data to international scholars and advocates working within less equitable citizenship frameworks. As Jürgen Habermas argues, arguments for liberalizing immigration and citizenship regimes worldwide can increasingly be made in a developing global public sphere.[87]

The Irish citizenship referendum suggests that what happens in American scholarship does have an impact on what happens in the rest of the world. Many of the referendum's most vociferous critics came from the academic legal community. In large part, their arguments pertained to universal or to specifically Irish concerns: the danger of hastily changing the Irish Constitution, the undesirability of affording privilege to pedigree, and the risk of undermining the Northern Ireland peace process.[88] Yet, perhaps surprisingly, many of the referendum's legal critics specifically appealed to *American* law and legal thought, including Aisling Reidy, director of the Irish Council for Civil Liberties, and legal scholar Cathryn Costello, who explicitly drew upon both *U.S. v. Wong Kim Ark* and upon Neuman's writings in her critique of the referendum.[89] Indeed, at a time when the United States government has ceased, in the minds of many international commentators, to be a leader on matters of global justice, American jurisprudence provided not just examples but inspiration to the referendum's critics. Citing Ronald Dworkin's phrase that constitutions are documents "*of principle*" and thus should constitute the highest aspirations of the state, barrister and law lecturer Neville Cox made this passionate plea for the rejection of the referendum: "I would wish that like Eleanor Roosevelt as she worked to create a Human Rights language for the world we would be able to say 'Save us from ourselves and show us a vision of a world made new.'"[90]

In contrast to the passionate criticism of Ireland's academic lawyers, however, scholars in the humanities and social sciences contributed little by way of organized resistance to the referendum.[91] This relative silence cannot be attributed to a generalized lack of political engagement on the part of Irish academics; its historians, for example, have taken a leading role in legal and political campaigns for heritage preservation. Rather, it seems that scholars in the humanities and social sciences did not see the referendum as "their battle." One of the likely reasons for this is that scholars in the humanities and social sciences lacked a body of scholarship on jus soli comparable to that available to legal scholars, who have also taken internationalism seriously for longer than scholars from history, political theory, and the social sciences have.

The second reason that we should pay more attention to jus soli is that neither it, nor the notion of permanence in immigration underpinning it, is unassailable in the United States. Ireland's massive turn to temporary migrant labor has an American parallel in the rash of new proposals—from the Bush administration, the House, and the Senate—for the large-scale issuing of limited-term visas, which come on the heels of a number of temporary visa programs for skilled workers in the past decades. Taken in the context of guest worker programs in other parts of Europe and in the Middle East, what this suggests is that the long era of permanent migration—and the long-term benefits to migrants that guarantees of permanence can provide—may be coming to an end. Revocations of jus soli only hasten this change and exacerbate its effects. Smith notwithstanding, such revocations are not made for the sake of a more egalitarian, consensual alternative. Rather, as can be seen from what has happened in Ireland, Australia, Britain, France, Malta, New Zealand, Sweden, and other democratic countries, revocations of jus soli no longer take place, as they did following the French Revolution, in the context of movements against feudal privilege. Rather, they take place within the context of inegalitarian campaigns to discourage permanence, to diminish rights, and to institute "caste division."[92]

Notes

1. Wesley Boyd, "An Irishman's Diary," *Irish Times*, May 22, 2004, 19.
2. Article 3 of the 1922 Constitution states: "Every person, without distinction of sex, domiciled in the area of the jurisdiction of the Irish Free State at the time of the coming into operation of this Constitution, who was born in Ireland or either of whose parents was born in Ireland or who has been ordinarily resident in the area of the jurisdiction of the Irish Free State and shall within the limits of the jurisdiction of the Irish Free State enjoy the privileges and be subject to the obligations of such citizenship." Available at http://www.ucc.ie/celt/online/E900003-004/ (accessed March 3, 2008). The Irish Nationality and Citizenship Act of 1956, http://www.inis.gov.ie/en/INIS/consolidationINCA.

pdf/Files/consolidationINCA.pdf (accessed March 3, 2008), Section 6 (1), states: "Every person born in Ireland is an Irish citizen from birth." See also Irish Nationality and Citizenship Act of 1935, http://www.irishstatutebook.ie/plweb-cgi/fastweb?state_id=1204551270&view=ag-view&numhitsf ound=1&query_rule=%28%28$query3%29%29%29%3Alegtitle&query3=The%20Irish%20National ity%20and%20Citizenship%20Act%20of%201935&docid=9936&docdb=Acts&dbname=Acts& dbname=SIs&sorting=none&operator=and&TemplateName=predoc.tmpl&setCookie=1 (accessed March 3, 2008).

3. The breakdown of voting was: Yes: 79.17%; No: 20.83%. Turnout was 59.95%. See http://electionsireland.org/results/referendum/refresult.cfm?ref=2004R (accessed March 15, 2008). Although the change also affected Northern Ireland, only voters in the Republic were eligible to cast ballots.

4. The 27th Amendment of the Constitution Act 2004, http://www.irishstatutebook.ie/2004/en/act/cam/0027/index.html (accessed March 15, 2008).

5. Mae M. Ngai, "The Architecture of Race in American Immigration Law: A Reexamination of the Immigration Act of 1924," *Journal of American History* 86.1 (June 1999): 67–92.

6. See Martin Ruhs, "Emerging Trends and Patterns in the Immigration and Employment of Non-EU Nationals in Ireland: What the Data Reveal," Working Paper No. 6 (Dublin: The Policy Institute, Trinity College Dublin), 15.

7. Applications for asylum subsequently fell from 11,634 in 2002 to 3,985 in 2007. See "Minister Hails Fall in Asylum Applications," *Irish Times*, January 4, 2008. This seems to be a result of *Lobe & Osayande v. Minister of Justice*, mentioned below. See also Angelique Chrisafis, "Country's Emigrant Past Lies Forgotten as Irish Accused of Racism," *The Guardian*, June 21, 2004, 3.

8. Because immigrants from the EU did not need work permits, the number of work permits issued began to fall, with 21,395 permits being issued in 2006. See http://www.entemp.ie/publications/labour/2006/permitsbynationality.xls (accessed March 15, 2008).

9. "Address by Minister for Labour Affairs, Tony Killeen, TD, at a Seminar on 'Migration of Workers in the EU—Economic, Social and Legal Issues,'" March 8, 2006. http://www.entemp.ie/press/2006/20060308.htm (accessed March 15, 2008).

10. *Lobe & Osayande v. Minister of Justice*, January 23, 2003.

11. The German citizenship reform also specified that "when they reach the age of 23, they must decide for one pass or another." Seyla Benhabib, "Citizens, Residents and Aliens in a Changing World: Political Membership in the Global Era," *Social Research* 66.3 (Fall 1999): 709–45, 718.

12. Christian Joppke and Ewa Morawska, "Integrating Immigrants in Liberal Nation-States: Policies and Practices," in *Toward Assimilation and Citizenship: Immigrants in Liberal Nation-States*, ed. Christian Joppke and Ewa Morawska, 1–36 (London: Palgrave Macmillan, 2003), 18; and Christian Joppke, "Response to Sassen," in *Displacement, Asylum, Migration*, ed. Kate E. Tunstall, 204–9 (Oxford: Oxford University Press, 2006), 205. On the liberalization of German and Belgian naturalization regimes, see Randall Hansen, "A European Citizenship or a Europe of Citizens? Third Country Nationals in the EU," *Journal of Ethnic and Migration Studies* 24.4 (October 1998): 757–58 [751–68]; and Patrick Weil, "Access to Citizenship: A Comparison of Twenty-Five Nationality Laws," in *Citizenship Today: Global Perspectives and Practices*, ed. T. Alexander Aleinikoff and Douglas Klusmeyer, 17–35 (Washington, D.C.: Carnegie Endowment for International Peace, 2001).

13. As of 1998 persons born in Austria do have a "privileged" access to citizenship, in terms of a reduced waiting period for naturalization. See Weil, "Access to Citizenship," 30.

14. Italy increased residence requirements for naturalization for non-EU nationals while simultaneously reducing it for people of Italian descent. Hansen, "A European Citizenship," 757–60; Malta revoked jus soli in 1989, but recently offered citizenship to all persons of Maltese descent with no residence requirement whatsoever. See "Citizenship law changes come into effect," http://www.maltamedia.com/artman2/publish/govt_politics/article_2905.shtml (accessed March 30, 2008).

15. See "Automatic Citizenship: Citizenship by Birth," http://www.citizenship.gov.au/automatic-citizenship/citz-by-birth.htm (accessed March 15, 2008).

16. Citizenship (Amendment) Act 1986. This was made more restrictive by denying citizenship to children one of whose parents was illegally resident by the Citizenship (Amendment) Bill, 2003. See http://rajyasabha.nic.in/legislative/amendbills/XXXIX_2003.pdf (accessed March 15, 2008).

17. See http://home-affairs.pwv.gov.za/sa_citizenship.asp (accessed March 15, 2008).

18. See http://www.citizenship.govt.nz/diawebsite.nsf/wpg_URL/Whats-new-Changes-to-Citizenship-by-Birth-in-New-Zealand-from-2006-FAQs (accessed March 15, 2008). This site's FAQs state:

"The Government chose to amend the *Citizenship Act 1977* to recognise the value of New Zealand citizenship. The changes mean that a person cannot travel to New Zealand on a temporary permit solely to give birth and gain New Zealand citizenship for the child born in this country. By restricting citizenship by birth to the children of citizens and permanent residents, the Act's new provisions ensure that citizenship and its benefits are limited to people who have a genuine and ongoing link to New Zealand."

19. *Citizenship Reform Act of 2005*, H.R. 698, 109th Cong.; H.R. 814, 109th Cong. (2005); H.J. Res. 42, 108th Cong. (2003); H.J. Res. 44, 108th Cong. (2003); H.J. Res. 59, 107th Cong. (2001); H.J. Res. 10, 106th Cong. (1999); H.J. Res. 4, 105th Cong. (1997); H.J. Res. 60, 105th Cong. (1997); H.J. Res. 56, 104th Cong. (1995); H.J. Res. 64, 104th Cong. (1995); H.J. Res. 88, 104th Cong. (1995); H.J. Res. 190, 104th Cong. (1995); H.J. Res. 117, 103rd Cong., (1993); H.J. Res. 129, 103rd Cong. (1993); H.J. Res. 396, 103rd Cong., (1993).

20. See "Anchor Babies: The Children of Illegal Aliens," http://www.fairus.org/site/PageServer?pagename=iic_immigrationissuecenters4608 (accessed March 23, 2008). See also Tom Tancredo, "Birth Rules Degrade U.S. Immigration," *The Mountain Mail*, January 30, 2006, http://www.themountainmail.com/main.asp?SectionID=7&SubSectionID=7&ArticleID=7180 (accessed March 20, 2008).

21. See "Illegal Immigration and Public Health," http://www.fairus.org/site/PageServer?pagename=iic_immigrationissuecenters64bf (accessed March 23, 2008); "Latin American Parasite Surfacing in U.S.," *Houston Chronicle*, March 15, 2007.

22. See http://www.cfau.org/hamdi/amicusmerits.html (accessed March 23, 2008).

23. "What Makes an American?" *Jewish World Review*, July 4, 2003, http://www.jewishworldreview.com/michelle/malkin070403.asp (accessed March 23, 2008).

24. Ellis Cose, "American-Born, but Still 'Alien'?" *Newsweek*, March 19, 2007; "More Apply to Be Citizens," *Dallas Morning News*, March 19, 2007. The text of the Bill, Texas HR 28, can be seen at http://www.capitol.state.tx.us/tlodocs/80R/billtext/html/HB00028I.htm (accessed March 23, 2008).

25. Referendum on British-Irish Agreement (Nineteenth Amendment of the Constitution Bill, 1998), May 22, 1998, viewable at ElectionsIreland.org, http://electionsireland.org/results/referendum/summary.cfm (accessed March 18, 2008).

26. Constitution of Ireland—Bunreacht na hÉireann, at http://www.taoiseach.gov.ie/attached_files/Pdf%20files/Constitution%20of%20IrelandNov2004.pdf (accessed March 18, 2008).

27. See Irish Nationality and Citizenship Act, 1956, Section 15, at http://www.inis.gov.ie/en/INIS/consolidationINCA.pdf/Files/consolidationINCA.pdf (accessed March 18, 2008).

28. See the explanatory notes of the proposed bill at http://www.oireachtas.ie/documents/bills28/bills/2004/4004/b4004d.pdf (accessed March 18, 2008), and the text of the act at http://www.oireachtas.ie/documents/bills28/acts/2004/a3804.pdf (accessed March 18, 2008).

29. See "Launch of the New Immigration Bill" at http://www.justice.ie/en/JELR/Pages/Launch%20of%20new%20Immigration%20Bill (accessed March 18, 2008).

30. Gerard Hogan, "Citizenship and the Constitution: 1922 to Date," (paper presented to The Citizenship Referendum: Implications for the Constitution and Human Rights conference, Trinity College Dublin, May 22, 2004).

31. To be eligible for citizenship beyond descent from an Irish grandparent, an applicant's parent must have taken up Irish citizenship before the applicant's birth. Oasis Information on Public Services, "Irish Citizenship Through Birth or Descent," http://www.citizensinformation.ie/categories/moving-country/irish-citizenship/irish_citizenship_through_birth_or_descent (accessed March 18, 2008).

32. Oran Doyle, "Citizenship and Equality," in *The Citizenship Referendum: Implications for the Constitution and Human Right* (Dublin: Trinity College Dublin, School of Law, 2004), 115–16 [101–24]; Hogan, "Citizenship and the Constitution," 6.

33. Brook Thomas, "*China Men, United States v. Wong Kim Ark*, and the Question of Citizenship," *American Quarterly* 50.4 (December 1998): 689–717, 705.

34. See Brian Lenihan, TD, "Citizen Change Common Sense," *Irish Times*, May 28, 2004, 18.

35. "YES Citizenship Matters," Fiona O'Malley, TD, *The Last Word*, June 3, 2004. See also Paul Cullen, "Citizenship Loophole Is Damaging Credibility of Entire Asylum System," *Irish Times*, June 3, 2003, 18; Constantin T. Gurdgiev, "Yes: Rejecting the Referendum Would Be a Betrayal of Those Who Truly Belong in Ireland through Effort and Achievement," *Irish Times*, June 8, 2004, 16.

36. Bertie Ahern, *The Last Word*, Today FM, June 2, 2004.
37. "Citizenship Tourists," *The Economist*, June 3, 2004; Denis Staunton, "Chinese Mother and Irish Baby 'Entitled to Live in EU,'" *Irish Times*, May 19, 2004, 9.
38. Mark Hennessy, "McDowell Insists His Action Heads Off 'Threat,'" *Irish Times*, May 19, 2004, 9; Carole Coulter, "European Finding Bolsters Case for Referendum Made by Government," *Irish Times*, May 19, 2004, 9.
39. Sean MacCarthaigh, "Government Provides the Sticks to Beat Itself," *Sunday Business Post*, April 25, 2004.
40. "Citizenship Referendum June 11th: Facts? No! Figures? No! Reasons? No! Vote NO!" Labour Party campaign leaflet, n.d. [May 2004]; Cllr. Leo Varadkar (FG), letter to the editor, *Irish Times*, May 25, 2004, 19; this charge was also leveled by Benedicta Attoh, Independent candidate for Louth County Council, on *The Last Word*, Today FM, June 3, 2004.
41. Fine Gael's campaign literature avoided specific mention of the referendum, but Mitchell and others publicly voiced their support for the referendum on the radio and in other media. Gay Mitchell, TD, "20 Questions on the European Union," campaign pamphlet, 2004; Mitchell, in debate with Ivana Bacik (Lab), Mary Lou McDonald (SF), Eoin Ryan (FF), *The Last Word*, Today FM, June 8, 2004.
42. Gay Mitchell, *The Last Word*, June 8, 2004.
43. Dr. Michael Geary, interview on *Morning Ireland*, RTÉ Radio 1, March 11, 2004; Senator Mary Henry, *The Last Word*, Today FM, May 31, 2004; Dr. Austin O. Carroll et al., "We wish to register our opposition to the upcoming referendum on citizenship" (open letter), published in "Doctors Launch No Vote Campaign," *Campaign against the Racist Referendum* press release, May 31, 2004; Kitty Holland, "Doctor to Raise Role of Three Masters," *Irish Times*, June 2, 2004, 5; Dr Muiris Houston, "Role of Masters to be Discussed Next Month," *Irish Times*, June 3, 2004, 3.
44. See Private Notice Questions of Roisin Shortall TD (Lab); Seymour Crawford TD (FG); John Gormley TD (Green); Dan Neville TD (FG); Paudge Connolly (Ind); all in *Dáil Debates*, vol. 559, December 12, 2002, 725–26.
45. In a letter to Micheál Martin on February 23, Geary apparently cited an "alarming" rise in cases of women from sub-Saharan Africa with HIV, claiming that "while we, as healthcare workers, will take the appropriate cautions to avoid transmission of HIV, it is obvious to all that I would not like to be in the position to have a member of my staff needing to change their career because of contracting HIV through an occupational incident." Arthur Beesley, "'Alarming' rise in HIV Cases in Maternity Care," *Irish Times*, May 28, 2004, 9. Alan M. Kraut, *Silent Travelers: Germs, Genes, and the "Immigrant Menace"* (Baltimore: Johns Hopkins University Press, 1994). See also Paul Cullen, "Rise in HIV among Non-nationals Highlighted," *Irish Times*, May 29, 2004, 5.
46. See http://www.stormfront.org/forum/showthread.php?t=129217 (accessed May 26, 2008).
47. Martin claimed in a radio interview that he supported the referendum because, in its absence, an immigrant child would die. *The Last Word*, Today FM, May 31, 2004. Progressive Democrat campaign literature included an anonymous quotation from "the Master of one of Dublin's leading hospitals" asserting that "'we have been fortunate that there have not been any maternal mortalities as a result of this but there have been some near misses.'" Progressive Democrats, "YES Citizenship Matters," n.d. [2004].
48. See "Report on Incidents Relating to Racism in Ireland, July–December 2007" at http://www.nccri.ie/pdf/RacistIncidentsJuly-Dec07.pdf (accessed March 20, 2008).
49. See Ronit Lentin, "Illegal in Ireland, Irish Illegals: Diaspora Nation as Racial State," *Irish Political Studies* 22.4 (December 2007): 433–53. See also Anwen Tormey, "'Everyone with Eyes Can See the Problem': Moral Citizens and the Space of Irish Nationhood," *International Migration* 45.3 (August 2007): 69–100; Steve Garner, "Babies, Bodies and Entitlement: Gendered Aspects of Access to Citizenship in the Republic of Ireland," *Parliamentary Affairs* 60.3 (July 2007): 437–51; Silvia Brandi, "Unveiling the Ideological Construction of the 2004 Irish Citizenship Referendum: A Critical Discourse Analytical Approach," *Translocations* 2.1 (Summer 2007) at http://www.translocations.ie/currentissue/volume1issue2-3.pdf (accessed March 20).
50. Ahern, *The Last Word*.
51. The racist incidents noted in note 48 indicate that while the majority of immigrants to Ireland come from other states in the EU, it is visible minorities, most especially black African males, who are the targets of racist incidents and attitudes. The sizable minority of Filipinos who have recently arrived in Ireland (the Philippine Embassy in London estimates there are approximately 11,500 Filipinos resident in Ireland, up from 500 in 1999; the Irish Central Statistics Office lists 9,548 Filipinos in

the 2006 census) do not seem to be particular targets of racial harassment or xenophobic sentiment. See www.philembassy-uk.org/default.asp?iId=KHEHL (accessed March 24, 2008). For the national composition of Irish migration, www.cso.ie/releasespublications/documents/population/non-irish/nonirishnationalscomplete.pdf (accessed July 3, 2008).

52. On the differences here, see the trenchant comments of former congressman Bruce Morrison (D-CT), author of a program that secured 48,000 green cards for Irish nationals in 1991: "During recent Irish media interviews, the hosts could not stop saying that my legislation had helped 48,000 Irish undocumented to get 'work permits' in the U.S. The number is right, but it was permanent resident 'Green Cards' they got, not temporary permits. . . . Canada and the U.S. make plenty of mistakes, but they have the basics right. Successful inclusion of immigrants requires permanent admissions and guaranteed citizenship for children born there. European use of ethnicity to define membership in the community is a recipe for segregation of newcomers and ongoing ethnic strife." Morrison, "No: There Is Nothing to Justify Citizenship Panic," *Irish Times*, June 8, 2004, 16.

53. Annual success rates of asylum applications in Ireland averaged below 11% before appeal, 1998 to 2001. See European Council on Refugees and Exiles, "Asylum in the European Union," 7. In 2004, the figure for "Convention Status" recognition was 6.02%. See "European Council on Refugees and Exiles—Country Report 2004—Ireland" at http://www.ecre.org/files/Ireland%20-%20FINAL_0.pdf (accessed March 23, 2008). On the education and work ban, see Irish Refugee Council, "The Right to Work = The Right to Dignity: Policy on the Right to Work for Asylum Seekers," http://www.irishrefugeecouncil.ie/policy01/righttoworkdignity.doc (accessed March 23, 2008).

54. For a critical view on how U.S. guest worker programs tie workers to employers, see Southern Poverty Law Center, "Close to Slavery: Guestworker Programs in the United States," available at: http://www.splcenter.org/pdf/static/SPLCguestworker.pdf (accessed March 23, 2008).

55. Yasemin Soysal, "Toward a Postnational Model of Membership [in Europe] [*sic*]," in *Readings in Contemporary Political Sociology*, ed. Kate Nash, 264–79 (Oxford: Blackwell, 2000), 270.

56. See William Binchy, "Citizenship and the International Remit of Constitutional Protection," in *The Citizenship Referendum*, 48–90.

57. Ruadhán Mac Cormaic, "Following Dreams Far from Home," *The Irish Times*, April 25, 2007.

58. This is suggested by the party affiliation of the noncitizens who contested local elections in 2004: 6 Independents, 11 Green Party, and 2 Labour. Kitty Holland, "Non-national Candidates Blaze New Trail," *Irish Times*, June 2, 2004, 9. At least one noncitizen candidate, Independent Rotimi Adebari, secured a local council position and has since become mayor of Portlaoise. Deaglán de Bréadún, "Nigerian Elected to Portlaoise Council," *Irish Times*, June 14, 2004, Election Supplement, 3.

59. See the Irish Congress of Trade Unions' document *Migration Policy and the Rights of Workers* at http://www.ictu.ie/html/publications/ictu/Migrant%20Policy.pdf (accessed March 24, 2008).

60. "Poles Unfair Dismissal Case Settled in Killarney," *Irish Times*, June 25, 2004, 4.

61. "Gov't 'Blocking' EU Worker Directive," *Irish Times*, December 5, 2007.

62. Patsy McGarry, "McDowell Says Inequality an Incentive in the Economy," *Irish Times*, May 28, 2004, 1.

63. Micheál Martin, *Last Word*, May 31, 2004.

64. The Department of Justice also made it difficult for work permit holders' families to secure even temporary visitor visas. Carl O'Brien, "Doctor's Parents Refused Entry Visas," *Irish Times*, June 23, 2004, 2.

65. Jim McDaid, *Questions and Answers*, RTÉ, May 24, 2004.

66. This is seen, for example, in the post-Reconstruction South, or in the provocative case of Native American whaling in Nantucket analyzed by Daniel Vickers in "The First Whalemen of Nantucket," in *American Encounters: Natives and Newcomers from European Contact to Indian Removal*, ed. Peter C. Mancall and James H. Merrell, 262–82 (London: Routledge, 2000).

67. Aristide R. Zolberg, "International Migrations in Political Perspective, in *Global Trends in Migration*, ed. Mary M. Kritz, Charles B. Keeley, and Silvano M. Tomasi, 3–27 (Staten Island: The Center for Migration Studies of New York, 1981), 15.

68. Robin Cohen, *The New Helots: Migrants in the International Division of Labour* (Aldershot, U.K.: Avebury, 1987), including his analysis of the Bracero Program in chapter 2. See also his more recent research, "Citizens, Denizens, and Helots: The Politics of International Migration Flows after 1945," in *Migration and Its Enemies* (Aldershot, U.K.: Ashgate, 2006), 137–53. See also Nigel Harris, *The New Untouchables* (London: I. B. Tauris, 1995).

69. Cohen, "Citizens, Denizens, and Helots," 152–53.
70. Joseph Stiglitz, *Globalization and Its Discontents* (New York: W. W. Norton, 2003).
71. Mae M. Ngai makes a criticism of Schuck and Smith similar to ours and notes the example of the Irish Citizenship Referendum, as well as the changes in New Zealand's citizenship regime in "Birthright Citizenship and the Alien Citizen," *Fordham Law Review* 75.5 (April 2007): 2524–25. We regret that Ngai's article only came to our notice as this article was going to press.
72. Linda K. Kerber, "The Asymmetries of Citizenship," *Common-place* 2.4 (July 2002).
73. See *Johnson v. Sullivan*, No. 1889, Circuit Court of Appeals, First Circuit, 8 F.2d 988; 1925 U.S. App. LEXIS 3423, November 16, 1925.
74. See H.R. 88, 108th Cong. (2003). See also *Johnson v. Sullivan*.
75. Cited in Kerber, "Asymmetries of Citizenship."
76. Rogers M. Smith, *Civic Ideals: Conflicting Visions of Citizenship in U.S. History* (New Haven: Yale University Press, 1997), 507n4 and 3, respectively.
77. Peter Schuck and Rogers M. Smith, *Citizenship without Consent: Illegal Aliens in the American Polity* (New Haven: Yale University Press, 1985).
78. Gerald L. Neuman, *Strangers to the Constitution: Immigrants, Borders, and Fundamental Law* (Princeton, N.J.: Princeton University Press, 1996), esp. chapter 9. See also Joseph Carens, "Who Belongs? Theoretical and Legal Questions about Birthright Citizenship in the United States," *University of Toronto Law Journal* 37.4 (Autumn 1987): 413; Gerald L. Neuman, "Back to Dred Scott?" *San Diego Law Review* 24 (1987): 485; David Martin, "Membership and Consent: Abstract or Organic?" *Yale Journal of International Law* 11 (1987): 278, 283; David Schwartz, "The Amorality of Consent," *California Law Review* 74.6 (December 1986): 2143.
79. Neuman, *Strangers to the Constitution*, 186–87.
80. *Weedin v. Chin Bow* (274 U.S. 657), 1927.
81. See Stephen Castles, *Citizenship and Migration* (Basingstoke, U.K.: Macmillan, 2000), 85. Castles emphasizes the integrative role of jus soli. This might be seen as the cultural aspect of the emphasis on political and economic integration of this paper.
82. On the complex relationship between citizenship and territory in an Irish context, see Brian O. Caoindealbhain, "Citizenship and Borders: Irish Nationality Law and Northern Ireland," Working Paper 68, Institute of British-Irish Studies, http://www.qub.ac.uk/cibr/WPpdffiles/MFWPpdf/w18_boc.pdf (accessed March 24, 2008).
83. Thus proposals by Senator Orrin Hatch (R-UT) and Congressman Barney Frank (D-MA) to grant Presidential eligibility for naturalized citizens would not change the Fourteenth Amendment. S.J. Res. 15, 108th Cong. (2003); H.J. Res. 47, 107th Cong. (2001).
84. Rainer Bauböck, *Transnational Citizenship* (Aldershot, U.K.: Edward Elgar, 1994), 35.
85. Jules L. Coleman and Sarah K. Harding, "Citizenship, the Demands of Justice and the Moral Relevance of Political Borders," in *Justice in Immigration*, ed. Warren F. Schwartz, 18–60 (Cambridge: Cambridge University Press, 1995), 38. Schuck has acknowledged this problem in "Membership in the Liberal Polity: The Devaluation of American Citizenship," in *Immigration and the Politics of Citizenship in Europe and North America*, ed. Rogers Brubaker, 51–65 (Lanham, Md.: The German Marshall Fund of the United States and University Press of America, 1989).
86. Coleman and Harding, "Citizenship," 39.
87. Jürgen Habermas, "Citizenship and National Identity," in *Between Facts and Norms* (Cambridge, Mass.: MIT Press, 1996), 514–15.
88. Aisling Reidy, "The Need for a Referendum Considered," paper presented at The Citizenship Referendum: Implications for the Constitution and Human Rights conference at Trinity College Dublin, May 22, 2004.
89. Reidy, "Need for Referendum"; Cathryn Costello, "Accidents of Place and Parentage: Birthright Citizenship and Border Crossings," in *The Citizenship Referendum*, 5–33.
90. Neville Cox, "The Language of Constitutional Debate," in *The Citizenship Referendum*, 91–100.
91. A notable exception was Piaras MacÉinrí of the Department of Geography and the Irish Centre for Migration Studies Institute of University College Cork.
92. Neuman, *Strangers to the Constitution*, 184.

New Americans or Diasporic Nationalists? Mexican Migrant Responses to Naturalization and Implications for Political Participation

Adrián Félix

[Immigrants] have to learn the language; they have to learn United States history and learn the way to do business. This is very difficult for Mexicans because they are too close to their country here and they try to remain Mexican while they stay in the United States. As a result there is this going and coming. What I want to say to Mexicans is that they have to get involved and assimilate into United States culture so that they can be part of the United States fabric.

—Arnold Schwarzenegger

We will never stop being Mexican. That cannot be taken away from you. In fact, we will continue to face discrimination simply because we are Mexican. Even if we become citizens, we will encounter prejudice.

—Don Juan, Mexican naturalizer

In the spring of 2006, anti-immigrant congressional legislation triggered immigrant rights protests that reverberated beyond the territorial confines of the United States.[1] The coordinated efforts between immigrant rights activists and the Spanish-language media allowed migrants and their allies to momentarily attain what Alfonso Gonzales describes as a counterhegemonic position powerful enough to prevent proposed punitive legislation from becoming law. Despite its initial success, Gonzales argues, the immigrant rights movement subsequently disintegrated due to a series of internal and external contradictions.[2] Whether the immigrant rights movement has dissolved or split into factions pursuing incongruous political outcomes, the mega-marches are fresh in the collective memory of immigrants who protested and even of some who did not participate, and such memories may be mobilizing them to take further political action. In addition to seeing a powerful entry into public politics by undocumented migrants, the period following the protests has witnessed an increase in the number of citizen-eligible immigrants seeking naturalization.[3] Between January and October 2007, the United States

Citizenship and Immigration Service (USCIS) received 1,029,951 naturalization applications, a 59 percent increase from the same period in 2006.[4] In light of the immigrant rights protests of 2006 and the attendant surge in citizenship applications, this article presents a political ethnography of a citizenship class in Southern California and discusses how Mexican immigrants experienced the naturalization process in the context of their transnational lives and identities.

Citizenship acquisition is conventionally understood as a landmark in the process of immigrant incorporation.[5] In his study of immigrant adaptation in early twentieth century Los Angeles, George J. Sánchez interprets Mexican immigrants' decision to naturalize as a sign of permanent resettlement in the United States and suggests that their mobilization in U.S. politics came at the expense of participation in Mexican politics.[6] The violence of the Mexican Revolution, the creation of the U.S. border patrol, and the repatriation of thousands of Mexican nationals during the Great Depression were some of the political and economic forces that led to a second-generation dominance in Mexican communities in Los Angeles. U.S.-born Mexicans and their political organizations broke with the former view against naturalization and called upon Mexican immigrants to become American citizens involved in American elections, making for a generation decidedly focused on events north of the border.

Today scholars point to transformations in communication and travel technologies, increased tolerance of ethnic pluralism in the United States, and home state rapprochement with their diasporas among other factors that facilitate cross-border interactions and identities. In the context of transnational migrations, there is debate among social scientists regarding the nature and degree of contemporary Mexican immigrant political incorporation in the United States, emphasizing failed assimilation on one end and a traditional pattern of political assimilation on the other.[7] Consistent with the first view, Mexican migrants' failure to assimilate is attributed to proximity to the homeland, cross-border activities, institutions of dual nationality, and other factors endogenous to "Mexican exceptionalism," as the Schwarzenegger epigraph suggests. Researchers of the second vein have argued that Mexicans are indeed assimilating, citing immigrant adherence to values such as economic individualism and U.S. patriotism. Under this view, immigrants who become naturalized citizens are believed to be as, if not more, patriotic to their new country than white Americans, adjusting for background and other factors.[8] An alternative perspective challenges these conventions. As the statement by Don Juan illustrates, cross-border loyalties and identities persist upon naturalization largely as a result of migrant self-identification in response to the institutional discrimination they face throughout the process of political enfranchisement.

In light of these studies, how do Mexican migrants experience the naturalization process? Why are they becoming U.S. citizens? What does it mean to them? Drawing on seven months of ethnographic fieldwork and twelve in-depth interviews with Mexican migrants who were preparing for the naturalization interview (or had already completed it) in a citizenship class in San Bernardino County, this essay presents preliminary responses to these questions.

In contrast to previous studies that attribute "failed assimilation" to forms of "Mexican exceptionalism," I argue that this pattern is a product of the anti-immigrant context of reception sustained and reproduced by U.S. society and politics. Moreover, while the anxiety, intimidation, and other negative factors attributed to low naturalization rates among Mexican migrants are well documented, such experiences are countered by the collective emotions, rapport, and solidarity of the citizenship classroom, positing it as a potentially empowering public space for the immigrant rights movement. Rather than operating as a conduit for Americanization, the citizenship classroom can be a space where migrants make the naturalization experience intelligible on their own cultural and political terms. As I will show, U.S. citizenship is indiscriminately negated to many migrants during the naturalization interview. In response to such bureaucratic inconsistency, the citizenship class functions as an alternative public space where migrants develop a counternarrative that exposes the arbitrariness of the naturalization process, creating an oppositional, rather than assimilative, relationship to citizenship and national identity. Regarding the incentives to naturalize, Ong and Lee note that securing tangible benefits in an anti-immigrant context leads to "defensive naturalization."[9] This article presents evidence of an added community empowerment motive driving a reactive naturalization, which is more politically purposeful and is more proactive than defensive. In such cases, when ethnic identity is perceived as the basis of shared discrimination, the resulting salience of ethnicity encourages naturalization as a means for furthering community interests via collective political action in ways that are not reducible to notions of assimilation.[10]

Unlike in the early twentieth century, Mexican naturalization in the twenty-first century cannot be viewed as a sign of permanent resettlement in the United States. As Sánchez notes, immigrants who secure legalization no longer face the institutional barriers to visit their home communities and re-enter the United States legally. To this we add the Mexican government's more recent dual nationality law and local policies like "La ley migrante" in Zacatecas, which allow migrants to participate in the civic life of their communities of origin. As Michael Jones-Correa demonstrates, immigrants from countries recognizing dual nationality average higher naturalization rates in the United States than their counterparts from countries that do not.[11] Far from being an impediment to political participation, ethnic identification and attachment to the homeland post-naturalization may drive migrant political participation across borders.

Political Context and Mexican Naturalization, 1990s–Present

Naturalization rates among Mexican immigrants (and Latinos more broadly) have been low relative to other ethnic groups. Citizen-eligible Latinos have been "characterized by their sluggishness between when they have been eligible to naturalize and when they actually undergo the process."[12] The 1990s are thought to have momentarily disrupted these patterns, setting an important precedent for the argument presented here. In 1990, more than 270,000 immigrants became U.S. citizens. Six years later, this figure soared to over a million, "with the proportion due to Mexican immigrants tripling from 6.5 percent to 20.8 percent."[13] By fiscal year 1999, this percentage had increased to 30 percent. The reasons for this change include a racially charged political climate and increased mobilization by ethnic and civic organizations, which are thought to have stimulated immigrant naturalization and political participation.[14]

In the post-9/11 context, immigrant advocates are concerned that developments within the Department of Homeland Security (DHS) and USCIS threaten to further discourage Latino naturalization, particularly among Mexican immigrants. Waslin indicates that "approximately 8 million legal permanent residents are now eligible to naturalize, and another 2.7 million legal immigrants will soon be eligible for naturalization but are unlikely to do so." Eligible immigrants who have not yet naturalized have lower English language skills and less formal education, and are more heavily Mexican than their newly naturalized counterparts. As of 2001, there were 2.3 million Mexican immigrants eligible to naturalize, ten times the number from any sending country. Moreover, "while Mexicans compose 28 percent of all currently eligible immigrants, they represent only 9 percent of recently naturalized citizens. Only 21 percent of eligible Mexicans entering the U.S. in the past twenty years have naturalized in comparison to 57 percent of Asians."[15]

It should come as no surprise that Mexican immigrants have been slow to naturalize. Mexican immigrants describe the naturalization process as one rife with patronizing officials, unreasonable criminalization, humiliation, fear, and anxiety. In addition, Mexican migrants have long been discouraged by feelings of disloyalty to the home country and misinformation about losing rights and privileges therein upon naturalizing.[16] However, this article suggests a shift in the popular conception of citizenship, signaling an emerging consensus in favor of naturalizing among noncitizens. The federal government's effort to make naturalization more difficult (for example, increased fee rates, higher English language requirements) may in fact be the impetus for immigrants to seek full de jure political membership in the United States. From an immigrant's perspective, the pragmatic reasons to naturalize include the hiking of fee rates, increased ability to obtain dual nationality, and the debunking of long-held myths about naturalization. On top of this, however, a hostile political climate and subsequent immigrant rights protests promoted by the ethnic media may account for the decision to "seek enfranchisement as an act of political expression."[17]

The current immigrant-hostile political climate is not without precedent. The mid-1990s temporarily disrupted stagnant naturalization patterns when citizen-eligible Latinos reacted to the confluence of an anti-immigrant political context and attendant political protests advertised by the ethnic media. Like current anti-immigrant legislation, Proposition 187, the 1994 California initiative, was punitive in nature in that it sought to deny public services to undocumented immigrants and required public officials to report suspected undocumented immigrants to the Immigration and Naturalization Service. In this context, citizen-eligible immigrants became more aware of immigration and ethnicity as salient issues.[18] Additionally, "because Proposition 187 was seen as a move against Latino immigrants, a large number of Latino non-citizens, perhaps out of fear of losing certain services or status, made the decision to begin the naturalization process."[19] An anti-immigrant political context resulted in "defensive naturalization." A similarly contentious political environment has emerged in California and beyond as evidenced by continued immigrant-focused initiatives and hostile public rhetoric from elected officials and pundits, albeit this time triggering a more politically purposeful reactive naturalization.[20]

In their study of Anglo and Mexican support for "core American values," Rodolfo de la Garza and his associates find that Mexican respondents were often more individually oriented and more patriotic than Anglos. When explaining why this is so, the authors state that "as the joyous tears shed at citizenship ceremonies indicate, immigrants who become naturalized citizens have undergone a major transition with intense emotional overtones."[21] The presumption is that legal immigrants who make the decision to naturalize do so out of patriotism to their new country. This essay complicates this picture. The findings suggest that, citizenship oath notwithstanding, these patriotic "new Americans" may in fact be long-distance or *diasporic* nationalists.[22] In other words, ethnic attachment and identification with the homeland do not cease or diminish upon naturalization, and this is consistent with other studies.[23] Unlike the "failed assimilation" and "traditional assimilation" camps that focus solely on factors endogenous to "Mexican exceptionalism" or the naturalization process exclusively, this analysis also considers the recurrent external factors of an anti-immigrant political context of reception. Additionally, the data has implications for earlier research that found that new citizens are not always civically minded.[24] Although they face a dearth of political information, the respondents suggest that newly enfranchised Mexican immigrants are likely voters.

Political Ethnography of a Citizenship Class

The data for this article come from seven months of ethnographic fieldwork and intensive interviews conducted in a citizenship class in San Bernardino County, from September 2006 to March 2007 and a follow-up visit in June of 2007. Citizenship instruction was offered Monday through Thursday, from 6 p.m. to 8 p.m. The venue was a small classroom that accommodated about twenty-five students. However, attendance was usually around thirty-five and sometimes as high as fifty. Although by a narrow margin, women often outnumbered men. This particular citizenship course was based on continuous enrollment, with no actual beginning or end date. The instructor was Benjamín, a naturalized Mexican immigrant for more than ten years, in his late forties, who was interviewed in the sample.[25] Class participants were mostly immigrants from Mexico, but there were a few students from El Salvador, Guatemala, and Honduras, as well as one from Peru and one from Argentina.

Twelve respondents were interviewed, six men and six women. With the exception of Benjamín and Felipe, who were interviewed the day of their citizenship interviews, all participants were potential naturalizers. The duration of the interviews averaged around sixty minutes and followed a structured guide. Six interviews were conducted on-site, during but separate from class instruction. The remaining six were conducted at the home of Doroteo and Adela, the only married couple in the sample. All interviews were conducted in Spanish.

Respondents, ranging in age from thirty to sixty-four, represented different immigrant cohorts (for example, different time of arrival to the United States and hence different experiences amid shifting political contexts). Occupations included housekeeping, maintenance, carpentry, construction, welding, and factory assembly work. One respondent was retired. Ten respondents came from rural regions in Mexico (Guanajuato, Michoacan, Jalisco, Zacatecas, Nayarit), while two came from large urban centers: Guadalajara and Mexico City. Education levels were generally low (elementary school) among the older respondents but slightly higher for the younger migrants, reflective of the educational variance among immigrant cohorts.[26] English proficiency was mostly low but ranged to intermediate. All respondents were married (one was widowed) with children born and/or raised in the United States.

How Do Mexican Migrants Experience the Naturalization Process?

Respondents emphasized how the naturalization process affected them in the private sphere, in their family and personal lives. Interview and observational data convey how the process was experienced emotionally and collectively in classroom interactions. Returning students added to this environment by sharing their experiences during the much anticipated and sometimes dreaded citizenship interview, the decisive moment of the naturalization process.

The Private Sphere

Permanent legal residents who make the decision to begin the naturalization process do not take it lightly and make it a priority to accomplish this goal. On top of class instruction, several respondents studied using audio aids and other materials at home or work. Doña María (age sixty-one), for instance, stated, "I listen to a cassette at home. I go over the questions and listen to the tape when I am at home." Don Juan (age fifty-two) relied on a "CD to practice the citizenship interview" when he was in the privacy of his home. Others practiced their English with their U.S.-born children, like Dolores (age forty-two), who exhorted her nine-year-old son, "Mi'jo, teach me how to write in English. Speak to me in English at home. I have to learn." Dolores was so consumed by the naturalization process that she had "dreams about the questions. I stay up late at night studying and I've had dreams about the immigration officer. He tells me I did not pass. He tells me I have to come back."

While the anxiety, fear, and intimidation involved in Latino naturalization are well documented, these negative emotions are often assuaged by encouraging remarks from friends and family.[27] Don Felipe (age forty-six) recalled some of this motivation: "You can do it," his friends said to him. "Those who are already American citizens would tell me, 'You have to accomplish it. If we did it, why can't you do it? You can do it.' Thanks be to God, I passed my exam today," he remarked. Likewise, Rosaura (age thirty), who married a U.S. citizen, reported that everyone in her family supported her attempt to naturalize. She said, "Everybody is happy because there is now a possibility for me to help them," signaling the prospect of legalizing her parents and siblings. "I have heard nothing but good remarks from friends and family," said Beatriz (age fifty-four). "They tell me, 'that is great. *Héchale ganas.* You can do it.'" Finally, Adela and Doroteo (age forty-three and forty-six, respectively), the only married couple pursuing naturalization in the sample, were equally supportive of one another. When Doroteo was reticent to seek naturalization and suggested Adela go at it alone, she replied:

No, we are both going to do it. If I become a citizen, I don't want you to remain as a resident. I don't want one of us to be higher and the other lower. I want both of us to be equal." More than anything, we are motivating one another to accomplish this goal. I try to help him and motivate him to learn. I tell him, "*Sí se puede.*"

Not everyone was as supportive, however. Adela and Doroteo decided not to inform other family members about their attempt to naturalize, "so that in case we don't pass, they won't make us feel bad." "I don't comment this to anyone," said Amparo (age fifty). Similarly, Don Juan avoided telling his co-workers, stating, "I am afraid to tell them because they will tease me if I don't pass the interview [laughter]." While in the past naturalizers may have feared being labeled disloyal to Mexico for seeking U.S. citizenship, here it is fear of embarrassment at not passing the exam, indicative of a shift in the popular conception of naturalization.

Potential citizens invested considerable amounts of time, energy, and money in the naturalization process. Most respondents agreed that the naturalization process required a huge sacrifice in their family and personal lives. "I have not missed time from work, but I have cut into my children's time and many other things I have to do around the house," Rosaura remarked. "I get out of work, I cook, and I come to class," Amparo explained. Similarly, Dolores stated:

> I wake up at 5 a.m., I clean my bathrooms and mop my floor, then I go to work [housekeeping], I pick up my children from school, I begin to cook for my husband once he returns from work. Then I bathe my children and I come to class. Sometimes my back hurts but I keep going. *Sigo adelante*. That is the only way.

Adela and Doroteo described a similar situation:

> We are making a huge sacrifice. I get up at 4 a.m. each morning, my husband at 5 a.m. I leave before he does and I try to make it home before he does and wait for my children to get home from school. It is hard. But God willing, we will make it. *Tenemos que salir adelante*.

On top of their long weekdays, students attended the citizenship course Monday through Thursday from 6 p.m. to 8 p.m. Remarkably, Adela and Doroteo offered their home for additional sessions on Friday evenings, suggesting the value that citizenship has assumed in the lives of these immigrants.

Monetarily, most respondents felt they had paid a handsome fee (then $400 for the application alone). "It is a little expensive because of the application fee, $400," Rosaura said. To make matters worse, "you only have two opportunities. If you do not pass in two attempts, you lose the $400," she lamented. Together Adela and Doroteo paid double that cost. For some, the rising fees are a real impediment to naturalization. Doroteo encouraged his brother to apply, "but he says he can't come up with the $400 fee. He is living paycheck to paycheck. It is not easy." Dolores agreed that the naturalization process was expensive, but said: "It doesn't matter. Even if we had to pay $1,000, so long as we become citizens, it is worth it," a sentiment echoed by most interviewees and indicative of the importance of citizenship in their lives. Acknowledging she was fortunate to have applied before the fee increased from $400 to $675 (effective July 2007), Beatriz stated, "I do not think it is expensive because we are taking a very important step that I think is priceless." As the data will show, the value of citizenship in the lives of immigrants has expanded beyond the quality-of-life benefits already noted in the literature, to include an added motive of collective political action.

The Classroom

Without a doubt, the classroom was the most propitious site to get at the question of how Mexican immigrants experience the naturalization process collectively. Academically, most students started off timid and performing low when it came to the history and government content of the naturalization exam. Not surprisingly, English proficiency was an obstacle. In the case of Doña María, she stated:

> I am concerned because I still don't know English very well. That is my main concern. I have a hard time understanding what they are asking me. Of course, in Spanish I understand perfectly. I know the material. But I have a hard time when they ask me in English.

The fact that persons with low English language skills have decided to begin the naturalization process suggests a sense of urgency to become citizens. Out of the sample, Dolores was the student with the lowest level of English skills. Regarding her decision to naturalize, she commented: "I hesitated until my sister-in-law told me that it was going to get more difficult. There were rumors that after this January (2007) they were going to require perfect English for citizenship and that is why I submitted my application promptly. I thought, if I don't do it now I never will and that is why I am here." Apparently, the federal government's effort to make the naturalization process more demanding has motivated eligible immigrants to seek citizenship immediately. If this trend endures, we can expect the time lag between when Mexican immigrants become eligible to naturalize and when they begin the process to narrow.

Emotions and the Naturalization Process

The naturalization process has been described as one rife with "intense emotional overtones."[28] My study reveals that a great deal of emotions unfold collectively in the classroom. The most memorable example was when two returning students shared their naturalization interview experience with the rest of the class. The following is an excerpt from my field notes on this occasion.

Pozole & Tears

> Rosa and Sandra arrived carrying a large *olla* [pot] of pozole, tostadas, beverages, and other treats. At this site, it is customary that students who take their interview return immediately (most of them returning the day of) to share their experience. The fact that Rosa and Sandra walked in with big smiles and carrying treats made it obvious to the class that they had passed their interviews and were now American citizens. Sandra had passed the day prior but waited to come in with Rosa, who passed on this day. It was clear that Rosa's interview had been that day as she was dressed more formally than usual. As the women walked in, the students jubilantly remarked "*¡Pasaron!*" [you passed!] and they congratulated their

former classmates. At this point, as is customary on these occasions, the instructor asked the women to come to the front of the classroom and share their experiences with their classmates, who were eager and full of questions.

The first question coming from the group was "*¿Quién te tocó?*" [Which officer did you get?] "*Una Americana*" [a white woman], Rosa replied. She proceeded to tell in detail the course of her interview. "*¿Tráes tu green card?*" [Do you have your green card?], the officer asked Rosa. "*Estaba nerviosa*" [I was nervous], Rosa admitted. "*¿Cuantas preguntas te hicieron?*" [How many questions did they ask you?], an impatient student asked. "*Once*" [eleven], Rosa replied. The officer also asked Rosa to read and write a total of five sentences. "*Cuando recién llegué a esta clase no sabía nada*" [when I first came to this class I didn't know anything], Rosa remarked. At this point, Rosa began to cry. "*Se me hacía tan difícil, pero el maestro nos levanta el ánimo*" [It seemed so difficult, but the instructor always gets our spirit up], she said as she wiped her tears. The students agreed, sympathized, and cheered for Rosa. "*Dale un abrazo*" [give him (the instructor) a hug], the students remarked. They all cheered as Rosa and the instructor embraced. Rosa smiled and wiped the remaining tears from her face. After sharing their thoughts and tears, I returned to my duties of serving and distributing refreshments to the students, who waited patiently in their neatly aligned desks. People chatted, joked, laughed, and enjoyed warm bowls of pozole. "*Parece cenaduría, como en México*" [it looks like a restaurant from México in here], somebody shouted from the back of the room. Once everybody was served, Rosa handed me a bowl; "*come*" [eat], she said. So I did. I sat and pondered about my project and the wonderful people around me who made it all possible over pozole and tears.

This incident was as memorable for Dolores as it was for me, as she recalled in her subsequent interview:

When somebody has his or her interview, I pray for that person. I pray, "Dear Lord help them pass" because they are in the same position as me. I pray to God that he gives luck to all of them, because at that moment we are all going to be the same, just as nervous. All of the people who come and give their testimony encourage the rest of us. They say, "*Si se puede, si se puede*" and that is very encouraging. Do you remember Rosa? She cried and she told us that she owed it to the instructor. I agree, we have a great instructor. And when we saw her cry, all of us also cried. Because like she said, when she first arrived to the class she did not know how to write, like myself. But she had the support of her husband, as do I, and thanks be to God she passed. And all of us are just as happy for her.

Such observational and interview data capture the collegial environment and general rapport that characterized the classroom. As evidenced above, the anxiety, joy and tears shed during the naturalization process are shared among the group, suggesting that the solidarity and synergy of the classroom counteract and perhaps trump the negative emotions that have long discouraged the process among Mexican immigrants.

It is important to highlight the instructor's role in creating a welcoming and vibrant learning environment for immigrants. During my follow-up visit, a younger instructor replaced Benjamín, much to the dismay of the students. U.S.-educated and hardly bilingual, the new instructor mandated that students speak English only. Immediately, the vibrant classroom dynamic that made it such a productive learning and cultural space diminished. Instead of being a conduit for "Americanization," the citizenship classroom can be a critical public space for the forging of a sustained "oppositional counterpublic" where migrants negotiate and understand the naturalization and political socialization processes on their own cultural terms. Given that noncitizens are excluded from public politics, the citizenship class constitutes an "alternative public sphere" for migrants to debate politics and new ideas about democracy more broadly and the naturalization process specifically.[29] As the following section illustrates, this citizenship class is a counterpublic insofar as it is a space for the production of a counternarrative that exposes the bureaucratic arbitrariness of the citizenship process. The production and validation of these alternative sets of knowledge in the classroom create an oppositional, rather than assimilative, relationship to citizenship and national identity, since both are denied to many immigrants legally and in everyday social interactions. When asked about relations in the classroom under Benjamín, Adela replied: "I think we are like a family. We all help each other. Nobody will make you feel bad. I hope it continues that way as new students arrive."

Racial Knowledge and the Naturalization Interview

Despite its standardized format, citizenship applicants perceive the naturalization interview as arbitrary and unpredictable. According to the accounts of those who have experienced the interview, the outcome is largely determined by the idiosyncrasies and prejudices of the officers. Some students are scrutinized; others are in-and-out in as little as five minutes. This adds to the anxiety of the students who await the interview and accounts for their desire to hear the experiences of others who have completed the process. When asked about the officers, María replied: "Some people say that they are nice, others say that they are mean. So, I don't know what to expect for my interview." Rosaura felt that some officers were more discriminatory toward individuals who were ill prepared or lacked English skills. Others who have completed the interview offered more mixed messages: "I have heard different things. Some people say it is hard. Some say it is easy. Some people say they do not really speak English and they passed it just fine. Others who do speak English have not passed it. So, I have heard both sides. Hard and easy." Regarding the officers: "Well, some say that the person was not too nice. Others say otherwise. I have heard both sides." Adela echoed the unpredictability of the officers stating: "One young lady said that out of ten questions she only answered three and the officer let her pass. So, it depends on the officer." Indeed, Benjamín often responded to students' anxiety over the interview by stating, "Every officer is different, every interview is different."

Negating Citizenship

This collective understating of the interview as subjective is largely predicated on the view that the outcome is shaped by the race of the examiner. Tellingly, the first question asked of Rosa was *who* interviewed her. There is concern among the students about the ethnicity of the officers who administer the exam, as some are reputedly more lenient than others. According to Don Juan, "there is one officer, an Asian American woman, who is particularly strict. Several people have said this." Beatriz recalled these statements in her interview: "They speak badly of an Asian American female officer. They say she does not pass anyone." When asked whether there were Latino officers, Juan replied: "Yes, there are Latino officers. They are racist [laughs]." On this point, Don Juan was not alone. Multiple times during site visits students remarked that Latino officers were customarily the hardest. When Luz, a student not interviewed, failed her exam, students attributed it to the unjust Latino officer who interviewed her. Reportedly, the first remark he made to Luz as she entered was, "How many lies are you going to tell me today?" Students were particularly dismayed about Luz's rejection as she was among the students with the greatest English competence and knowledge of the history and government content. In contrast to Sandra and Rosa, who returned to share their experience, Luz did not return to the classroom, perhaps out of shame or disillusionment.

Among her listed sources of anxiety over the interview, Dolores mentioned her English and writing skills. "Unless I get an officer who is a despot, ego-tistical. That has happened to a lot of people. Or a racist officer as well," she added, suggesting that this is a major concern that can ultimately determine the outcome. Conversely, Dolores recalled hearing about "two people who got a Filipino officer and they said they are very nice." However, she concluded, "the best we can do is to be ready. The officers can tell when a person is well prepared. Likewise, we can also tell how the officer is, how he looks at you, how he speaks to you, how he treats you."

Finally, the gender of the officer and test taker play a role. These played out in Sandra's experience, as per my field notes. "I was interviewed by a Filipino officer. He was nice to me. I would say he even winked at me." Despite being a standardized process, race and gender dictate a big portion of the naturalization interview and in some cases the outcome. Given the nature of the naturalization interview in the lives of immigrants, their experience may have lasting implications on their subsequent views and incorporation in the host country. In response to such "inconsistent bureaucratic treatment," the citizenship class enables students to collectively navigate the arbitrariness and inequality of the naturalization process, an experience that can potentially inform future political action.[30]

Why Are Mexican Migrants Becoming U.S. Citizens?

As Waslin points out, several of the factors historically involved in low Latino naturalization include

> lack of outreach to eligible immigrants, confusion about the naturalization process, fear of mistreatment by the U.S. immigration service, feelings of disloyalty to the home country, the loss of property rights and other rights and privileges in the home country, and a continuing desire to eventually return to the home country.[31]

Regarding future outlook and return ideology upon arrival to the United States, Don Felipe remarked, "I think that a lot of people who come, all of us who come, arrive and never think that we will stay in this country. Usually, we all think that we will stay for some time and then we will return. But we don't have a deadline, a specific date to return. We always think that one day we will return and in the end, we don't go back." "I thought I was coming for five years and I have been here for fifteen," said Beatriz. On top of this, many Mexican immigrants eschewed naturalization out of fear of losing rights in the home country. "In the past I have heard that a lot of people thought they would lose their Mexican nationality by becoming U.S. citizens. Therefore, they did not want to become U.S. citizens. But today I don't hear much about that," recalled Rosaura. Don Juan provided further insight: "When I became a resident, a lot of people would say that persons who became citizens would lose their rights in Mexico. I am not sure if that is true. Now the rhetoric has changed. Now they say that you don't lose any rights in Mexico. I think you can now have dual citizenship." When asked whether he knew individuals who do not want to naturalize, Jose Alfredo (age fifty-five) replied, "Yes, there are a lot of people because they fear losing who knows what. But that is not so. Now, you no longer lose your Mexican citizenship." Don Juan remembered popular conceptions of naturalization among his *paisanos* as follows: "People used to say that if you went to Mexico, you could not be there for more than six months. After that, you had to return to the U.S. I am not sure if that was true. In any case, most of us ended up living here in the U.S. and we only return to Mexico to visit and for vacation."

Yet another reason that dampened prospects for naturalization among Mexicanos was the belief that "if you became a U.S. citizen you could not own property in Mexico." However, Don Juan dismissed this and other myths: "But that is not true. It is in Mexico's interest for people to invest in property, homes. A lot of people refused to become U.S. citizens in the past because they thought that meant rejecting their rights as Mexicans. But, fortunately, Mexico has facilitated dual citizenship. So, this is no longer a problem." Likewise, Jose Alfredo, who plans to return to Guanajuato once he retires, stated: "Previously, an American citizen could not own property in Mexico. They could not own a house. They could not be an *ejidatario* and now you can . . . have land." While previously an ideology of return discouraged naturalization, Mexico's dual nationality law seems to free up migrants who desire an eventual return to seek citizenship in the United States.[32]

When asked why they were seeking citizenship, most respondents immediately listed the need to legalize relatives, secure tangible benefits (employment, health care) and/or the right to vote. Don Juan and Benjamín, the only two respondents in the sample who were already citizens, replied respectively: "The motive is the right to vote but I have another reason that compelled me further, that is to legalize my wife" and, "that was one of the reasons why I became a citizen, because [my family was] here illegally. So in order to fix their papers, that was the reason why I became a citizen sooner." Indeed, family reunification is a major component of the transnational migrant experience. To put it in Don Ignacio's (age sixty-four) words, "We are here but we are never complete. We are here and our people are over there."

Among the tangible benefits listed by respondents were health care, better employment, and a pension. Dolores said she sought citizenship for benefits, a better salary, and perhaps a "government job one day." She also associated citizenship with access to health care, which can otherwise be "taken away from you. But if you are a citizen, they continue to help you." Dolores lamented that her brother "can't get Medi-Cal for his children because they don't have papers, except for his daughter who was born here [in the United States]."

She was grateful that her children, who are U.S.-born, have basic health care. About her nine-year-old son's speech impediment, she stated that "the therapists say they will help him as long as he needs it. And it is all because he is a U.S. citizen." Lastly, Dolores recalled an anecdote about a friend who took her elderly mother to the doctor and was denied treatment because she was not a citizen. "I don't want that to happen to me," Dolores said solemnly. "I have to think ahead. I don't want to be a burden for my children." Finally, many migrants also thought ahead to their retirement. "Once I retire, I am going back to my homeland," Doroteo exclaimed. "But I want to make sure they send my check over there, to La Barca [his hometown]." When calculating the benefits of being a permanent resident versus a citizen, Jose Alfredo stated: "If you retire one day, and you want your money sent to Mexico, a sum will be deducted. On the other hand, if you are a citizen, you get the entire sum with nothing deducted."

Finally, there is reason to believe that Mexican naturalizers "seek enfranchisement as an act of political expression."[33] While it is not surprising that most respondents listed voting as a top motive, and while self-reported intent to vote should be viewed cautiously as such claims do not always materialize, this was a recurring theme that received ample justification without much probing. Some interviewees were outright enthusiastic about voting. When asked whether she planned to register, Beatriz exclaimed, "Yes, I have received voter registration forms and I say, 'when will I be able to fill you out!'" On top of naturalizing in order to legalize his wife, Felipe stated he is also doing it "for the right to vote because we do witness a whole lot of injustices and we need to become a majority so that they can take us into consideration." Felipe had unsuccessfully attempted to naturalize in the mid-1990s. When asked why he waited ten years to give it another shot, he replied: "Now is when things are getting hot, with the whole driver's license issue," referencing the highly publicized bill proposed by California senator Gil Cedillo, and alluding to the resurfacing of a contentious political climate. When asked why she felt voting was important, Dona María replied, "Well, because these are things that we have to do. That is precisely why we are seeking citizenship so that we can all be the same or equal." Rosaura echoed these beliefs: "It's like they say, the Latino vote counts a lot and perhaps we can make a difference and help our people by voting," again, signaling a desire to redress community needs. When asked why he planned to vote, Don Ignacio, the only respondent who was retired, replied, "They say that one more vote *es la fuerza*."

This theme of Latino voting and collective political clout was perhaps most remarkable in my interview with Juan. While Don Juan acknowledged that he sought naturalization to legalize his son, he was also "aware of the needs of the Latino community. I think it is important for Latinos to seek citizenship so that we can exercise our rights, so that we can vote and so that we can be taken into consideration." Clearly, Don Juan's decision to naturalize is indicative of this dual stimulus: on the one hand, he wanted to legalize his son, and on the other, he had an added political motive that he felt he owed to his community. He later generalized this logic to other Latino naturalizers.

> A lot of us are motivated to naturalize because of the discrimination that we face. Elected officials discriminate Latinos frequently. Latinos have such a strong presence here. Imagine if we were all citizens. We would have clout. If we were to unite, like we did May 1st, that would be powerful. I think it is good that Latinos are naturalizing. It is in our interest and in the interest of our children.

Don Juan concluded by stating, "The way I see it is that by becoming a citizen I will have more clout to defend the rights that many Latinos lack. I feel that it will give us more authority to speak out for our rights." Contrary to earlier research that found immigrants who associate mostly with noncitizens to be less likely to naturalize, it appears that because all respondents were formerly undocumented, they are in solidarity with the millions of co-ethnics who currently have no legal pathway to legal residence or citizenship in the United States and seem to imagine future political action with community-wide interests in mind.[34]

Regarding the immigrant rights protests of 2006, although nobody in the sample marched because of work or other obligations, most overwhelmingly sympathized with the cause and several cited the protests as an additional impetus for naturalizing. Felipe recalled feeling "terrible" when he encountered a pro-immigrant march in San Bernardino that he was unaware of.

> One day that I came here, there was a march that I did not know about and I felt terrible. I thought they were only going to have them in Los Angeles, but they also had one here. And when I saw the march proceeding here, I felt like, all of these people, and I wasn't even aware of it . . . But that time I did feel terrible. I didn't even want to go out because I thought they would say, "Why isn't this fool marching?" [laughter].

This echoes Don Juan's earlier statement of a shared responsibility that they owe their community. When asked whether the immigrant rights protests motivated him to naturalize, Felipe said that on top of his urgent need to legalize his wife, the marches "pushed me further to do it." Don Juan, who was not present at the protests and who had already made up his mind to naturalize prior to them, candidly stated, "Honestly, no. I couldn't be there . . . I had already made up my mind [to naturalize] long before. But I thought it was great for the Latino population. It was a strong sign of unity."

Other respondents echoed such opinions. Dolores remarked, "I did not participate, but my neighbors did. They were very excited to march. If I could have, I would have been there too. I thought it was a very good idea. It was a great cause, to ask for immigration reform. The more people we can unite, the better chances we have of being heard." Likewise, Adela and Doroteo were unable to attend because of work. "But if we had the time, we would have gladly been there. Especially because it was a great cause. It was very important for us Latinos," Adela exclaimed. When asked whether the protests affected her decision to naturalize, Adela replied assertively: "Yes. It motivated you. A lot of the people who marched do not have papers, and those of us who do have them, we should not let them go to waste, and we should not be complacent. We should strive to reach higher." Clearly, there is evidence of a sense of collective action, solidarity, and shared responsibility with migrants who are barred from participation in formal politics. Doroteo, Adela's husband, agreed: "I heard that a lot of people were becoming citizens and that encouraged me even more. That motivated me further." To borrow from Guidry and Sawyer, the 2006 protests and subsequent migrant solidarity and collective action have the potential to transform the meaning and possibility of U.S. democracy and citizenship, in this case, via the legalization of millions of undocumented immigrants and their families.

What Does Naturalization Mean to Mexican Migrants?

In contrast to studies that associate acquiring citizenship with political assimilation, this data suggests that cross-border loyalties and attachments do not wane upon naturalization. Benjamín, who was the citizenship class instructor and a U.S. citizen for more than a decade, stated, "I think that we can take the [citizenship] oath [of allegiance] but never be completely loyal. I think that you can never deny your roots or origins." When asked how she will identify upon naturalization, Rosaura replied assertively, "Oh, well, *Mexicana* obviously. I will always be *Mexicana*. One hundred percent." Upon further probing, she elaborated,

> Well, I don't know, but I feel that, yes I am becoming a U.S. citizen, but I am *Mexicana*. Even if I was told that I can no longer be *Mexicana* I will continue to be *Mexicana*. That is what I believe. If the government were to tell me, "you are no longer *Mexicana*," well okay, they can believe that if they wish, but I feel that my family is *Mexicana*. I am *Mexicana*.

Rosaura concluded, "To be Mexican is to be Mexican. Even if you become an American citizen, you have it in your blood, in you, in everything. You have to say it [the oath], you will say that you will renounce it, but you know that you cannot stop being what you are."

Similarly, Dolores argued, "I am *Mexicana*. I will always be *Mexicana*. Because of my roots. Just because I become a citizen doesn't mean that I will stop being *Mexicana*." This question was seemingly as important for Adela, who remarked:

> We will never stop being Mexican. You always have it in your heart. When I go to Tijuana, and I see the Mexican flag, I feel like crying, because we are not in our country. When I see the American flag, I feel joy, but I don't feel the same way as when I see the Mexican flag. I think that even if you become a citizen, you will never stop being Mexican. No matter what you say in the oath.

While there is evidence of dual loyalties "under two flags" here, to use Michel Jones-Correa's language, Adela's reaction to her native flag was more emotive than her response to the U.S. flag. Upon further probing, she offered an interesting metaphor:

> Well, when I am in the states, I can say I am a citizen. But when you are in your country, all it is a piece of paper that makes you a U.S. citizen, but in reality you were born in Mexico. And I think you are never going to leave Mexico. It is like a marriage. Even if you are married, you cannot forget about your parents. It is very similar. Even if I become a citizen, I will never forget where I came from.

Her husband, Doroteo, agreed, "I will continue being Mexican. The papers have nothing to do with that. I will always be Mexican. Nothing can take that away from me."

The Prospect of Enduring Diasporic Roots

Furthermore, there is evidence that the apparent diasporic nationalism and cross-border loyalties can have enduring effects. This is best represented when respondents spoke about their children who were born and/or raised in the United States. Felipe stated:

> I want my children to never forget their roots. I don't want them to forget where they came from. There are some people who don't want their children to speak Spanish, only English. But in my eyes, it is better for them never to forget their roots. Because this way, our children, if they are to one day make something of themselves, if they represent us in some government branch, they can do something for us because they are informed about

the kind of life we have, how we come here, how much we suffer to come here. Otherwise, they will forget about their roots, and later on they could even be against us. So perhaps my grandchildren would say, "Throw out all those old people" [laughter]. Because he is not going to be aware of his roots and he will not sympathize with how much we suffer to come to this country.

Don Juan, who said his children self-identify as Mexican, stated, "Well, I think they fight for their place in the U.S. and for establishing themselves in the U.S. but they also feel that they are Mexican." When asked why she identified her U.S.-born children as Mexican, Dolores replied: "Well because their parents are Mexican and because of their roots. The same way we were brought up as children, we raise them in the same way." When asked whether she thought her children would have the same degree of ethnic attachment to Mexico as she does, Dolores replied, "Yes, I think so. I am going to instill that in them. That they have to go to Mexico, and visit their uncles and get to know all of Mexico; it is beautiful." Likewise, Doroteo and Adela have four U.S.-born children. "They are Mexican," Doroteo said assertively. "If they are the children of Mexican parents, then they have to be Mexican. And they have to maintain our customs from Mexico and our roots."

Racial Naturalization

Among respondents who said they would retain ties to Mexico upon naturalizing, there is evidence of what the legal scholar Devon Carbado calls *racial naturalization*. Carbado defines racial naturalization as the social practice by which "all of us are Americanized and made socially intelligible via racial categorization."[35] Effectively, Don Juan stated, "We will never stop being Mexican. That cannot be taken away from you." Among the reasons for this enduring Mexican identity is the fact that "we will continue to face discrimination simply because we are Mexican. Even if we become citizens, we will encounter prejudice." Similarly, Dolores argued that "a person could very well be a citizen but he/she is treated based on appearance." While Don Juan and Dolores implied that their phenotypic cues trumped formal or legal citizenship, there is reason to believe that Mexican immigrants are not "Americanized" in the way that black immigrants are. Conversely, Mexican immigrants likely undergo what Claudia Sandoval calls *racial alienization*, the purely exclusive corollary of racial naturalization, which makes ethnic Mexicans vulnerable to detention, deportation, and state violence.[36]

Of course not everyone agrees on the point of enduring ethnic identifications post-naturalization. While there was nobody in my sample who resembled this view, Rosaura described a fellow co-worker who recently naturalized as follows.

> There is one person at my work who became a U.S. citizen and he says that although he was born in Mexico, he is now one hundred percent American citizen. He says that since he became a U.S. citizen he is an American. I always argue with him. I would fight him if he weren't a man [laughter]. I don't understand how he can be racist; I feel he is racist toward his own people. I ask him, how can it be that you feel this way if you came here like the rest of us did? You suffered like the rest of us. And now that you were able to obtain citizenship, you should thank God, but that should not make you feel that you are better than those of us who do not have papers. But he is the kind of person who is narrow-minded. The kind that lets it get to his head—the fact that he is a citizen gets to his head.

This discussion bears similarities to a comment made by Doroteo. With regard to whether he will change upon naturalization, Doroteo replied assertively, "In my opinion, I will be the same person, regardless if I pass or don't pass. A piece of paper is not going to change who I am." Doroteo was aware that other migrants, like Rosaura's co-worker above, did not agree.

> A lot of people think otherwise. They even change their name. They even use American names. But I think that is wrong. It is not like you can change your face. It is not like you can wear a mask. What are you going to do, wear a mask? If I have money or don't have money, I will continue being the same person."

Most respondents actively retained their Mexican identity and nationalism/regionalism upon naturalization and disapproved of co-ethnics who did not. In this context, migrants' enduring Mexican identity is a product of their perception of how race and gender structure both the naturalization process and their everyday life experiences in the United States more broadly.

Conclusion: Implications for Political Participation

As the Schwarzenegger epigraph illustrates, policymakers and commentators in the United States vocally disapprove of Mexican migrant cross-border identifications and loyalties. The institutionalization of these transnational ties has evoked public outcries from observers bemoaning the fact that dual nationality undermines national sovereignty and singular loyalty to the United States. An alternative explanation suggests that for immigrants, dual nationality can be a means to reconcile memberships in both their countries of residence and of origin, leading to higher naturalization rates in the United States, and making dual nationality consistent with membership in the American polity.[37]

Regarding allegiance, Don Juan stated, "By seeking citizenship I have to obey this country's standards. It would be contradictory for me to seek membership in a country whose principles I did not agree with." Dolores added, "Once you become a citizen you have to respect the laws of this country." Adela said naturalization is a commitment, "legally and before God, that you will accept that oath. No matter what, we want to be in this country, so we have to accept the laws the way they have them." As these statements suggest, ethnic attachment to the homeland post-naturalization does not necessarily equate with disloyalty to the host country. U.S. commentators and policymakers who demand loyalty from immigrants should focus on granting first-class citizenship to ethnic Mexicans rather than the noncitizenship or second-class citizenship historically conferred upon them regardless of nativity.[38]

This essay challenged the assertions that, regarding Latinos in the United States, "a traditional pattern of political assimilation appears to prevail" and that "the intention to become an American citizen increases identification with the United States," pointing to a sustained anti-immigrant context and discrimination throughout the naturalization process.[39] From the perspective of immigrants, there is more to naturalization, understood as the legal rituals of U.S. political belonging, than newfound patriotism and singular national allegiance.[40] With regard to immigration history, this article suggests that the decision to naturalize today cannot be understood as a sign of resettlement in the United States or an indication that immigrant mobilization in U.S. politics comes at the expense of participation in Mexican politics. These patterns have implications for identity politics. In the twenty-first century, scholars will have to fight the tendency to use the terms *Mexican, Mexican American,* and *Chicano* interchangeably.[41]

As the data show, among immigrants who were once reticent to seek U.S. citizenship, there seems to be a shift in favor of naturalization. Similarly, the newly eligible also share a sense of urgency to naturalize in an immigrant-hostile and increasingly precarious political environment. However, ethnic attachment to the homeland does not always wane over time or upon naturalization. Naturalizers retain cross-border identifications and attachments in a way that does not preclude political engagement in their new country. To put it in Jose Alfredo's words when asked how he will identify upon naturalization: "If I am in the United States, I am an American citizen. If I am in Mexico, I am Mexican, upon entering. We can be both; they are not mutually exclusive. There is nothing unlawful there." Don Juan responded to the same question, stating, "I will be Mexican, but I will have the rights of an American citizen." Just like migrants who were civically minded in their home country are likely to be engaged in the host country, there is nothing to say that reactive naturalization cannot drive political participation across international boundaries.

Notes

The opening Schwarzenegger quote is from an article by Araceli Martínez-Ortega, "Arremeten contra Schwarzenegger: Los demócratas lo atacan por cuestionar la asimilación de los Mexicanos a este país," *La Opinión*, October 6, 2006. All translations are mine.

1. In a gesture of transnational solidarity, immigrant sympathizers boycotted Wal-Mart in Zacatecas, Mexico, on May 1, 2006. This was one of multiple such demonstrations occurring concurrently on Mexican territory. I thank professors Miguel Moctezuma and Rodolfo García Zamora of Universidad Autónoma de Zacatecas for providing information on this point.

2. Alfonso Gonzales, "Anti-Migrant Hegemony in a Transnational North America: The Politics of Immigration Control from 1986 to 2006" (PhD diss., University of California, Los Angeles, 2008).

3. On public politics and democracy, see John A. Guidry and Mark Q. Sawyer, "Contentious Pluralism: The Public Sphere and Democracy," *Perspectives on Politics* 1.2 (June 2003): 273–89.

4. Carlos Avilés, "Más de un millón pide ciudadanía," *La Opinión*, January 7, 2008.

5. Irene Bloemraad, *Becoming a Citizen: Incorporating Immigrants and Refugees in the United States and Canada* (Berkeley: University of California Press, 2006).

6. George J. Sánchez, *Becoming Mexican American: Ethnicity, Culture, and Identity in Chicano Los Angeles, 1900–1945* (New York: Oxford University Press, 1993).

7. Respectively, Samuel P. Huntington, *Who Are We? The Challenges to America's National Identity* (New York: Simon & Schuster, 2004); and Jack Citrin, Amy Lerman, Michael Murakami, and Kathryn Pearson, "Testing Huntington: Is Hispanic Immigration a Threat to American Identity?" *Perspectives on Politics* 5.2 (March 2007): 31–48.

8. Rodolfo de la Garza, Angelo Falcon, and F. Chris Garcia, "Will the Real Americans Please Stand Up: Anglo and Mexican-American Support of Core American Political Values," *American Journal of Political Science* 40.2 (May 1996): 335–51, 347.

9. Paul Ong and Joanna Lee, "Defensive Naturalization and Anti-Immigrant Sentiment: Chinese Immigrants in Three Primate Metropolises" (paper delivered at the 2007 Immigration and Politics Workshop, Los Angeles, California).

10. For a discussion of community empowerment and Latino politics, see Matt A. Barreto, "*¡Sí Se Puede!* Latino Candidates and the Mobilization of Latino Voters," *American Political Science Review* 101.3 (August 2007): 425–43.

11. Michael Jones-Correa, "Under Two Flags: Dual Nationality in Latin America and Its Consequences on Naturalization in the United States," *International Migration Review* 35.4 (Winter 2001): 997–1029.

12. Matt A. Barreto, Ricardo Ramírez and Nathan D. Woods, "Are Naturalized Voters Driving the California Electorate? Measuring the Effect of IRCA Citizens on Latino Voting," *Social Science Quarterly* 86.4 (December 2005): 797.

13. Kelly Stamper Balistreri and Jennifer Van Hook, "The More Things Change the More They Stay the Same: Mexican Naturalization before and after Welfare Reform," *International Migration Review* 38.1 (March 2004): 113.

14. Adrian Pantoja, Ricardo Ramírez, and Gary M. Segura, "Citizens by Choice, Voters by Necessity: Patterns of Political Mobilization by Naturalized Latinos," *Political Research Quarterly* 54.4 (December 2001): 729–50.

15. Michele Waslin, "Latino Naturalization and the Federal Government's Response," unpublished manuscript, written for the National Council of La Raza, 2005, 2–3.

16. Ibid., 3.
17. Pantoja, Ramírez, and Segura, "Citizens by Choice," 729.
18. Shaun Bowler, Stephen P. Nicholson, and Gary Segura, "Earthquakes and Aftershocks: Race, Direct Democracy, and Partisan Change," *American Journal of Political Science* 50.1 (January 2006): 146–59.
19. Pantoja, Ramírez, and Segura, "Citizens by Choice," 731.
20. Gonzales ("Anti-Migrant Hegemony") discusses the consolidation of anti-immigrant politics at the local, national, and transnational levels.
21. De la Garza, Falcon, and Garcia, "Will the Real Americans Please Stand Up," 347.
22. Diasporic nationalism is expressed by migrants as attachments to hometowns and localities within Mexico. Hence, the term diasporic nationalism can be read as diasporic localism or regionalism. Additionally, the term does not imply uncritical loyalties to the Mexican state. Most of my respondents expressed disillusionment and skepticism toward the Mexican government, a sentiment consistent with the idea that diasporic nationalism is not an identity entirely rooted in or fostered by the Mexican state.
23. José Itzigsohn and Silvia Saucedo, "Immigrant Incorporation and Sociocultural Transnationalism," *International Migration Review* 36.3 (Fall 2002): 766–98.
24. Louis DeSipio, "Making Citizens or Good Citizens? Naturalization as a Predictor of Organizational and Electoral Behavior Among Latino Immigrants," *Hispanic Journal of Behavioral Sciences* 18 (May 1996): 194–213.
25. The names of all participants in this study were changed by the author for purposes of anonymity.
26. The 2005 Pew Hispanic Center "Survey of Mexican Migrants" found that 72% of respondents lack a high school education, but the youngest and most recently arrived have higher levels of schooling than long-term migrants.
27. Robert Alvarez, "A Profile of the Citizenship Process among Hispanics in the United States," *International Migration Review* 21.2 (Summer 1987): 327–47.
28. De la Garza, Falcon, and Garcia, "Will the Real Americans Please Stand Up," 347.
29. Guidry and Sawyer, "Contentious Pluralism," 276.
30. Louis DeSipio, "Transnational Politics and Civic Engagement: Do Home-Country Political Ties Limit Latino Immigrant Pursuit of U.S. Civic Engagement and Citizenship?" in *Transforming Politics, Transforming America: The Political and Civic Incorporation of Immigrants in the United States*, ed. Taeku Lee, S. Karthick Ramakrishnan and Ricardo Ramírez (Charlottesville: University of Virginia Press, 2006), 110.
31. Waslin, "Latino Naturalization," 3.
32. DeSipio, "Transnational Politics," 110.
33. Pantoja, Ramírez, and Segura, "Citizens by Choice," 729.
34. DeSipio, "Transnational Politics," 110.
35. Devon Carbado, "Racial Naturalization," *American Quarterly* 57.3 (September 2005): 633–58.
36. Claudia Sandoval, "Allies or Aliens? Black-Latino Relations and Perceptions of Political Membership in the U.S" Unpublished Manuscript, University of Chicago. See also Nicholas P. De Genova, "Migrant 'Illegality' and Deportability in Everyday Life," *Annual Review of Anthropology* 31 (October 2002): 423.
37. Jones-Correa, "Under Two Flags," 2001.
38. David G. Gutiérrez, *Walls and Mirrors: Mexican Americans, Mexican Immigrants, and the Politics of Ethnicity* (Berkeley: University of California Press, 1995).
39. Citrin et al., "Testing Huntington," 41.
40. Josh Kun, *Audiotopia: Music, Race, and America* (Berkeley: University of California Press, 2005), 7–11.
41. See Nicholas De Genova, *Working the Boundaries: Race, Space, and "Illegality" in Mexican Chicago* (Durham, N.C.: Duke University Press, 2005), 3.

Transnationalism: A Category of Analysis

Laura Briggs, Gladys McCormick, and J. T. Way

Transnationalism is a much abused word. Is it the same thing as globalization? As internationalism? Is neoliberalism a particular period in the history of the political economy of transnationalism, or something else? Was the colonial period transnational or prenational? Anna Lowenhaupt Tsing, in her brilliant ethnography of environmental movements, *Friction*, writes that "the concept of 'globalization,' at its simplest, encourages dreams of a world in which everything has become part of a single imperial system," which she calls a theory "of suffocation and death." Transnationalism, in contrast, she identifies as the work she is doing, centering difference, coalition, misunderstanding, the alternating voraciousness and stuttering and failure of multinational capitalism.[1] So can we follow Tsing, and agree that transnationalism is the name of longings on the left, and globalization the imperial universalism of the right? Alas. A participant in a recent conference on "transnational history" said she almost did not come, because for her as a Latin American, "transnational" could not mean anything except (primarily U.S.-based) rapacious corporate dominance and its associated knowledge systems. If only the proliferating meanings could be sufficiently contained that we could all agree on a single naming system—if only, in fact, processes within and across nations were so easily divided into good and bad, left and right.

Clearly, one key distinction in the deployment of these terms is political valence—Immanuel Wallerstein and Coca-Cola may both be working in transnational frames, but with very different consequences; one is a critique of more than five centuries of capitalist transformation, the other, its realization. Within academe, there is also the question of discipline. Diverse fields are talking about transnationalism, but those working in these fields are not even necessarily mutually conversant; terms such as *glocal*, so crucial to geography's working out of what is meant by transnationalism in that field, is only occasionally even intelligible to historians. Influential formulations, such as Arjun Appadurai's notion of fluid cultural flows, ideoscapes, and ethnoscapes, may be in their particulars fundamentally opposed to the kinds of transnationalism proposed by, say, a sociologist of migration such as Yen

Le Espiritu, who is interested in the hard-edged and violent legal exclusions and differential inclusions produced by U.S. migration policy.[2] This lends debates about transnationalism as theory a certain boxing-with-shadows quality; one can say a great many contradictory things about what is wrong with transnationalism and they will all be true about someone's transnationalism, and those of us who think the paradigm productive feel compelled to defend ourselves against charges of complicity with work with which we disagree. Hence, the precise things that some find inadequate about transnationalism as a paradigm—its inability to think about the force of nationalism, say, or imperialist aggression—others see as precisely its strength—nationalism and imperialism as above all transnational processes, for example.

There are, of course, concrete material reasons for this conceptual confusion. As Bruce Cumings, Aihwa Ong, and Andrew Ross have all mapped in different ways, in the aftermath of the cold war, increasingly cash-strapped academics, universities, and fields (conspicuously area studies) were all invited to map the transnational. Cumings points to two specific incidents in the United States: the National Security Education Act (NSEA) in the first half of the 1990s, providing funding for graduate and undergraduate students (and hence, indirectly, to departments) for post–cold war area studies research, organized through the Defense Intelligence Agency ("an outfit that makes the CIA look liberal and enlightened," says Cumings) with a requirement that those students serve an intelligence agency after receiving a grant; and, at the Social Science Research Council (SSRC), a restructuring plan for academic funding that includes "a desire to move away from fixed regional identities given that globalization has made the 'areas' more porous, less bounded, less fixed."[3] Cumings' point is that in many ways academic transnationalism has had to serve the goals of the U.S. government or business. Those of us who early hoped that we could ride the transnationalism funding horse to a different destination were largely disappointed. "Us and IBM! We'll all be transnational!" one of our colleagues said as she dashed off grant proposals—only to find that the Ford Foundation, for example, was not interested in funding a "transnationalism" conference in Mexico—especially not if the goal of the funding was to fly in Latin American scholars. Transnationalism, apparently, was something done in the United States by U.S. American scholars. The irony apparently escaped Ford.[4]

This article is the product of that conference, in fact of four years of conversations at the Tepoztlán Institute for the Transnational History of the Americas, a tremendously productive annual week-long scholarly gathering.[5] Although even in that context the concept of transnationalism has been regularly and vigorously abused (as an ahistorical term implying that there were always nations to transverse, as never more than a celebration of neoliberal or corporate globalization, as just another Yankee imperialist assault on productive Third World nationalisms . . .), we want to keep the notion in play as a crucial corrective to academic ways of doing history. Even scholarship on centuries prior to the eighteenth that might seem to pose an alternative to the nation by historicizing it are regularly transformed into prehistories of the nation—"colonial Guatemala," for example, or "colonial U.S."—as if these colonies were always nations in fetal form. If the intellectual work in history, literature, and area studies (like American studies) has been more than a handmaiden to the ideological work of producing the imagined communities of nations, then at a minimum these fields and the nation have a common root. As is clear in U.S. policy debates about national history standards for public schools, conservative ideologues have been winning the fight over whether history has a role beyond inspiring young citizens in their nationalist faith. In this article, we argue against writing histories or analyses that take national boundaries as fixed, implicitly timeless, or even always meaningful, and for a quite different role for history-writing and criticism—one that directly challenges the nation by revealing nationalism as ideology.

We want to suggest that, even if we stipulate that transnationalism is a notion underpinned by the goals of the U.S. state or multinational corporations, its possibilities are multiple, and so are its histories. Rather than argue for what seems in this context an elusive linguistic clarity about the relationship of transnationalism, globalization, neoliberalism, colonialism, and internationalism, we will argue here, first, for a genealogy that centers some meanings of transnational and displaces others and, second, for a way of thinking the conceptual work of the "transnational," leaning on an analogy with the intellectual work of feminists in thinking gender. We want to suggest that "transnationalism" can do to the nation what gender did for sexed bodies: provide the conceptual acid that denaturalizes all their deployments, compelling us to acknowledge that the nation, like sex, is a thing contested, interrupted, and always shot through with contradiction.

As American studies scholars know well, none of the imputed attributes of the nation—the people, the language, the literature, the history, the culture, the environment—is the "pure" object that nationalisms take them to be. The notion of the transnational enables us to center certain kinds of historical events as the emphatically non-national but indisputably important processes that they are, including colonialism; the travels of the Enlightenment, science, liberalism, socialism, major religions, such as Christianity and Islam; an international (sexed) division of labor; the production of migrants, slaves, coolies, and other strangers and unfree peoples as racialized minorities; resource extraction and environmental degradation, as well as the more contemporary productions of non-governmental organizations; human rights discourses; free trade agreements; refugee and migrant "crises"; and the production of national security states in a global "war on terror." As much as it belongs to the worlds of free trade agreements and export processing zones, transnationalism belongs to genealogies of anti-imperial and decolonizing thought, ranging from anticolonial Marxism to subaltern studies to Third World feminism and feminisms of color. Transnationalism has been a diverse, contested, cross-disciplinary intellectual movement that in some of its manifestations has been bound together by a particular insight: in place of a long and deeply embedded modernist tradition of taking the nation as the framework within which one can study things (literatures, histories, and so forth), the nation itself has to be a question—not untrue and therefore trivial, but an ideology that changes over time, and whose precise elaboration at any point has profound effects on wars, economies, cultures, the movements of people, and relations of domination.

As historians, we do here what historians always do when confronted with tangled, unclear ways of conceiving the world: we tell a story. Edward Said observed that the first task of any intervention is to create a beginning. In what follows, we begin by naming or inventing an anti-imperialist, politically left intellectual tradition within which we understand the work of transnational paradigms. As historians of the United States, Mexico, and Guatemala, respectively, we draw primarily from work in and on the Americas. There are at least three different conversational strands. The first is rooted in anticolonial thinkers, from Fanon and Wallerstein to peasant and subaltern studies. The second is work that draws on those traditions, but is explicitly concerned with struggles over gender, race, and ethnicity. The third, not always entirely separable from either of the other two, is in labor history and migration. We then turn to an exploration of what transnationalism can do, conceptually and theoretically. Finally, we turn to a discussion of the kinds of work transnationalist paradigms have enabled for us.

Genealogies

As part of a broader set of conflicts over power in the Third World from the 1930s through the 1960s, a new generation of scholars pressed a research agenda that resonated with decolonization movements from Latin America and the Caribbean to Africa to Asia, particularly Vietnam and Algeria. One of their innovations was to decenter previously territorialized and localized subjects—antifascism, Marxism, literature, the exploration of psychic distress, and modern economies. Not only did they call attention to the vibrant existence of such phenomena in the Third World (not just Europe and the United States), but they also implicitly and explicitly reconceptualized them as rooted in transnational processes—colonialism and the resistance to it. Intellectuals such as C. L. R. James, Frantz Fanon, and Alejo Carpentier wrote powerful texts that centered transnational processes and retooled familiar narratives: antifascism, but from the perspective of Ethiopia; Marxism, but from the point of view of black nationalism; psychiatry, but mapping the effects of racism, imperialism, and anti-imperialist activism; the radical avant-garde and the liberatory potential of the imaginary and the marvelous, but from the perspective of Haiti.[6] Historians of Latin America began examining the effects of imperialism and forms of migration through such themes as the evolution of economic relations and power struggles within colonial institutions, most prominently the slave trade, mining, and other forms of mercantile investment. Immanuel Wallerstein, looking to bring closure to the debate over feudalism and capitalism in explaining the supposed "lag" in economic development the "Third World," proposed his world systems model in the mid-1970s.[7] In it, he extended the center/periphery proposition of Ernesto Laclau, Raúl Prebisch, and André Gunder Frank, and forced into the "development" debates the possibility that impoverished economies were not isolated islands awaiting the coming of modernity, but part of a continuous, interconnected, historical process that enriched some at the expense of others.[8]

One presupposition of these antifascist and cold war texts was that if imperialism and capitalism were the problem, then some form of socialism might well be the answer. After 1989, though, we saw the emergence of a radical formation that was openly critical of postcolonial socialist regimes, although still Marxist, via Gramsci: subaltern studies, a powerful South Asian critique, rooted in peasant studies.[9] Subaltern studies disrupted the fundamental underpinning of the decolonial nation-building process by insisting that postcolonial nations were still fundamentally shaped by historical colonial processes, epistemologically, institutionally, and in their processes of citizen subject-formation. In *Provincializing Europe*, Dipesh Chakrabarty intervened in India's national-history writing project, arguing compellingly that history writing itself is a European enterprise, founded in epistemologies and cosmologies foreign to other places before colonization and, to some extent, after. Ranajit Guha and other members of the subaltern studies group argue that a recovery of the agency of Indian peasants requires a rejection of *both* a historiography that focuses on elite actors and a too-simplified account that insists that the people always really want socialism, disrupting the apparent natural-ness (and vertical integration) of the evolution of India's state-socialist project. In "Can the Subaltern Speak?" Gayatri Chakravorty Spivak brilliantly theorizes the problem as one not only of socialisms, but also of Foucauldian, Deleuzian, and U.S. ethnic studies and women's studies in which the subjectivity of the subaltern (especially the subaltern woman) is homogeneous and transparent, showing how the nationalist project of defending *sati* in the name of history and the authentic desires of the good wife is a ventriloquist trick that can equally justify imperialist intervention as well as nationalism, while "white men are fighting with Brown men over Brown women's bodies."[10]

South Asian subaltern studies had a great effect on Latin American scholarship, particularly as the end of the cold war and the violent defeat of communism in Central America occasioned a requestioning of the paradigms of the 1960s and 1970s. Scholars studied the ways in which subaltern groups organized around alternative interpretations of dominant political and economic paradigms, including their noninclusion or partial inclusion in specifically national projects like citizenship, socialism, and liberalism.[11] A Latin American subaltern studies group formed, born of the desire to "recover voices" without homogenizing or oversimplifying the experiences of those living at the margins or assuming that their longings were coterminous with the nation. This group wrote about the triumphalist, capitalism-is-all post-Sandinista moment of 1991 as productively directing critical attention away from national projects, recentering questions of the unrepresentability and ungovernability of the Latin American popular classes (interestingly prefiguring *Zapatismo*).[12] In his 1992 ethnography, *Life Is Hard*, Roger Lancaster studies the intimacy of power in a poor urban neighborhood during the Sandinista revolution, and finds that even in that period of crisis, the nation could not contain or even describe the forms of life and power he found there. Sexuality, gender, and class emerge as lines of fracture, with *machismo* constructed as much by U.S. American popular culture (like Rambo) as by any national culture.[13] Another Latin Americanist response to the challenge of subaltern studies and the disappointments of the postrevolutionary period is Diane Nelson's *Finger in the Wound*, which transforms what she calls the "transvestite trick" of the U.S.-based solidarity movement, which, she points out, relied on the premise of a homogeneous "people" in Guatemala (and Nicaragua and El Salvador), oppressed by U.S. foreign policy and military campaigns, who longed for the realization of the authentic form of their nations (some form of socialism, undistorted by U.S. interventionism) and could be protected, championed, and defended by U.S. solidarity activists (including prominently, for Nelson, feminists). With the defeat of the revolutionary Unidad Revolucionaria Nacional Guatemalteca (UNRG) in Guatemala and the emergence of a self-consciously Mayan movement in contradistinction to the guerrillas, Nelson suggests, this position shattered. Hence, she suggests "fluidarity," a practice of alliance with identities-in-formation.[14] Nelson proposes a transnational politics that uses innovative ways of getting at what Raymond Williams called "structures of feeling," by looking at jokes, for example, and ties together global discourses and the world of specific subjects by using the body, and "body politics," as a central metaphor.[15] Works such as these suggest the productivity of Foucauldian approaches that underscore the messy (often gendered), on-the-ground articulations of power with a nation-based analysis that would highlight economic systems, points of production, and class, armies, nations, states and institutions.

As Nelson's work underscores, an *internacionalista* feminism on the left has long been a crucial piece of the transnational anti-imperialist critique we are characterizing here. The "Third Wave" periodization, which imagines that feminists discovered racism, political economy, and imperialism only in the nineties, is wrong. On the contrary, there was a fight; where some feminists (in North America, Latin America, Asia, and Africa) prioritized questions of gender to the exclusion of race, class, and imperialism—from the 1970s to the present—others struggled for an analysis that understood these things as mutually imbricated and simultaneous. These struggles, in academic scholarship and international conferences, came to a head in the seventies and eighties over issues such as development, genital cutting, missionaries, and the colonial studies field. In 1984, Robin Morgan proposed that there was a "global feminism," and Pratibha Parmar and Valerie Amos rejoined that its proper name was "imperial feminism."[16] While the existence of an "imperial feminist" formation for some seemed to limit the utility of feminism, nevertheless, feminism has been crucial to understanding the transnational deployments of women's labor, woman-as-symbol-of-the-nation, and women who take up revolutionary roles. For a time in the 1960s and '70s, it was a romance of (female/feminist) insurrectionism, and photographic images of women as gun-toting *guerilleras* circulated widely, influencing both revolutionary movements and feminist scholarship. Frantz Fanon's essay "Algeria Unveiled" was especially influential in this regard, positing as it did women taking up radical, revolutionary roles. In the 1980s, we saw texts like Margaret Randall's *Sandino's Daughters*, which constructed the revolutionary Nicaraguan woman in the context of the Sandinista struggle. Other efforts theorized the role of women in neocolonial development and Reagan-era imperialism, such as Cynthia Enloe's influential *Bananas, Beaches, and Bases*, about women and the military, from sex workers to file clerks. This is also the moment when texts like Yamila Azize-Vargas's *La Mujer en la Lucha* emerged, focusing on recovering a strong anti-imperial tradition among Latin American women in a context of an imperial history. In the 1990s, another current in this revolutionary-inspired historiography traced social movements. For example, Emma Pérez's *The Decolonial Imaginary* conceptualizes Mexican and Chicana/o feminism in the United States as a descendent of the Mexican Revolution; Jennifer Nelson, in *Women of Color and the Reproductive Rights Movement* wrote about the Young Lords Party—a Puerto Rican nationalist party on the mainland, styled after the Black Panthers—as the site of a fight in which feminists won, transforming the party's platform to one that contained demands for an end to *machismo*, coerced sterilization, and an affirmative right to abortion. Other works, such as Diana Taylor's *Disappearing Acts*, on Las Madres de la Plaza de Mayo, have looked to transnational solidarity networks among women's movements in the late twentieth century, especially those formed in response to human rights crises.[17]

Much work by Chicana feminist theorists has centered the simultaneity of the *transfrontera*/transnational together with the hard-edged and sometimes violent ways that gender collides with and is refigured by race, class, and the trans/nation. One of the most influential Chicana/Latina feminist formulations was Gloria Anzaldúa's *Borderlands/La Frontera*, from 1987, which imagined neither a "here" nor a "there," a Mexico nor a United States, but an in-between, formulated on the one hand as an actual place, a geography of *mestizaje* in the context of the U.S. Southwest, and on the other as a metaphor for locations and imaginaries of impurity, hybridity, and queerness.[18] Anzaldúa's generative formation suggested to scholars of the Caribbean ways of thinking the restless migration of individuals, here one day, there the next, as Alberto Sandoval-Sanchez's "guagua aérea" (air bus) would have it, or, as Orlando Patterson posited, the existence of the Third World within the First. In the eighties and nineties, these scholars challenged us to think of the unfolding of Latin American and Caribbean history within the United States and vice versa. They underscored the "back and forth" movements of people and ideas within spaces that challenged our notions of discrete domains.[19]

Other theorists like Mary Pat Brady, Norma Alarcón, and Sonia Saldívar-Hull have suggested that a transnational sensibility lets scholars see the movement of goods, individuals, and ideas happening in a context in which gender, class, and race operate simultaneously.[20] In this context, the process of empire building in Latin America and the Caribbean took place inside a world economy that placed individuals into discrete categories that could easily migrate into different settings, albeit often with significant changes. In this way, we can see how policies such as social engineering and eugenics were not exclusively about either race or class, but were also mobile gender ideologies (and discourses of reproduction) aimed at creating a more modern citizenry. We also see the gendered, class, and racial dimensions behind populist politics and social reform projects geared at civilizing the popular masses pressuring for inclusion via reform or revolution.

A Few Recent Interventions: Mapping Neoliberalism, Feminism, War

Influenced by the wars in Central America, Latin American, and the Caribbean, leftist activists developed a critique of neoliberalism that irrupted into international headlines in 1994, when the implementation of the North American Free Trade Agreement (NAFTA) was met with the Zapatista revolt in Chiapas, the impoverished and significantly indigenous southern state of Mexico. The Zapatista movement's critique of neoliberalism spread rapidly—through newspapers, the Internet, and European and U.S. American activist circles—in significant part because its vision and aspirations were transnational. Although on the one hand it offered itself as a fulfillment of the national project of the Mexican Revolution, of Zapata's dream of land and full cultural citizenship for impoverished, peasant Mexico, it simultaneously directed itself outward, "a revolution that makes revolution possible," in one of its memorable aphorisms. International solidarity activists were welcomed, but also transformed into students of forms of privatization, neoliberal governance, and alternative, deep forms of democracy. Naomi Klein writes about the kinds of hopefulness Zapatismo inspired in international activist circles, calling it "a global call to revolution that tells you not to wait for the revolution, only to stand where you stand, to fight with your own weapon . . . It's a revolution in miniature that says, 'Yes, you can try this at home.'"[21] It emerged in anarchists' squats in Italy, in the WTO protests against globalization in Seattle in 1999, and, increasingly, in a critical scholarship on neoliberalism.

Some of the most innovative new scholarship linking transnationalism, neoliberalism, and war has also come from, or derived from work about, Africa and Asia. James Ferguson's recent work on Africa leaves the concept of the nation in tatters—neither the state, the economy, territory, nor publics are national, as he understands them. Following Achille Mbembe's arguments about the ongoing brutalization of Africa and African subjects, and the ever deepening of the processes initiated under colonialism, Ferguson offers a map of neoliberalism's transformations of these postcolonies. In the aftermath of International Monetary Fund (IMF) structural adjustment in the 1980s, states were stripped of many development-era functions (health care or education, for example), and these functions were taken over by institutions that exercised a form of transnational sovereignty, NGOs. As state workers followed their jobs and salaries to NGOs, many states essentially shifted their function, gathering income and power from forms of criminalization. While international capital refused to invest in nations governed by weak states, poor infrastructure, and little security apparatus, it did not disappear from the continent—appearing instead in enclaves like Angola's, where oil companies claim territories governed by corporations and private armies. Populations, far from longing for national renewal, channel their desires for improved standards of living and an end to sharply declining life spans in transnational directions, migration on the one hand and modernity and development for "Africa" on the other (that concept so rejected by academics, in favor of national specificity, but which Ferguson compellingly argues is alive and well on the continent).[22]

From the post–cold war perspective of the "Asian Tiger" markets, Aihwa Ong expands on two of the most influential accounts of recent forms of transnationalism—Giorgio Agamben's (particularly in *Homo Sacer*) and Michael Hardt and Antonio Negri's (in *Empire* and *Multitude*)—in her brilliant *Neoliberalism as Exception*.[23] She suggests that Agamben, charting a Europe awash in refugees and other migrants, offers too simple an account in producing only two categories—the "citizen" and the exception. In contrast, she argues that there are (of course) multiple kinds and qualities of dispossession, and that even those who are not citizens are not necessarily reduced to the status of "bare life," as Agamben suggests, but rather have many kinds of claims on states. Ong maps the ways that NGOs, human rights groups, and Islamic religious groups advocate for those who are dispossessed through a specifically moral language. Ong also complicates and expands on the work of postcolonial critics like Ferguson and Mbembe in charting the limits of state sovereignty. Not all such limitations, she argues, are historically derived from colonialism; some of them are new, such as China's "Special Economic Zones," where the state's economic regulation does not apply. Finally, she suggests that the conditions of labor (and labor's forms of resistance) are vastly more differentiated than Hardt and Negri's account of a global multitude allows for. If you theorize too far away from empirical work, she suggests, you wander into a fantasy that is logical but wrong. What emerges in *Neoliberal as Exception* is an image of how neoliberalism is producing sovereignty, citizenship, public cultures, and forms of labor that are striated across multiple "zones" that are not nations, but which articulate with nations and with other, transnational forces.

There is, too, a restaging of the global feminism/imperial feminism debates here, but with ever increasing urgency as a form of "imperial feminism" provides one of the rationales for the U.S. war in Afghanistan (ventriloquized memorably by Laura Bush, not a public figure otherwise known for her feminism). So, where Ong is interested in the ways those advocating human rights form unlikely alliances with Islamic feminists, Inderpal Grewal is far less sanguine about the work of human rights discourses, especially with respect to women. Akin to Spivak's postcolonial critique, Grewal's concern is with the ways human rights discourse constructs a female object of imperial intervention, as in the U.S. project of "rescuing" Afghan women from the Taliban (by bombing them). Lisa Yoneyama productively reframes the question as "national feminism" versus "critical feminism," a formulation that reiterates our concern here with the reified frame of the nation as the problem. Yoneyama notes that there is nothing new in the deployment of "national feminism" by otherwise antifeminist policymakers—she points to MacArthur. Noting that U.S. policymakers claim to have modeled the occupation of Iraq on the U.S. occupation of Japan after World War II, she recalls that that occupation, too, found legitimacy in a claim to be liberating women from (Japanese) oppression.[24] In a weird reversal, one that could scarcely have been conceived in the 1970s and '80s struggles over global feminism, now, in the context of the war in the Middle East, neoconservative ideologues have constructed themselves as the arbiters of what is good for women, and actual feminists have become the problem—in October 2007, David Horowitz announced "Islamo-Fascist Awareness Week" on U.S. university campuses, in which he urged students to organize "sit-ins in Women's Studies Departments and campus Women's Centers to protest their silence about the oppression of women in Islam."[25]

Another intriguing and provocative recent intervention in thinking the fever-dream of the nation has been a feminist- and queer-inflected account of the ways publics and desiring subjects are produced in relationship to nationalisms and transnationalism, which extends Benedict Anderson's "imagined communities" in new and unexpected ways to diagnose the neoliberal moment. Inderpal Grewal's *Transnational America* renders "America" as a consumer culture, bought and produced in many places (India and the United States interest her in this work), through a particularly female instantiation of the consumer. Lisa Rofel's *Desiring China* notes the ways that for China and its citizens the production of desiring subjects—longing for consumer objects on the one hand and kinds of sex or partners that might include gay and lesbian desires on the other—are mobilized in specifically national ways, on behalf of China's neoliberal experiments. That these are forms of desire and kinds of public cultures produced in relation to forces outside the nation goes without saying for Rofel. Neferti Tadiar incisively and helpfully describes the project of understanding desiring publics as they interact with the nation, joining the national economy—a thing so foundationally naturalized in neoliberalism—to the nationalist political project, and calling them both fantasy productions, "part of the dream-work of an international order of production founded upon the conjoined, if sometimes contradictory, logics of nationalism and multinational capitalism." Jasbir Puar's *Terrorists Assemblages* asks, against what others are LGBTQ subjects being recognized and incorporated into the U.S. nation? Could it be the perversely sexualized (although deficient with respect to gay rights) Muslims and Arabs, who engage in practices such as honor killings and female veiling?[26]

Despite the ways "transnationalism" or "globalization" has declared itself as a new theoretical, economic, or political project, then, we are suggesting a continuous and productive tradition of analyzing against the naturalized frame of the nation. As Stuart Hall writes,

> when we are talking about globalization in the present context we are talking about some of the new forms, some of the new rhythms, some of the new impetuses in the globalizing process . . . located within a much longer history. We suffer increasingly from a process of historical amnesia in which we think that just because we are thinking about an idea it has only just started.[27]

A considerable amount of work in anti-imperialist and decolonial traditions, in feminist, antiracist, and ethnic studies scholarship, and in economic and labor history has prefigured and provided a foundation for the project of transnationalism. What remains, if transnationalism is to be a coherent category of analysis, is to chart its theoretical direction.

Writing Transnational History

We see feminist theory as providing a useful analogy for ways of theorizing the transnational. Two decades ago, Joan Scott made the argument that gender is a crucial category of analysis for any study of politics, society, and culture.[28] Scott suggested that we understand gender as having significance far beyond sexed bodies (read: women), shifting instead to a framework that understands gender as "a constitutive element of social relationships based on perceived differences between the sexes, and . . . a primary way of signifying relationships of power."[29] In so doing, Scott denaturalized male and female, masculinity and femininity, suggesting instead that they are always cultural ideologies applied to bodies. As such, these ideologies not only underpin interpersonal relationships, but also extend outward in all directions to condition far more wide-ranging and abstract social structures and events, such as economies, political paradigms, and even wars. Similarly, the nation is an ideology applied to a territory, its people, and its economic and social institutions that extends far beyond the naming of a piece of land. It is, in short, another "primary way of signifying relationships of power." Scott's simultaneous abstraction of the meanings of gender *and* materializing of gender holds great promise for how we might think about the nation.

Scott identified four elements of gender: (1) culturally available symbols; (2) normative concepts that set forth interpretations of the meaning of the symbols; (3) social institutions and organizations thus conditioned (ranging from kinship, the household, and the family to more formal institutions); and, finally, (4) subjective identity.[30] With just a few changes in wording, Scott's formulation of gender as a category can also apply to the nation. The work of the "nation concept" far exceeds the bounds of problems of the state or diplomacy. It produces endlessly proliferating related terms, such as homeland, security, traitors, minorities, family, culture, home, immigrants, and so on. Are nations and nationalities composed through something that is actually fairly unified and coherent, an identity etched on states, individuals, and communities by geography and history? Or are they rather much more contingent and fragile, sometimes in play and other times not, and sometimes a cover story, a patriotism that persuades people to act against their own interests? Here we make the case for "transnationalism" as a strategy for identifying the ideological work of the nation by offering a series of provocations derived from our own work about what might be seen as the self-evidently "national."

Take, for example, the case of the Guatemalan national economy. In this moment of free market fundamentalism, nothing could be more foundationally real, more naturalized than the national economy—especially in critiques of its backwardness in places like Central America, where the vast majority of economic activity takes place in the informal sector, which is held to be a symptom of its fundamental weakness. But what if, as J. T. Way argues in his forthcoming book, the predominant "real" economy in Guatemala is precisely the so-called informal economy—produced through small-scale capitalism within Guatemala and outside it? Further, perhaps this "backward" and "antimodern" nation is hypermodern, a laboratory of the future of neoliberal privatization and militarization in the name of crime, gangs, and security, with the involvement of familiar entities such as Texaco and the U.S. Drug Enforcement Agency. Guatemala's putative underdevelopment, one could argue, is part and parcel of the transnational process of corporate capitalist development. In this sense, the economy is simultaneously bigger (extending beyond national boundaries) and more local (the informal economy) than the nation; in this sense, the "national economy" emerges as an ideological invention that constructs national "underdevelopment."

The nation's identity as a land of premodern, indigenous farmers (who serve collectively as a "culturally available symbol" buttressing the "normative concept" of national backwardness and informing hosts of "social institutions and organizations," to use Scott's terms) is in no way incompatible with globalization writ large. The notion of an "informal economy" does a particular kind of ideological work, rendering some people's—primarily women's—economic activity illegal or unreal, in need of capture by transnational economic entities. Popular articulations such as *oficios de su sexo*, a commonly used phrase for women's labor that elides its centrality to the economy, evidence a widespread fetishism that also lies behind the feminized naming of the economy that supports nearly 80 percent of the population as "informal," and therefore backward and in need of change. The unquestioned gender ideology lurking behind *oficios de su sexo* also bolsters the near-hegemonic myth of a stable, nuclear family—a now apparently "disintegrating" family that historical evidence indicates was never a social norm to begin with. It conditions everyday politics in markets and neighborhood associations and lies behind the evolution of contemporary moral outrage over young male *mareros* (gang members). The word *development* itself is a product of the transnational, capitalist culture industry—a word that straddles a paradoxical mix of unquestioned acceptance and fierce contestation in Guatemala, where neoliberalism was imposed by genocide, torture, and war on a country only allowed to return to "democracy" when the left wing of the body politic had been effectively clipped by violence.[31] The precise structures that are deployed to characterize Guatemala as a nation—the interlocked characteristics of its economic "backwardness," its gender ideologies, families, and development—are transformed when we see them as transnational.

The story of modern Mexico told through cooperatives in the 1940s and 1950s suggests that the process of naturalizing the nation was much more contentious, violent, and negotiated than previously assumed. History remembers these decades as Mexico's heyday of economic growth and cultural production, bookended by the earlier revolutionary moment and the ensuing post-1960s economic and political upheavals. Gladys McCormick explores the uneven and contested production of the "subjective identities" of peasants as fully subjects of the Mexican Revolution's progressive tradition. In her work on the development of state-sponsored sugar production cooperatives throughout Mexico, McCormick argues that these years were anything but peaceful.[32] She delves into the struggles and negotiations between rural peoples determined to preserve some autonomy and state officials intent on laying down the contours of what became arguably the most successful instance of authoritarian modernization in twentieth century Latin America. Cooperatives (as an example of Scott's culturally available symbols) conveyed an image of national collaboration and brought together thousands of peasants and industrial and white-collar workers in a project to industrialize the countryside and connect each group to the state's corporatist structure. Through cooperatives, the state purported to give the means of production to previously disenfranchised groups and thereby invest them in the nation's modernization. In practice, however, the state adopted a top-down approach that included divisive strategies to ensure its control over cooperative members. While the state afforded workers effective means of representation and met their demands as a class, in essence domesticating them, it chose to disregard and marginalize peasant claims. Peasant leaders thus opted for innovative strategies to make their voices heard: they reached out to other popular groups, including teachers and railroad workers, and formed their own organizations to compete with ineffective state-sponsored unions.

Increasingly frustrated, some peasant leaders chose radical paths to stymie the state's deliberate neglect and to recover the revolutionary legacy underpinning modern Mexico. The fact that several of these leaders fought in the peasant army of Emiliano Zapata during the 1910–1919 Revolution made their call to arms all the more threatening to a social order supposedly founded on the memory of national heroes such as Zapata. In response, the ruling regime unleashed unprecedented repressive tactics on peasant movements that it later employed against worker and student activists in urban centers, most shockingly in the 1968 student massacre at the Tlatelolco Plaza in Mexico City. As far back as 1947, with the support of the U.S. government, the Mexican state set up a new intelligence agency, the Dirección Federal de Seguridad, to act as a form of secret police to bring in line popular opposition. To do so, the agency complemented its surveillance activities with more aggressive strategies to co-opt, subvert, and eliminate dissent against the regime. The authoritarian social order easily identified and distinguished between "enemies" and "friends," even as Mexico kept up its progressive image in the international arena and conveyed a sense of social peace. Taking then what appears to be a perfect case of national integration and nation formation, the vertical class integration and enfranchisment of the rural poor in Mexico through a vision of progressive collectivism, in the heyday of Mexico state-sponsored economic and cultural development, McCormick shows that these rural workers were anything but integrated into either state projects or a united imaginary of Mexican-ness. Even the Mexican state, it turns out, is not bounded by the nation, but is rather shot through by efforts of the U.S. intelligence agencies to produce bureaucratic efficiency in the production of an anticommunist security state.

Using the family as a starting point, Laura Briggs has argued that, far from being private or national affairs, reproduction and sexuality are key ways that relations between nations are negotiated, both symbolically and materially; there is no "domestic" that is not extensively transected by the transnational. Although we think of the family and the household as the opposite of the transnational, as that which above all is domestic (a word we not incidentally use to describe both the inside of the nation and the inside of the home, suggesting something of their symbolic importance to each other), the boundaries of the "domestic" are illusory and ideological. From the colonial to metropolitan household, it is not difficult to think of ways that domestic and sexual labor are transnationalized (indeed, in the wake of scandals involving various Clinton and Bush cabinet-level appointees that have gone awry because of "problems" involving undocumented household workers, it is tempting to say, counterintuitively, that the family is not "domestic" at all, but the most explicitly transnational of spaces).[33] Turning to the newspapers, one finds that sexuality and reproduction are frequently topics of importance to transnational publics, in part because reproductive and sexual labor are stratified by nation. That is, questions regarding, for example, military sexual politics are periodically but explosively transnational subjects of interest (think, for example, of the movement on Okinawa to get rid of U.S. military bases when three servicemen raped a twelve-year old girl in 1996, or how the market in sex outside the Subic Bay Naval Base spurred the movement in the Philippines to close it).[34] Although these might at first glance appear to be isolated examples, other questions of sex, household, and kinship are equally transnational: au pairs, nannies, and other domestic laborers are almost by definition transnational migrants, coming to households in Europe, the United States, Australia, New Zealand, and Canada, but also to places like Costa Rica and Puerto Rico. These forms of ("domestic") labor migration are not random, but extend along the lines of colonialism, capitalism, and trade; differences in labor's value are not a function of separation or isolation but of familiarity, so to speak—there is a relationship between the domestic relations of the colonial household and domestic work in London or Los Angeles. Contemporary sites of transnational adoption, likewise, have historic and contemporary relationships to the displacements of this century's hot wars—think Korea, Vietnam, El Salvador, Guatemala—and cold ones—for instance, China, Russia, or Romania.

These "domestic" international relations are more than the passive fallout of (implicitly more real) transnational relations; they are a constitutive part of them. As Christina Klein argues in *Cold War Orientalism*, caring for "their" orphans from China in the 1950s shored (and shores) up a U.S. American sense of benevolence and responsibility toward Asia.[35] Remittances from transmigrants doing domestic labor of various sorts have a significant impact on local and national-level economies in places like Nicaragua, El Salvador, and the Dominican Republic. As Briggs argued in *Reproducing Empire*, the demographic production of "overpopulation" was ideologically key to erasing the history of Western colonialism during the cold war, and the production of a "new" policy of help for the "Third World" called development (a combination of industrialization and reforming reproduction through birth control)—as if it were not a continuation of older, colonial policies.[36]

Military, colonial, and public policies are constantly called upon to develop ways of policing transnational intimacies, regulating institutions such as the brothel, the orphanage, the lock hospital.[37] As Ann Stoler has argued, laws structuring the nationality and mobility of mixed race children, war orphans, and other unclaimed (adoptable?) children are crucial colonial and postcolonial institutions.[38] Transnational domestic spheres also require laws governing who can make whom a citizen in the context of heterosexual marriage, as well as medical tests and policies regulating the mobility, labor, and social interaction of those suffering from TB, syphilis, or AIDS. Furthermore, not only do censuses and demographers try to determine where children belong, but they also, since the 1930s, simply quantify them, giving rise to the social science of "overpopulation," spurring the science of birth control research, and engaging in the taxonomies of quality associated with eugenics—which are also transnational discourses.[39] Notwithstanding all the ways that the family as a social institution is asked to stand for the nation and so underpins subjective identity ("as American as mom and apple pie," "soccer moms," "security moms," the "American family," "family values," even "working families"—and non-U.S. examples could serve equally well), the family is as flexibly trans/national a space as any other.

The examples we have given from our own work suggest that economics, politics, subjectification, and the family all exceed the nation, and offer points of entry into transnational analysis. Race is another example. Conceived within a U.S.-based formation of "minorities," race seems above all national (one is minoritarian or majoritarian only with reference to a certain population or demographic reference point—a stat-istic, a number kept by the state). But other evidence points differently if, for example, we looked to the wealth of scholarship on the ways Asian Americans are constructed as permanently foreign to the United States.[40] Nor is this paradoxical state of affairs unique to U.S. Americans. Mexican national subjects may be paradigmatically *mestizo*, and Brazilians engaged in a process of whitening, while Central Americans may understand indigenous people only as those who wear traditional dress, and most everyone else might be acknowledged to be mixed. But each of these examples simultaneously points to racial difference as constitutively *inside* the nation and also indicates that certain racial formations exceed the nation. Indigenous people in Mexico, Guatemala, or Bolivia are construed as signs of a colonial moment before the nation, or, if acknowledged to exist in the present, an unruly and ungovernable people who cannot be fully incorporated in the citizenry or the national economy. Indigenous people point beyond official state nationalisms.

This contradictory nature of racialized subjectivities in the United States (as both within and outside the nation or, better, of nationalism as a strategy for containing the "excesses" of racial justice claims) was played out in one of the more ingenious efforts of liberal newspapers to minimize the nature of racial protest in the aftermath of the April 2006 marches for immigrant rights. It seemed in general like a moment of naked ideological containment. To take only one example of a move that was repeated in the national press for weeks, the *New York Times* described the federal legislative district that includes Tucson, home to the largest march in southern Arizona's history, as "majority Latino." Tucson is represented by a politically left Mexican American congressman, Raúl Grijalva, and the *Times* used the designation "majority Latino" to explain both the march and Grijalva's election when in fact the largest single group in the district is composed of Anglos, with Latinos and indigenous people making up somewhat less than a third each.[41] But the possibility that justice for immigrants was a *politics*, rather than a racial identity, was being rapidly shut down at that moment. Not only did various commentators try to foreclose the possibility of a multiracial alliance in the pro-immigrant movement on the left, but in Republican circles, the hard right tried to discredit the Bush administration's proposal for guest workers by construing the desire for an end to restrictive immigration laws as essentially foreign, as inimical to U.S. national interest and hence brought to us by foreigners. In the immediate aftermath of the protests, newspapers began asking whether these marchers, recast as all "Mexicans" or Mexican Americans (and probably "illegals") were actually inheritors of the civil rights tradition they claimed.[42] African Americans were duly found to speak on behalf of an uneasy, potentially economically displaced *national* subject.[43] Latinos were thus construed as the foreign, diasporic racialized group and contrasted with African Americans, who were represented as a U.S. minority.

These brief examples are meant to suggest some of the possibilities of thinking the nation as a category of analysis, to understand some of the ideological effects of the nation, well beyond what we obviously and instantly think of as the work of nationalism, constructing the national population, or simply as a frame for other kinds of stories. The nation does all sorts of ideological work, and when we take it for granted as the frame of U.S., Guatemalan, or Mexican history, for example, that work becomes invisible. Those who work on social movements or the welfare state sometimes claim that concepts such as "national liberation" or the redistributive state are not necessarily bad. That may be true. But that does not mean that we are better off when we take the nation for granted.

Transnational scholarship opens possibilities and raises new questions, but is also fraught with potential problems. One important avenue that transnational intellectual work can open up is the possibility of collaboration among academics and intellectuals located in publishing's First World (the United States and Europe, with access to international publics) and Third World (where knowledge, however erudite, seems to be of strictly "local" provenance).[44] This piece is itself the product of a transnational collaboration in one sense—we met each other in Mexico, McCormick is Costa Rican by birth, Way lives in Guatemala, Briggs is a U.S.-based academic—and it has crossed many national borders in its travels among us, and is based on research that, for each of us, has been done in more than one country. Yet in another sense, our collaboration is not transnational at all, built as it is on the fact that each of us has sturdy ties to U.S. universities, and more importantly, the funding structures that flow from that. And therein lies the rub. Transnational scholarship, to the extent that it requires jetting around to multiple nations (with all that implies about easy access to visas), is potentially just another imperial vantage point.

There is also the risk of being U.S.-centric in our studies of empire or hegemonic power and failing to recognize the influences of non-U.S. groups. Thinking of the Americas, Mexico, for instance, has long played a pivotal role in the historical record of Central America. European powers, such as Spain (of course), but also France and Germany, have also long wielded political, cultural, and economic pressures in the region. But if we pull back the lens to look at nations in this way, how do we account for larger, global forces without being reductive about the local and regional specificities? Or, alternatively and contradictorily, where do we put an analysis of how the nation signifies in people's lives that is not deterministic? In their provocative article "Unfinished Migrations: Reflections on the African Diaspora and the Making of the Modern World," Tiffany Ruby Patterson and Robin D. G. Kelley argued that "the African diaspora itself exists within the context of global race and gender hierarchies which are formulated and reconstituted across national boundaries" and other kinds of borders—which is to say, the nation is only one among several forms of power, meaning, and containment, and not always the dominant one at that.[45] We need to keep in tension a focus on the power of the heroic narratives of nationalism without, as it were, taking them too seriously and thus participating in renaturalizing the nation.

Finally, though, it seems crucial to reiterate the importance of making the nation and nationalism an explicit question, and how the nation's ideologies and institutions are in play in countless obvious and not obvious ways in diverse struggles, symbols, institutions, and identities. To do otherwise is to risk engaging in scholarship that unwittingly does the work of nationalism, whether it is in the form of American exceptionalism, naturalizing the national economy, or any in a host of related moves. History, in particular, we would argue, needs to be more than just another way to teach young people to love their country. Literary study likewise ought not reify the national culture by making it singularly wonderful, stunningly racist, or even just unique; rather, scholars might be about the business of noting how literary traditions in fact are constructing the fiction of the national community. This is more than a claim that nationalism is perhaps bad for human communities—we are perfectly willing to agree that it is sometimes good. Rather, it simply asks our scholarship to make us sensible of when nationalism and ideologies of the nation are in play, rather than being complicit with them.

Notes

1. Anna Lowenhaupt Tsing, *Friction: An Ethnography of Global Connection* (Princeton, N.J.: Princeton University Press, 2005), xiii, 3.
2. Yen Le Espiritu, *Home Bound: Filipino American Lives across Cultures, Communities, and Countries* (Berkeley: University of California Press, 2003); Arjun Appadurai, *Modernity at Large: Cultural Dimensions of Globalization* (Minneapolis: University of Minnesota Press, 1996).
3. Andrew Ross, "The Survival of American Studies in the Era of Financialization," American Studies Association Annual Meeting, Philadelphia, October 11–13, 2007, and *Fast Boat to China: Corporate Flight and the Consequences of Free Trade: Lessons from Shanghai* (New York: Pantheon Books, 2006); Aihwa Ong, *Neoliberalism as Exception: Mutations in Citizenship and Sovereignty* (Durham, N.C.: Duke University Press, 2006); Bruce Cumings, "Boundary Displacement: The State, the Foundations, and Area Studies During and After the Cold War," in *Learning Places: The Afterlives of Area Studies*, ed. Masao Miyoshi and H. D. Harootunian, 261–302 (Durham, N.C.: Duke University Press, 2002), 185.
4. In 2007, "transnationalism" is in the title of literally hundreds of academic journal articles; a search of commercial academic databases suggests that the overwhelming majority of them are on human migration. For monographs, see, for example, Thomas Bender, *A Nation among Nations : America's Place in World History* (New York: Hill and Wang, 2006); Charles S. Maier, *Among Empires: American Ascendancy and Its Predecessors* (Cambridge, Mass.: Harvard University Press, 2006); and Denise Segura and Patricia Zavella, *Women and Migration in the U.S.-Mexico Borderlands: A Reader* (Durham, N.C.: Duke University Press, 2007).
5. It has, for example, produced the Fall 2007 transnationalism issue of *Social Text*, as well provided the context for sustained and thoughtful discussion of the work of literally dozens of forthcoming books.
6. For example, C. L. R. James's *The Black Jacobins: Toussaint L'Ouverture and the San Domingo Revolution* is one key work marking these discussions over imperialism (New York: Vintage Books, 1963); others include Frantz Fanon, *The Wretched of the Earth* (New York: Grove Press, 1965); Frantz Fanon, *A Dying Colonialism* (New York: Grove Press, 1967); and Alejo Carpentier, *El reino de este mundo* ([Santiago de] Chile: Editorial ORBE, 1972).
7. Immanuel Wallerstein, *The Modern World System: Capitalist Agriculture and the Origins of the European World Economy in the Sixteenth Century* (New York: Academic Press, 1974).
8. Challenging Wallerstein in 1988, Steve Stern argued against the world system's view and the formulation of "periphery" because its European-centered perspective failed to account for economic diversification and overemphasized the feudal features in the evolution of Latin America's history. For a more recent formulation of Stern's critique, see his contribution, "The Decentered Center and the Expansionist Periphery: The Paradoxes of Foreign-Local Encounter," in *Close Encounters of Empire: Writing the Cultural History of U.S.-Latin American Relations*, ed. Gilbert M. Joseph, Catherine C. Legrand, and Ricardo D. Salvatore, 47–68 (Durham, N.C.: Duke University Press, 1998).

9. As in James Scott, *Weapons of the Weak: Everyday Forms of Peasant Resistance* (New Haven, Conn.: Yale University Press, 1985); and James Scott, *Domination and the Arts of Resistance: Hidden Transcripts* (New Haven, Conn.: Yale University Press, 1990).

10. Dipesh Chakrabarty, *Provincializing Europe: Postcolonial Thought and Historical Difference* (Princeton, N.J.: Princeton University Press, 2000); Gayatri Chakravorty Spivak, "Can the Subaltern Speak?" in *Marxism and the Interpretation of Culture*, ed. Cary Nelson and Lawrence Grossberg, 271–314 (Urbana: University of Illinois Press, 1988); Ranajit Guha, *Elementary Aspects of Peasant Insurgency in Colonial India* (1098; Durham, N.C.: Duke University Press, 1999).

11. Florencia Mallon, "The Promise and Dilemma of Subaltern Studies: Perspectives from Latin American History," *American Historical Review* 99 (December 1994): 1491–515; and *Peasant and Nation: The Making of Postcolonial Mexico and Peru* (Berkeley: University of California Press, 1995).

12. Ileana Rodríguez, *The Latin American Subaltern Studies Reader* (Durham, N.C.: Duke University Press, 2001).

13. Roger N. Lancaster, *Life Is Hard: Machismo, Danger, and the Intimacy of Power in Nicaragua* (Berkeley: University of California Press, 1992).

14. Diane M. Nelson, *A Finger in the Wound: Body Politics in Quincentennial Guatemala* (Berkeley: University of California Press, 1999). See esp. 41–48. The author attributes the term *fluidarity* to anthropologist Mark Driscoll.

15. On structures of feeling, see Raymond Williams, *The Long Revolution* (1961; London: Penguin, 1965), esp. 64, along with his later works.

16. Valerie Amos and Pratibha Parmar, "Challenging Imperial Feminism," *Feminist Review* 17 (1984): 3–19; Robin Morgan, *Sisterhood Is Global : The International Women's Movement Anthology* (Garden City, N.Y.: Anchor Press/Doubleday, 1984). One of the arenas in which this fight took place, memorably, in these decades, was at the three U.N. conferences on the decade of women, in Mexico City (1975), Copenhagen (1980), and Nairobi (1985). *The* issue at Copenhagen was the question of the relationship of feminism to oppression by race, class, or nationalism/colonialism. For a flavor of the conversation, see Nilüfer Çagatay, Caren Grown, and Aida Santiago, "The Nairobi Women's Conference: Toward a Global Feminism?" *Feminist Studies* 12.2 (Summer 1986): 401–12.

17. Emma Pérez, *The Decolonial Imaginary: Writing Chicanas into History* (Bloomington: Indiana University Press, 1999); Yamila Azize Vargas, *La Mujer En La Lucha* (Río Piedras, P.R.: Editorial Cultural, 1985); Margaret Randall and Lynda Yanz, *Sandino's Daughters: Testimonies of Nicaraguan Women in Struggle* (Vancouver: New Star Books, 1981); Fanon, *A Dying Colonialism*; Cynthia H. Enloe, *Bananas, Beaches and Bases: Making Feminist Sense of International Politics* (London: Pandora, 1989); Diana Taylor, *Disappearing Acts: Spectacles of Gender and Nationalism in Argentina's "Dirty War"* (Durham, N.C.: Duke University Press, 1997); Jennifer Nelson, *Women of Color and the Reproductive Rights Movement* (New York: New York University Press, 2003).

18. Gloria Anzaldúa, *Borderlands/La Frontera*, 2d ed. (San Francisco: Aunt Lute Books, 1999).

19. Alberto Sandoval Sanchez, "Puerto Rican Identity up in the Air: Air Migration, Its Cultural Representations, and Me 'Cruzando El Charco,'" in *Puerto Rican Jam: Rethinking Colonialism and Nationalism*, ed. Frances Negrón-Muntaner and Ramón Grosfoguel, 189–208 (Minneapolis: University of Minnesota Press, 1997); Orlando Patterson, "The Emerging West Atlantic System: Migration, Culture, and Underdevelopment in the U.S. and the Circum-Caribbean Region," in *Population in an Interacting World*, ed. William Alonzo, 227–61 (Cambridge, Mass.: Harvard University Press, 1987).

20. Sonia Saldívar-Hull, *Feminism on the Border : Chicana Gender Politics and Literature* (Berkeley: University of California Press, 2000). Norma Alarcón, "Traddutora, Traditora: A Paradigmatic Figure of Chicana Feminism," *Cultural Critique* 13 (Autumn 1989): 57–87; Mary Pat Brady, "The Fungibility of Borders," *Nepantla: Views from South* 1.1 (2000): 171–90.

21. Naomi Klein, "The Unknown Icon," in *¡Ya Basta! Ten Years of the Zapatista Uprising*, ed. Ziga Vodovnik, 15–23 (Oakland, Calif.: AK Press, 2004).

22. J. A. Mbembe, *On the Postcolony* (Berkeley: University of California Press, 2001); Roderick A. Ferguson, *Aberrations in Black: Toward a Queer of Color Critique* (Minneapolis: University of Minnesota Press, 2004); James Ferguson, *Global Shadows: Africa in the Neoliberal World Order* (Durham, N.C.: Duke University Press, 2006); James Ferguson, "Seeing Like an Oil Company: Space, Security, and Global Capitalism in Neoliberal Africa," *American Anthropologist* 107.3 (2005): 377–82; James Ferguson and Akhil Gupta, "Spatializing States: Toward an Ethnography of Neoliberal Governmentality," *American Ethnologist* 29.4 (2002): 981–1002.

23. Ong, *Neoliberalism as Exception*; Michael Hardt and Antonio Negri, *Multitude: War and Democracy in the Age of Empire* (New York: Penguin, 2004); Michael Hardt and Antonio Negri, *Empire* (Cambridge, Mass.: Harvard University Press, 2000); Giorgio Agamben, *Homo Sacer: Sovereign Power and Bare Life* (Stanford, Calif.: Stanford University Press, 1998).

24. Lisa Yoneyama, "Liberation under Siege: U.S. Military Occupation and Japanese Women's Enfranchisement," *American Quarterly* 57.3 (September 2005): 885–910; Ong, *Neoliberalism as Exception*; Inderpal Grewal, *Transnational America: Feminisms, Diasporas, Neoliberalisms* (Durham, N.C.: Duke University Press, 2005).

25. For a humorous riff on this, see Barbara Ehrenreich, "It's Islamo-Fascism Awareness Week," October 22, 2007, http://www.thenation.com/doc/20071105/ehrenreich (accessed October 2007).

26. Benedict R. Anderson, *Imagined Communities: Reflections on the Origin and Spread of Nationalism* (London: Verso, 1983); Neferti Tadiar, *Fantasy-Production: Sexual Economies and Other Philippine Consequences for the New World Order* (Hong Kong: Hong Kong University Press, 2004), 7; Lisa Rofel, *Desiring China: Experiments in Neoliberalism, Sexuality, and Public Culture* (Durham, N.C.: Duke University Press, 2007); Jasbir K. Puar, *Terrorist Assemblages: Homonationalism in Queer Times, Next Wave* (Durham, N.C.: Duke University Press, 2007); Grewal, *Transnational America*.

27. Stuart Hall, "The Local and the Global: Globalization and Ethnicity" in *Culture, Globalization and the World System*, ed. Anthony D. King, 19–39 (Minneapolis: University of Minnesota Press, 1997), 19–20.

28. Joan Wallach Scott, "Gender: A Useful Category of Historical Analysis," *American Historical Review* 91.5 (December 1986): 1053–75.

29. Ibid., 1067.

30. Ibid., 1067–69.

31. John T. Way, "The Mayan in the Mall: Development, Culture and Globalization in Guatemala, 1920–2003" (PhD diss., Yale University, Department of History, 2006), forthcoming, Duke University Press.

32. Gladys McCormick, "Challenging the Golden Age: The Mexican Sugar Industry, Popular Mobilizations, and the Rise of an Authoritarian State, 1935–1965" (PhD diss., University of Wisconsin-Madison, Department of History, forthcoming 2009).

33. See Pierrette Hondagneu-Sotelo, *Doméstica: Immigrant Workers Cleaning and Caring in the Shadows of Affluence* (Berkeley: University of California Press, 2001); Barbara Ehrenreich and Arlie Russell Hochschild, *Global Woman: Nannies, Maids, and Sex Workers in the New Economy* (New York: Metropolitan Books, 2003).

34. Halina Todd, "Prostitution," *The Mobilizer* (Mobilization for Survival), http://feminism.eserver.org/prostitution.txt (Summer 1993). See also the Web page of the Okinawa Peace Network of Los Angeles (Buddahead Productions): http://www.uchinachu.org.

35. Christina Klein, *Cold War Orientalism : Asia in the Middlebrow Imagination, 1945–1961* (Berkeley: University of California Press, 2003).

36. Laura Briggs, *Reproducing Empire: Race, Sex, Science, and U.S. Imperialism in Puerto Rico* (Berkeley: University of California Press, 2002).

37. For a magnificent study of the regulation of brothels and lock hospitals, see Philippa Levine, *Prostitution, Race, and Politics: Policing Venereal Disease in the British Empire* (London: Routledge, 2003).

38. See, among others, Ann Laura Stoler, *Carnal Knowledge and Imperial Power: Race and the Intimate in Colonial Rule* (Berkeley: University of California Press, 2002), and "Tense and Tender Ties: The Politics of Comparison in North American History and (Post) Colonial Studies," *Journal of American History* 88.3 (2001): 829–65.

39. Briggs, *Reproducing Empire*.

40. See Lisa Lowe, *Immigrant Acts: On Asian American Cultural Politics* (Durham, N.C.: Duke University Press, 1996); Robert G. Lee, *Orientals : Asian Americans in Popular Culture* (Philadelphia: Temple University Press, 1999).

41. David Kirkpatrick, "Demonstrations on Immigration Are Hardening a Divide," *New York Times*, April 17, 2006, 1.

42. Ibid.

43. Jennifer Harper, "Americans Take Stern View of Illegal Immigration," *Washington Times*, April 12, 2006, 1.

44. For a forceful and compelling argument along these lines, see Suresh Canagarajah, *A Geopolitics of Academic Writing* (Pittsburg: University of Pittsburg Press, 2002).

45. Tiffany Ruby Patterson and Robin D. G. Kelley, "Unfinished Migrations: Reflections on the African Diaspora and the Making of the Modern World," in *African Studies Review* 43.1 (April 2000): 11–50, quote on 20. Also see Kim D. Butler, "Defining Diaspora, Refining a Discourse," in *Diaspora* 10.2 (2001): 189–219.

"The Birth of a European Public": Migration, Postnationality, and Race in the Uniting of Europe

Fatima El-Tayeb

> The fact is that the so-called European civilization—"Western" civilization—as it has been shaped by two centuries of bourgeois rule, is incapable of solving the two major problems to which its existence has given rise: the problem of the proletariat and the colonial problem.
>
> —Aimé Césaire, 1955

I

Europe appears to be in a unique position in this post–cold war, post-9/11 world, both with regard to its internal reconstruction and to its potential role in current world politics. Seemingly having overcome the state of crisis famously analyzed by Césaire in his *Discourse on Colonialism*, at a time when "postnational" and "end of the nation-state" have become favorite buzzwords within academic and nonacademic discourses of globalization, it is Europe, and Europe alone, that has created a material manifestation of this new world order: the European Union appears as the first supranational system fit for the twenty-first century, meant to magnify the virtues and minimize the vices of the nation-states that built it. As concerns grow over the unilateral policies of the United States as the one remaining superpower, the inefficiency of the United Nations, and the apparent rise of antidemocratic movements and regimes worldwide, the perception of the European Union as a vanguard form of post-statehood rapidly gains ground.[1]

The "European vanguard" model has temporal as well as spatial dimensions, assessing Europe's position both geographically and in relation to its own history. Current discussions in Europe emphasize that essential to the success of the continental union is a sense of a transnational European identity, based on common values, rooted in a common past, distinguishing the continent from the rest of the world while connecting nations with vastly different cultures.[2] The quest for this European identity however, seems to have fallen far behind the process of creating a common legal and economic system. While changes in national laws and the introduction of the Euro passed relatively smoothly, the rejection of a European constitution in a number of national plebiscites led to renewed debates, a search for an existing "European consciousness" able to hold the union together. All too often however, these debates devolve into an assessment of what, or rather who, is certainly *not* European. Migration in particular gains a central position here by functioning both as a threat uniting the beleaguered European nations and as a trope shifting the focus away from Europe's unresolved identity crisis.

In this essay, I briefly analyze discourses on the continent's future and past as they pertain to memory, identity, and migration. In order to do so, I will trace some of the complicated interactions resulting from the simultaneous construction of a European space, both materially and discursively, in the contemporary global landscape and of a normative European historical memory. My starting point is the notion of an emerging European "public space" and its role in creating a common continental identity. I focus on two recent incidents of what could be defined as the emergence of a "transnational" European public: the widespread antiwar demonstrations in the spring of 2003 and the "riots" in the French *banlieues* in the winter of 2005. Both events not only reflect on the ways in which the Second World War and colonialism are (not) evoked in the process of Europeanization, but also place the European public within the discursive space of two dominant tropes of current global politics, "the war on terror" and "the clash of civilizations," both tied to renewed attempts to create transatlantic Western unity. I believe that the emerging dynamic between migration and post-nationhood that I focus on here might be relevant beyond the European context, offering insights into developments on the other side of the Atlantic as well.

I will approach the events at the center of my analysis partly by way of their assessment by two of Europe's foremost "public intellectuals," Jürgen Habermas and Jean Baudrillard. Habermas's reflection on the meaning of the Western European resistance to the Iraq war and Beaudrillard's view of the uprising on the margins of French society can be seen as emblematic of two versions of postwar Europe—one in which the European Union stands for the successful construction of a civil society out of the ruins left behind by World War II, the other documenting the failure of this attempt. Ultimately, however, I will argue, both interpretations fail to place Europe's post- (and pre-) war history in a global context as they remain caught up in an outdated, solipsistic perspective that continues to place racialized migrant and minority populations outside "Europe."

Worldwide movements of migration have already emerged as one of the central issues in the new millennium. Apart from the material reality of dwindling resources, economic globalization, and internationalized migration regulations, immigration has gained increasing importance as a symbol of the various social, economic and political fears plaguing contemporary Western societies. Migration, both in its material and its discursive incarnation, possesses additional relevance within the European context, where the collapse of the Soviet empire and the process of economic and political unification generate a massive redefinition and reconstruction of borders. Europe is a densely populated continent with ostensibly clearly separated national and cultural, and often by implication ethnic, spaces. The tension between those imagined pure spheres of national identity and actual cultural and ethnic pluralities is not a new phenomenon.[3] It has been intensified, however, in the context of recent developments both within and beyond the continent's borders, which have created a renewed need to define what "Europe" means.

Current debates on the continent's identity seem to indicate that the twentieth century division between insiders and outsiders based on the model of the nation-state is not necessarily diminishing with the European unification, but often merely appears to be shifting to reconfigure migration as a European "problem" that threatens continental as well as national identities. The unified Europe manifests itself increasingly through ethnicized economic bonds: belonging to the Union primarily means having access to economic privileges not available to non-Europeans. In order to prevent or control the access of those non- (or, in the case of the East, not yet) Europeans, the continent's external borders are increasingly fortified.[4] "Fortress Europe," in turn, means that non-Europeans may break the law—and accordingly might be treated as criminals—simply by being present.[5] While the elimination of borders within the union produces increased freedom of movement for some, for others the border is now everywhere. Theoretically, "belonging to" Europe is a question of one's passport, but in everyday life this status is determined along different lines: if there are no systematic border controls regulating access to a particular national space and its resources, these controls must be replaced by informal, widely accepted definitions of (not) belonging. In practice, this frequently translates into racial and religious profiling.[6] The perception of "visible minorities" in European public discourse is still largely determined by long-standing pseudo-biological or implicitly racialized concepts of national, and by extension European, identity that invariably position them as other. Within the new types of omnipresent border policing, two main geographical, cultural, and racial threats are identified, both long-standing European tropes: one in the South, with African migration representing the quintessential racial difference from white Europe; and the other in the Middle East, where Muslim migrants embody the religious/cultural opposition to Christian/enlightened Europe.[7]

Within continental Europe, where nations cling to the notion of Europe as a multiethnic but "white" space, a European seems to be accepted as such only if able to merge with the majority in a rather literal sense. While present for centuries, communities of color continue to be perceived as "foreign matter," stand-ins for the masses beyond the continent's borders. The resistance to accepting the fragile, arbitrary, and ideological nature of these borders is reflected in the peculiar European definition of the term "migrant," at once implying a temporary and a permanent condition: migration appears as always reversible, coming with an expiration date, but at the same time stretching over several generations. Persons born in a European nation, of parents born and raised there as well, are thus routinely identified as "third-generation migrants," manifesting their position outside the community of citizens.[8] The notion that this is a deeply racialized concept is supported by the less than indiscriminate application of the "hereditary" migrant status, which is overwhelmingly attributed to the descendents of nonwhite postcolonial and non-Christian labor migrants.[9] Race and religion thus function as central but largely invisible factors in European concepts of identity.[10] Rather than entering new territory, debates around European identity and political rights are thus frequently sidetracked by discussions of the "Europe compatibility" of particular homogenized and marginalized groups, as if minorities of color could be returned to their "place of origin" if they fail to pass the integration test (and of course, within this racialized setup, they are inevitably doomed to fail).[11] This exclusionary discourse, one could argue, indeed manifests a specific European consciousness in its mobilization of images that have been central to constructing a European identity since the early Middle Ages: the racial threat of Africa and the religious/cultural threat of Islam reappear as key themes in contemporary Europe, constituting a commonality that indeed seems to transcend all national differences (it does not appear coincidental that immigration policies were the first part of the future European legal system that the member states could agree on).[12]

There is little awareness of the actual ethnic diversity in not only contemporary, but also historical Europe—rather, the supposed ethnic homogeneity of the latter is seen as an explanation for the persistent resistance to a multi-ethnic and multireligious conceptualization of the former. National identity revolves around the construction and institutionalization of a common past, whether minorities find a place in the larger community thus also depends on their relation to its narrative of national origin.[13] Usually, migrants are denied "possession" of this common history.[14] At the same time, they and their descendants live the national past as much as the "native" population, while frequently simultaneously functioning as its other. This multidimensional position is turned into its opposite by the exclusionary approach of national historiography which, from its most populist to most sophisticated versions, tends to firmly place migrants of color outside of Europe's past and present. Historiography ascribes "the migrant" (including succeeding generations to the nth level) a flat, one-dimensional existence in which s/he has always just arrived, thus existing only in the present, but like a time traveler simultaneously hailing from a culture that is centuries (or in the case of Africa, millennia) behind, thus making him/her the representative of a past without connection to or influence on the host society's history.[15]

The "European memory" currently debated and constructed as a basis for a transnational continental identity could offer a perfect opportunity to overcome the structural (self-)exclusion of migrants and minorities so often lamented in mainstream discourses. Despite the professed desire to integrate inexplicably reluctant and hostile "foreigners" however, so far it seems as if the internalist focus of national histories will instead be reinscribed in twenty-first century "postnational" discourses, leaving unexplored the myriad ways in which minorities and migrants are part of this history. In current debates, the French Revolution, the Second World War, and the totalitarian systems of fascism and Stalinism, with their implications that obviously reach beyond the nation-state, are used as foundations for a continental European identity, incorporating as well as transcending national experiences. Their postnational Europeanization can also be read however as a continuation of exclusions that already shaped the European nation states. This exclusion is based on what Haitian anthropologist Michel-Rolph Trouillot calls "archival power," that is, "the power to define what is and what is not a serious object of research and, therefore, of mention."[16] By deeming irrelevant the involvement of non-Western and nonwhite populations in World War II and that conflict's effect on them, the proponents of a postnational Europe again reproduce the ideas that "world history" really is white history and that events of global importance take place in the West alone while excusing Western ignorance about the rest of the world. Equally important, this model is necessary to the claim that migrant cultures and European cultures did not touch until the post-war period and thus do not share a common, interdependent history (and by implication, no common, interdependent future). In what follows, I will show how such an "internalist" narrative of Europe is constructed, how it adversely affects migrant and minority communities, and how it is being deconstructed by exactly those groups it is meant to exclude.

II

> Two dates we should not forget: the day when the newspapers presented to their baffled readers the oath of loyalty to Bush by the coalition of the willing, orchestrated by Spain behind the back of the other EU nations; but neither February 15th, 2003, when the protesting masses in London and Rome, Madrid and Barcelona, Berlin and Paris reacted to this surprise coup. The contemporaneity of these overwhelming demonstrations—the largest since the end of World War Two—could in hindsight enter history books as the signal for the birth of a European public.
>
> —Jürgen Habermas, 2003

After the collapse of the Soviet Union and the disappearance of the communist Other within Europe's limits, the extent to which ideological cold war debates were in fact often a reworking of the experience of World War II becomes increasingly obvious.[17] Support for the European unification process is frequently framed within an older model of postwar Western Europe that sees the Second World War in general and the Holocaust in particular as the "end of innocence" of modernity, the (temporary) collapse of Western civilization. The challenge and moral obligation that the postwar West thus faced was to recover and modify the Enlightenment project in a way that would reestablish it as the basis for an international regime of universal human rights. In this view, Europe appears as the driving force in creating a network of international relations and treaties effectively preventing a return to the state of "absolute war" that marked the birth of postmodern Europe.[18] It is this distinctive, paradigmatic European experience that in the eyes of many contributors to current discussions predestines the European Union for a key role in world politics.[19] Aimed at justifying (and demanding) a leading role for a united Europe in twenty-first century global politics, this argument also presents an interpretation of the Second World War that offers a happy ending of sorts: it was after all exactly the descent into anti-Enlightenment and thus ultimately un-European barbarism that motivated the unique success story of the European Union: during the second half of the twentieth century (Western) Europe has repented, has proven that it learned from its mistakes and should thus be granted another shot at world leadership.

While this position becomes increasingly common, it might have been expressed most forcefully in a piece that Jürgen Habermas and Jacques Derrida published in 2003, as part of a concerted action of European intellectuals in response to the Iraq war and the popular Western-European opposition to it.[20] The European public made explicit references to World War II (rather than Vietnam) in its antiwar rhetoric, claiming a voice based on an experience with "total war" that Europeans (but not Americans) share. This position implies a superior moral authority that in fact becomes quite explicit in the Habermas/Derrida piece—and the argument for a European (intellectual) intervention certainly gained weight after being expressed by two of the most influential European philosophers, representing different schools of thought, known for their disagreement on almost everything of philosophical importance, but now united by the urgency of the occasion: Europe having to save the world. Again. Derrida characterized the essay, copublished but written by Habermas, as "the designation of new European political responsibilities beyond any Eurocentrism, the call for a renewed affirmation and effective alteration of international law and its institutions, particularly the United Nations, a new concept and a new practice of the separation of powers etc. in a spirit based on the Kantian tradition."[21] In addition to thus designating the European Union a central role in newly popular cosmopolitan theories, the text touches on many of the key arguments brought forward in favor of united Europe as model for a future world order.

It is entirely justified and potentially useful to ask about the particular role a united Europe might play in contemporary global politics, about the possibilities created by an association that intends to respond to the more than obvious crisis of the nation-state. The dominant answers as expressed in the Habermas/Derrida essay pose a number of problems however, both in their characterization of Europe's past and in their suggestions for a future world order. Of course, the Habermas/Derrida argument did not go unchallenged, but criticism focused primarily on the exclusion of Eastern Europe and the authors' wholesale dismissal of U.S. strategy.[22] Less critical attention was devoted to the matter of course way in which Europe appears as entirely self-contained, the eternal engine of historical development, and the world as divided between "the West" and those who reject its values. In a seemingly generous gesture, Europe's achievements are shared with the world, which thereby is effectively divided along very familiar lines—hardly the same as a departure from Eurocentrism:

> Because Christianity and capitalism, science and technology, Roman law and code Napoleon, a civil-urban lifestyle, democracy and human rights, the secularization of state and society

have spread over other continents, they are not Europe's property anymore. The Western spirit, rooted in Judeo-Christian traditions, certainly has characteristic properties. But the European nations share this way of thinking, defined by individualism, rationalism, and activism, with the United States, Canada, and Australia.[23]

Apart from peculiarly linking "the Western spirit" to European descent, this characterization of Europe as always creating, never receiving repeats a favorite trope of Eurocentrism: that of the continent continuously recreating itself, shaping other cultures but never fundamentally touched by them, a trope tying all "universal" concepts to the West, rejecting notions of "other" modernities, downplaying the influence of Islam on the European renaissance. In short, erasing any sense of a world in which Europe was not the center of "progress." As Stuart Hall has observed, "this has been the dominant narrative of modernity for some time—an 'internalist' story, with capitalism growing from the womb of feudalism and Europe's self-generating capacity to produce, like a silkworm, the circumstances of her own evolution from within her own body."[24] Europe's amazing ability to continuously give birth not only to itself but to every idea and movement of world historic relevance necessarily establishes the European as the normative type of human. Habermas's characterization of the European mentality can be seen as exemplary of this narrative:

Here, citizens are distrustful of transgressions between politics and religion. Europeans have rather a lot of faith in the organizational and governing capacities of the state while being skeptical of the market. They have a distinct understanding of "the dialectic of enlightenment," are not overtly optimistic towards the possibilities of technological progress. They favor the securities of the welfare state and of joint guarantees. Their level of tolerance towards violence against persons is comparatively low. The desire for a multilateral, regulated international order joins in with the hope for an effective world domestic policy [*Weltinnenpolitik*]—through a reformed United Nations. (33)

This rather idealized representation of the European public consciousness is traced back directly to the French Revolution: "The emission of the French revolutionary ideal throughout Europe explains why here politics in both senses, as the medium that secures freedom and as structural power, have a positive value" (33). The French revolution thus functions both as the source of modern European difference and of Eurocentric universalism, since it is assumed that the idea of universal human rights was born there. One could argue however that the promise of the French revolution has been taken nowhere more seriously or put into practice more radically than on the French slave island of St. Domingue that transformed itself into the independent black republic of Haiti—against the violent resistance of Europe's most powerful nations and without any support from either the French revolutionaries or those Enlightenment thinkers whose passionate commitment to the human quest for freedom inspired both the French and the American revolution but was bizarrely detached from contemporary racial slavery.[25] The obvious double standard applied to the black liberation struggle led Michel-Rolph Trouillot to the scathing yet accurate conclusion that "the Haitian revolution was the ultimate test to the universalist pretensions of both the French and the American revolutions. And they both failed."[26]

The immediate application and expansion of the French revolutionary ideals by Europe's colonized, enslaved subjects could have been interpreted as a sign that the "Western spirit" referenced by Habermas is no European property and as an indication of the complex interconnectedness of world cultures before the current "globalization." The contemporary reactions to the uprising on the other hand can draw attention to severe limitations of the European conception of universal rights, challenging the notion of a sudden "fall from grace" in the twentieth century. The Haitian revolution, despite its far-reaching consequences, however, is conspicuously absent from standard accounts of the age of revolutions, the Napoleonic wars (after all, more than a decade before Waterloo, Napoleon's army experienced a devastating defeat in Haiti, prompting him to give up all colonial ambitions in the Americas), or Western history in general. The investment in keeping invisible what challenges fundamental tenets of the Enlightenment narrative continues to limit the ability to envision a non-Eurocentric humanism. Discussions of the meaning of Europe's legacy such as Habermas's, while meant to envision new political formations beyond nationalism, reinforce rather than challenge the existing one that insists that "individualism, rationalism, and activism" are white, "Western" properties.

Just as the Haitian revolution is excluded from the list of universally significant events—which overwhelmingly happen to take place in the West, a West that, as these examples show, is a racial as much as a geographical location—so are people of color excluded from all the markers of Europeanness. This is evident, for example, in the ways the two world wars become a completely Western affair through a denial of the link between the war and colonialism, which provided Europe with non-Western resources, battle sites, and cannon fodder.[27] But of course colonialism itself is the big blank of European history, though it certainly qualifies as a common and identity-shaping experience. Again Habermas's essay summarizes a dominant position that acknowledges and at the same time erases Europe's colonial past:

> Each of the big European nations went through a prime of imperial power, and, more important in our context, through the experience of losing an empire. In many cases, this descent went along with the loss of a colonial empire. With the growing distance from imperial power and colonial history, the European nations received the chance of critically reflecting on themselves. Thus they could learn, from the perspective of the defeated, to see themselves in the dubious position of winners who are held responsible for the violence of an enforced and rootless modernity. This might have advanced the rejection of Eurocentrism and fed the Kantian hope for a *Weltinnenpolitik*.[28]

This position does imply some guilt or rather regret over colonialism. Not for the exploitation, enslavement, and forced underdevelopment of large parts of the world however, but for an "enforced modernity" that although positive overall in retrospect might have been introduced more gently.[29] This image not only denies, or at least minimizes, the disastrous effects of colonialism on the colonized, but also the continued postcolonial exploitation from which Europe profits as much as the United States.[30] This deeply ambivalent attitude, attempting to "save" colonialism while admitting, at least to some degree, that it was wrong is a structural part of Europe's self-representation, also reflected in the European Union declaration on colonialism in the wake of the 2001 Durban conference against racism or the short-lived 2005 French law ordering high school teachers to instruct students on the positive effects of French colonialism (particularly in North Africa).[31] This whitewashing of the colonial past has obvious implications for Europe's perceived role in contemporary global politics in which it appears as a benevolent, neutral mediator, wizened by past mistakes and without a stake in current power struggles. But the effects of this distorted perception of the colonial past are just as stark for intra-European developments: the "internalist" European narrative could not survive an honest scrutiny of the impact of knowledge, resources, and manpower from the global South on European "progress." Furthermore, by excluding colonialism from the list of the key events shaping European identity, the complex effects of colonial rule on contemporary Europe can be ignored or externalized as can its postcolonial populations.

   Instead, Europe continues to imagine itself as an autonomous entity, simultaneously part and whole of the dialectic of progress, untouched by "race matters," occasionally wizened but fundamentally unchanged by its contact with various Others who remain forever outside; a colorblind continent in which difference is marked along lines of nationality and ethnicized Others are routinely ascribed a position outside the nation, allowing the permanent externalization and thus silencing of a debate on the legacy of racism and colonialism. The fact that those who are most emphatically presented as "Others-from-Without"[32] (Jews, blacks, Muslims, Roma, and Sinti) are always (also) "Others-from-Within," and that the "ethnic cleansing," aimed at achieving an already proclaimed national homogeneity has been a key feature of twentieth century European population politics long before the Yugoslavian war introduced the term into the common European vocabulary does not change this binary perception of cultural and national belonging any more than does the long-standing, naturalized European claim to other parts of the world.

What appears thus as an urgent task within the oft-proclaimed quest for a twenty-first century European identity is the exploration of the impact of these neglected aspects of Europe's history (and present), and more so of their inextricable link to the foundational elements of Europeanness. There are a number of possible, symbolically charged, entry points for such an exploration in recent history: 1945, 1989, 2001, or, possibly less obvious, 1961, the year of the Eichmann trial in Jerusalem, marking the end of the "postwar" period and the beginning of a new assessment of the Holocaust; the beginning too of the hot phase of the cold war marked by the building of the Berlin wall and the failed Bay of Pigs invasion; a year also in which more than a hundred Algerians were murdered by French police in the streets of Paris, a largely uncommemorated event exemplifying the repression of European colonial history (and echoing the French army's massacre of Algerian civilians on May 8, 1945);[33] the same year finally that the West German government signed a "guest worker" treaty with Turkey that brought to Europe what is now its largest ethnic and religious minority community, a community, however, that is still perceived as representing whatever is *not* European.[34] The events of 1961, all remembered in varying degrees but rarely together, could be seen as symbolizing the link between colonialism, World War II, cold war politics, and migration that is routinely ignored in discussions of either subject. Instead, in public narratives, colonialism is remembered as having taken place outside of Europe (if it is remembered at all), the war appears as a European event (while there is a dim awareness of the Pacific theater, this is certainly not true of the war's implications for colonized nations and Latin America), the cold war is seen as shaping Europe's postwar history, but not so decolonization, which in turn seems unrelated to migration, appearing as a recent, reversible phenomenon. While the detrimental effects of this compulsively compartmentalized perception of postwar European history are obvious on many levels, they are most urgently felt in the legal, social, and discursive treatment of "migration."[35]

III

> The French can reassure themselves that it is not just theirs but the whole Western model
> which is disintegrating; and not just under external assault—acts of terrorism, Africans
> storming the barbed wire at Melilla—but also from within.
>
> —Jean Baudrillard, 2006

As a result of the provincializing of the world wars, the externalization of colonial rule, and the dehistoricizing of migration, the majority of people of color currently living in Europe are officially and unofficially defined as being part of a "migrant population," even when they were born there. In fact, while the peak of postcolonial and labor migration from the Middle East, North Africa and South Asia occurred in the early 1970s, the children and grandchildren of these migrants are perceived as at least as "un-European" as their ancestors. The context in which this exclusion is currently framed in Europe, even more than in the United States, comprises clash of civilization scenarios that, although far predating 9/11, since then have become the dominant framework for discourses on migrants, especially those of Muslim background, who form Europe's largest religious minority and a substantial part of its migrant population.

The 2005 "riots" in France can function as an illustration of both the culturalist framing of the economic, social, and legal exclusions Europeans of color are facing and of the continent's repressed colonial and racist legacy.[36] The events unfolding in the French *banlieus* seemed to be in complete accordance with dominant discourses: urban minority and migrant youth after all play a prominent role in debates on Europe's demographic and economic future, usually as targets of alarmist discourses around an essentially different, dangerous other within, threatening both Europe's liberal and modern identity and its economic stability. Popular and academic discussions of minority youth focus largely on the male population, usually equating "minority" with "migrant" and migrant with "Muslim." Girls and women remain marginal, noticed almost exclusively as mute, passive victims of their culture, mainly in the context of "honor killings" and in revived debates on headscarf bans, granted a voice only after they, like Ayaan Hirsi Ali and others, have explicitly broken with their community and religion. Male agency on the other hand is framed largely in terms of aggression: Muslim men appear as intolerant and violent, against their communities' women, each other, and the state.[37]

After the death of two teenage boys running from the police, Zyed Benna and Bouna Traore, one of North African the other of West African descent, in the Paris suburb Clichy-sous-Bois on October 27, 2005, long-standing tensions and frustrations erupted in three weeks of unrest that quickly spread from Paris all over the nation (and into neighboring countries such as Germany and Belgium). Violence was concentrated in the larger cities' *banlieus*, officially known as *zones urbaines sensibles*—structurally neglected, isolated neighborhoods with a high concentration of populations originating in France's former African colonies—resulting in about ten thousand torched cars and almost half as many arrests.[38] The conservative government under President Chirac reactivated a state of emergency law first introduced in 1955 in response to the colonial war in Algeria and then French minister of the interior, and current president, Nicolas Sarkozy took a strong man approach in defense of the nation (and Europe), threatening the deportation of the "ringleaders," as if the vast majority of protesters hadn't been French.[39]

The riots garnered Europe-wide media attention, resonating with fears of migrant populations throughout Europe, especially in the Western nations. The question "Could it happen here?" became a constant refrain in a debate that drew on images of violent, criminal minority youths recognized throughout the continent. The destructive rampage of young men of color in the suburbs seemed to validate this perception, offering an almost perfect inversion of the public space created by the white and middle-class protesters against the Iraq war: here the "civil" and "civilized," nonviolent antiwar demonstrations of a liberal European citizenry, there the violent, inarticulate, self-destructing, antidemocratic, and anti-European riots of a black and Muslim underclass. While the European media initially had difficulties classifying the rioters—Arab, African, migrant—most reports, especially those published outside of France, quickly focused on "Muslim" as a central characteristic, as if the young men's religion was an incentive for their violence (this was after all, only a couple of months after the London bombings). The search for the roots of the riots was visibly shaped by this perception: radical Islam, hip-hop gangs were identified as culprits.[40] And while the marginalization of black and Muslim French youth was admitted, their own explanations for the riots were dismissed as insufficient justification for their violent response:[41]

> The police come and hassle us all the time. They ask us for our papers 10 times a day. They treat us like delinquents—especially Sarkozy. That's not the answer. It would be good to have youth clubs and other places to go - then there would be less trouble. It's not good to burn cars but that's one way of getting attention, so people can come and solve our problems.[42]

The coverage of the "riots" was symptomatic in its homogenizing of a hetero-geneous group, externalizing representatives of a postindustrial European ur-banity as a foreign, hostile other. The *banlieus*, though invisible in Habermas's vision of a new Europe, are a public space in many ways symptomatic of the European postindustrial condition of spatial segregation, of borders running through urban centers. Containing superfluous populations, they became foreign territory, an enclave of the non-West, finally invading Europe itself. The Mouvement de l'Immigration et des Banlieues (MIB), founded in 1995, puts the media reports into context:

> Today we are told about these "young people from the suburbs" (by which we are to un-derstand "these Blacks and Arabs") who burn things down as if they were foreigners who came to pillage France.
> And yet from Minguettes (1981) to Vaulx-en-Velin (1990), from Mantes-la-Jolie (1991) to Sartrouville (1991), from Dammarie-les-Lys (1997) to Toulouse (1998), from Lille (2000) to Clichy, the message is plain and clear:
> Enough with unpunished police crimes, enough with police profiling, enough with crappy schools, enough with planned unemployment, enough with rundown housing, enough with prisons, enough with humiliation! And enough with the two-tier justice system which protects corrupt politicians and consistently convicts the weak.[43]

More sympathetic analyses of this decade-long history of failed communication and of conscious structural neglect, creating and containing a native under-class, nonetheless tend to retreat to established "lost between cultures" and "nation within nation" tropes. Accusing the French state (and often European societies in general) of failing the "second generation," the latter is nonetheless naturalized as "foreign," denied the right to become European by the only agent able to grant this right: the majority of "real Europeans." The criticism of European integration policies thus falls short by assuming the existence of a distinct, separate, non-European "culture of poverty" dominating minority communities who are granted little agency in claiming a space within the nation and the continent. Failing to note, as MIB does, the long history of resistance against racialized oppression in France (and Europe), the inability to contextualize within Europe's history minority communities in general and the riots in particular is reflected in the media's frequent reference to 1960s uprisings in the United States. Supported neither through a closer look at U.S. structural racism, nor through a detailing of the supposed parallels, it seems instead that the similarity of "black riots" speaks for itself, leaving the United States as the paradigmatic site of "racial conflict," with Europe drifting dangerously in its direction.[44]

The most prominent dissenting opinion in this Europe-wide public debate, that for the most part granted a voice only to members of the majority culture, used the riots to condemn an unjustified European arrogance, seeing them as the final proof of the failure of liberal democracy. Seemingly taking its inspiration from Aimé Césaire's scathing condemnation of post–World War II bourgeois Europe, but not sharing his concern with the fate of the global South, in this negative Eurocentrism the riots appear as a mere backdrop for the grander narrative of the West's decline. Jean Baudrillard, in his "The Pyres of Autumn," published in the *New Left Review* in early 2006, exemplifies this attitude that condemns Europe for its oppressive and exclusionary policies, but is not able to see those excluded as anything but a fundamentally different Other, ultimately existing only in relation to and for the benefit of greater self-realization for the majority:

> This society faces a far harder test than any external threat: that of its own absence, its loss of reality. Soon it will be defined solely by the foreign bodies that haunt its periphery: those it has expelled, but who are now ejecting it from itself. It is their violent interpellation that reveals what has been coming apart, and so offers the possibility for awareness.[45]

From this internalist perspective, the material and discursive exclusion of minorities becomes equal, and ultimately secondary, to the existential alienation of a European citizenry for whom the nation cannot offer sufficient meaning anymore and whose only remaining power lies in the rejection of Europe—the rejection of the European constitution that is, not that of actual membership:[46]

> Their No was the voice of those jettisoned by the system of representation: exiles too, like the immigrants themselves, from the process of socialization. There was the same recklessness, the same irresponsibility in the act of scuppering the EU as in the young immigrants' burning of their own neighbourhoods, their own schools; like the blacks in Watts and Detroit in the 1960s. Many now live, culturally and politically, as immigrants in a country which can no longer offer them a definition of national belonging.[47]

The blending of drastically different kinds of disenfranchisement and homelessness at play here is problematic on a number of levels, not the least the epistemological (mis)use of "the migrant" as a mere foil for deliberations on the European condition. This account is very different from, for example, Zafer Şenoçak's reflections on how the Turkish minority presence in Germany and its negotiation of a place in the nation's past and present could productively reconfigure the national memory.[48] For Baudrillard, through its daring and convenient refusal to be integrated the minority remains outside Europe and unaffected, its "recklessness" proving a point from the margins while leaving the white center intact:

> Perhaps they consider the French way of life with the same condescension or indifference with which it views theirs. Perhaps they prefer to see cars burning than to dream of one day driving them. Perhaps their reaction to an over-calculated solicitude would instinctively be the same as to exclusion and repression.[49]

The subaltern stubbornly refusing to be domesticated, boogeyman of conservative migration discourses, becomes a romantic hero of this left Eurocentrism. But while he (this is definitely a male figure) might exist, the focus on the modern urban outlaw conveniently keeps intact a clear separation between "French" and "foreign" and ignores the larger context of the riots, born out of the frustration of a population for whom integration is not an option:

> The problem with French-style Republicanism is that you are accepted as long as you fit a certain mould. As soon as you have something that comes from outside, you are no longer viewed as entirely French. You are suspicious.[50]

Rather than religious difference or cultural alienation, economic disparities are at the center of the continued marginalization of Europeans of color. The massive deindustrialization of European urban centers since the 1980s especially affected migrant and minority communities. While postwar industrial metropolises had been in need of unskilled migrant work, contemporary postindustrial centers have moved to the service sector. As a consequence, a working migrant population has been replaced with a multiethnic underclass that represents an example of what Etienne Balibar and others have called "disposable populations," considered superfluous from the moment they are born, with no realistic prospect of being integrated into the system. In postindustrial Europe class thus not only is racialized but also (de)nationalized, placing an ethnicized underclass literally outside of the nation.[51]

The "riots" in the French suburbs were based on the economic desperation of a heterogeneous, racialized, and native underclass (of North and West African descent), their desperation caused exactly by the fact that they *are* French, not migrants. Despite the fact that the "migrant problem" routinely invoked in recent debates over Europe's future usually refers to native Europeans, that is, the second and third generations of migrants, these "visible minorities" remain invisible in the unambiguous discursive divide of "Europeans" and "migrants." It is this persistent exclusion that creates an explosive situation that the culturalist framing of migration discourses works to cover up as much as it does the continued reality of postcolonial exploitation.

IV

> March 25th, 2006, Los Angeles. A multitude of migrants took over the streets and claimed their rights in this biggest demonstration ever seen in the history of the city. This was not an isolated event but rather the culmination of hundreds of other mobilizations taking place in every corner of the US. Millions were involved and they raised simple questions: Can you imagine the US without its migrant population? Can you imagine the impact on the US economy of a single-day strike of all migrant workers? . . . It is . . . worthwhile to raise the same questions in Europe. In fact, it is movements and struggles of migration that are raising these questions in Europe. We believe the answer on the both sides of the Atlantic to be the same.
>
> —The Frassanito Network[52]

If the French "riots" showed the failure of European integration policies, the vast majority of mainstream responses manifest the failure to envision the truly postnational, inclusive Europe postulated by Habermas and Derrida. After the events in France 2005, public attention briefly turned to the obvious consequences of the decade-long economic segregation underlying discourses of cultural Otherness and religious difference. But even while the need for more infrastructure, employment programs, and so on, was conceded, funding for existing measures was cut.[53] Like the momentary attention granted after the *march de beurs* in 1983 or the riots in Les Minguettes in 1996, the "rediscovery" of the *banlieus* by the majority had no lasting consequences. There still is no European framework of analysis for these events; instead the dialectic of amnesia and memory characteristic of European racializations seems in full effect. Punctual analyses warning of a "European apartheid" lead to no lasting change in public attitudes or polices and the only longtime effects are repressive measures, inevitably met with new violent responses.[54]

This pattern proves drastically that the postindustrial minority communities in Europe's metropolises can lay little claim on the universal human rights that a more optimistic sociology of migration attributed to them in the 1990s.[55] It is the lack of recognition within the nation that makes any effective claim to supranational rights difficult, if not impossible. Despite all postnational rhetoric, it is still largely the state's prerogative to grant or withhold these rights. The precarious situation of communities of color lies precisely in their uncertain position within the nation. This precariousness notwithstanding, however, neither the mobilization of anti-immigrant sentiment in the United

States nor the European scapegoating of minority communities can be fully understood in a national context. The fight over who or what is granted free global movement and the ways in which mobility, geographically and socially, across national and internal borders, is restricted and contained, follows patterns that are shaped but not determined by the logic of the nation-state. Movements of resistance, in the United States, Europe, and elsewhere have responded by creating structures both below and above the level of the nation in order to circumvent and counter their marginalization. In order to grasp this complex interaction of commonalities and exclusions, scholarship will have to follow and move beyond the national paradigm and, in the European case, beyond the "postwar" moment. If it includes a break with its internalist tradition, the process of "postnational Europeanization" obviously offers a chance to include formerly excluded populations and narratives. However, it appears as if marginalizations that already shaped the nation state will continue. The interventions of Habermas, Derrida, and Baudrillard, while they should not be given undue importance, do show the complicity of European theory with exclusionary state and social practices, preventing the emergence of a "new European identity" by excluding exactly those groups central to the continent's changed, transnational culture and from whom, against all apparent odds, one might most reasonably expect a constructive intervention. Only a European public that incorporates these voices, as well as its own repressed history, might indeed become postnational.

Notes

1. See Ulrich Beck and Anthony Giddens, "Europa kann nicht auf den Ruinen der Nationen errichtet warden," *Die Welt Online Edition*, October 1, 2005, http://www.welt.de/print-welt/article168315/ Europa_kann_nicht_auf_den_Ruinen_der_Nationen_errichtet_werden.html (accessed June 16, 2008); Perry Anderson, "Depicting Europe," *London Review of Books*, September 20, 2007.

2. See, for example, "Constitution 'Key for EU Success,'" BBC News, January 17, 2007, http://news. bbc.co.uk/2/hi/europe/ 6269349.stm (accessed June 16, 2008).

3. See Etienne Balibar and Immanuel Wallerstein, *Race, Nation, Class, Ambiguous Identities* (London: Verso, 1991); and Rogers Brubaker, *Citizenship and Nationhood in France and Germany* (Cambridge, Mass.: Harvard University Press, 1992).

4. See European Council on Refugees and Exiles, http://www.ecre.org; People Flow: Migration in Europe, open democracy dossier, http://www.opendemocracy.net/people-migrationeurope/issue.jsp (accessed June 16, 2008).

5. European Union refugee policies are part of the increasing use of prisons and internment camps as a means of population management, and incarceration is not based on an individual criminal act or even a court sentence but on belonging to the wrong group, that is, on lacking "legitimate" ties to privileged spaces. See the recent United Nations High Commission on Refugees (UNHCR) condemnation of

Germany's refugee policy, "UNHCR wirft Deutschland in Flüchtlingsfrage Völkerrechtsbruch vor," *Neue Rhein Zeitung*, August 10, 2007, http://rhein-zeitung.de/a/ticker/t/rzo35543.htm (accessed June 4, 2008).

6. The extended jurisdiction of border police now includes the right to exert control anywhere, independent of "suspicious circumstances," if the patrol suspects a violation of immigration laws. Numerous complaints indicate that this translates into profiling of people of color and Muslims—while in fact the majority of "illegal" immigrants in the Union are white and Christian: Eastern Europeans, Ukrainians, and Russians. See Jochen Becker, http://www.moneynations.ch/topics/euroland/text/bahn. htm, *Euroland*, http://www.moneynations.ch/texte (accessed June 16, 2008).

7. One could argue that in recent years, these two groups are used to represent the internal and external threat migration presents for Europe: Muslim communities in Europe have come to stand for all the "migrants" already there or, rather, for those migrants that will remain "unassimilated" due to their inherently foreign culture, while West Africans, trying to reach Southern Europe by boat from North Africa (with as many as ten thousand people drowning in the process each year) stand for potential migrants, the vast masses in the global South threatening to overrun the wealthy West. See below.

8. Despite the obvious failure of the concept behind the original "guest worker" program, which assumed that a large number of people could be transplanted temporarily into another society without becoming part of it, ready to be returned unchanged after some years, the current European Union negotiations around "controlled" migration from West Africa are based on the very same idea. See Dominic Johnson, "Afrika schmiedet Europa zuammen," *Die Tageszeitung*, November 23, 2006, http://www.taz.de/index.php?id=archivseite&dig=2006/11/23/a0139 (accessed June 16, 2008).

9. The opposition between second-generation "French" Catholic Nicolas Sarkozy (whose Hungarian father acquired citizenship by serving in the French Foreign League in Algeria) and the "third-generation migrants" of North and West African descent is a case in point. See Michel Gurfinkiel, "A Battle Royal," *Weekly Standard*, February 26, 2007 (vol. 12, no. 23).

10. In the wake of the admission of ten new European Union members from the eastern part of the continent and renewed negotiations with Turkey, and in reaction to the assassination of Dutch filmmaker Theo van Gogh by a young Muslim, the religious undertones of current European debates have become much more explicit. See Alan Travis and Madeleine Bunting, "British Muslims Want Islamic Law and Prayers at Work," *The Guardian*, November 30, 2004; Ilya Meyer, "*Swedish Children for Sale*," *FrontPageMagazine*, November 29, 2004; Dominik Cziesche et al., "*Fighting the Preachers of Hate*," *Der Spiegel*, November 26, 2004; Tom Hundley, "*Europeans in No Mood to Welcome Turkey*," *Chicago Tribune* and Yahoo! News, November 26, 2004; "*A Civil War on Terrorism*," *The Economist*, November 25, 2004; William Pfaff, "*Europe Pays the Price for Its Cultural Naïveté*," *International Herald Tribune*, November 25, 2004; "*Some 20,000 Protest in Cologne Against Violence in the Name of Islam*," AFP and Yahoo! News, November 21, 2004; Anthony Browne, "*Belgian MP Goes into Hiding After Criticising Muslims*," *The Times*, November 19, 2004; and Mary Riddell, "The Roots of Prejudice," *The Observer*, November 7, 2004.

11. Again, this is especially obvious in the case of black Europeans, who are stubbornly considered "migrants," and European Muslims, whose presence is discussed as if they were not already an integral part of the continent's makeup. A special case is presented by Roma and Sinti, who have been present in most parts of Europe since the fifteenth century but are nevertheless still denied the right of belonging (European Commission Directorate-General for Employment and Social Affairs, *The Situation of Roma in an Enlarged European Union* [Luxembourg: Office for Official Publications of the European Communities, 2004]; Andrey Ivanov et al., *At Risk: Roma and the Displaced in Southeast Europe* [Bratislava: United Nations Development Programme 2006]; European Roma Rights Center, *The Glass Box: Exclusion of Roma from Employment* [Budapest, 2007]).

12. It is certainly no coincidence that not a single European nation has signed the "International Convention on the Protection of the Rights of All Migrant Workers and Members of Their Families," http://www.unhchr.ch/html/menu3/b/m_mwctoc.htm (accessed June 16, 2008).

13. This narrative has lost none of its importance in these postnational times: in part it reappears in debates around a European identity, and in part, as Etienne Balibar claims, the discourse on the "end of the nation-states" is really one with its origins in *We, the People of Europe? Reflections on Transnational Citizenship* (Princeton, N.J.: Princeton University Press, 2004), 14.

14. As Zafer Şenoçak writes about the specific situation of Turkish Germans: "One can immigrate into a country, but not to its past. In Germany, history is read as a diary of the 'community of fate,' the

nation's personal experience, to which Others have no access." Zafer Şenoçak and Leslie A Adelson, *Atlas of a Tropical Germany: Essays on Politics and Culture 1990–1998* (Lincoln: University of Nebraska Press, 1999), 53.

15. See Maurice Crul and Hans Vermeulen, "The Future of the Second Generation: The Integration of Migrant Youth in Six European Countries," *International Migration Review*, Special Issue 37.4 (2003): 965–86; Mark Terkessidis, *Die Banalität des Rassismus Transcript* (Bielefeld: Verlag, 2004).

16. Michel-Rolph Trouillot, *Silencing the Past: Power and the Production of History* (Boston: Beacon Press, 1995), 99.

17. See the special issue of *National Identities* The Re-thinking of the Second World War since 1989 (August 4, 2006).

18. For an influential critique of this understanding of modernity from the perspective of diaspora studies, see Paul Gilroy, *The Black Atlantic: Modernity and Double Consciousness* (Cambridge, Mass.: Harvard University Press, 1993), 420.

19. See Slavoj Žižek, "A Leftist Plea for 'Eurocentrism,'" in *Unpacking Europe*, edited by Salah Hassan and Iftikhar Dadi (Rotterdam: NAI, 2001), 112–30; Anderson, "Depicting Europe."

20. Jürgen Habermas and Jacques Derrida, "Unsere Erneuerung. Nach dem Krieg. Europas Wiedergeburt," *Frankfurter Allgemeine Zeitung*, May 31, 2003. Simultaneously, articles were published by Umberto Eco in *La Repubblica*, Adolf Muschg in the *Neue Zürcher Zeitung*, Fernando Savater in *El País*, Gianni Vattimo in *La Stampa*, and Richard Rorty in the *Süddeutsche Zeitung*.

21. Habermas and Derrida, "Unsere Erneuerung," 33, my translation.

22. See Ivan Krastev, "Nicht ohne mein Amerika," *Die Zeit*, August 14, 2003; Harold James, "Aussenpolitik missverstanden: Europa schwelgt in gefährlicher Sehnsucht," *Sueddeutsche Zeitung*, June 3, 2003. For a more thorough critique see Marion Iris Young, "Europe and the Global South: Towards a Circle of Equality," August 20, 2003, www.opendemocracy.net (accessed June 16, 2008). Young points out, among other things, that the starting point of Habermas's argument, the huge antiwar protests all over Western Europe on February 15, 2003, which he terms the birth of a new European public, were in fact part of a *global* movement in which Europe was involved but not central (ibid., 2).

23. Habermas and Derrida, "Unsere Erneuerung," 33.

24. Stuart Hall, "Europe's Other Self," *Marxism Today*, August 1991, 18.

25. See, for example, Trouillot, *Silencing the Past*; Susan Buck-Morss, "Hegel and Haiti," *Critical Inquiry* 26 (2000): 821–65.

26. Trouillot, *Silencing the Past*, 88.

27. This history left its traces within Europe as well as outside of it, including, for example, the Muslim burial ground in the German town Mainz, housing the graves of French colonial soldiers who died during the post-WW I occupation of the German Rhineland.

28. Habermas and Derrida, "Unsere Erneuerung," 33.

29. This sentiment was echoed almost verbatim by French president Nicolas Sarkozy in a speech on Africa's future given in Senegal in the summer of 2007—to the understandable dismay of his audience. See Dominic Johnson, "Sarkozy befremdet Afrika," *Die Tageszeitung*, August 1, 2007, 1.

30. See Young, "Europe and the Global South"; Jean Ziegler, *L'empire de la honte* (Fayard: Paris, 2005).

31. European Commission, Council Conclusions 2001. The EU commission statement failed to define colonialism as a crime against humanity and instead condemned only aspects of it. The French law, passed in February 2005, was repealed a year later after massive protests; see, for example, *Claude Liauzu*, "*Une loi contre l'histoire*," *Le Monde diplomatique*, April 2005, 28.

32. Michelle Wright, *Becoming Black: Creating Identity in the African Diaspora* (Durham. N.C.: Duke University Press, 2004).

33. Since October 17, 2001, a plaque on St. Michel bridge in Paris does commemorate the event, whose near-complete suppression for 40 years nonetheless seems both stunning and characteristic (BBC News, October 17, 2001, http://news.bbc.co.uk/2/hi/world/monitoring/media_reports/1604970. stm (accessed June 16, 2008).

34. This is a community, moreover, that despite its longstanding presence in Western Europe is still primarily, if not exclusively, perceived to belong with the Turkish nation-state, whose attempts to enter the European Union in turn have been denied for half a century largely due to its majority Muslim population.

35. This is exemplified by the Dutch case: the dates of both the invasion of and the liberation from the German occupiers are keystones of ritualized national memory formations, the internment of Dutch

colonizers in Indonesia after the Japanese invasion is marginal by comparison but nevertheless part of the mainstream narrative. Surinamese soldiers fighting in Europe on the other hand have been written out of this narrative. Only in the 1990s were they for the first time included in the annual honoring of the war veterans, while the suffering of the Indonesians at the hands of the Dutch is rarely if ever related to the Dutch suffering at the hands of the Japanese.

36. Despite the central place of the Holocaust in European rituals of remembrance, its lasting effects on European societies remain understudied. In an astonishing act of suppression the "ethnic homogeneity" of postwar Europe upset by the beginning of large-scale labor migration often remains unrelated to the unprocessed "disappearance" of the Jewish minority population. See Amira Hass, *Drinking the Sea at Gaza: Days and Nights in a Land Under Siege* (New York: Holt 2000), 8.

37. See Fatima El-Tayeb, "Urban Diasporas: Race, Identity, and Popular Culture in a Post-Ethnic Europe," in *Motion in Place/Place in Motion: 21st Century Migration*, JCAS Symposium Series 22, Population Movement in the Modern World, October 2006, Tokyo.

38. See, for example, Yves Coleman, "The French Riots: Dancing with the Wolves," http://www.solidarity-us.org/node/33 (accessed June 16, 2008), January 1, 2006; Michael Kleeberg, "Apartheid in Europa," *Die Welt*, November 12, 2005; Anne-Marie Vaterlaus, "Les Minguettes," *Neue Zürcher Zeitung*, December 9, 2006.

39. Alain Morice, "Comprendre avant de juger: à propos des émeutes urbaines en France," January 24, 2006, samizdat.net.

40. See Sylvia Poggioli, "French Rap Musicians Blamed for Violence," NPR World, August 6, 2006.

41. See, for example, Craig Smith, "France Has an Underclass, but Its Roots Are Still Shallow," *New York Times*, November 6, 2005. The article is also indicative in its historical analysis, contrasting the marginalization of African Americans, based on centuries of racial oppression, with the new "phenomenon of post-war ethnic minorities in France, completely ignoring the effects of centuries of colonial rule on the structural racism shaping the relationship between the majority and these groups."

42. Mehmet Altun, 15, from Clichy-sous-Bois, interviewed for BBC News during the riots, http://news.bbc.co.uk/2/shared/spl/hi/picture_gallery/05/europe_paris_riot_suburb_residents/html/6.stm.

43. I am using here the English translation published at http://sketchythoughts.blogspot.com/2005/11/communique-from-mouvement-de.html#jumpto. For the French original of the MIB statement, published on November 9, 2005, see http://lenumerozero.lautre.net/spip.php?article743.

44. See Kleeberg, "Apartheid in Europa"; Isolde Charim, "Wirklichkeit wird sichtbar," *Die Tageszeitung*, August 11, 2005; and Jean Baudrillard, "The Pyres of Autumn," *New Left Review* 37 (Jan/Feb 2006).

45. Baudrillard, "The Pyres of Autumn," 6.

46. See, for example, Anderson, "Depicting Europe."

47. Baudrillard, 7.

48. Zafer enoçak and Leslie A. Adelson, "Atlas of a Tropical Germany," in *Essays on Politics and Culture, 1990–1998* (Lincoln: University of Nebraska Press, 1999).

49. Budrillard, 7.

50. Samia Amara, a twenty-three-year-old youth worker, interviewed by BBC News during the riots (http://news. bbc.co.uk/2/hi/europe/4376500.stm). The riots took place twenty-two years after the *March of Beurs*, attended by more than 100,000 people, the high point of a nonviolent movement demanding equal rights for French minorities (Doug Ireland, "Why Is France Burning?" *The Nation*, November 28, 2005). According to a 1995 poll, 70% of second-generation Maghrebis said they felt closer to the French than to their parents' culture and 90% wanted to be integrated into French society. At the same time, less than a third of the majority population saw the *beurs* as French, and almost 80% of acts of racist violence and more than 90% of racist murders were committed against Maghrebis (Hargraves 1997, 19).

51. This happens both legally, through denying citizenship to (some) descendents of migrants, with all the implications for access to jobs, social services, and so on this has, and discursively through the persistent definition of minority youth as "migrants."

52. The Frassanito Network is a Europe-wide coalition of migrant activist groups founded in 2003.

53. Doug Irelands counts "60 percent cuts over the past three years in subsidies for neighborhood groups that work with youths, and budgets slashed for job training, education, the fight against illiteracy

and for neighborhood police who get to know ghetto kids and work with them. After the first riots in Toulouse, Sarkozy told the neighborhood police there, "Your job is not to be playing soccer with these kids; your job is to arrest them!" (Ireland, "Why Is France Burning?").

54. See Coleman, "The French Riots." Most recently, French President Sarkozy, whose "zero tolerance" stance during the 2005 riots arguably both helped to escalate the situation and helped to win him the presidential elections, ordered a sweep of the Parisian suburb of Villiers-le-Bel, center of the 2007 riots. The deployment of more than 1,000 police systematically searching the neighborhood and arresting several dozen people hardly qualifies as a change of policy ("French Police Target Riot Leaders," *BBC News*, February 18, 2008, http://news.bbc.co.uk/w/hi/europe/7250102.stm).

55. See Yasemin N. Soysal, *Limits of Citizenship: Migrants and Postnational Membership in Europe* (Chicago: University of Chicago Press, 1994); and Miriam Feldblum, "'Citizenship Matters': Contemporary Trends in Europe and the United States," *Stanford Electronic Humanities Review* 5.2 (1997).

Enforcing Transnational White Solidarity: Asian Migration and the Formation of the U.S.-Canadian Boundary

Kornel Chang

In the summer of 1909, hundreds of migrant Japanese laborers from Washington State besieged the offices of the Japanese consul in Vancouver. Due to what one observer described as a "peculiar operation of the United States immigration law," these Japanese, who had migrated from Washington to work for several months in Canada, were barred from reentering the United States. Described as "mostly men who have worked on farms, sawmills and other laboring employment in the state of Washington," they had come to the Fraser River in Vancouver, anticipating a prolific salmon run. Denied the privilege of returning to their homes and with their future plans in doubt, the men held "indignation meetings" and discussed "vigorously every possible suggestion that affords a way out of their dilemma." In their appeals to the Japanese consul, they insisted that they had "lived a number of years in the United States" and had "made such trips before returning to the south without hindrance heretofore."[1] Indeed, the claims made by the Japanese laborers were supported by none other than the Immigration Bureau itself. In an earlier report from the field, immigration inspector C. A. Turner confirmed that "it is the custom to allow all of these aliens to cross the boundary at will for trading or other purposes, there being no watch of any kind kept on roads leading into Blaine from Canada and no check obtained of the number who came or returned."[2]

The Japanese migrant workers, as this story suggests, were caught in the midst of broader spatial and social transformations unfolding in the Pacific Northwest. The fluid and imprecise transborder world they once knew and experienced was slowly receding as North American regimes, in efforts to regulate and discipline Asian mobility, drew and enforced a new racialized geography of exclusion. The Pacific Northwest borderlands once associated with cross-border labor opportunities, commercial exchange, and social visits gradually faded giving rise to a more hardened spatial discipline. Facing an ever-expanding system of surveillance and control, Asian migrants soon discovered they could no longer freely transgress the boundary as they once had. What was formerly a poorly coordinated amalgam of customs officers and local deputies had evolved into a complex web of institutions and practices including courts, processing and detention centers, border patrolmen, and immigration inspectors. These developments allowed the state to collect information, distribute regulations, and impose spatial order, all of which had the effect of legitimizing and expanding the reach of sovereign power into the everyday life and community of Asian immigrants on both sides of the boundary line.

At the turn of the twentieth century, Canada and the United States elaborated new forms of sovereignty in an attempt to control Asian migration around the Pacific and across landed borders in North America. This joint effort at Asiatic exclusion helped codify immigration and boundary controls as rightful prerogatives of the nation-state, which in turn, reconstructed racial and national borders through its practical enforcement. The process transformed the U.S.-Canadian boundary from an imaginary abstraction to a social reality on the North American Pacific Rim. The mutual opposition to Asian migration wove Canada and the United States together into an Anglo-American alliance in defense of a "white man's country"—the ideology of settler colonialism that declared the western frontiers the exclusive preserve of Anglo-American civilization.[3] In contrast, on the southern boundary, where illegal Asian border-crossings also raised concern, the United States, because of conflicting national interests and historically strained relations with Mexico, unilaterally enforced the border.[4] The comity of whiteness, on the other hand, encouraged bilateral cooperation and coordination between Canada and the United States in the north. Indeed, bound by their commitment to white supremacy, Anglo-American governments of North America worked in collaboration to construct and maintain the U.S.-Canadian border as a bulwark against Chinese, Japanese, and South Asian migrants. This jointly invented border, then, was the spatial expression of transnational white solidarity in the Pacific Northwest.

The evolution of this hardened border, however, rather than the simple culmination of coercive state policies and regulations, was instead the outcome of a protracted struggle between white workers, Asian migrants, labor-contractors, smugglers, capitalist interests, and local civil servants who were locked in a contest over the permeability of the boundary. Indeed the border was constructed from above and below with everyday interactions, conflicts, and negotiations between migrants, the state, and local society being integral to the process. These struggles were transnational in scope, involving contests over Asian migration that extended across the Pacific world. This account, therefore, examines the role of transpacific and transborder labor recruitment, white labor activism, racial politics, and state practices and regulations in the construction of the U.S.-Canadian boundary. In doing so, it highlights the contested and contingent history of border-formation in the Pacific Northwest, as well as the transnational context in which it took shape.

Chinese Exclusion and the Rise of Illegal Immigration

Between 1882 and 1917, the United States and Canada instituted a series of immigration policies designed to restrict and regulate Asian immigration to North America. Taken together, the various exclusion laws, head taxes, and executive agreements facilitated a process by which Asian groups beginning with the Chinese—and later, Japanese, Koreans, and South Asians—emerged as the nation's first "illegal" immigrants.[5] Yet even as these measures aimed to restrict Asian migration and movement to North America, they also created new and unintended problems and consequences for the modern state. The U.S. architects of the Chinese Exclusion Act (1882), which excluded Chinese immigrants with the exception of certain exempt classes, did not anticipate that excluded Chinese laborers would exploit the nation's landed borders to secure admission.

Following the passage of the Exclusion Act, the Federal Government assigned the task of enforcing the exclusion laws to the United States Customs Service which up to that point had no prior experience in such matters. Within this department, the government created an official position known as the "Chinese inspector," responsible for screening Chinese immigrants entering the United States. In the Pacific Northwest, this small cadre of inspectors determined the eligibility of Chinese immigrants seeking admission, primarily in Seattle and other seaports, while leaving the border for the most part, unguarded. Although first made aware of the problem of illegal Chinese border-crossers in the 1880s, U.S. Customs Inspectors cited limited resources as the primary reason for the lack of proper border enforcement.[6]

The situation was not much different on the British Columbian side. Apart from the occasional sighting by the North-West Mounted Police, movement across the U.S.-Canadian boundary went virtually unregulated. The Mounties were more concerned with the movement and activities of indigenous Indian groups and militant industrial laborers in the Canadian West than with migrant Asian workers.[7] There was good reason for this: in Canada, after all, Chinese immigrants found it less trouble to simply pay the head tax of fifty dollars than to attempt more clandestine means of illegal entry.[8] This policy difference—with Canada instituting a poll tax as opposed to outright exclusion—decisively shaped the direction of illegal Chinese immigration, which flowed from north to south or from British Columbia to Washington State.

The white-working class, fresh off its successful political campaign to exclude Chinese immigrants, culminating in the passage of the Chinese Exclusion Act in 1882, objected vehemently to the cross-border migration and movement of Chinese transients. Certain that they were rid of the so-called coolie problem, reports of illegal Chinese laborers migrating across the northern border riled the region's white-working class, inspiring a new round of labor agitation and unrest. Indeed, the cross-border passages of Chinese sojourners from Canada helped precipitate the race riots that swept through and paralyzed the Pacific Northwest region in the mid-1880s.

Washington pioneer Frederic Grant attributed early anti-Asiatic sentiments and organizing to Chinese transborder labor and mobility. "During the construction of the Canadian Pacific railroad," Grant wrote, "large numbers of Chinamen had been at work in British Columbia," however, "on the completion of that work they were discharged and crossed into Washington Territory, congregating principally at Seattle, Tacoma, and Olympia," and "their presence swelled the number of Chinese laborers at these points and furnished to anti-Chinese orators additional arguments to excite the laboring element of the population."[9] The riots proved to the state that it needed to take a more active role in enforcing its territorial boundaries. Commissioner-General of Immigration Terence Powderly initiated this process by expanding the force of immigration inspectors in the northern Pacific region and by establishing tighter controls over the U.S.-Canadian border under his tenure.[10] As we shall see, the anti-Asian politics of the white-working class was crucial in promulgating the northern boundary. The process of elaborating national borders and boundaries required the elucidation of social distinctions between "citizens" and "aliens"—defining those who were included and excluded from the body politic. The region's white-working class was at the center of producing these inclusions and exclusions on the U.S.-Canadian boundary.

The labor unrest and social upheaval resulting from the unanticipated flow of Chinese migrants also prompted the U.S. government to seek the collaborative assistance of their northern neighbors in rooting out what they believed to be a problem common to both nations. As reported by a Dominion official in the foreign ministry: "The United States Minister called at this Office today and spoke to me respecting the exclusion of Chinese subjects from the United States. The Chinese, he said, were in the habit of using Canada as a stepping stone to enter the territory of the United States and his government would be glad if the Canadian government could give their assistance in preventing this practice."[11] With the initiation of this exchange, a long, productive, and yet at times, contentious partnership over the issues of unauthorized Asian immigration and border management was born.

The U.S. Immigration Service, in what was known as the "Canadian Agreement," extended its bureaucratic powers and laws beyond its own borders. While the arrangement went through several revisions during the 1890s and 1900s, the core of the agreement was to have all U.S.-bound Chinese immigrants traveling through Canada directed to designated ports along the Canadian border, where they would be subject to U.S. immigration protocol and standards, before being allowed to proceed to the United States. Upon passing inspection, Chinese immigrants received certificates of admission which would then be presented to border authorities on the U.S. side. The intent behind these measures was to "establish the same level of control over Chinese immigration through Canada as it had over Chinese sailing directly into the United States." The goal was to preempt illegal cross-border migrations.[12] According to historian Erika Lee, this was part of a larger strategy which "centered on border diplomacy based on a historically amicable diplomatic relationship and a shared antipathy for Chinese immigration." Lee argues that this approach contrasted markedly from the one the U.S. government took for the southern boundary where they relied "more upon border policing, a system of surveillance, patrols, apprehensions, and deportation."[13]

However, this dichotomy between border diplomacy and policing fails to capture the full complexity of U.S. border policies during this period as the state's disjointed efforts to consolidate territorial sovereignty defied easy categorization. First, efforts to solve the problem through diplomatic channels ran up against the subversive mobility of Chinese immigrants who were intent on circumventing the international agreements designed to keep them out. Devising new cross-border migratory strategies and networks, the Chinese contested the policies of "border diplomacy," forcing the state to come up with different tactics and approaches for enforcing the northern boundary. Secondly, the border was not simply the invention of governmental policies, resulting from diplomatic negotiations between nation-states, but was also the outcome of everyday contests over space and mobility. Finally, other Asian groups, besides the Chinese, shaped and informed the process of border-formation in the Pacific Northwest. The arrival of Japanese and South Asian migrants created the impetus for a renewed emphasis on border control and management at the turn of the twentieth century.

The "Canadian Agreement"—the supposed diplomatic solution to the problem of Chinese migration—had major flaws, which the Chinese were quick to exploit. It failed to account for the Chinese already residing in the region, and, more importantly, for newly arriving immigrants who were increasingly claiming British Columbia as their final destination, paying the poll tax, and then surreptitiously crossing the largely unguarded border into the United States. This issue would later become a source of tension between the neighboring nations. An often heard complaint within official U.S. circles was that "British Columbia gets the money and we get the Orientals."[14] Thus, despite their diplomatic efforts, the problem of illegal Chinese migration across the U.S.-Canadian border persisted. Therefore, the United States, while continuing to cooperate with Canada over the issue of unauthorized Chinese border migrations, developed a parallel system of policing and surveillance to detect and apprehend illegal Chinese border crossers in the Pacific Northwest. As this suggests, border enforcement strategies were fluid as the state reacted and revised their policies according to shifts in Chinese migration patterns in a cat-and-mouse-like game.

The border region extending from west of the Cascade Mountains to the Pacific Ocean presented authorities with enormous challenges. Aside from the problem of sheer size and space, these vast expanses of rugged and varied terrain provided would-be border crossers with a labyrinth of dirt roads and forest trails leading back and forth across the international line. If that was not enough, the natural waterways of the Puget Sound furnished yet another avenue for smugglers and illegal aliens. The broad and deep Puget Sound, which hooked far into Washington, was cluttered with tiny islands and ragged peninsulas and teemed with fishing trawlers, sail boats, and oceangoing ships, prompting Immigrant Inspector John Sargent to call the "district one of the most difficult in the United States to guard against the surreptitious entry of unlawful aliens."[15]

From the outset, Chinese merchant contractors played a major role in creating and sustaining the cross-border traffic of unauthorized immigrants. In the late nineteenth and early twentieth centuries, Chinese labor brokers in Seattle and Vancouver imported workers from along the Asia-Pacific Rim and across landed borders in North America, acting as chief suppliers of cheap foreign labor to the region's resource-based economy.[16] Developments which acted to curtail this migration, such as the anti-Chinese riots of 1885 and the Exclusion Act of 1882, led to a sharp reduction in the supply of labor available to Chinese contractors on the U.S. side. Labor smuggling across the border became one of the ways Chinese merchants in Washington attempted to make up the difference. Consider the following cross-border smuggling scheme arranged by several Chinese merchants in 1900:

> Acting on information already gained, C. K. and Colonel Hill left Blaine, Washington, for the farm of Hop Lee, located some 9 miles from Blaine, and in B.C., and near the small town of "Cloverdale." [Hop Lee] was in the smuggling of Opium, and Chinese, that he made his farm, a depot for the Chinese to rest in, until their contractors could secure their landing, by guiding them over the border. That he had then, some 40 Chinamen, waiting to be landed, in this way. That these Chinamen belonged to Toy Wing, Wong Good, Yong Goon, and Goon Me Kan, smugglers who reside in Seattle, when at home.[17]

The *Seattle Union Record*, complained bitterly about the illegal cross-border trafficking of Chinese. "The Chinese cheerfully pay the Canadian poll tax of $50, but 90 percent of them do not stay more than a week, but go immediately to the other side of the line, where by law their entrance is barred."[18] U.S. immigration officials estimated that several thousand Chinese gained admissions surreptitiously through the northern border from the 1880s to the early 1900s; many of those were undoubtedly assisted or coordinated by merchant-contractors of the Pacific Northwest. The bureau's 1902 annual report stated alarmingly that the "Canadian border has become the most prolific field for the introduction into the United States of the Chinese coolie."[19]

U.S. customs inspectors lacking the manpower and resources to address the problem at the point of entry responded by scrutinizing the status of Chinese laborers in the interior of the state. On this front, the passage of the Geary Act in 1892, which required that all Chinese laborers possess a certificate of residency or be subject to deportation, made such a strategy possible. On a routine basis, inspectors conducted unannounced inspections and raids of canneries, laundries, merchant stores, and other major business operations suspected of employing illegal aliens to check and validate the certificate of any and all Chinese. This policing of everyday life put all Chinese peoples and communities—including those with proper documentation—under a cloud of suspicion as they became increasingly associated with what anthropologist Nicholas De Genova calls "migrant illegality."[20]

It was a well-known fact that contractors smuggled Chinese migrants from Victoria, B.C. to the Puget Sound canneries during the salmon season.

"The average amount of Chinese employed by each Cannery [is] about 300, therefore you may judge as to the amount admitted each year. This traffic has been carried on for many years, I am told, and they feel very safe."[21] On a typical tour in 1898, Inspectors Sargent and Schulyer paid visits to canneries in Anacortes and Fidalgo Island, reviewing several hundred Chinese certificates in the process but unable to make a single arrest.[22] The reason for the lack of arrests may be explained by Inspector Fisher's findings in a subsequent visit in the fall of 1899. When making a similar tour of canneries in Fairhaven and Whatcom, he learned that the Chinese knew of his inspection a week prior to his arrival. Chinese cannery workers had developed an organized network of communication for sharing information and tipping off fellow workers to potential inspections and raids. Inspector Fisher was informed that "they were on the watch for him, and the first call that he made, word was sent to all other Canneries, and the Chinese hid themselves by opening up the floor and sliding down the piling, to the water below where they remained until after the Inspector's departure."[23]

While authorities were actively engaged in everyday efforts to police and check illicit Chinese in their midst, other Asian nationalities not subject to legal exclusion—more specifically, the Japanese and to a lesser extent, South Asians—began to migrate and settle in significant numbers.[24] Like their Chinese predecessors, Japanese—and later South Asian—migrant laborers were drawn by the opportunities created by railroad construction and the rise of extractive industries in the Pacific Northwest. Many of the new Asian immigrants occupied the bottommost positions formerly held by the Chinese. "Chinese hands have become so scarce," remarked one Canadian cannery owner, "that we simply have to take any labor that offers itself and the Hindus may aid us in solving the problem of how to provide ourselves with robust labor to do the hundred and one odd jobs around a cannery which in the past have been performed by the Chinese."[25]

The growing presence of these new Asian immigrants did not go unnoticed however. Albert Johnson, who would later become chair of the House Committee on Immigration and Naturalization and chief architect of the National Origins Act of 1924, launched his political career as an exclusionist by writing against Japanese immigration for the *Tacoma Daily News*. With the assistance of an informant in Victoria, British Columbia, Johnson was able to "receive the first information as to the number of Japanese coolies arriving on each Northern Pacific packet." The title of one of his many articles on the subject reads as follows: "(SPECIAL DISPATCH)-PASSED IN AT 10 A.M. S.S. TACOMA WITH 1,763 JAPANESE COOLIES ABOARD."[26]

In a familiar discourse, fastened earlier to the Chinese, white nativists linked the Japanese and South Asians to a host of social ills, charging them with depressing wages, displacing white workers, breeding and carrying disease, and debasing moral standards. "From every part of the coast complaints are made" of the undesirability of newly arriving Asian immigrants including "their lack of cleanliness, disregard of sanitary laws, petty pilfering, and insolence to [white] women," declared the Asiatic Exclusion League.[27]

Despite this sentiment, there was no specific legal proscription against Japanese migration at this time and it was not until the Gentleman's Agreements of 1907 that the U.S. and Canadian governments placed any formal limitations on immigration from Japan. Prior to these diplomatic accords, in which the Japanese government pledged to issue passports only to certain exempt classes, the Japanese emigrated and settled the North American West without restriction. Japanese sojourners exploited this freedom of mobility to pursue and sustain familial, cultural, and economic interests and ties on both sides of the imaginary line, and in the process, were part of circular networks of migration and exchange that connected the American Pacific Northwest and Canadian West at its common border in the late nineteenth and early twentieth centuries.

In the absence of formal exclusionary laws, the Immigration Bureau attempted to construct Japanese-migrant illegality by enforcing existing statutes and regulations within U.S. immigration law regarding foreign contract labor. Local immigration authorities alleged that the Japanese coming across the border from British Columbia were contract laborers, imported by capitalists and industrialists on the U.S. side. Immigrant inspector C. W. Snyder, for example, reported that:

> Port Blakely, located nine miles across the bay from here, is becoming the popular place for smuggled Japanese to be landed. I have been over there several times and have done all in my power to intercept them but I am known and I can see no way of accomplishing the results desired but by having some good man employed for one month to watch the beach where it is reported the boats land them, and catch them in the act. A gang of twelve to fifteen at a time can be safely landed and as soon as they can get within the village confines of their countrymen it is impossible to identify them.[28]

Puget Sound companies like the Port Blakely Mills employed Asian labor contractors, who regularly recruited and imported Chinese and Japanese workers from across the border in British Columbia. The bureau, therefore, considered these Japanese to be in the country unlawfully in violation of the Foran Act of 1885, which prohibited the hiring of foreign workers prior to their emigration.

These immigration policies and procedures increasingly pushed Japanese cross-border movements underground. Masato Uyeda of Seattle told interviewers that his father, Masajiro, who was initially residing in the mining town of Nanaimo, British Columbia, entered the United States surreptitiously via Port Blakely in 1900.[29] Fumiko Uyeda Groves recounts a similar story involving her grandfather and his friends.

> And then so one night they all spent five dollars for a boat trip, and it was a rowboat. And in the dark they rowed from, somebody rowed them from Vancouver Island to Port Blakely on Bainbridge Island because there was a very thriving community in Port Blakely, and thriving Japanese community.[30]

The transborder mobility of Asian migrants engendered new concerns and anxieties over a border that had, in a practical sense, never existed before. White residents began to bemoan the loss of control over their national boundaries and spaces. One Seattle newspaper, for example, argued that, due to governmental neglect, "Orientals go back and forth practically unmolested," and consequently, "more Orientals get into this country through Puget Sound ports than all of the rest of our coast line combined."[31] On the other side, the Vancouver tabloid, *The Province*, reported similarly that there

> appears to be, to say the least, an impression prevailing among the Chinese scattered along the border line from the Rockies to the coast that papers issued to them in either Canada or the United States entitle them to pass out of one country into the other and return when they feel like it.[32]

This transient way of life was, of course, not unique to Asian migrants; other groups also experienced life on the move. The steady stream of Euro-American and Canadian immigrants traveling by way of the northern boundary was an invariable fixture on the Pacific Northwest landscape.[33] Coastal Native communities in British Columbia were also known to migrate seasonally to southern hop fields in Washington State in order to supplement their traditional mode of living.[34] Yet it was the Chinese, Japanese, and South Asian who would ultimately be defined by Anglo-American law and culture as the "alien," the racialized "other" in the borderland region. Moreover, it was the decisively Asian nature of migrant transborder mobility and labor which drew the attention and opposition of white residents, eventually becoming the object of the states' disciplinary strategies and power.

Pacific World Borders

The rising emphasis on border control and surveillance in the Pacific Northwest was fueled by the intensifying migratory links between the North American West and the Asia-Pacific world. In 1907, the Northwest region experienced a record influx of Japanese and South Asian immigrants. From January 1, 1907 to September 12, 1907, more than eight thousand Asian immigrants landed at the British Columbia ports of Vancouver and Victoria, with more than half applying for admission to the United States. Among the Japanese arrivals, almost all were migrating from the recently U.S.-annexed territories of Hawai'i. In search of new sources of overseas labor, Japanese contracting firms in Seattle and Vancouver imported thousands of migrants as contract workers from the sugar plantations of Hawai'i throughout the course of the year. Seizing on the opening created by U.S. imperial expansion into the Pacific, they generated new global circuits of labor cutting across multiple imperial and national boundaries.

For the Seattle-based Oriental Trading Company, this was a complex, multiple-step process necessitated by an executive order issued by President Theodore Roosevelt several months earlier that elaborated a new form of sovereignty in an attempt to exert control over Asian migrants crossing the empire. It authorized the immigration bureau to refuse entrance to Japanese and Korean laborers whose passports were issued for any destination other than the continental United States. U.S. immigration authorities hoped this would end the practice among Asian laborers of using alternate routes through the empire to enter the country. To circumvent this measure and the new boundaries it delineated, the firm had migrant laborers from Hawai'i first shipped to British Columbia, where they were processed for admission into Canada, and kept in boarding houses in Victoria and Vancouver until runners hired by the company were ready to guide them over the border. This elaborate labor-recruiting scheme brought Japanese migrant laborers from Hawai'i through Canada to different points in the American West where they performed seasonal work in railroad construction, fishing, and salmon canning.[35]

Meanwhile, U.S. immigration officials in Seattle watched this new wave of immigration to British Columbia with concern, predicting quite correctly that many of the new Asian arrivals would attempt to enter the United States surreptitiously via the border. Moreover, they worried that the influx of Japanese and South Asian immigrants would generate public agitation and social unrest, especially among the white working-class, reproducing the tumultuous scenes from twenty years earlier. One U.S. Immigration Inspector warned that

> the number of Japanese and other aliens who are now in British Columbia and the state of public feelings on both sides of the border in this vicinity against these aliens is such that an emergency has arisen, whereby it is absolutely necessary to have additional men appointed, if the border is to be properly guarded."[36] In August 1907, the bureau responded to this threat by hiring six temporary watchmen and forming a border detail led by Immigrant Inspector C.A. Turner. This newly created unit patrolled and guarded the border between Steveston, British Columbia, and Point Roberts, Washington, on a full-time basis.[37]

The concerns over unlawful cross-border passages prompted the U.S. Immigration Bureau to commission Inspector-at-Large Marcus Braun to investigate conditions along the northern border. Braun was a leading proponent of border management and control, believing them to be vital operational features of the modern state. In a highly sensationalized report, he described the Northwest region as an open border, highly susceptible to Asian immigrants determined to enter the country illegally. "There is undoubtedly a large number of Japanese, Hindus and other aliens now in British Columbia, many of them near the boundary line who are awaiting opportunities and the proper time to effect surreptitious entries into the United States." He proposed that at least sixty officers be posted in the Puget Sound District along the northern border of Washington "in order to effect proper control of the territory . . . in view of the fact that so many Japanese and other Orientals are now landing in British Columbia with the object of entering the United States."[38] In calling for these numerous patrolmen, Inspector Braun proposed to have as many officers stationed around the Washington-British Columbia border as there were patrolling the entire length of the 1,900-mile-long U.S.-Mexican boundary.[39]

The problem of Asian migration to the Pacific Northwest evolved into an international crisis with the race riots of September 1907. While anti-Asiatic racism was already a constitutive feature of Northwest borderland culture, it reached, in the words of one Canadian minister, "almost hysterical" proportions by this time. This racial hysteria culminated with upheavals and demonstrations in the borderland cities of Bellingham and Vancouver, occurring within days of each other in September 1907. These hostilities were fueled by the prevailing belief that the dominant social order, founded upon the notion of a "white man's country," was under siege. One British Columbia newspaper played to these racial anxieties and fears when it asked rhetorically: "Are we to have this great big province—a land virtually flow-ing in milk and honey—conserved for the best interests of the white British subject—English, Scott, Irish, Welsh, etc.—or must it be given over entirely to the yellow and brown hordes of China and Japan?"[40] Assertions of white racial destiny and entitlement animated the politics of anti-Asian agitation on both sides of the U.S.-Canadian divide. Ernest Crawford, writing for the *American Federationist*, explained that "men on both sides of the international line feel that the continent of North America is intended to afford the largest democratic development to the white men of the earth," and "is the region that the common finds his last chance; it is the land of the monogramic homestead, high wages, men at work on the soil, women toiling in the home, the scene of the square deal for every square."[41] Responding to the foreign menace that threatened to usurp their inheritance, white men claimed their birthright through racial violence.

In Bellingham, tensions between white and South Asian laborers, already simmering for months, finally came to a spectacular head in the first week of September. Incited by sensational newspaper reports and the growing public hysteria over the so-called Hindu invasion, a mob of some four hundred to five hundred white men stormed the quarters of the South Asian community on the night of September 5 and proceeded to perpetrate acts of racial violence. This led to a mass exodus of South Asians from the city: some recrossed the border to the North traveling to Vancouver while others migrated southward to California.[42] The following day, the Asiatic Exclusion League of Seattle sent an ominous letter to President Theodore Roosevelt threatening that "if something were not done soon the agitation started in Bellingham would spread all over the Sound country and massacres of the Eastern aliens were likely."[43]

Two days later on September 7, the Vancouver branch of the Asiatic Ex-clusion League organized an anti-Asiatic demonstration in the city with the assistance of a number of white labor activists from south of border as well as across the Pacific world. Organizers hailed from Australia, New Zealand, Canada, and the United States. Assembled in front of City Hall, the protesters included about twenty-five thousand people and representatives from fifty-eight labor organizations. During the rally, several of the participants marched into the Chinese and Japanese districts in downtown Vancouver instigating a clash with Asian residents. This small flare up eventually led to several days of intense conflict between white laborers and Chinese and Japanese residents.[44] When the dust finally settled, the Chinese and Japanese in Vancouver sustained tens of thousands of dollars in damages to their homes and businesses and several Chinese and Japanese reported physical injuries.[45]

Popular support for tighter immigration restriction against Asian groups swelled in the wake of the riots. These demands included an appeal for stricter border enforcement in the Pacific Northwest. The *Seattle Times*, for example, described the situation concerning the border in dire terms and called for swift state intervention:

It is claimed that by those in touch with the situation that although over 4,000 Japanese have come to British Columbia the past summer, practically all contract laborers, it would be hard to find one-fourth of that number there now, and the balance will be found in this country to which they have sneaked across the line, contrary to immigration laws. The troubles of local immigration officials with Mongolians who insist upon entering this country either lawfully or unlawfully were never more numerous than at the present time, and it is apparent that the present force of inspectors and watchmen is totally inadequate, even with the unusual zeal with which is shown, to cope with the horde of Japanese and Chinese who are making their way across the border.[46]

In an attempt to quell social unrest on the west coast, both the United States and Canada consummated agreements with the Japanese government, known as the "Gentleman's Agreements," which set numerical limits on immigrants coming from Japan. The Japanese government agreed to limit passports to certain categories of people including diplomats, merchants, students, and tourists. The U.S. Gentleman's Agreement became official policy in the summer of 1908 while the Canadian version, also known as the Hayashi-Lemieux Agreement, went into effect several months earlier.[47]

As for the northern border, U.S. immigration officers lobbied for new powers and resources that would change the scale and nature of boundary policing in the Pacific Northwest. Efforts to control the boundary in a more systematic manner began with increasing the size of the border force and positioning them along the international line dividing Washington and British Columbia. Immediately following the riots, U.S. Commissioner-General of Immigration Frank Sargent secured funding for a new team of border inspectors. Sargent instructed the bureau in Washington to "utilize their services in guarding the British Columbia boundary, bending every effort towards preventing the illegal entry of Japanese."[48] Despite this upgrade in border personnel however, local public opinion demanded even further state intervention. One borderland newspaper wrote:

If the Japanese so choose to smuggle into this country they can easily do so because it is impossible to watch every foot of the boundary line and it is equally impossible to patrol every part of the sea. Additional watchmen have been placed on duty by the immigration department, but more are needed."[49]

Correspondence between local inspectors and the U.S. Immigration Bureau in Washington D.C. shows there was a significant expansion in the border force at this time. U.S. Immigrant Inspectors in British Columbia and Washington estimated that more than ninety percent of unauthorized border-crossings in the Pacific Northwest occurred somewhere between Port Angeles on the west and Sumas on the east. Based on this information, the U.S. Immigration Service deployed border inspectors and mounted watchmen at Ferndale, Lynden, Everson, and Blaine. Each of these towns was strategically important because they represented different points along the Nooksack River—flowing westward from the Cascade Mountains to the Puget Sound—a key venue, with various routes, passageways, and bridges for would be border-crossers.[50] In Bellingham, located some twenty miles south of the border, agents stationed at the Great Northern, Northern Pacific, and the Bellingham Bay and British Columbia Railway depots daily inspected all trains coming from the north. On the Puget Sound, inspectors patrolled the waters, monitored the myriad small islands, and checked and observed for ships and boats arriving from British Columbia. The Immigration Service maintained regular contact with the different transportation lines and was alerted to the arrival times of steamships, boats, and railroads coming into Washington.

A year after the anti-Asiatic riots and the initial augmentation of the border force, Inspector-in-Charge John Sargent wrote confidently to the commissioner-general of immigration that "the [northern] border is being better guarded than ever before."[51] According to a 1910 roster, the immigration force in the Washington jurisdiction alone consisted of close to fifty full-time Immigrant and Chinese inspectors and border watchmen. To match the increase in the size of the force, the Service also expanded their facilities to include substations in almost every border town along the boundary.[52]

The institutionalization of the border also involved the construction of a dense, state-organized system of surveillance. The bureau established regular contact with numerous government agencies in Washington and British Columbia regarding Chinese, Japanese, and South Asian communities. They also hired mobile informants who toured the borderlands—including Steveston, Vancouver, and Westminster on the Canadian side and Blaine, Anacortes, Bellingham, and the San Juan Islands on the U.S. side—in order to report on the movements and activities of Asian groups. Finally, the Service relied on the eyes and ears of the local population to help monitor the border. As one U.S. immigration inspector reported: "There are several thousand people living in Whatcom County . . . many of whom are in possession of telephones and most of whom are willing to give our officers any information they may secure regarding aliens passing their residences or places of business."[53] Similarly, in British Columbia, Canadian immigration authorities sought the cooperation of borderland residents by installing telephones along roads and byways thought to be traveled by illegal Asian migrants.[54] Taken together, they formed an information network that enabled state bureaucrats to put Chinese, Japanese, and South Asian immigrants under surveillance with the objective of restricting their mobility.

The problem of illegal Asian immigration moved in both directions across the boundary. In 1908, Canada enacted the Continuous Journey Order barring admission to all immigrants not traveling directly from their country of origin. Despite its broad language, the intent behind the measure was to restrict South Asian immigration to Canada.[55] South Asian migrants circumvented the law by first migrating to the United States and then surreptitiously crossing the border into Canada at some later point. "It is the understanding of the Dominion Agent that many of them who have landed at San Francisco and Seattle are in reality destined to British Columbia points, and ultimately succeed in effecting surreptitious entry into Canada."[56] Similarly, the *Vancouver Ledger* obtained information that smuggled Japanese were also a part of the underground traffic from south of the border. "Latest reports state that an unusually large number of Japanese are arriving from the Orient at Seattle, and it is expected that many of these will come across the unprotected boundary into British Columbia."[57]

As in Washington State, the force of public opinion compelled the Province to institute several reforms. First, the Canadian Immigration Bureau assigned a small number of personnel to border detail. This involved the stationing of Dominion officers alongside U.S. inspectors in Washington State and the placing of ethnic informants amongst the different Asian communities. They also began requiring seasonal workers from the United States to undergo inspection with the bureau, though the lack of personnel ensured that most seasonal laborers residing south of the border would continue to enter Canada without examination.[58]

The efforts to define and institutionalize the border invariably led to struggles between the state and the Chinese, Japanese, and South Asian immigrants who were intent on maintaining control over their mobility. Asian migrants, whether on their own or with the assistance of professional smugglers and guides, found creative ways to defy the borders and boundaries designed to keep them out. In one scheme, Japanese and South Asian immigrants in

Washington State sold their passports to countrymen in British Columbia seeking to enter the United States. Once the Japanese or South Asian immigrant secured entrance, the individual would perpetuate the cycle by selling or circulating it to yet another immigrant across the border:

> Ten Japanese caught at the international boundary line in one week with bogus passports shows the wholesale extent to which coolie laborers of the Mikado's empire are attempting to deceive the United States Immigration department. The favorite system is that of the use of the same passport over and over again. Nine out of the ten men who were detained at the boundary last week and finally refused admittance to the United States confessed that they had been supplied with the passports of Japanese now in the United States. These had been mailed back to Vancouver and were resold at from five to twenty-five dollars each.[59]

One of the more imaginative ploys to gain entry from Canada into the United States involved the complicity of unsuspecting border inspectors. Issei Izo Kojima recounts how Japanese seeking entry from British Columbia deceived U.S. border inspectors into believing they were residents of the United States. "There were many iron bridges, and those who tried to get into America from Canada thought up many tricks to get across. There was the trick of walking backwards inconspicuously. Sooner or later such a walker would be discovered by the American guards, and when called he would turn around, as if trying to escape from America to Canada."[60]

Border inspectors thinking that the Japanese immigrant was unlawfully crossing the border to Canada would apprehend the suspect and "return" the person to the United States. There was also the use of racial disguise in attempts to surreptitiously cross the border. "When questioned the Oriental gave his name as R. Abe and said he wanted to go to Seattle to look for work. Before crossing the line near Blaine, he smeared his face with grease and blackening, giving him the appearance of a Negro."[61]

Some Asian transients in British Columbia relied on family and kinship networks to make it across the boundary. Take the case of Sahuro Iguchi, who traveled on the transpacific steamship liner "Athenian" and arrived in Vancouver on May 30, 1907. About a month later, he applied for admissions to the United States but was rejected on account of having contracted a degenerative eye-disorder known as trachoma. It is very likely that his intent all along was to immigrate to the United States, but Iguchi probably took the indirect route through Canada to avoid the stricter regulations of the U.S. Immigration Service. Unable to deport him back to Japan, the Service returned him to Vancouver where he received treatment for trachoma. He applied for admissions two additional times in October 1907 and March 1908 and each time U.S. immigration authorities denied him entry based on his medical condition. Desperate to gain entry, Iguchi contacted a friend in Seattle, Nada Tokujiro, "to find some way by which [Iguchi] could enter the United States." Tokujiro sent one Mr. Hashizume to Vancouver with the intention of having him escort Iguchi across the border and into Seattle, Washington. The plan comprised several steps. They took a train from Vancouver to Cloverdale, British Columbia and from there they walked by foot across the international line to Blaine, Washington and spent the night at a nearby hotel. In the morning, they left for Bellingham where they were supposed to take a boat to Seattle; unfortunately for them, U.S. border inspectors apprehended the Japanese migrants before they could complete the final leg of their journey.[62]

Precisely because of cases like this, the U.S. government applied pressure on Canada to modify its immigration standards and regulations to conform to that of the United States. U.S immigration inspectors often complained that the less rigorous inspection standards encouraged Chinese, Japanese, and South Asian immigrants to exploit Canada as a back door into the United States. Eventually, the Canadian Immigration Bureau agreed to end the policy of allowing diseased Asian immigrants to receive treatment in their detention hospitals. In 1909, Canadian immigration authorities began to summarily reject Asian arrivals diagnosed with "loathsome disease" and prohibited them from landing at their ports of entry.[63]

In the Pacific Northwest, professional smugglers and ethnic-labor contractors facilitated the cross-border trafficking of illegal Asian migrants. Prior to the boundary enforcement buildup in the late 1900s, Chinese, Japanese, and South Asian immigrants could pay a small fee to be navigated across the international line. Native Indians in British Columbia, for example, piloted Chinese and Japanese transients to the United States for as little as three dollars. By 1914, Special Immigrant Inspector Roger O'Donnell testified before the House Committee on Immigration that the Chinese were willing to pay anywhere between one hundred and one thousand dollars to be smuggled into the United States.[64] While inspector O'Donnell may have exaggerated the figures, he was accurate in suggesting that Asian smuggling had become big business in the new era of the border. Noted Asian smuggler George Nelson told authorities that he charged between $125 and $150 per Chinese alien. Working as a fireman for the Great Northern, Nelson concealed his human contraband in the tool box within the engine tender, and once his train made it safely across the border, Nelson delivered the immigrants to a Chinese labor agent in Seattle.[65]

Asian labor contractors contributed to the cross-border flow of illegal immigrants by importing them as workers from across the international line. Labor agent T. Sengoku unknowingly confided to an informant for the U.S. Immigration Service that he had "taken three hundred Japanese across the Border at Blaine" and "placed [them] at work in the state of Idaho in the building of the Great Northern Railway." In the same conversation, Sengoku boasted that "he would be able to get Hindoos across the border without examination provided they were first taken down and put to work on the Canadian side for a few days' time."[66] In a different case, U.S. immigration officials suspected the Green Investment Company based in Walla Walla, Washington, of recruiting and smuggling South Asian laborers across the border. The bureau intercepted a company letter addressed to Gurdit Singh encouraging him to recruit South Asian laborers to the Pacific Northwest. Gurdit Singh helped charter the *Komagata Maru*, which sailed from Hong Kong to Vancouver in May 1914 with close to four hundred South Asians on board. The Green Investment firm was one of the rising numbers of South Asian-owned lumber businesses surfacing throughout the Greater Pacific Northwest. The company assured Gurdit Singh that they could find employment for these men in the state of Washington.[67]

Policing the Boundaries of a White Man's Country

The seemingly intractable problem of Asian migration brought together officials from the United States and Canada who were equally intent on preserving a "White Man's Country." The *Vancouver World* declared that the "Asiatic invasion" represented the "most serious attack on this continent" and threatened both "Republic and Dominion alike."[68] With a mutual interest in maintaining the boundaries of race and nation, the two countries engaged in collaborative transnational policing and enforcement of Asian immigration. Canadian immigration officer Malcolm Reid boasted that

> the utmost harmony prevails between the United States Immigration officers and our own officials, not only in Vancouver but throughout this whole district, especially in Oriental matters; as it seems to be realized that the Oriental question is a menace both to the United States and Canada, hearty cooperation is necessary to deal with this momentous question adequately."[69]

A number of U.S. and Canadian bureaucracies including local law enforcement, customs houses, and immigration departments coordinated joint efforts to address the problem of illegal immigration across the border. One U.S. official described the working agreement with Canadian officials to the Congressional Committee on Immigration and Naturalization in 1913. "American immigration officers board boats and examine passengers landing in Canadian ports, join in border patrols, and obtain the assistance of Canadian immigration officers in investigating records of immigrants coming from Canada."[70]

The transnational process of raising the border both reflected and engendered racial ideas and practices in the Northwest borderlands. While the boundary emerged as a barrier to Asian migrants, it remained porous and open to white Euro-Americans and Canadians during this time. In 1912, the Seattle-based *Industrial Worker* observed:

> Thousands of migratory workers have gone to Canada in the past year, there to work for American contractors. Thousands of Canadians come here to work for American employers. In either case the lives of the workers were not influenced by the form of government, by tariff laws, by income taxes, by municipal ownership or any other legal enactment. Industrial relations alone ruled.[71]

This fluid situation was, in part, related to the selective manner in which state immigration authorities applied and enforced border policies in the Pacific Northwest. In determining who possessed the privileges of border-crossing, immigration bureaucrats distinguished between "undesirable" and "desirable" groups, and in the process, North American border regimes became entangled with the larger project of defining national belonging taking place at the turn of the twentieth century.

U.S. and Canadian immigration officials stationed in the Pacific Northwest treated the cross-border flow of white Americans, Canadians, and European immigrants mostly with benign neglect and in some cases outright support. Recent scholarship shows that illegal European immigrants frequently entered the United States across the northern border. Historian Marian Smith notes that unauthorized European migration across the U.S.-Canadian boundary first became an issue in the 1890s and 1900s. U.S. lawmakers responded by instituting formal inspection regimes along the northern boundary, starting on the eastern seaboard. According to Smith the "immigrants simply moved further west or to some other unguarded point" in order to avoid inspection, although by 1908, "a string of entry posts dotted the northern boundary line from east to west."[72] Yet the correspondences of local inspectors and border watchmen in Washington State rarely, if ever, mention any groups other than

Asian immigrants crossing the border unlawfully. This discrepancy suggests that U.S. border inspectors likely ignored or overlooked European immigrants coming into the Pacific Northwest from Western Canada.

Race also played an important role in the construction of the border on the Canadian side. When designing their immigration and border policies, Dominion authorities in British Columbia considered how they could meet the demands of the labor market without compromising the racial ideal of whiteness. Indeed, they endeavored to attract immigrant laborers, who were essential to economic development and growth, while maintaining a "White Man's Province" at the same time. In 1908, the Dominion passed what was known as the Continuous Journey Act which barred immigrants not traveling directly from their country of origin. The legislation was a subtle attempt to exclude South Asians, as there was not a single steamship line at the time traveling directly from British India to Canada. However, the act, unbeknownst to those drafting the law, also prohibited Euro-Americans in the United States from entering Canada. Dominion authorities remedied the situation by passing an Order-in-Council allowing non-Asians to emigrate from places other than their country of origin, and in doing, so reopened the border to Euro-American migration while keeping it closed to Asian immigrants.[73]

The Immigration Bureau in British Columbia also implemented more explicit measures in order to promote the migration of "desirable" groups. Immigration authorities, for example, distributed a departmental circular to all boundary inspectors in 1914 encouraging them to allow European migrants from the United States to enter Canada. More specifically, it authorized Canadian inspectors stationed in Washington and other bordering states to issue letters of entry to European immigrants interested in settling in Western Canada.[74] As historian Bruno Ramirez explains, "Canada had to resort massively to immigration" because workers "were needed in new mining districts and lumber camps, on railroad lines, and in the construction of urban infrastructures."[75] The Canadian government used the head taxes collected from Chinese immigrants to subsidize and promote immigration from Europe. Furthermore, in March 1913, the superintendent of immigration temporarily suspended monetary qualifications for prospective immigrants provided that "they are natives or citizens of Great Britain, or Ireland, or if natives or citizens of some other European country . . . and that they are not persons of Asiatic origin."[76]

Canadian immigrant inspectors regularly manipulated border policies in the hopes of "whitening" the labor force in British Columbia. Reflecting the racial sensibilities of the Province, they considered the cross-border migration and labor of U.S. and European workers far more desirable than Asian sojourners. "For many years past Japanese fishermen have monopolized the catching of the fish for the salmon-packing industry, and have driven white fishermen of all kinds almost all out of the waters. Some of the canneries however appear to have become tired of the Japanese alleging that they are far from straight, and are attempting to replace them with white men." Canadian boundary inspectors tried to accommodate the canneries by relaxing their border regulations in regards to American and European migration from the U.S. Northwest.

> Of the white men on the coast, both on the Canadian and American sides, Greeks are probably the most numerous class, and many of them, as well as other American and European fishermen, have been yearly frequenting the Fraser River, some of them going back and forth through port of entry and being inspected by our officers, and others traveling in their own boats and thus entering Canada without inspection.[77]

Even though the latter was in violation of immigration law, the Canadian Immigration Bureau was "fairly well at ease" with these groups of immigrants and therefore gave sanction to their transborder movements.[78]

The border remained fluid to immigrants from Southern and Eastern Europe as well, even as their social desirability and inclusion in the nation was being questioned on the eastern seaboard.[79] As scholars have recently explained, ethnic Europeans in the North American West obtained the status of "white" persons before their counterparts in the East. Historian Linda Gordon argues that "what made the West a land of opportunity was the chance to become white."[80] Cross-border mobility was among the many privileges associated with whiteness. Highlighting the complex interplay between race and space, it appears that the border, as far as ethnic Europeans were concerned, became softer the farther west they traveled.

In the summer of 1912, Canadian boundary inspectors stationed in Seattle suspected a large number of Greek and Italian immigrants of illegally crossing the border from Bellingham, Washington, to Steveston, British Columbia. Immigration officials therefore dispatched inspector Hopkinson to investigate the situation, who upon reaching the fishing town of Steveston, discovered a group of unauthorized Greek migrants from Seattle working in one of the canneries. He promptly arrested them on the grounds that they had violated immigration laws by entering Canada without inspection. They were later convicted of the charge and levied a fine of $5.00. More interestingly however, Canadian immigration inspectors recommended that the undocumented Greeks be allowed to stay in British Columbia. "The men in question, appeared to be fair class of fishermen, and because it was impossible for their employers to secure white men of this type in this Province, I have no hesitancy in recommending that they be permitted to proceed with their season's contract, and so have taken no steps securing their deportation."[81] While still requiring the Greek immigrants Nick Vallas, Angelo Keane, Nick Dupont, and John Maleson to pay the nominal fine, border practices such as this one served to distance ethnic Europeans from the so-called status or category of "illegal aliens," facilitating their national and racial assimilation as "white" Americans and Canadians in North America.

Conclusion

In the late nineteenth and early twentieth centuries, Chinese, Japanese, and South Asian migrants were brought to the Pacific Northwest through new transpacific and transborder systems of mobility and exchange. Drawn by railroad construction and the rise and mix of extractive industries, Asian laborers, merchants, and entrepreneurs helped create and sustain a transborder world of motion in the Pacific Northwest during this period. These manifold movements and circulations were embedded in a larger Pacific world of migration, trade, and empire that increasingly connected the region to Asia and the South Pacific—indeed, it was where a North American borderland met and intersected the Asia-Pacific world.

The intensifying movements and linkages with the Asia-Pacific, however, led Canada and the United States to consolidate their respective national-state sovereignty, giving rise to a new emphasis on border policing and surveillance at the turn of the twentieth century. Yet, as I have argued, delineation of the U.S.-Canadian boundary was neither about drawing rigid lines of division, nor enforcing strict notions of national difference between Canada and the United States. Rather, the process of border formation in the Pacific Northwest was primarily concerned with defining an outer limit against the encroachment of an Asia-Pacific world. North American regimes adopted political, diplomatic, and legal measures to restrict and regulate the transpacific as well as the transborder movement of Chinese, Japanese, and South Asian migrants. This binational effort to systematically control transnational Asian migration involved the construction of transpacific borders—a process that included enforcing an imaginary line between the Asia-Pacific world and the North

American West, as well as consolidating a territorial boundary between the United States and Canada.

Notes

For their helpful comments and suggestions I would like to thank Mae Ngai, Adam McKeown, Paul Sue, Henry Yu, Mark Overmyer-Velazquez, David Gutierrez, Lisa Lowe, Curtis Marez, and the anonymous readers at the *American Quarterly*.

1. *Daily Colonist*, September 11, 1909.
2. Letter from C. A. Turner to Inspector-in-Charge John H. Sargent, September 14, 1907, United States, National Archives (Washington) (hereafter NARA), Record Group (hereafter RG) 85, Entry 9, File 51630, Folder 44-B.
3. Marilyn Lake and Henry Reynolds, *Drawing the Global Colour Line: White Men's Countries and the International Challenge of Racial Equality* (Cambridge: Cambridge University Press, 2008).
4. Erika Lee, *At America's Gates: Chinese Immigration during the Exclusion Era, 1882–1943* (Chapel Hill: University of North Carolina Press, 2003), 151–88.
5. Mae M. Ngai, *Impossible Subjects: Illegal Aliens and the Making of Modern America* (Princeton, N.J.: Princeton University Press, 2004).
6. Letter to Walter S. Chance, October 6, 1899, NARA.
7. Andrew Graybill, "Texas Rangers, Canadian Mounties, and the Policing of the Transnational Industrial Frontier, 1885–1910," *Western Historical Quarterly* 35.2 (2004): 167–91.
8. See Patricia E. Roy, *White Man's Province: British Columbia Politicians and Chinese and Japanese Immigrants, 1858–1914* (Vancouver: University of British Columbia Press, 1989); Peter Ward, *White Canada Forever: Popular Attitudes and Public Policy toward Orientals in British Columbia*.
9. Frederic J. Grant, *History of Seattle, Washington: With Illustrations and Biographical Sketches of Some of Its Prominent Men and Pioneers* (New York: American Publishing and Engraving Company, 1891), 188.
10. *U.S. Report of the Commissioner General of Immigration, 1905*, 66.
11. February 11, 1891, Office Memorandum, National Archives of Canada (Ottawa) (hereafter NAC), RG 7, Series G-1, File 22.
12. Lee, *At America's Gates*, 177.
13. Ibid., 152.
14. "Restriction on Immigration," House Immigration Committee hearings, 63d Congress, 2d sess. (Washington, D.C.: Government Printing Office, 1914).
15. Letter from Inspector-in Charge John H. Sargent to F. H. Larned, October 2, 1909, NARA, RG 85, Entry 9, File 52999, Folder 26.
16. See Gunther Peck, *Reinventing Free Labor: Padrones and Immigrant Workers in the North American West 1880–1930* (Cambridge: Cambridge University Press, 2000); Chris Friday, *Organizing Asian American Labor: Pacific Coast Canned-Salmon Industry, 1870–1942* (Philadelphia: Temple University Press, 1994).
17. Letter to Walter S. Chance, October 6, 1899, NARA.
18. *Seattle Union Record*, October 19, 1901.
19. "Digest of, and Comment Upon, Report of Immigrant Inspector Marcus Braun," September 20, 1907, NARA, RG 85, Entry 9, File 51360, Folder 44-D.
20. Nicholas De Genova, "Migrant 'Illegality' and Deportability in Everyday Life," *Annual Review of Anthropology* 31 (2002): 419–47.
21. Letter to Walter S. Chance, October 6, 1899, NARA.
22. Letter from the Chinese Inspector to F. D. Huestis, October 13, 1898, NARA-PA, RG 36, Box #105, Folder 5.
23. Letter to Walter S. Chance, October 6, 1899, NARA.

24. There was not a significant South Asian colony in the Pacific Northwest until 1903 when more than four hundred immigrants from the Punjab region of northern India arrived in Vancouver, British Columbia. The next wave of South Asians migrated several years later with their numbers peaking in 1907 and 1908. See Hugh Johnston, *The East Indians in Canada* (Ottawa: Canadian Historical Association, 1984).

25. *The Province*, May 12, 1909.

26. *Tacoma Daily News*, January 16, 1899.

27. Asiatic Exclusion League, *Proceedings of the Asiatic Exclusion League, 1907–1913* (New York: Arno Press, 1977). See the meeting minutes for February 1908.

28. Letter from Immigrant Inspector Snyder to F. D. Huestis, January 3, 1900, NARA-PA, RG 36, Box#106, Folder 4.

29. Ito Kazuo, *Issei: A History of Japanese Immigrants in North America*, trans. Shinichiro Nakamura and Jean S. Gerard (Seattle: Japanese Community Service, 1973), 87.

30. Fumiko Uyeda Groves interview, June 16, 1998, Densho, Japanese American Legacy Project.

31. *Seattle Union Record*, June 22, 1901, and *Seattle Union Record*, October 19, 1901.

32. *The Province*, September 6, 1901.

33. Bruno Ramirez with Yves Otis, *Crossing the 49th Parallel: Migration from Canada to the United States, 1900–1930* (Ithaca: Cornell University Press, 2001); Beth Ladow, *The Medicine Line: Life and Death on a North American Borderland* (New York: Routledge, 2001).

34. Paige Raibmon, *Authentic Indians: Episodes of Encounter from the Late-Nineteenth Century Northwest Coast* (Durham, N.C.: Duke University Press, 2005).

35. See Correspondences between the Oriental Trading Company and the Great Northern Railway, UWSC, Northern Pacific Railway Company, Accession #4415, Reel 1; and William Lyon Mackenzie King, Royal Commission Appointed to Investigate Into the Losses Sustained by the Japanese Population of Vancouver, B.C., on the Occasion of the Riots in That City in September 1907, *Report* (Ottawa: King's Printer, 1907).

36. Letter from Inspector-in-Charge John H. Sargent to Commissioner-General of Immigration Frank P. Sargent, September 19, 1907, NARA, RG 85, Entry 9, File 51360, Folder 44.

37. Ibid.

38. "Digest of, and Comment Upon, Report of Immigrant Inspector Marcus Braun," September 20, 1907, NARA.

39. Neil Foley, *White Scourge: Mexicans, Blacks, and Poor Whites in Texas Cotton Culture* (Berkeley: University of California Press, 1997), 47.

40. Quoted from Roy Ito, *Stories of My People: A Japanese Canadian Journal* (Hamilton: Ontario Nisei Veterans Association, 1994), 59.

41. Ernest Crawford's article was republished in the *Everett Labor Journal*, May 6, 1910.

42. Joan M. Jensen, *Passage from India: Asian Indian Immigrants in North America* (New Haven, Conn.: Yale University Press, 1988), 42–56.

43. *American Reveille*, September 6, 1907.

44. Roy, *White Man's Province*, 185–226.

45. William Lyon Mackenzie King, Royal Commission Appointed to Investigate Into the Losses Sustained by the Chinese Population of Vancouver, B.C., on the Occasion of the Riots in That City in September 1907, *Report* (Ottawa: King's Printer, 1907); King, Royal Commission Appointed to Investigate Into the Losses Sustained by the Japanese Population, *Report*.

46. *Seattle Times*, September 22, 1907; and *American Reveille*, September 24, 1907.

47. See Roger Daniels, *The Politics of Prejudice: The Anti-Japanese Movement in California and the Struggle for Japanese Exclusion* (Berkeley: University of California Press, 1977), 33–35, and 37–41.

48. Letter from Commissioner-General of Immigration Frank P. Sargent to Commissioner of Immigration, Montreal Canada, September 10, 1907, NARA, RG 85, Entry 9, File 51686, Folder 17-A.

49. *American Reveille*, September 24, 1907.

50. Letter from Inspector Charles Babcock to Inspector-in-Charge John H. Sargent, November 4, 1908, NARA, RG 85, Entry 9, File 52999, Folder 26.

51. Letter from Inspector-in-Charge John H. Sargent to Acting Commissioner-General of Immigration F. H. Larned, September 24, 1908, NARA, RG 85, Entry 9, File 52999, Folder 26.

52. Letter from Everett Wallace to Commissioner-General of Immigration Daniel J. Keefe, December 6, 1909, NARA, RG 85, Entry 9, File 52999, Folder 26-B.

53. Letter from Henry M. White to the Commissioner-General of Immigration Anthony Caminetti, March 16, 1914, NARA, RG 85, Entry 9, File 52999, Folder 26-G.
54. *Vancouver World*, April 15, 1908.
55. Dominion authorities passed the order knowing that there was not a direct passage from India to Canada at the time. See Johnston, *The East Indians in Canada*.
56. Letter from Daniel Keefe to Commissioner of Immigration, San Francisco, California, March 8, 1910, WNA, RG 85, Entry 9, File 51388, Folder 5.
57. *Vancouver Ledger*, June 6, 1903.
58. Letter to Superintendent of Immigration W. D. Scott, March 1, 1912, NAC, RG 76, Series I-A-1, vol. 578, File 817172.
59. *The Province*, January 20, 1908.
60. Quoted in Kazuo, *Issei*, 87.
61. *American Reveille*, October 17, 1907.
62. Letter from the Seattle Immigration Office to the Commissioner-General of Immigration Frank P. Sargent, May 18, 1908, NARA, RG 85, Entry 9, File 51893, Part 2.
63. Letter from Superintendent of Immigration W. D. Scott to Medical Superintendent M. Chishild, November 15, 1909, NARA, RG 85, Entry 9, File 51630, Folder 44-D.
64. "Restriction of Immigration of Hindu Laborers," House Immigration Committee hearings, 63d Congress, 2d sess. (Washington, D.C.: Government Printing Office, 1914).
65. "Industrial Relations," vol. 7 (Asiatic Smuggling), Final Report and Testimony, Commission on Industrial Relations, 64th Congress, 1st sess. (Washington, D.C.: Government Printing Office, 1916).
66. Letter from Immigrant Inspector P. L. Prentis to the Commissioner-General of Immigration Frank P. Sargent, August 22, 1907, NARA, RG 85, Entry 9, File 51686, Folder 17-A.
67. Memorandum to the Secretary of State Williams Jennings Bryan, June 12, 1914, NARA, RG 85, Entry 9, File 51388, Folder 5.
68. *Vancouver World*, August 26, 1907.
69. Report of Malcolm Reid, April 1, 1914, City of Vancouver Archives (hereafter CVA), MSS. 69, 509-D-7, File 1.
70. "Restriction on Immigration," House Immigration Committee hearings, 63d Congress, 2d sess. (Washington, D.C.: Government Printing Office, 1914).
71. *Industrial Worker*, December 19, 1912.
72. Marian Smith, "The INS at the U.S.-Canadian Border, 1893–1933: An Overview of Issues and Topics," *Michigan Historical Review* 26 (Fall 2000): 127–47.
73. Jensen, *Passage from India*, 81–82.
74. Circular to Boundary Inspectors, January 16, 1914, NAC, RG 76, Series I-A-1, Vol. 561, File 808722.
75. Ramirez, *Crossing the 49th Parallel*, 37.
76. Circular, Immigration, March 12, 1913, NAC, RG 76, Series I-A-1, Vol. 561, File 808722.
77. Letter to Superintendent of Immigration W. D. Scott, March 1, 1912, NAC.
78. Ibid.
79. See John Higham, *Strangers in the Land: Patterns of American Nativism, 1860–1925* (New Brunswick, N.J.: Rutgers University Press, 1955).
80. Linda Gordon, *The Great Arizona Orphan Abduction* (Cambridge, Mass.: Harvard University Press, 1999), 104. Also see Tomas Almaguer, *Racial Fault Lines: The Historical Origins of White Supremacy in California* (Berkeley: University of California Press, 1994).
81. Letter to Superintendent of Immigration W. D. Scott, March 1, 1912, NAC.

Flexible Citizenship/Flexible Empire: South Asian Muslim Youth in Post-9/11 America

Sunaina Maira

Nasreen

"I came to the U.S. on January 17, 1999. I remember the date, because it was the first time I saw snow . . . My father had been here for twelve or thirteen years; he was in New York for a few months, then he came to Wellford. He liked it here because it is not so crowded, and he thought the schools are better for us . . . My father works at the Passage to India restaurant. He's been there a while, so now he's the manager. My mother works in a Store 24 close to Prospect Square.

We're from Bangladesh—from Sylhet, a city there. There are many people from Sylhet in America, in New York and also here. I have four sisters and three brothers. . . . I came here with all of them, except my oldest sister who was over twenty-one. She couldn't get the papers to come with us, so I don't know if she'll be able to come here.

My father told me what New York and Wellford are like, and he said it's good to study here. One thing is that in my country, I didn't have to work, but here I do. It's not really hard, and my family doesn't really care if I work or not. But I always give my check to my parents. If I go to college, my brother is going to help me pay for it. He works in a hotel in the city, and the older one used to work there too, but he kinda got laid off after September 11.

I used to work in a dental clinic last summer . . . thirty-five hours a week. They knew my father at the clinic and I liked the job; I got to do different things. I had to help the doctor do the suction thing, clean up after the patient leaves, answer the phone, and play with the dog. Yes, if you want to work there, you have to love the dog! After I graduate from high school, I'm not sure what I want to do. I used to say that I want to work in a bank, but when I started working in the school bank downstairs, I read the rules and became afraid of all the risk. . . . My father went to college, and when he was in Sylhet he used to teach my aunties at home because he really wanted women to have an education. My mother told me that my father also taught her. She finished tenth standard but my father wanted her to go to college. She never went, even though my mother's mother was a teacher. So Muslim women are not like what people here think.

After 9/11, I felt very, very sad about what happened. . . . I was also sad about the war in Afghanistan because they were killing poor people who did not have anything to do with 9/11. I was scared for the first week after 9/11, because I was wearing my salwar kameez [traditional South Asian dress] and people always looked at me funny, even before 9/11 happened. Then one day, some students were talking in class about why Muslims hate the U.S. and Miss Scott said that just because a few Muslims did the attacks, it doesn't mean all of them think that way. If some African Americans did something, you wouldn't bomb all African Americans, would you?

I think of myself as Bangladeshi. . . . I'm already a U.S. citizen, and so is my father, so I'm not so worried about him. I became a citizen when I was sixteen years old, and my sisters are all citizens too, but not my brothers, because they are over eighteen so they have to wait. My mother was also sponsored by my father but she failed her English test the first time. For me, citizenship is not that different from having a green card, but I heard it's better if you want to go to college, because you get financial aid. But the laws keep changing so I hope I can stay here. The reason people came here is because of the laws and the rights they get, and they like the way they live. But things are changing, and the laws are changing. If the rights are gone, then what's the point of living here?"

Ismail

"My relatives came to America twenty years ago; both my father's sisters are here and they live in Dunbury. My father works in a factory; he makes car parts. My aunt's daughter is a lawyer, and the other is doing a PhD degree, I'm not sure in what. I went to school in Dunbury for two months, and then I transfered to Wellford. My family is from Valsar, in Gujarat, and there are a lot of Gujarati people in these two buildings; they're all from Valsar. Now, there are a lot of people coming from villages around there . . . a lot of people want to come here because of the education. . . .

When I got to America I was a bit shocked, I was confused; I didn't know how I'd do in my studies. And no one here knew me. My brother came here too, and he is doing his second bachelor's, in information technology. My sister had already been to the high school for a year, so she told me about everything. And now all these new students are coming to the school, so they come to me in the same way, ask me questions. . . . I tell them how to get a work permit so they can get a job, help them fill out the forms.

I do a phone card business with my brother, where I sell phone cards to these Indian stores and convenience stores, and I also work at the university doing tech support. One of my friends is working at Dunkin' Donuts, the other one has left and he's now working with his father in a store. The other boys—Pakistani boys—work at security jobs, and they work from five to twelve at night. So we don't really have the time to do things, everyone's busy with their own thing. . . . We don't have the time to go to the Gujarati events in Billtown, or to do the dandiya raas [Gujarati folk dance]. . . . I'm just occupied with work, and with helping my mother. My sister's not at home much now since she's at college, so I have to do the housework, shopping, laundry. So there's not much time, but I listen to music and watch films for fun, mostly.

I'm thinking that after I finish school, maybe I'll go to India for six months and then I'll come back here for six months and work. Maybe I'll buy a gas station or a convenience store. I might do a business with my uncle, who works in McDonald's. My auntie works in a laundry. They're not very educated, but they have some money to invest. Actually, the thing is I'd like to stay here, but this place doesn't need me more than my country, because in India there's a lot of poor people who need our help and our education. If we study here, then we'll go back to our country, open up some kind of company or something, that'll be really good for them there because our economy is really down right now, you know. So most people are unemployed in India right now. If I at least learn some computer stuff and my brother and me open up a company there, and one here, that'll be a great thing because people can work and they can come here; they can support their whole family.

I don't really mind if I call myself Indian or American, as long as I feel comfortable with the people. So I'm going to become an American citizen next month. 'You're not a citizen yet? How come, if you've been here seventeen years?' I got my green card four and a half years ago, so now I can apply for citizenship. My relatives were U.S. citizens, so that's why they called us here. They've been here twenty-two years. I have relatives in Florida, and my aunt is in London, my mother's sister.

Here, in my building, it's very international; there are Chinese people, Moroccan, black. But for blacks and others who live here, it's not a problem that we are Muslim. . . . I've talked to some friends of mine about the war, and they said this is all wrong, the American government is just causing more violence and we don't want this war, we should solve the problem peacefully. . . . See, if bin Laden has killed them, just get bin Laden. Why are they bombing Afghanistan and killing innocent people?"

This article focuses on the ways in which young South Asian Muslim immigrants living in the United States express ideas of national and transnational belonging and cultural citizenship during the War on Terrorism waged both within and beyond U.S. borders. In the wake of the September 11, 2001, attacks, questions of citizenship, racialization, religion, and transnational identities took on new, urgent meanings for Muslims, South Asians, and Arabs in the United States. The narratives above are excerpts from interviews I conducted with South Asian Muslim immigrant students in a public high school in a New England town I call Wellford.[1] These Muslim youth are grappling with issues of displacement, belonging, and exclusion that extended well before and after 2001, but were heightened in the post-9/11 moment. Nasreen, Ismail, and other Muslim immigrant youth are coming of age at a moment when their religious and national affiliations are politically charged issues, exacerbating the crises generated by transnational migration, global capitalism, and U.S. political and economic hegemony consolidated in this moment of empire. The national allegiances of Muslim, Arab, and South Asian Americans have come under intense scrutiny for signs of betrayal to the nation and for any wavering in allegiance to the project of "freedom" and "democracy" as defined in the neoconservative vision for the "New American Century." Cultural citizenship, or the everyday experience of national belonging beyond legal citizenship, is thus a crucible for many of the key issues facing Muslim immigrant youth.

This article explores the transnational dimensions of cultural citizenship for South Asian Muslim youth in the United States, but it also questions the ways in which transnational practices of citizenship, mobility, and flexibility are produced, imagined, and idealized in the post-9/11 moment. Generally missing in much of the research literature on immigration and transnationalism has been an analysis of U.S. imperialism as a larger framework that shapes processes of migration, racialization, and marginality.[2] Domestic histories of race and class relations cannot be isolated from the broader rubric of U.S. empire, as the case of Muslim immigrant youth after 9/11 makes only too evident. The "war on terrorism" overseas and the War on Terror "at home" are linked because empire works on two fronts, the domestic and the foreign. U.S. foreign policy is linked to the "policing of domestic racial tensions" and disciplining of subordinated populations through race, gender, and class hierarchies at home.[3] The national consensus for U.S. foreign policies is strengthened through historical processes of scapegoating "outsiders" and conflating internal and external enemies through racial and gendered discourses, as apparent during the cold war.[4] However, the transnational link between the two realms of imperial power are generally obscured in everyday discussions and representations, even if they are alluded to implicitly, and sometimes problematically, in the suspicion of Muslim communities with "overseas" ties. The fissure between the two fronts of empire effectively prevents marginalized groups in the United States from understanding how their subjugation within the nation is connected to dominance overseas.[5] This analysis is important for understanding questions of citizenship for immigrant youth after 9/11, for it has always been the case that imperial power maintains dominance outside the nation by maintaining dominance over subordinated groups at home, such as racial minorities, women, workers, and immigrants.[6]

This article is drawn from a larger study that analyzes young people's own understandings of citizenship, transnationalism, empire, war, and dissent in the social contexts they inhabit in their everyday lives. The research demonstrates how the micropolitics of citizenship practices and performances of immigrant youth in these everyday contexts are linked to the macropolitical processes of the imperial state and global capital. As part of my ethnographic study in Wellford from 2001 through 2003, I interviewed South Asian Muslim immigrant students, second-generation South Asian youth as well as Muslim immigrant students from other countries, parents of both immigrant and nonimmigrant students, teachers, staff, youth program organizers, community and religious leaders, and activists working on immigrant and civil rights. I did fieldwork in the school and at a range of sites in Wellford, including homes, workplaces, social gatherings, and cultural and political events. At the time of this research, I was also involved with a volunteer program for South Asian immigrant students in the high school, SAMTA (South Asian Mentoring and Tutoring Association), that organized workshops on academic, social, and career issues, so the students knew me as someone semi-officially involved with the school and also as a researcher, a much more ambiguous identity.

Wellford is a small, predominantly white city that was transformed in the 1990s by accelerated gentrification and by increasing immigration, which expanded the population of immigrant workers from different parts of the world.[7] The Wellford public high school has an extremely diverse student body, with students from Latin America, the Caribbean, Africa, and Asia.[8] Students from India, Pakistan, Bangladesh, and Afghanistan constituted the largest Muslim population in the school, followed by youth from Ethiopia, Somalia, and Morocco.[9]

South Asian students have been coming to the high school since they started migrating to Wellford about fifteen years ago, as part of a second wave of labor migrants from South Asia beginning in the 1980s, many entering on family reunification visas rather than through the professional/technical categories that drew an influx of upwardly mobile, highly educated South Asian immigrants after the Immigration Act of 1965.

The South Asian immigrant student population in the school is predominantly working class to lower-middle class, recently arrived (within the last five to seven years), and with minimal to moderate fluency in English. These youth seem to socialize mainly with other South Asian immigrant youth, of diverse national and religious backgrounds, and with other immigrant students in the bilingual education program. The majority of the Indian immigrant youth are from Muslim families, most from small towns or villages in Gujarat in western India. Several of the South Asian Muslim youth are related to one another, as their families have sponsored relatives as part of an ongoing chain migration. Entire families have migrated from the same village in Gujarat, re-creating their extended family networks in the same apartment building in Wellford. The parents of these youth generally work in low-income jobs in the service sector, and they themselves work after school, up to thirty hours a week, in fast food restaurants, gas stations, retail stores, and as security guards. The families of the South Asian (Sunni) Muslim youth are not very involved in local Muslim organizations or mosques in the area, largely because they are so busy struggling with work and survival, and generally do not affiliate with the local Indian American or Pakistani American community organizations, which primarily involve middle- to upper-middle-class suburban families.[10] The expressions of citizenship of these immigrant youth are rooted in the specificities of their urban, working-class experience, an experience that is often completely unknown to their more privileged South Asian American counterparts in the area.

Cultural Citizenship and Flexible Citizenship

The narratives of the South Asian immigrant youth, such as Nasreen and Ismail, suggest that the cultural dimensions of national belonging were part of their everyday experiences of inclusion, exclusion, and engagement with the school, workplace, and public sphere. Ismail and Nasreen echoed the views of other students who critiqued the scapegoating of Muslims after 9/11 as a form of collective punishment for the Twin Tower attacks and the scrutiny of Muslim Americans as somehow "un-American." Cultural citizenship, according to Lok Siu, refers to the "behaviors, discourses, and practices that give meaning to citizenship as lived experience" in the context of "an uneven and complex field of structural inequalities and webs of power relations," the "quotidian practices of inclusion and exclusion."[11] Recent work on citizenship has shed light on "the tension between citizenship as a formal legal status and as a normative project or an aspiration" that remains unfulfilled in countries such as the United States despite the "formal equality" guaranteed to citizens.[12] Cultural citizenship is a key notion for South Asian Americans, because legal citizenship is clearly not enough to guarantee protection under the law with the state's War on Terror, as Nasreen observed, and as is clear from the profiling, surveillance, and even detention of Muslim Americans who are U.S. citizens. The larger study explores the different kinds of cultural citizenship performed by South Asian Muslim immigrant youth, but in this article I focus on one mode of cultural citizenship, in particular, that emerges from the transnational experiences of these youth in relation to migration, family, labor, and cultural consumption.

"Flexible citizenship" was the form of cultural citizenship most consistently evident in these young people's stories about their experiences of migration and citizenship. The concept of flexible citizenship is used to describe the emergence of new uses of citizenship by migrants in response to the conditions of transnationalism, specifically, the use of transnational links to provide political or material resources not available within a single nation-state, as has been demonstrated for affluent Chinese migrants by Aihwa Ong.[13] For these South Asian immigrant youth, flexible citizenship is part of a carefully planned, long-term, family-based strategy of migration in response to economic pressures on those living in, or at the edge of, the middle class in South Asia. Nasreen, Ismail, and other immigrant youth spoke about feelings of belonging in relation to several nation-states, such as Bangladesh and Pakistan; regional or linguistic identifications, such as Gujarati and Sindhi; and villages or towns, such as Sylhet and Valsar. Their stories moved between these places, threaded together by strands of family and friendship and desires for work and education. Their desires for U.S. citizenship and permanent residency were not seen as conflicting with their affiliations with their home nation-states but layered in a flexible understanding of national belonging, embedded in mobility and migration.

Saskia Sassen points out that practices of citizenship are no longer based in the arena of the nation-state alone, as the national state has been transformed, but extend to "international arenas." Actors now make claims that express what some call "postnational citizenship," which is partly outside the national realm, or "denationalized citizenship," based on a transformation of the nation itself, but both forms coexist as the nation-state continues to be significant.[14] Flexible citizenship, in my view, is a manifestation of both postnational and denationalized citizenship, for it emerges in response to changes in the institution of citizenship within nation-states as well as to shifts in power on national and global scales. This concept is different from traditional notions of dual citizenship, which imply an actual legal status as citizen of two nation-states; in contrast, flexible citizenship leaves open questions of national loyalty or strategic uses of citizenship status for legal and economic purposes. It is a form of citizenship that responds to the conditions of globalization and U.S. domination, although not in the romanticized sense of Michael Hardt and Antonio Negri's "multitude" of immigrants resisting empire by crossing national borders.[15] But it is also true that empire needs the labor power of the mobile multitude, so flexible citizenship has emerged in tandem with the flow of labor across national borders that benefits the U.S. economy, in some cases facilitating labor migration and in other cases developed strategically by migrants moving between different labor markets, as Ismail's story suggests. Despite the interest in transnational movements, the political potential of "postnational citizenship"[16] or "global citizenship"[17] remains an abstract ideal, given that individual and collective rights still remain largely tied to territorially bounded nation-states.[18] Political movements, too, continue to address their claims for immigrant and civil rights to the nation-state as the guarantor of rights, as evident in the mass immigrant rights marches in the United States in 2006.

Ong argues that the flexibility of state sovereignty allows it to use the logic of "exception to create new economic possibilities, spaces, and techniques for governing the population," and "the neoliberal exception thus pries open the seam of sovereignty and citizenship, generating successive degrees of insecurity for low-skilled citizens and migrants who will have to look beyond the state for the safeguarding of their rights."[19] Ong extended her work on flexible citizenship to develop the concept of "latitudinal citizenship," embedded in "horizontal spaces of market rights" and emerging from ethnic networks and labor relations that span national borders under neoliberal capitalism, tying together an analysis of Asian American communities and global capitalism.[20] Flexible citizenship does not only resist or only serve global capitalism but often manages to do both, as illustrated by the stories of the youth above and their transnational family networks. They migrated to the United States with their families to try to avail themselves of perceived economic and educational opportunities but ended up as low-wage workers in the service sector—with the exception of Ismail, whose family was slightly more affluent and educated, but whose aspirations to transnational entrepreneurship were still a distant vision.

There has been a "globalization" and "flexibilization" of citizenship with the increasing flows of people and capital across national borders, but this has not led to greater flexibility of rights for all.[21] South Asian Muslim immigrant youth understood that their transnational vision for mobility and collective advancement, as well as re-creation of family ties, was necessarily linked to formal citizenship and legal belonging in the nation-state. Nasreen's family was one of several that had been divided by immigration regulations of entry and citizenship and so all these immigrant youth acknowledged the importance of nation-state membership in defining who could travel, work, or vote. About half of these immigrant youth had green cards already; the remaining were a mix of citizens and undocumented immigrants. Nearly all of them desired a U.S. passport because of what they perceived as economic and civic benefits, including the right to vote. For example, Nasreen said that she wanted to take advantage of federal financial aid for college, and several said that they wanted to be able to travel freely between the United States and South Asia, to be mobile in work and family life. After 9/11, of course, naturalization seemed to become less a matter of choice for immigrants—particularly Muslim, South Asian, and Arab Americans—than a hoped-for shield against the abuses of civil rights, which Nasreen worried were being eroded even for U.S. citizens. In fact, students such as Ismail were surprised that I had not obtained citizenship yet in the fall of 2001 and wanted to know why it had taken me so long to obtain the vital documents. I had to explain that by the time my own parents became naturalized and could sponsor me for a green card, I had already advanced into the "adult children over twenty-one" category that was a low priority for permanent residency; I was still waiting for U.S. citizenship, which I had decided to apply for only after 9/11. This reflexive discussion of citizenship momentarily shifted my relationship with these young immigrants, as they perceived themselves to have advanced a small step further on the legal road to official belonging to the state, and worried about my own vulnerability.

Legal citizenship and immigration documents were understood by these youth as artifacts created by the state that they needed in order to move across national borders and to be reunited with their families, but they were also the source of disruption of family ties and cleavages of emotional bonds. In some cases, these immigrant youth had fathers who migrated alone many years earlier; at least three students, Faisal, Osman, and Nasreen, had been separated from their fathers for twelve to fifteen years and so had basically spent their childhood years without them. For Nasreen's father, migration was supposedly an investment in his children's education, first and foremost, but this aspiration was ironically undermined in some cases by the difficult process of migration. Faisal, who was from Pakistan, said his father had left Peshawar for the United States right after he was born and worked there, returning to visit his family occasionally, till their visas were approved. By the time Faisal came to the United States, however, his older brother was too old to enroll in high school and had to struggle to get a GED certificate and find a job with his limited English skills.

Flexible citizenship is a strategy driven by family and based on family relationships, which are used to sponsor relatives for permanent residency and citizenship, but it is also a strategy that divides and disperses families and alters the meaning of kinship ties. These youth seemed to take these transnational family arrangements matter of factly, but they also spoke longingly of the friends and familiar places they had left behind. There is an affective dimension to flexible citizenship rooted in a geography of loss, sorrow, and memory, and in feelings of alienation or disorientation. For these youth, there is, at some level, an ambivalence about the biopolitics of migration, or the ways in which migrants are "a form of human life upon which the sovereignty of states, of ethnic/religious communities . . . can be performed and 'natured'"; if migrant lives are considered anomalous, drawing on Giorgio Agamben's work, they are also the "spaces of exception" that help define notions of " 'normal' citizenship and community life."[22]

It is ironic that South Asian immigrants, and Asian Americans more generally, are held up in the United States as "model minority" citizens who embody traditional "family values," presumably promoting stable family units with two parents. Yet one could also view these immigrants as the model citizens of global capitalism who are willing to scatter family members across the globe and separate parents from their children. These are the actual "family values" that the globalized free market engenders, even as "broken families" are paradoxically denounced by conservatives, for immigrants rely on transnational family networks created through chain migration and the pursuit of flexible citizenship. There are other, complex shifts in "cultural values" that the often reductionist debate about immigration and immigrant cultures in the United States fails to note. For example, Ismail spoke of how the pressure of trying to juggle school and work gave him little time to socialize with other South Asian friends, let alone participate in cultural events such as "traditional" folk dances. An Indian girl, Zeenat, spoke of the difficulties of learning what it meant to work outside the home, which she did not have to do in India; she noted a shift in gender roles in an immigrant community in which middle-class women may not have traditionally worked for wage labor outside the home—although this is changing in India—and where it is now common for immigrant girls and women to work because of economic pressures in the United States. This is an example of how "tradition" in South Asian Muslim immigrant communities, which are perceived as conservative or unchanging, is actually flexible in arenas linked to work and citizenship, challenging Orientalist discourses about "immigrant traditions" or "Muslim cultures" as somehow outside of the influence of global capital and media. Cultural practices and ideals are enmeshed with the demands of neoliberal globalization, for transnational labor networks and ethnic ties draw these immigrant youth and families into what Aihwa Ong calls "lateral spaces or latitudes," spanning national borders that promote ethnicization, but also a persistent self-disciplining and flexibility in response to the demands of the market.[23]

Working-class South Asian migrants enact practices of flexible citizenship, if at greater cost and with fewer material benefits to themselves and their children than those of elite migrants and "parachute kids."[24] Some of these youth in Wellford, such as Ismail, imagine their lives spanning national borders and speak of returning to South Asia in the future, at least temporarily, once they have become U.S. citizens and perhaps after their parents have retired there. Ismail wanted to set up a transnational hi-tech business so that he could live part-time in Gujarat and part-time in the United States while supporting his parents. This was not just an instrumentalist strategy, but also a way to express his nationalist attachments and feelings of obligation to the home nation-state, using the benefits of U.S. citizenship. Transnational marriages and social ties are common in these immigrant families, but this does not mean they happen easily or smoothly. Despite these struggles to realize flexible citizenship, some of the immigrant youth I spoke to still expressed hope that they could create the transnational future they imagined, for themselves and their families, a future curtailed by restrictions in both home and host nation-states and contested in debates about national allegiance in both places. For example, the anti-Muslim massacres in Gujarat in spring 2002, and the military standoff between India and Pakistan that preceded it, reinforced for Indian Muslim youth their ambiguous position between religious and national identifications.

Official practices of flexible citizenship for the benefit of home nations have been encouraged by South Asian states, including the Indian government, which developed policies to encourage Indian citizens living overseas, or Non-Resident Indians (NRIs), to invest in the Indian economy, especially as foreign currency reserves were declining in the early 1990s.[25] PIO (Persons of Indian Origin) cards were created in 1999, representing an interim category of flexible citizenship that could be purchased for three hundred dollars, and conferred the right to acquire property but not the right to vote; this is not available, however, to persons of Indian origin in Pakistan and Bangladesh, thus excluding Muslim populations that were displaced by the partition of the subcontinent but are not officially recognized as part of the Indian diaspora.[26] The Constitution of India still does not allow dual citizenship, but in 2006 the government introduced the Overseas Citizenship of India (OCI) scheme to allow foreign citizens easier travel to India and limited economic rights (but no voting rights), continuing to exclude citizens of Pakistan and Bangladesh.[27] While on the one hand the Indian government was issuing PIO cards to wealthy diasporic Indians, on the other hand it was planning to develop identity cards to identify and deport "illegal settlers" from Pakistan and Bangladesh to combat "terror threats," using language remarkably similar to that of the U.S. government after 9/11.[28] So the challenges to national belonging for South Asian Muslims, in particular Indian Muslims, need to be considered on both sides of the transnational terrain in which citizenship is claimed and contested, in the United States and also in South Asia itself.

Practices of Flexible Citizenship

I found that the transnational affiliations of these immigrant youth were based on at least three related processes of "self-making and being-made" in relation to different nation-states.[29] First, their everyday identifications with India or Pakistan were based largely on transnational popular culture: on Bollywood (Hindi) films, South Asian television serials, and Hindi music that they accessed through video, DVDs, satellite TV, and the Internet. Many of the South Asian boys, for example, regularly surfed the Internet for Hindi film and music Web sites either at home or on computers in the International Center. Jamila, a Bangladeshi immigrant girl, talked of visiting Internet chat rooms for diasporic Bangladeshi youth as well as youth in Bangladesh who are part of a transnational Bangladeshi community. She commented that Bangladeshis "in London, they're like, they're almost the same as me." Some of the girls regularly watched episodes of Hindi TV serials on DVD or satellite TV, and everyone watched Indian films on video. An Indian girl, Sara, was an avid fan of *Kusum*, the Hindi TV serial, and knew all the details of the intricate relationships of the extended families in the serial. These films conjured up an imagined India that was both remote and close, since she and other youth were themselves living in extended or "joint" families reconstituted in the United States, though these were now spread across apartment buildings and city blocks.

The home is an important site for consuming South Asian popular culture, since few of these youth had the money or time to go to movie theaters or other public spaces of cultural consumption, with the exception perhaps of shopping malls, where they strolled with friends. In almost all of the homes I visited, large-screen televisions and entertainment centers occupied a prominent place in the living room, and some also subscribed to satellite links with South Asian Zee-TV. It became apparent that national and transnational identities were explored and fashioned by these youth through the consumption of popular culture. Néstor García Canclini has observed that "for many men and women, especially youth, the questions specific to citizenship, such as how we inform ourselves and who represents our interests, are answered more often than not through private consumption of commodities and media offerings than through the abstract rules of democracy or through participation in discredited legal organizations."[30]

Second, flexible citizenship is necessarily intertwined with labor and education, issues that are interrelated for working-class, immigrant youth. Work on Muslim immigrant youth, however, has generally privileged religious and cultural identities but underemphasized the role of labor. Understanding the particular position of different groups of South Asian Muslim immigrant youth in the labor market and neoliberal economy is important for analyzing the processes that have constructed South Asian, Muslim, or Arab Americans, especially undocumented and working-class immigrants, as targets of detention and deportation after 9/11. The assumption that certain groups are "aliens" who can be expelled from the nation emerges from processes that are cultural and political as well as economic, and that extend well before the events of 2001. Mae Ngai and others, for example, have shown how the historical need for cheap Mexican labor in the Southwest made "illegality" constitutive of a "racialized Mexican identity" that was considered outside of the national polity, based on cultural and national factors central to modern racism and definitions of national identity.[31]

The South Asian immigrant youth in this study came to the United States with their families as migrant workers, in some sense, and worked in low-wage, part-time jobs in retail and fast food industries. These young workers thus provide the flexible labor that the globalized U.S. economy relies on for maximum profit, but they also find that the opportunities available to migrant workers through immigration and citizenship policies discriminate between U.S. and foreign-born workers. The increasing reliance on part-time, low-wage, or flexible labor in the service sector economy, fueled by immigrant labor, accompanied the rise of neoliberalism, or the reorganization of global capitalism according to free market principles, supposedly free of state intervention.[32] These neoliberal state formations are accompanied by neoliberal notions of citizenship that celebrate "individual freedom" and self-reliant citizens as well as mask social inequalities and U.S. imperial policies. The privatization of citizenship in the neoliberal state has diminished the right of citizens to public goods and services that are allocated according to individual "worthiness" and not by right. "Good" immigrants deserving of citizenship who can affirm the myth of a nation of hard-working immigrants are distinguished from "bad" immigrants who are a threat to society and deserve to be expelled. This is evident in the frame contrasting "good" (loyal, productive, politically "moderate") and "bad" (anti-U.S., militant, or fundamentalist) Muslim or Arab immigrants and the ongoing discourse about immigration reform focusing on "legalization" or amnesty for Latin American immigrants that reflect "assumptions about citizenship and alienage."[33] The threat of deportation suppresses wages but also helps keep undocumented labor compliant, a strategy that was used to maximum effect after 9/11, since the detentions and raids selectively targeted undocumented Arab and Muslim immigrants and simultaneously stifled political dissent in their communities.[34]

Working-class South Asian immigrant youth entered the labor market to support their families economically and saw education in the United States as an avenue to a "better life," as Zeenat and Nasreen remarked, expressing aspirations for class mobility that had driven their migration across national borders. This "aspirational citizenship," a desire for economic advancement and educational credentials, was evident in the hopes and career ambitions of Nasreen, Ismail, and other immigrant youth. Yet these aspirations for upward mobility and achieving the American Dream are tempered by their awareness of the many constraints in realizing their goals: their daily struggles to try to keep up in school, improve their English, find even an entry-level service job with low wages, learn about the U.S. college system, and find financial aid to go to college. Soman, an Indian immigrant student, worked in his family's Bengali restaurant in Prospect Square after school and often waited on more affluent South Asian customers. He said, "Here, you live in a golden cage, but it's still a cage. . . . my life is so limited. I go to school, come to work, study, go to sleep." Soman's poignant comment about being trapped in the "golden" illusion of the American Dream also reveals the paradox in notions of "freedom" and "mobility" that shape the cage of work under neoliberal capitalism.

Third, nearly all these youth understood flexible citizenship to be a form of cultural citizenship embedded in larger global conflicts and questions of international human rights. Ismail, Nasreen, and several other youth challenged the premise of the War on Terror and thought that waging war on Afghanistan as retribution for the 9/11 attacks was unjust and would only intensify the spiral of violence. They were critical of the profiling of Muslims in the United States and concerned about the erosion of civil rights under the PATRIOT Act, appealing to legal rights, but also expressed a pragmatic concern with the limits of flexible citizenship and skepticism of the notion of the United States as a land of "freedom" and "democracy." These observations suggest a transnational analysis focusing on citizen and human rights within the United States, or India and Bangladesh, and also in other nation-states, but also an awareness of the limitations of "rights." Thus these young immigrants' experiences of flexible citizenship were necessarily layered with the politics of racialization, rights, war, and dissent.

It became clear to me that these young immigrants thought about citizenship in ways that were themselves flexible, shifting, and contextual. In some cases, religious identity actually prompted youth to think of themselves as belonging to the United States or at least identifying with its concerns, if not identifying as "American." Ismail said to me in the fall of 2001, "Islam teaches [us that] what country you live in, you should support them. . . . See, if I live in America, I have to support America, I cannot go to India." Interestingly, he seemed to connect Islam to a notion of territorialized cultural citizenship based on loyalty to the nation-state of residence. This, of course, is the same student who said that he ultimately wanted to return to India and support its economic development, but his statements about national allegiance are not as contradictory as they first appear. Ismail was able to frame his relationship to Islam in a way that would help him think through questions of loyalty at a moment when Muslims in the United States were being framed as noncitizens *because* of a particular suspicion of Muslim identity as superseding all other national identities and loyalties. Ismail, instead, seemed to be using Islam to counter this technology of exclusion and to support a flexible definition of citizenship. In his view, being Muslim actually required loyalty to the nation-state regardless of national origins. While Ismail did not speak directly to larger debates about the "relationship between state, society, and religion" among U.S. Muslims, he seemed to voice a pragmatic and also rather sophisticated understanding of citizenship as necessarily mobile, drawing on different ideological resources to respond to the exigencies of diverse moments and places.[35]

Flexibility and Control

After 9/11, however, flexible citizenship can be a tenuous or even potentially dangerous strategy for Muslim immigrant youth, for transnational ties and shifting national allegiances are precisely what have come under scrutiny for Muslim Americans by the state in the era of the PATRIOT Act. "The privilege of transnational identification," according to Sally Howell and Andrew Shryock, "has been, for Arabs in Detroit, the first casualty of the War on Terror."[36] After 9/11, ties to Muslim communities and organizations outside the nation cast Muslim and Arab immigrants as potential security threats to the United States, even if only through transnational businesses or charities, or at least as immigrants whose political loyalties were suspect.[37] Travel across national borders; money transfers, including donations to Islamic charities; and transnational businesses and organizations have all been monitored and used to detain Arab and Muslim immigrants, as the state has broadened its definitions of involvement with "terrorism" through the PATRIOT Act.[38] In late 2001, U.S. Customs launched "Operation Green Quest" to seize currency and cashier's checks being sent out of the country by Arabs and Muslims, supposedly to fund terrorists, including individuals and groups who had never threatened the United States.[39] Small businesses owned by South Asian and Arab immigrants in the United States were investigated on the suspicion that their owners were somehow funding "militant" groups, leading to nationwide arrests of Indian Muslims and Pakistanis working in jewelry stores and raids of Indian-owned convenience stores in California in 2002, although no links were found to terrorist groups.[40] The impact of all of this, of course, is that Muslim and Arab entrepreneurs and workers have suffered economically for taking advantage of their transnational networks.

After 9/11, the Bush administration shut down "three of the largest Muslim charities in the United States, on the charge that they provided 'material support' for terrorist activity without a criminal charge or hearing."[41] The government used the International Emergency Economic Powers Act to ban all transactions with the charities and freeze millions of dollars, as President Bill Clinton had done in 1995 to block funding for several political organizations in the Middle East, including ten Palestinian groups who were critical of the "peace process."[42] This selective clamping down of transnational flows of funds is clearly political, as it has restricted the donations that many Muslim and Arab Americans send to support relief for those suffering from war and occupation in Iraq, Palestine, and other zones of conflict in which the United States has strategic interests. The flow of money to the Middle East is now carefully monitored, and funding from overseas to organizations, businesses, and mosques in the United States is suspect, creating an additional layer of frustration and anxiety for Muslim, South Asian, and Arab American entrepreneurs, political advocates, and religious clerics.[43]

There is also greater fear among Muslim and Arab immigrants about sending money to support family members in their home countries, particularly through money-transfer agencies run by Muslim Americans. It is not just immigrant families in the United States who have been affected by the War on Terror, but also families overseas who depend on economic remittances from relatives working there and, on a larger scale, their homeland economies. For example, one estimate suggests that at least 95 percent of Somali immigrants in the United States send money home and more than 40 percent of war-torn Somalia's GDP is from remittances from Somalis abroad.[44] The family ties, immigration networks, financial connections, and political links that constitute Muslim and Arab diasporas have been constrained by monitoring and repression.[45] Increasingly, diaspora is not just viewed by these communities as a site of hoped-for cultural and economic flexibility and opportunity but also a zone of increased state suspicion and repression.

While not all the youth in this study were engaged in institutionalized transnational practices involving business or organizational ties, they felt the power of the state to limit their mobility across national borders and to interrogate their national allegiances, and also experienced the anxiety felt by their families and community as their businesses and immigration histories come under state scrutiny. Flexibility, then, is always in tension with *control*, and it is a strategy that is in practice constrained by the state and by ideologies of who can and cannot move or waver. Doreen Massey describes this as "the power-geometry of time-space compression" in globalization, which shapes not just "differentiated mobility," but also which groups initiate, or are altered or imprisoned by, flows of capital and labor.[46] Much has been said in the academic literature, and also in popular discourse on globalization, about the movement of bodies, commodities, capital, and images that is part of a "transnational" world.[47] But these discourses sometimes underemphasize how this movement and crossing of national spaces is also powerfully controlled, and coercive, especially as flexible labor is used to discipline and exploit immigrant workers. Ong's recent work on immigrant labor in the Silicon Valley suggests that there is a "splintering of cosmopolitan privilege" for low-wage or undocumented workers, as well as Indian "technomigrants" on H1-B visas who are "semi-indentured" through insecure contracts. Some migrants clearly enjoy the rights and privileges of sovereign subjects more than others.[48]

Furthermore, the War on Terror has been waged primarily against immigrants, heightening the distinction between citizens and noncitizens and making legal citizenship a crucible for the post-9/11 crackdown. Nasreen, Ismail, and all the other Muslim immigrant youth I spoke to were anxious about getting legal citizenship for themselves and their family members in a climate of repression and erosion of civil rights. David Cole points out that since 9/11, "the government has repeatedly targeted noncitizens, selectively denying them liberties that citizens rightfully insist upon for themselves."[49] Immigration law is intentionally used in lieu of criminal law to execute the domestic crackdown in order to avoid the constitutional requirements applied to citizens.[50] The contradictions between discourses that celebrate global flows of people, capital, and commodities and the realities of detention, deportation, and involuntary migration highlight the tension between flexibility and coercion, mobility and immobility.

This does not mean that there is a stark dichotomy between the flexibility of transnationalism and the inflexibility of regulation by state and capital, but there is often an acute tension in the way time, not just space, is experienced by those who move and those who hope to stay. Mobility and temporality can feel powerfully, even painfully, constraining for those who are circumscribed by immigration laws, state documents, and racialized perceptions of those who belong and those who do not. Flexible citizenship is layered with this tension of immobility and with complex feelings—of ambivalence, anxiety, frustration, desire, fear, and fantasy—that the South Asian immigrant youth in this study expressed as they grappled with the demands of neoliberal capitalism. In the larger study, I explore the ways in which these working-class immigrant youth struggled with the expectations of self-reliance, autonomy, and individual freedom encoded in neoliberal citizenship and the stark realities of their low-wage, part-time service sector jobs—even more tenuous in a weak economy—that shattered their beliefs in the American Dream. The ideals of neoliberal citizenship mystify policies of privatization of social services and erosion of the welfare state and mask the social inequalities generated by the "Washington Consensus" on structural adjustment and U.S. imperial policies.[51]

Flexible Empire

The ideologies and practices of flexible citizenship are in dialectical relationship with those of what I call "flexible empire"—the imperial regimes of governmentality that regulate bodies and ideas of belonging, excluding certain subjects who are deemed undeserving of rights under national or international law due to the threat they pose to Western "civilization" or "our way of life." One of the arguments I make in the larger project is that U.S. empire is itself characterized by flexibility and secrecy in its political and military interventions; it is historically based on indirect rather than direct territorial control, relying on covert operations, proxy wars, and client states. The ambiguity of this "flexible empire" has contributed to the collective denial of U.S. imperial power that is being challenged by a new generation of theorists of U.S. empire, building on earlier work on this peculiar form of "imperialism without colonies."[52] Amy Kaplan points out that the U.S. brand of imperialism led to the creation of new designations of overseas territories, under varying degrees of U.S. control, and new categories of persons and citizens serving imperial interests while obscuring the nature of U.S. imperialism.[53] This process has continued to the present day and is illustrated by the contradictory national space occupied by Guantánamo Bay, neither fully under Cuban or U.S. sovereignty but clearly under U.S. control, and ambiguous designations of "enemy combatants" not entitled to the legal rights of the Geneva Convention.[54]

The dispersed, often de-terrioritalized nature of U.S. imperial power is in many ways mirrored by the dispersed, transnational networks that resist it.

One way to describe the politics of the War on Terror, according to Enseng Ho, is in terms of a confrontation between empire and diaspora. Ho argues that there is a tension between the transnational social, political, economic, and religious networks established by diasporic communities and the imperial forces that try to suppress transnational political movements viewed as oppositional.[55] Ho points out that diasporas often emerge from histories of Western colonization, trade, marriage and kinship, and religious ties that stretch across national borders and that also bind together communities of resistance to empire. In fact, it is the awareness of these transnational political movements that underlies the U.S. government's suspicion and monitoring of transnational economic, religious, and political ties of Muslim Americans after 9/11. However, the specific regional or local grievances that animate these transnational networks are generally not acknowledged by state officials in the civilizational rhetoric of the War on Terror.

Ho observes that the resistance of many in these transnational Muslim or Arab networks is based on their opposition to imperial policies in the regions they inhabit or originate from, such as bin Laden's demand that the United States withdraw its troops from Saudi Arabia and end its support for Israeli occupation of Palestine.[56] (This is not to mention the fact that bin Laden and his followers were, in fact, supported by the United States when they were helping to drive the Soviets out of Afghanistan, and so the transnational layers of the conflict are thicker and more complex than they are portrayed in U.S. mainstream discourse.) Ho does not condone Al Qaeda's methods or endorse their religious ideology, but he suggests that there is a historical, anti-imperial analysis evident in their actions that has a global appeal and that makes flexible citizenship a strategy of oppositional movements. This is the rationale, explicit as well as unspoken, for why flexible citizenship is both an economic necessity in a global economy and a political threat to the U.S. regime's efforts to establish a new global order serving U.S. imperial interests.

Thus flexible citizenship in the post-9/11 era raises questions about for whom citizenship is flexible, why, and how. The notion of flexible citizenship is, and always has been, politicized and has had disastrous consequences for immigrant communities in a time of national crisis. Berlant argues that cultural citizenship in the United States has become defined through the idea of crisis: the theme of a nation that is morally, culturally, and politically under attack and whose national identity must be defended, as has been propagated by conservatives for the past several decades and, most dramatically, after 9/11.[57] Flexibility in national loyalty is viewed as potentially threatening when national security is perceived to be at risk, and there is a fear that this threat is both from without—from foreigners who oppose the United States—and from within—from treacherous immigrants or "un-American" citizens. This is what drove the internment of over 100,000 Japanese Americans during World War II who were considered to be inherently loyal to the Japanese government, even if they were third-generation U.S. citizens; the detention of 10,000 immigrants, who were also legal permanent residents, detained during the Palmer Raids of 1919 because of fears of ties to Bolshevik Russia;[58] and the witch hunt by Senator McCarthy against Communists during the cold war in the 1940s and 1950s.[59] In each of these cases, citizenship was not enough to guarantee the protection of civil rights by the state, but the idea of flexible national loyalties was highlighted and exaggerated in fanning xenophobia and national hysteria and targeting particular groups as scapegoats for larger national anxieties.

Conclusion

The paradox of flexible citizenship in the current moment is that it is considered desirable for some and dangerous for others, underscoring that sovereign rights to "freedom" and "mobility" are unevenly distributed. Transnational ties have been encouraged, and produced, by global capitalism and global media as not just desirable, but necessary and even glamorous. The question is for whom flexibility of citizenship is considered favorable and supported by the state, and for whom it is seen as a threat to the nation, to be scrutinized and circumscribed at certain moments. This is a key tension as the aspirations of these immigrant youth for spatial and class mobility collide with the limits of immigrant rights and citizenship policy, especially in the War on Terror. As they negotiate these contradictions, South Asian Muslim immigrant youth draw on their experiences of labor, popular culture, work, and education to grapple with the realities of neoliberal citizenship; they develop their own critical understandings of cultural citizenship in ways that are often nuanced and flexible enough to both desire and critique the rights and opportunities promised by the nation-state and global capitalism.

Notes

This research was funded by a grant from the Russell Sage Foundation. I wish to thank my able research assistants, Palav Babaria and Sarah Khan, and Kathleen Coll for her helpful suggestions.

1. Given that the profiling of Muslim Americans for political speech and criticism of the U.S. government after 9/11, and the fact that there was only one public high school in Wellford, I changed the name of the site to try to protect the identities of these young immigrants (a couple of whom were undocumented), as much as realistically possible.

2. See notable exceptions in Asian American studies such as Sucheng Chan, *Asian Americans: An Interpretive History* (New York: Simon & Schuster Macmillan, 1991); and more recently, Mai M. Ngai, *Impossible Subjects: Illegal Aliens and the Making of Modern America* (Princeton, N.J.: Princeton University Press, 2004).

3. Donald Pease, "New Perspectives on U.S. Culture and Imperialism," in *Cultures of United States Imperialism*, ed. Amy Kaplan and Donald Pease, 22–37 (Durham: Duke University Press, 1993), 31.

4. Ann L. Stoler, "Intimations of Empire: Predicaments of the Tactile and Unseen," in *Haunted by Empire: Geographies of Intimacy in North American History*, ed. Ann L. Stoler, 1–22 (Durham, N.C.: Duke University Press, 2006), 12.

5. Pease, "New Perspectives"; Robert Young, *Postcolonialism: An Historical Introduction* (Malden, Mass.: Blackwell, 2001), 28.

6. Ediberto Román, "Membership Denied: An Outsider's Story of Subordination and Subjugation Under U.S. Colonialism," in *Moral Imperialism: A Critical Anthology*, ed. Berta E. Hernández-Truyol, 269–84 (New York: New York University Press, 2002).

7. Wellford's population is 68.1% white American, 11.9% African American, 11.9% Asian American, and 7.4% Latino (U.S. Census Bureau, 2000, http:factfinder.census.gov/bf/_lang=en_...2000 [accessed November 13, 2002]). The median household income in 1999 was $47,979, which is above the national median, but 12.9% of the population was living below poverty level, slightly above the national level, which some say is due to the significant presence of students.

8. The high school has approximately 2,000 students, of which about 40% are white and 60% are students of color. African Americans form the largest group of students of color (about 25%), followed by Latino/as (15%), and Asian Americans (about 7%). From 2000 to 2002, 33% of students spoke a language other than English as their first language, and 14% were in the bilingual program, which suggests that the immigrant student population in the school is somewhere between these figures.

9. There were about sixty students of South Asian origin, including a few Nepali and Tibetan youth, who are almost evenly split between immigrant students and second-generation youth.

10. The 2000 Census reported 2,720 Indian immigrants (2.7% of the population), 125 Pakistanis, and 120 Bangladeshis in Wellford. This, of course, does not include undocumented immigrants. The "native" population is 74.1% and foreign-born population is 25.9%; 17.7% are not citizens and 31.2% speak a language other than English (U.S. Census Bureau, 2000).

11. Lok Siu, "Diasporic Cultural Citizenship: Chineseness and Belonging in Central America and Panama," *Social Text* 19.4 (2001): 9.

12. Saskia Sassen, "The Repositioning of Citizenship: Emergent Subjects and Spaces for Politics," in *Empire's New Clothes: Reading Hardt and Negri*, ed. Paul A. Passavant and Jodi Dean, 175–98 (London: Routledge, 2004), 184; Siu, "Diasporic Cultural Citizenship."

13. Aihwa Ong, *Flexible Citizenship: The Cultural Logics of Transnationality* (Durham: Duke University Press, 1999). For a discussion of transnationalism, see Linda Basch, Nina Glick Schiller, and Cristina Szanton Blanc, eds., *Nations Unbound: Transnational Projects, Postcolonial Predicaments, and Deterritorialized Nation-States* (Amsterdam: Gordon and Breach, 1994).

14. Sassen, "The Repositioning of Citizenship," 190–91.

15. Michael Hardt and Antonio Negri, *Empire* (Cambridge, Mass.: Harvard University Press, 2000), 399.

16. Yasemin N. Soysal, "Changing Citizenship in Europe: Remarks on Postnational Membership and the National State," in *Citizenship, Nationality, and Migration in Europe*, ed. David Cesarani and Mary Fulbrook, 17–29 (London: Routledge, 1996).

17. Hardt and Negri, *Empire*.

18. Gershon Shafir, "Citizenship and Human Rights in an Era of Globalization," in *People out of Place: Globalization, Human Rights, and the Citizenship Gap*, ed. Alison Brysk and Gershon Shafir, 11–25 (London: Routledge, 2004).

19. Aihwa Ong, *Neoliberalism as Exception: Mutations in Citizenship and Sovereignty* (Durham: Duke University Press, 2006), 7, 19.

20. Ibid.,122.
21. Thomas B.Hansen and Finn Steputat, "Introduction," in *Sovereign Bodies: Citizens, Migrants, and States in the Postcolonial World*, ed. Thomas B. Hansen and Finn Steputat, 1–36 (Princeton, N.J.: Princeton University Press, 2005), 10; Barry Hindess, "Citizenship and Empire," in *Sovereign Bodies*, ed. Hansen and Steputat, 241–56, esp. 255–256.
22. Cited in Hansen and Steputat, "Introduction," 35–36.
23. Ong, *Neoliberalism as Exception*, 121–23.
24. Ong, *Neoliberalism as Exception*; Christy Chiang-Hom, "Transnational Cultural Practices of Chinese Immigrant Youth and Parachute Kids," in *Asian American Youth: Culture, Identity, and Ethnicity*, ed. Jennifer Lee and Min Zhou, 143–158 (New York: Routledge, 2004).
25. Aradhana Sharma and Akhil Gupta, "Rethinking Theories of the State in an Age of Globalization," in *The Anthropology of the State: A Reader*, ed. Aradhana Sharma and Akhil Gupta, 1–41 (Malden, Mass.: Blackwell, 2006).
26. See http://www.indianembassy.org/policy/PIO/Introduction_PIO.html (accessed September 15, 2006).
27. See http://www.indianembassy.org/New_Template/oci.asp (accessed September 15, 2006).
28. "Advani Asks States to Deport Illegal Settlers," *Times of India*, January 8, 2003, 1; "Illegal Immigrants Cause Alarm in South Mumbai," *Times of India*, Downtown Plus edition, January 10, 2003, 1.
29. Ibid.
30. Néstor García Canclini, *Consumers and Citizens: Globalization and Multicultural Conflicts* (Minneapolis: University of Minnesota Press, 2001), 5.
31. Ngai, *Impossible Subjects*, 58. Compared to South Asian and other Asian immigrants who were excluded from citizenship and also immigration on the grounds of not being legally white in the 1920s, Ngai argues that during the same period Mexicans fulfilled the need for agricultural and mining labor and were not excluded from immigration or citizenship but were racialized through a discourse that viewed them as simultaneously "white" and subjects of U.S. conquest (Ngai, *Impossible Subjects*, 58).
32. David Harvey, *A Brief History of Neoliberalism* (Oxford: Oxford University Press, 2005).
33. Susan Bibler Coutin and Phyllis P. Chock, "Your Friend the Illegal: Definition and Paradox in Newspaper Accounts of U.S. Immigration Reform," *Identities* 2.1-2 (1997): 125.
34. Sunaina Maira, "Deporting Radicals, Deporting La Migra: The Hayat Case in Lodi," *Cultural Dynamics* 19.1 (March 2007): 39–66.
35. See Ingrid Mattson, "How Muslims Use Islamic Paradigms to Define America," in *Religion and Immigration: Christian, Jewish, and Muslim Experiences in the United States*, ed. Yvonne Haddad, Jane Smith, and John Esposito, 19–215 (Walnut Creek, Calif.: AltaMira, 2003), 199.
36. Sally Howell and Andrew Shryock, "Cracking Down on Diaspora: Arab Detroit and America's 'War on Terror,'" *Anthropological Quarterly* 76.3 (2003): 445.
37. Neil MacFarquhar, "Muslim Charity Seeks Dismissal of Charges of Terrorism," *The New York Times*, December 12, 2006.
38. Neil MacFarquhar, "Fears of Inquiry Dampen Giving by U.S. Muslims," *New York Times*, October 30, 2006.
39. John Mintz and Douglas Farah, "U.S. Terror Probe Reportedly Targeting Muslim, Arab Stores," *Boston Globe*, August 12, 2002, A8.
40. Moni Basu, "Atlanta Muslims Recoil After Federal Raids," *Atlanta Journal-Constitution*, July 18, 2002, http://www.accessatlanta.com/ajc/news/0702/13probe.html (accessed October 16, 2006); Irina Slutsky, "Indian Couple Seeks Release: Jewelry Store Investigation," *The Bradenton Herald*, July 17, 2002, http://www.accessmylibrary.com/premium/0286/0286-6880641.html (accessed August 31, 2007).
41. David Cole, *Enemy Aliens: Double Standards and Constitutional Freedoms in the War on Terrorism* (New York: New Press, 2003), 76.
42. Ibid., 77.
43. Press release issued by the American-Arab Anti-Discrimination Committee (ADC), "ADC Calls Upon FBI to Explain Timing of Raids," Washington, D.C., September 21, 2006, received via e-mail on September 21, 2006.
44. Tram Nguyen, *We Are All Suspects Now: Untold Stories from Immigrant Communities After 9/11* (Boston: Beacon Press, 2005), 34; Nathalie Peutz, "Embarking on an Anthropology of Removal," *Current Anthropology* 47.2 (2006): 217–41.

45. Sally Howell and Andrew Shryock, "Cracking Down on Diaspora: Arab Detroit and America's 'War on Terror,'" *Anthropological Quarterly* 76.3 (2003): 455.

46. Doreen Massey, *Space, Place, and Gender* (Minneapolis: University of Minnesota Press, 1994).

47. Arjun Appadurai, *Modernity at Large: Cultural Dimensions of Globalization* (Minneapolis: University of Minnesota Press, 1996); Basch, Schiller, and Blanc, *Nations Unbound*.

48. Aihwa Ong, "Splintering Cosmopolitanism: Asian Immigrants and Zones of Autonomy in the American West," in *Sovereign Bodies*, ed. Hansen and Steputat (Princeton, N.J.: Princeton University Press, 2005), 257–75, 274.

49. Cole, *Enemy Aliens*, 21.

50. Ibid., 24.

51. Harvey, *A Brief History*.

52. Harvey, *A Brief History*; Amy Kaplan and Donald Pease, eds., *Cultures of United States Imperialism* (Durham: Duke University Press, 1993); Harry Magdoff, *Imperialism Without Colonies* (New York: Monthly Review Press, 2003); William A. Williams, *Empire as a Way of Life: An Essay on the Causes and Character of America's Present Predicament* (New York: Oxford University Press, 1980).

53. Amy Kaplan, "Where Is Guantánamo?" in *Legal Borderlands: Law and the Construction of American Borders*, ed. Mary Dudziak and Leti Volpp, special issue of *American Quarterly* 57.3 (September 2005): 831–58.

54. Ibid.

55. Enseng Ho, "Empire Through Diasporic Eyes: A View from the Other Boat," *Comparative Studies of Society and History* 46.2 (2004): 210–46.

56. Ibid., 234.

57. Lauren Berlant, *The Queen of America Goes to Washington City: Essays on Sex and Citizenship* (Durham, N.C.: Duke University Press, 1997). See also Alyson M. Cole, *The Cult of True Victimhood: From the War on Welfare to the War on Terror* (Stanford, Calif.: Stanford University Press, 2007).

58. Alan Brinkley, "A Familiar Story: Lessons from Past Assaults on Freedoms," in *The War on Our Freedoms: Civil Liberties in an Age of Terrorism* (New York: Century Foundation, Public Affairs Reports, 2003), 32–34; Nancy Chang, *Silencing Political Dissent: How Post-September 11 Anti-Terrorism Measures Threaten Our Civil Liberties* (New York: Seven Stories/Open Media, 2002), 39.

59. Ellen Schrecker, *Many Are the Crimes: McCarthyism in America* (Princeton, N.J.: Princeton University Press, 1998).

Beyond Mexico: Guadalupan Sacred Space Production and Mobilization in a Chicago Suburb

Elaine Peña

¡Ay, Virgencita Morena! Guadalupe, mi esperanza, del Cielo tu amor alcanza para aliviar toda pena; cuídame con tu alma Buena y dame en esta ocasión tu sagrada bendición pues con cariño constante, para venir de migrante, te traje mi corazón.
[Oh, young, dark-skinned virgin! Guadalupe, my hope, your love reaches down from the heavens and alleviates my worries; take care of me with your good soul and give me your sacred blessing, your constant affection, I came as an immigrant, I brought you my heart.]
—"Virgen de los Migrantes," prayer recited
at the Second Tepeyac of North America

One crisp fall day in a northwest suburb of Chicago, Mexican, Salvadoran, Guatemalan, and Honduran *Guadalupanas/os* gathered in the gymnasium-cum-sanctuary at the "Second Tepeyac of North America"—a sanctioned replica of the hill in Tenochtitlán (present-day Mexico City) where la Virgen de Guadalupe first made herself known to Juan Diego Cuauhtlatoatzin. Between December 9 and December 12, 1531, the Virgin appeared four times to ask Juan Diego for one thing: a temple constructed in her honor. Not only did this colonial figure—the embodiment of Iberian and indigenous spirituality—receive a shrine atop the hill of Tepeyac, but she also inspired outposts across North America and as far away as the Philippines, Kenya, and Korea.[1]

Devotees celebrated Juan Diego, the unsung hero of the apparition story, that day at the Second Tepeyac.[2] The cover of a special issue of *El Católico*, the Chicago archdioceses' official Spanish-language periodical, featured an illustration of Pope John Paul II holding Juan Diego's hand and la Virgen de Guadalupe's luminous figure in the background. The accompanying headline read: "*Canonización de Juan Diego Cuauhtlatoatzin: ¡Nuestra Señora de Guadalupe ha cumplido lo que ha prometido!*" [The canonization of Juan Diego Cuauhtlatoatzin: Our Lady of Guadalupe has accomplished what she promised!][3] Fulsome reports of the cult's historical and contemporary influence in Mexico and beyond filled the pages of the glossy magazine. Positioned between each article were job notices—"Cooks: Applebee's Zion, Illinois. Flexible Schedules, Excellent Pay, Health Insurance"—as well as advertisements for schools, shops, services, and congratulatory notes from various social clubs operating in Chicago and its suburbs.

Second Tepeyac committee members and the officiating priest had also designated this particular Sunday to formally welcome *Guadalupanas/os* from El Salvador. After the prayer service, the priest asked Salvadorans in the audience to raise their hands. A handful in a room of five hundred responded. A couple of those devotees let out a prideful holler. Giggles and applause rolled in soft waves across the crowded gym. Next, he called out for families of *Guadalupanos* from Honduras to respond, and then motioned toward a small group of believers from Guatemala. Each party responded in turn, equally proud, if underrepresented. The priest then asked the mexicanos to declare their presence. More than 90 percent of the attendees offered an assortment of *gritos*, cheers, whistling, and outstretched arms. Nervous giggles and reserved approval were now roars and toothy smiles. Finally, he called for *Americanos* to make their presence known. A wave of silence fell over the crowd. Standing against the back wall of the gymnasium, I timidly began to raise my hand with the three other "Americans" I saw positioned in the crowd like the cardinal directions of a compass. Being marked as an American, I thought, didn't really capture the fact that I was raised on the U.S.-Mexico border, traversed both Tamaulipas and Texas with ease, and that I was a U.S. citizen because I was born, literally, less than a mile north of the Rio Grande. José, my *compadre* with dual citizenship, sensing my apprehension, grabbed my thinking hand and raised it far over my head.

I attended prayer assemblies at the Second Tepeyac of North America over a two-year period (2002–2004). These experiences were familiar but always a bit strange. No longer surrounded exclusively by border-Mexican and Tejano-American devotees in South Texas but by *Guadalupanas/os* from across North and Central America, my understanding of piety, devotion, and the sacred became infused with diverse cultural perspectives, distinct idioms, and different life experiences. I spent the majority of my time working alongside immigration lawyers and shrine coordinators whose primary objective was to mitigate the pressures of undocumented life in the United States. Oftentimes, I traveled to Des Plaines with *Guadalupanas/os* from the North Side of Chicago, many of whom are "unauthorized migrants" originally from dominant sending states such as Michoacán and Guanajuato, while others hail from Veracruz and Nuevo Leon.[4] They did not necessarily find themselves aligned with fellow devotees at the Second Tepeyac on the basis of nationality or even regional affiliation. What connects adherents in Des Plaines is their allegiance to la Virgen de Guadalupe and their determination to rise above the xenophobic realities of life in "*el Norte*." This is the underlying point of the following discussion.

Framing Devotion and Migration: Theoretical, Historical, and Geographical Considerations

This article examines the dynamics that produce a transnational *sacred* space. In particular, I focus on the ways in which devotional performances used to develop sacred space—"[the] moment[s] of instability and possibility in which the spoken word or an embodied act transforms place into [sacred] space"—also contour relations of migration and nation.[5] Although scholars have attended to the intersections among the cult of Guadalupe, resettlement, and national affiliation, those efforts position Guadalupan devotion, and justly so, as an evocation of Mexican spirituality, culture, and history.[6] As early as 1754, for example, Pope Benedict XIV declared *la Virgen de Guadalupe* to be "*patrona de Nueva España*" and designated the 12th of December as her feast day. His famous proclamation, taken from Psalm 147—"*Non fecit taliter omni natione*" [It was not done thus to all nations]—differentiated Mexico from all other colonized/Christianized territories and positioned the Virgin as a Catholic icon for subjects of the crown throughout New Spain, which then stretched from northern California to El Salvador.[7] In 1935, Pope Pius XI, following his predecessor's declaration, reconfirmed *la Virgen de Guadalupe's* position as empress of Latin America *and* the Philippines.[8]

A plethora of texts interpret, substantiate, celebrate, and/or criticize the Virgin's impact on the Americas. Of particular importance to the following discussion is scholarship that focuses on Guadalupan devotees' identity formation outside of Mexico, specifically the nationalistic elements underwriting the development of ethnoreligious spaces.[9] Renderings of Mexican exiles in the 1930s escaping religious persecution, for example, and their conceptualization of México de Afuera, "unyielding dedication to nationalism, Mexican national symbols, the Spanish language, Mexican citizenship, and the Catholic faith rooted in devotion to Mexico's national patroness, Nuestra Señora de Guadalupe," set a precedent for contemporary analyses.[10]

Although Mexican *Guadalupanas/os* in Des Plaines display analogous convictions, the intercultural and multinational dynamics sustaining the

Second Tepeyac demand that we refocus our optic. That Guadalupe is an inherent part of Mexico's identity is undeniable. Her presence, however, does not represent a solely "Mexican" perspective; the Second Tepeyac provides an atmosphere in which communities are encouraged to celebrate their distinct heritages and homelands. Devotees, many of whom learn about and circulate religious practices along migration circuits, acknowledge each other's nationalist affiliations, but their religious principles exceed secular nationalist identifications.[11] Further, they appeal explicitly to the sacred when expressing collective pro-immigrant subjectivities. As Manuel A. Vásquez and Marie F. Marquardt argue:

> Released from the disciplinary power of the modern secular nation-state, religion is free to enter the globalizing, regionalizing, and localizing dynamics described here to generate new identities and territories. . . . Cities [and suburbs] become places where those displaced by globalization—be it Latino immigrants in the United States or peasants migrating to growing metropolises in Latin America—try to make sense of their baffling world by mapping and remapping sacred landscapes through religious practices like making pilgrimages, holding festivals, and constructing altars, shrines, and temples.[12]

In this way, inter-American sacred space development allows adherents to circumvent secular limitations dictated by the nation-state. Further, ethnoreligious community formation, even at its early stages, encourages polyvalent expressions of the sacred that enable devotees to address the debilitating material and societal effects of anti-immigration narratives. The following considers how *Guadalupanas/os* from across North and Central America manage the politics of integration at the Second Tepeyac through a multisited examination of the architectural, rhetorical, and performance-oriented dynamics that produce sacred space in Des Plaines *and* Mexico City. The conclusion reviews the ways in which sacred space functions as a political sanctuary in which devotees may learn about immigration legislation and future mobilization opportunities.

Guadalupan devotion in the suburb of Des Plaines continues a long history of ethnoreligious community in Chicago. Migrant laborers traveled between western Mexico and the Midwest in the early twentieth century, for example, and many practiced their specific cultural and religious ideals in the urban landscape. External factors also helped guide the settlement process. The Illinois Steel Company and the Archbishop of Chicago, Cardinal Mundelein, organized the construction of Our Lady of Guadalupe Parish in 1923. Illinois Steel donated twelve thousand dollars to finance the construction project while the archdiocese, which had previously denied the merit of establishing a parish, "blessed" the project.[13] Founding institutional spaces in immigrant neighborhoods such as the Back of the Yards and the Near West Side continued the legacy of the church's strategy for catering to diverse communities. In 1846, for example, the archdiocese offered St. Peter's and St. Joseph's to German settlers and St. Patrick's church to the Irish population. In 1880, the Italian community received Assumption BVM and in 1889, John Augustine Tolton, the first African American to be ordained in the United States, helped build St. Monica's for the black community.[14]

Pierrette Hondagneu-Sotelo and her colleagues use the term "religio-ethnic cultural expansion" to describe "the ways in which a distinctively ethnic and religious form is adopted, transformed, and expanded to new inclusiveness in the United States."[15] Karen Mary Davalos's Chicago-based study of the Via Crucis (Stations of the Cross) in the Pilsen neighborhood, which demonstrates how generations of residents continue to use this port of entry to perform rituals, offers a terrific exemplar.[16] Since 1977, that Easter Holy Week ritual, in which devotees reenact Jesus Christ's agonizing walk toward crucifixion, has attracted thousands of "Mexicanos and other Latinos" from the Chicago area and the Midwest. "The crowd itself," Davalos suggests, "has become a symbol of the event and the people comment on its size, strength, and security for 'the undocumented who normally remain hidden.' . . . Pilsen residents and other Mexicanos forge a relationship as a community, speak in a nearly unified voice against forms of oppression, and transcend space and time from Mexico to Jerusalem, Mexico to the United States, Chicago to Calvary."[17] Similar to Guadalupan devotional rituals enacted at the Second Tepeyac, the Via Crucis offers disenfranchised communities an opportunity to mobilize in which they not only celebrate their respective culture and homeland but also articulate a collective political subjectivity that appeals to the sacred.

There are productive differences, however, that relate to the site-specific components of each case study. Davalos argues that "material barriers, physical dangers, and social inequalities [in Pilsen] constitute the architecture of domination."[18] With the term "architecture of domination," she critically pinpoints Chicago's problematic race/urban space politics, specifically how basic city services and infrastructure upkeep are selectively applied according to neighborhood demographics shaped by industrialization processes.[19] By contrast, and pivotal to this study, are the ways in which Chicago's deindustrialization has transformed the suburbs. The metropolis entered a period of economic restructuring following World War II. Lower land costs and unionization rates, a growing labor pool, an expanded highway system, and the shifting consumer market led to the repositioning of industry outside of the city. Race, particularly the "explosive political militancy of the civil rights struggles of the late 1960s," equally influenced Chicago's deindustrialization.[20] By 1981, Chicago had lost 25 percent of its factories and 27 percent of its manufacturing jobs to the wider metropolitan area. Many laborers followed work to the suburbs, while others entered the tertiary labor market: retail, restaurants, and hotels. The development of the city's transit system and O'Hare International Airport, which is adjacent to Des Plaines, attracted raw material and product distribution centers, corporation headquarters, and the laborers who sustain these industries and accompanying service sector needs.[21]

A predominantly white suburb, Des Plaines seems a peculiar choice for a sanctioned replica of Mexico's most important colonial-era sacred space.[22] Likelihood aside, Maryville Academy, the isolated ninety-seven-acre property that hosts the Second Tepeyac, offers a secure communal space where people may worship and mobilize (simultaneously if they wish). Initially opened to help orphaned children displaced after the Great Chicago Fire in 1871, Maryville, which is currently comanaged by the Archdiocese of Chicago and the state's Department of Children and Family Services, is one of Illinois' largest facilities for treating battered and neglected children.[23] The verdant campus surrounding "*el Cerrito*" [little hill; Tepeyac] draws thousands of devotees on foot, on bicycles, on buses, and even on planes. This is not to suggest that this institutional space is ideal. The Catholic Church, with her modes of production and expansion, is a power industry laden with hierarchies and stratification. Although coordinators and volunteers are committed to social justice issues and to advancing cultural, economic, and educational development within the congregation, the situation is far from perfect. Community members do not talk about gay rights, for example, not in public at least. Nor do I wish to imply that Chicago's suburbs are immune to "urban" problems: xenophobia, poverty, gang and police violence, and so on. Instead, I seek to acknowledge the varying trajectories of transmigration circuits and to distinguish suburban-based sacred space production.

Constructing Sacred Space

In October 2001, the Institute for Historical and Theological Worship for the Virgin of Guadalupe in Mexico City, under the guidance of Cardinal Norberto Rivera Carrera, proclaimed the Church of Maryville in Des Plaines the "Second Tepeyac of North America."[24] The reproduction of sacred space, however, does not commence with proclamations alone. In 1987, Joaquín Martinez, then a lay volunteer at a church in the Chicago suburb of Northbrook, solicited a statue of la Virgen de Guadalupe from relatives in San Luis Potosí. Inspired by a call for a Marian year by Pope John Paul II, Martinez organized a tour that took the statuette to various Chicago-area schools, parishes, seminaries, convents, hospitals, and retirement homes, as well as to Daley plaza, Mayor Daley's home, and eventually, after much uncertainty, Maryville Academy. In 1991, Martínez, using the apparition story as a primary point of reference, conceptualized the construction of a Second Tepeyac. He enlisted Chicago-area architects to study Tepeyac's physical layout, which was a formidable challenge considering its colonial-era roots.[25] Deliberating among multiple options, a shrine committee, organized and led by Martínez, decided that reproducing Tepeyac's outdoor sanctuary—el Jardín de la Ofrenda [the Offering Garden]—would best fit Maryville's resources and devotee's needs. After securing authorization, donations, and fund-raising support, the burgeoning Guadalupan community oversaw the ten-year construction period.

Maryville's outdoor structure displays an eight-by-six-foot copy of the "ayate de Juan Diego" on "el Cerrito" that serves to legitimate the replication process. According to the apparition myth, the Virgin filled Juan Diego's *ayate*, a garment made of maguey fiber worn across the torso, with roses and miraculously imprinted her likeness underneath them. Its aged appearance, the contrast between the deep warm tones of her aura and the tranquil blue of her robe, and the multihued haze of pale sky that seems to maintain her form in perpetual levitation encapsulate the historic moment in which Christianity secured its place in the New World. This *ayate* (which is currently protected behind a bullet- and fire-proof structure in Mexico City) and not, for instance, an interpretation featuring an altered color scheme, roses, a Mexican flag, and/or a close-up of the Virgin cuddling Pope John Paul II, is the only representation that has the historical and symbolic currency to legitimize the replica. For this reason, Maryville officials insist that it remain front and center on the simulated landscape.

Directly to the right of the image stand two bronze statues representing the Virgin's fourth apparition atop the hill of Tepeyac in which Juan Diego discovered the roses on his *ayate*. Maryville-contracted architects drew the likeness of these statues directly from the seventeen bronze statues mounted in Tepeyac's Offering Garden (est. 1986). The original in Mexico City, designed by Aurelio G. D. Mendoza and sculpted by Alberto Pérez Soria and Gerardo Quiróz, symbolize and celebrate the conquered peoples' rapid acceptance of the cult of Guadalupe and the birth of a new mestizo population—the sons of Indians and Spaniards. Among those immortalized are Fray Juan de Zumárraga and generic indigenous devotees offering Guadalupe *maíz*,

Figure 1.
Replica of the *Ayate de Juan Diego* behind bulletproof glass, Des Plaines, Illinois. Photo by author, September 2002.

flowers, and incense (figure 2). Maryville designers imitated the aesthetic of the statues precisely, but the message is different from that of the statues in Mexico City—not because the el Cerrito shrine has two instead of fifteen bronze statues, but because la Virgencita's gaze rests on Juan Diego and not on Fray Zumárraga (figure 3). By focusing on the upright Spanish church official and not on the kneeling indigenous man, the original offering garden reinforces the superiority and authority of the church over the conquered. In Des Plaines, the statue's focused gaze on Juan Diego emphasizes the Virgin's position as mother and protector of the conquered. Promoting the latter idea, I would argue, is the most effective approach for unifying an ethnically and culturally diverse congregation. The most recent addition to the shrine, two large stones engraved with the words "In Memory of Blessed Mother, St. Juan Diego, Indians & Emigrantes," memorializes the Virgin's benevolent role—her deep connection and commitment to those experiencing hardship. By placing *"emigrantes"* alongside Juan Diego and "Indians," committee members combine the foundations of the colonial cult and the diverse requirements of a U.S. congregation to produce a transnational sacred space that is distinct from the original.

Many *Guadalupanas/os* with whom I have worked explain that they are drawn to the serenity and sanctity of the landscaped gardens. Some who have

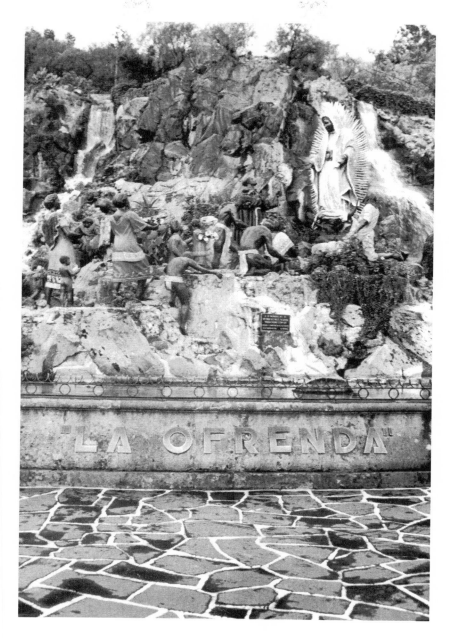

Figure 2.
Bronze statues atop of *El Jardín de la Ofrenda*, Mexico. Photo by author, August 2003.

Figure 3.
Bronze statues of the Virgin and Juan Diego
atop *El Cerrito*, Des Plaines, Illinois. Photo
by author, September 2002

worshipped at the shrine in Mexico City
readily admit that the replica is not as awe
inspiring as Tepeyac's gardens; but no one
denies that the Second Tepeyac is a sacred
space, despite the fact that there is no tradition there of a Marian apparition.
As two women from Michoacán (via Pilsen) explained to me while we were
selling tamales and cups of *champurrado* to *peregrinos* [pilgrims] on a bitterly
cold December 12 morning, "*Ella, sí está*" [She is here]. It takes only "*un grano
de arena*" [one grain of sand], they agreed emphatically. This saying literally
suggests that any measure of sacred space, no matter the size, when transposed,
will make its new surroundings sacred, like making tap water instantaneously
holy by mixing it with water blessed in a church.[26] The Second Tepeyac's popular appeal and authority owes much to this adage. This expression, however,
also suggests a localized form of time-space compression.[27] Building on David
Harvey's concept that describes the acceleration and wide-reaching potential
of business and communication networks, we can imagine how notions of
the sacred, like global capital, can transcend the nation-state.[28] Maryville's
built environment inspires these women to transcend time and space on their
own terms, to link the original with its counterpart in a way that surpasses a
state-based framework.

There are additional ways, however, that the Virgin appears in different locations—through performance. Consider these lyrics from "*Las Apariciones Guadalupanas*" [The Guadalupan Apparitions]

Desde el cielo una hermosa mañana
[One beautiful morning from heaven]
(repeat)

La Guadalupana, la Guadalupana, La Guadalupana, bajó al Tepeyac
[the Virgin of Guadalupe, the Virgin of Guadalupe, the Virgin of Guadalupe descended to Tepeyac]

Suplicante juntaba las manos
[She clasped her hands together pleadingly]
(repeat)

Y eran mexicanos, y eran mexicanos, y eran mexicanos
su porte y su faz
[Her bearing and her face were Mexican,
and they were Mexican, and they were Mexican, and they were Mexican]

This song, which relates the Virgin's sixteenth century apparitions on the hill of Tepeyac, has local and transnational significance.[29] Devotees, clergy members, and lay leaders alike perform this mythic story to celebrate the cult of Guadalupe across national borders and for international communities. Paradoxically, the text pinpoints the nationalist components inherent in the cult. In practice, however, adherents do not necessarily subscribe to the composition's implicit secular distinction but to the Virgin's power to protect them. We shall see in the following sections, performances shift shapes; practitioners modify meaning to accommodate their immediate and long-term needs.

Securing History / Legitimizing Sacred Space: Guadalupe's Apparition Made Flesh

At Tepeyac in Mexico City, tourists/devotees/employees have multiple opportunities to witness *la Virgen de Guadalupe's* apparition story. Every hour, the clock tower, el Carillón, located at the easternmost point of the Plaza de las Américas, becomes a stage from which Guadalupe's story is reenacted by mechanical bodies. Life-sized figures of the Virgin, Juan Diego, Juan Bernandino, and Fray Juan de Zumárraga present the four-part apparition story to spectators standing in the atrium. The space in the middle of the tower opens up to show Juan Diego, a soft-spoken, humbly dressed brown man. In other presentations, such as posters, postcards, prayer booklets, and church statues, this iconic Indian has been mysteriously whitened—his skin tone has been lightened and his facial features Europeanized. But in this performance his colored body is a key element of this daily reenactment. He remains native for the natives who sustain the shrine. These figures move seamlessly from left to right, guided along a circular track custom-designed in Holland. There are no special light or sound effects. Their gestures are simple; their facial expressions singular. But the dioramas these robotic dolls create are effective. This performance, combined with the presence of the "*ayate de Juan Diego*" in the New Basílica, allows each visitor the opportunity to consume the myth and the evidence in one location.

By contrast, when *Guadalupanas/os* in Des Plaines perform the apparition story, they embody it and make it flesh. In the early morning hours of December 12, between 3:00 and 4:00 a.m., select devotees present a theatrical version of the apparition story in the gymnasium-cum-chapel. Festival organizers choose the actors from the congregation based on their participation in Cerrito activities and their institutional connection with Maryville Academy. The young pregnant woman who portrayed *la Virgen de Guadalupe* during the 2005 celebration, for example, worked as a secretary in the Maryville office. The participants use all of the gym space to present the story and often inadvertently involve spectators in the telling. The elevated altar, which priests, bishops, and other official figures of the Catholic Church use for the duration of the twelve-day celebration, doubles as the sixteenth century quarters of Fray Juan de Zumárraga. Devotees use the area during the most pivotal moment of the apparition story—which is Juan Diego's presentation of the Virgin's image to Zumárraga—and to honor congregation members who have made exceptional contributions to the shrine. In December 2005, for instance, two devotees constructed a large gold crown for *la Virgencita*, which they placed behind her image on *el Cerrito*. At the altar, the devotees publicly presented their labor to the congregation and, in turn, Father Miguel gave them their gift, a special blessing.

The devotee-actors use a freestanding mural of the Tenochtitlán hillside and an archway/portal to frame Guadalupe each time she converses with Juan Diego. The scenery is particularly effective because it gives only an impression of the surrounding landscape—the hill of Tepeyac and the sky from which Guadalupe descended—thereby foregrounding the living actors who tell the narrative. This scenic arrangement gives a curious valence to the story. Depending on one's perspective, the spectator may juxtapose the apparition scenes with an image of a national flag—Brazil, Spain, the United States, or Japan for instance (figure 4). Staging the action in this way mixes multiple frames of reference and reinforces Tepeyac/Maryville's appeal as a transnational sacred space. And the production and consumption of the myth by members of the community from diverse places underlines Guadalupe's presence among them.

Following a tradition practiced at Tepeyac, the congregation in Des Plaines stages a *docenario* [a twelve day prayer cycle] to build toward the aforementioned theatrical reenactment of the Virgin's apparition. In Mexico City, officiating priests dedicate each day to a particular faction of society—employees and volunteers, the faithful, able and disabled persons, the sick, the young, families, colleges and universities, seminarians and novices, San Juan Diego Cuauhtlatoatzin, and the Republic of Mexico. At the Second Tepeyac, organizers use this technique to reinforce the shrine's dual role as a sacred space and as an inclusive transnational political haven. In addition to dedicating the mass to an extensive list of laborers (construction workers, gardeners, waiters, cooks, secretaries, bakers, athletes, carpenters, journalists), the congregation recognizes countries from across the Americas and families, individuals, or businesses that have performed as the *padrinos* [benefactors] of the day's events. On the tenth day of the 2005 celebration, for instance, the Guadalupan community dedicated religious ceremonies to artists and musicians from Guanajuato, Sinaloa, Zacatecas, and Surinam, and they credited Angel Córtez and his family, as well as the communications corporation Telemundo, as *padrinos*. The differences between Tepeyac and el Cerrito—the strategies by which both shrines cultivate devotion, who is given a voice, and where these voices may come from—are significant. By naming a wide range of occupations and geographic locations, while keeping the structure of tradition, the Second Tepeyac is identifying itself as a U.S.-based sacred space that caters to an ethnically, financially, and culturally diverse congregation.

Guadalupan coordinators are intent on creating a culture of inclusion. According to Martínez, one of the main objectives in founding the Second Tepeyac is to celebrate *la Virgencita's* presence with others, regardless of race, citizenship, or class status. He and his colleagues want an international meeting place for Catholics from the five continents who reside in the Chicago area and to officially title the annual December gathering "*La Fiesta Guadalupana de los 5 Continentes del Mundo.*" Much like the Basílica's Plaza de las Américas, which displays flags from each American nation and one flag representing

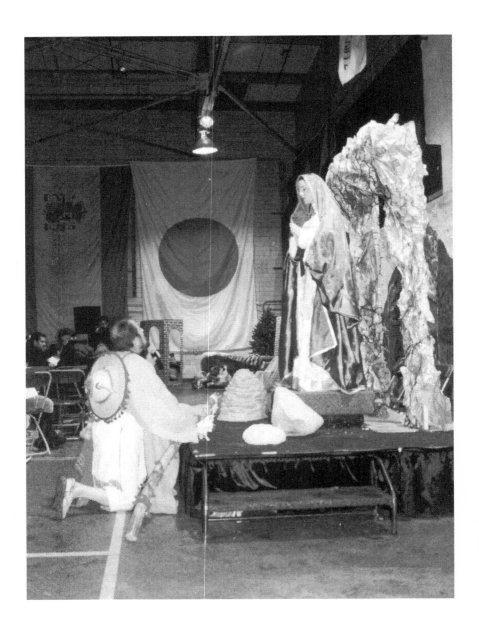

Hispanic America, Maryville officials have created an attractive global space by adorning the shrine with an array of flags from around the world, including Switzerland, Mali, Austria, Jamaica, Brazil, China, Great Britain, and Greece. Juxtaposing these banners with prayer services, devotional performances, and political speeches produces interesting, and at times confusing, results. Placing Sweden's flag behind *la Virgen de Guadalupe's* image in the gymnasium for aesthetic reasons, for example, effectively illustrates how intentionality and arbitrariness overlap, particularly at the beginning stages of sacred space development.

"[Sacred] Space Is a Practiced Place"

The number of *Guadalupanas/os* who worship and network at the Second Tepeyac has grown exponentially since its inaugural ceremony in 2001. In December 2002, approximately 20,000 devotees journeyed to Des Plaines. There were three walking pilgrimages from the Chicago suburbs of Cicero, Rolling Meadows, and Northbrook as well as pilgrimages from Michigan, Wisconsin, and California. The next year, between 50,000 and 60,000 votaries visited the shrine. In 2005, Maryville officials estimated that 130,000 *Guadalupanas/os* participated in Guadalupan feast day activities. Institutional

Figure 4.
History made flesh, Des Plaines, Illinois. Photo by author, December 2005.

involvement and media coverage have also intensified in response to the sacred space's growing and diverse congregation. In 2005, Auxiliary Bishop Gustavo García-Siller, John R. Manz—an administrator of the Migration and Refugee Services Church in Latin America based in Chicago, Father Claudio Díaz from the Office for Hispanic Catholics, Bishop José Trinidad González from the Archdiocese of Guadalajara, and local clerics Father John Smyth and Father Miguel Martínez celebrated mass during the *docenario.* Univision Chicago now covers the annual celebration with a special program called "Desde el Cerrito del Tepeyac" [From the Little Hill of Tepeyac] and popular Spanish-language radio stations, including La Ley 107.9 FM, broadcast the arrival of walking, bicycling, and caravanning pilgrims from across the Chicago area.

At 10:00 p.m. on December 11, 2003, for example, approximately two hundred Guadalupan devotees left their respective parishes on Chicago's Lower West Side and walked more than seven hours in single-digit weather toward the Second Tepeyac. Upon arriving at 5:30 a.m., they first paid homage to the Virgin at el Cerrito, serenading her with song and prayer, before entering the gymnasium. The moment this walking pilgrimage of young and old devotees entered the space of celebration was unforgettable. An older volunteer opened the industrial-sized doors, letting in blasts of below zero wind, and announced the *peregrinos* would arrive soon. Mariachi band members rose to attention, lifting their instruments in anticipation, and the congregation rustled in their seats. Coordinators instructed us to clear the first four rows of the seating space for the tired and cold *Guadalupanas/os* "who walked the entire night to get here," they emphasized. There was a moment of hesitation before they entered the space. We could hear the faint sound of their voices getting stronger as they approached the building. It could not have been more than two minutes, but this pause, in which bodies were moving from one space to another, was tangible within this improvised religious space. If I were to construct a spatial ethnopoetic transcription marking this pause, it would not be a blank space on the page. Rather, it would be like a moment in a performance when an ultra dim light slowly becomes brighter to expose an important object or a person, redirecting and focusing the spectator's gaze.

The arrival of the travelers was overwhelming. They walked down the center aisle of the gymnasium to loud applause and the synchronized sound of trumpets. Once the crowd settled, Martínez invited members of the pilgrimage to speak. Dolores de los Angeles, a woman perhaps in her late forties, was the most articulate. She commented that the walk was cold and long, and she was tired, but her love *for la Virgencita* was greater than her discomfort. De los Angeles also spoke of the necessity of keeping and teaching "*nuestra cultura, nuestra lenguaje*" [our culture, our language] to our children. "We cannot lose where we come from." At this point, the space performed on multiple levels. The celebration was no longer solely about religious devotion; de los Angeles had invoked the cultural politics that parallel devotion to *la Virgen de Guadalupe.* Her statements made layers of time and history, culture and migration, spirituality and politics explicit. The specters of past performances are always active.

Michel de Certeau's claim that "space is a practiced place" provides an optic through which to examine the embodied dynamics supporting sacred space production. Space, as de Certeau suggests, is always in the process of transformation.[30] The Second Tepeyac's development is contingent on the multiple layers of institutional and popular history, shifting political and economic climates, and the living, breathing bodies that give meaning and make sense of the space. The act of reproducing a place—the replication of physical/aesthetic elements from Mexico City to Des Plaines—is only the first step. Left at this initial stage, the shrine would remain a superficial structure invoking, but never realizing, the vibrancy and legitimacy of its counterpart. The replicated place becomes a sacred space only when devotees' embodied performances—their voices raised in ecstasy, their praying and dancing bodies in motion, the labor and care they offer to maintain the shrine—initiate the succession of transformative moments that give meaning to the Second Tepeyac.

In addition to conducting pilgrimages on foot and by bus, *Guadalupanas/os* also enact bicycle pilgrimages. In 2005, devotees from Chicago's South Lawndale, Uptown, Lower West Side, and Northwest side neighborhoods braved bitterly cold weather conditions to adore the Virgin. Most *peregrinas/os* wore nondescript puffy jackets, gloves, and jeans, but one young man, originally from Jalisco, Mexico, used the journey to demonstrate his faith and his national pride (figure 5). In addition to draping a Mexican flag around his shoulders like a cape, he had adorned his bicycle with two Mexican flags, one on each handle, and had placed his *distintivo* [pilgrimage badge], which featured an image of *la Virgencita*, above the front wheel. The act of adorning body and vehicle is one example of the transposition of the sacred space and patriotic sensibilities that occurs at the Second Tepeyac. Similarly, in 2004, while conducting fieldwork at Tepeyac in Mexico City, I met a young *peregrino* from Tlaxcala who had placed an image of Guadalupe on his bicycle and wore a T-shirt with an image of *la Virgencita* framed by the word *Mexico* in white boldface (figure 6). It bears mentioning that while this incorporation of the Mexican flag evokes a particular expression of patriotism, it is a diasporic form of Mexican cultural identity that is not reducible to state nationalism.

These two devotees arrived at their destinations exhausted, with their bodies battered and stomachs empty. Both were actively contributing to the sanctification of space but their devotional labor also imbued their bodies and keepsakes with a form of the sacred.[31] Many *peregrinos* with whom I have worked in the Midwest and central Mexico explain that their relics become important elements on their home altars or deeply personal gifts for loved ones who could not journey. The powerful presence of calluses, scabs, and scrapes, however ephemeral, also evinces the journey and these become markers for others of the pilgrims' devotion.

Chicago-area Guadalupan *danzantes* also legitimize sacred space and perform political subjectivities by putting their suffering and/or artistic expression on public display. Matechine dancers bless the space through ritual movement. Even though their costumes, dance steps, instruments, and headdresses may

Figure 5.
Peregrino on bike, Des Plaines, Illinois. Photo by author, December 2005.

not replicate exactly those found beyond the United States, their presence is evocative (figures 7 and 8). These dance troupes provide exceptional examples of ritualized worship. Not all *Guadalupanas/os*, of course, worship in such a public way and the regenerative effects of embodied devotion are not always obvious, but each act counts. Volunteer workers, the persons who keep the sacred space tidy, for example, are backstage players who are indispensable at both shrines (figures 9 and 10).

Envisioning the Future: Political Mobilization and Other Regenerative Effects of the Sacred

On a chilly November morning in the fall of 2003, I did not join the congregation gathered for Sunday service but walked toward a back area of the gymnasium-cum-sanctuary, which a mock wall hid from plain sight. Entering a cold, concrete space, I faced a line of waiting *Guadalupanas/os*, several people seated at long brown tables, a photographer, and a woman binding documents near a copy machine in the far corner of the room. Congregation

Figure 6.
Peregrino on bike, Mexico.
Photo by author, December
2004.

members, shrine officials, volunteers, and local immigration lawyers, I soon found, had transformed the
back room of the gymnasium into an assembly line
for U.S. naturalization. The organization of the room
allowed lawyers and bilingual volunteers to walk devotees through every step of
the N-400: Application for Naturalization process. At the end of the assembly
line, a volunteer handed each participant a ready-to-mail package addressed
to the Department of Homeland Security that included: (1) form N-400,
(2) copy of Resident Alien card of applicant, (3) photograph of applicant,
and (4) a money order for $310 for the filing fee, which rose to $675 in June
2007. That morning, like many others thereafter, I translated N-400 forms
for Spanish-speaking Guadalupan devotees seeking free legal assistance.

In addition to offering free consultation and supervision, lawyers sold a
twenty-five dollar "citizenship" box complete with bilingual flash cards featuring questions such as "*¿Cúantas estrellas aparecen en la bandera de los Estados
Unidos?*" [How many stars appear on the American flag?] Answer: *cincuenta
estrellas* "fifty stars." This kit also included a bilingual answer booklet and a
compact disc intended to prepare Spanish speakers for their citizenship inter-

Figure 7.
Danzante performing piety,
Des Plaines, Illinois. Photo by
author, December 2005.

view in English. As the head lawyer explained between consultations: "You do not have to learn this material, you have to memorize it. This kit gives you all the tools to learn the questions in Spanish but answer confidently in English. At the interview it is all about confidence."

This *taller de ciudadanía*, or citizenship workshop, was undetectable to anyone who was not aware of the developing connection between *el Cerrito* as a sacred space and as a platform for immigration reform and legal services. Shrine organizers did not offer this opportunity as part of the front-stage activities of Sunday church service; only active and embedded members of the Guadalupan community were privy to this knowledge. In tandem with the recent wave of immigrant rights rallies and public discourse on comprehensive immigration reform, this type of activity at the Second Tepeyac evinces its dual role as religious sanctuary and political safe haven. It demonstrates one of the many ways in which devotees use the sacred to address secular issues—or, put another way, challenge a sacred/secular binary. By frequently cohosting naturalization workshops with the National Immigrant Justice Center, Maryville has become part of a city and statewide circuit of centers, academies, and high schools that perform as improvised legal centers for both

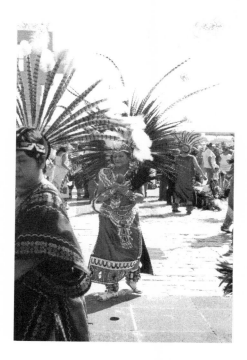

Figure 8.
Danzante performing piety,
Mexico. Photo by author,
December 2004.

newly arrived and established migrants. In addition, *el Cerrito* is now considered to be not only a destination point for *peregrinas/os,* but also a starting location for caravans of volunteers and devotees traveling to rallies in downtown Chicago and the state capital or participating in nationwide events such as the Immigrant Workers Freedom Ride across America.

The sacred space also hosts events in which devotees can learn about pending legislation. On October 12, 2003, two attorneys from the American Immigration Lawyers Association (AILA) gave compelling speeches at the foot of *el Cerrito.* Lawyers Rosalba Piña and Royal Burge used the Second Tepeyac on Día de la Raza as a platform from which to encourage Guadalupan devotees to support the amendment of the Immigration and Nationality Act to Promote Family Unity 240A (b). On this day of solidarity with citizen-children, the lawyers, priests, and Guadalupan officials staging the gathering asked parents to dress their children in white shirts and blue pants or skirts. Differentiating them from other participants would make for a powerful press photo. Coordinators aimed at gathering one thousand children at the shrine to send a message to Congress, which was discussing the amendment or rejection of the proposal. As written, the act recommends that citizen-children

Figure 9.
Male devotee struggling to keep sacred space slush-free, Des Plaines, Illinois. Photo by author, December 2005.

under the age of eighteen should relocate to their parents' nation of origin in the event of the parents' deportation. A judge would allow undocumented parents to stay in the United States only if they had resided in the country for more than ten years, had demonstrated good moral conduct, did not have convictions and/or a police record, and could prove that the family would face "exceptional, extreme, or unusual suffering" in the home country. Piña argued that "extreme or unusual suffering" would begin at "the moment of deportation." The act of one judge, one human being, she suggested, would deny the child's rights as a citizen—specifically their right to life, liberty, and the pursuit of happiness. Because these children are minors, Piña reasoned, they do not have a voice, and their parents, who are undocumented, cannot speak for them. "Therefore, we must send a message to Congress. We must give our children a voice. We must promote our right to family unification."[32]

As these lawyers spoke passionately in English and Spanish, I listened from a small table collecting signatures. Auxiliary Bishop John R. Manz, a key representative for the diocese regarding immigration issues, sat among the children on the raised platform in front of the hill.[33] Approximately two

Figure 10.
Women workers keeping the Modern Basílica immaculate, Mexico. Photo by author, August 2004.

hundred Guadalupan devotees listened patiently to the statements, but only those devotees with citizenship, about 10 percent, were able to sign the petition. Regardless of the success of this gathering, shrine coordinators, the archdiocese, and these immigration lawyers collaborated to educate devotees who would have otherwise remained uninformed about specific laws directly affecting their day-to-day existence.

These ethnographic vignettes reflect what several historical and contemporary studies have shown: the transposition of sacred space and/or religious practices often creates transnational, intracultural, and cross-cultural interactions.[34] Spanish speakers intent on practicing Catholicism in the nineteenth century, for example, produced intracultural and cross-ethnic encounters across the United States. As Timothy Matovina and Gerald E. Poyo suggest, "in the face of oppositional forces such as military conquest and occupation, indiscriminate violence and lawlessness, political and economic displacement, [and] rapid demographic change," Mexican, Central, and South American immigrants practiced "Spanish-speaking Catholic feasts and devotions [that] provided ongoing means of communal expression."[35] One of the earliest documented mobilization efforts occurred in 1871, when an alliance of Spanish-speaking Catholics in San Francisco successfully lobbied for the establishment of a national parish. Consuls of Chile, Perú, Nicaragua, Colombia, Bolivia,

Costa Rica, and Spain, as well as various other Hispanic residents, formed this coalition to accommodate Spanish-speaking communities.[36]

The combination of transposing sacred space and cultural practices can create multicultural and multilingual environments thriving under a singular vision. At the Second Tepeyac, ethnic, class, generational, and citizenship differences run the gamut. Mexican *Guadalupanos* physically and symbolically claim the space with their sheer numbers, but shrine coordinators avoid conflating their histories or the specificities that make up their national identities. There is always an explicit effort on the part of organizers to produce an atmosphere of inclusiveness among the congregation—a space in which devotees may retain their individual affiliations or preferences and work toward securing workers' rights, health care, legal documentation, and increased human rights via religious practice. Celebrating the shrine's place within a global context via "the blessing of the five continents of the world," employing an international-themed decorating strategy, and publicly recognizing that the Guadalupan community is a mix of various nationalities and histories are only some of the ways in which the shrine is not solely a Mexican or Latino phenomenon. Polite and ambitious terminology such as pan-Latino or generalized social scientific processes of becoming—assimilation, ethnic-resilience, or accultura-tion—although conceptually useful, do not attend to the complex intracultural and cross-cultural processes that engender such community formation.[37] Yes, utilizing pan-Latinoism for mobilization purposes is strategic. Yet, as many pro–pan-Latino theorists have suggested, when U.S. government agencies, mass media, and marketing agencies invoke the mythologies of pan-Latinoism, the results can be detrimental. The implicit homogenizing power of this term makes stigmatizing, categorizing, and disciplining across the board easy for self-interested parties. Beyond external complications, there are also internal conflicts and hierarchies—the ways in which one Latino group may have more power, numbers, or influence than another—that complicate any rosy vision of pan-Latinoism. By acknowledging and working with these complex realities, however, we can continue to learn a great deal about the politics of inclusion and exclusion informing diasporic community formation.

Notes

I am indebted to the editors and readers of *American Quarterly*, especially Pierrette Hondagneu-Sotelo, David Gutiérrez, and Curtis Marez, for challenging me to develop this article and to Marisela Chávez, José Luis Ledesma, and José María Muñoz who inspired me to make it legible across disciplines. I dedicate this essay to my mother, Sandra Ojeda Martínez (October 31, 1953-October 2, 2007), with whom I spent many late nights contemplating memory, analysis, and representation.

1. See Esteban Martinez de la Serna, *Los santuarios de la virgen de Guadalupe* (Mexico City: Editora Escalante, 2003), 7; Jorge Durand and Douglas S. Massey, *Miracles on the Border: Retablos of Mexican Migrants to the United States* (Tucson: University of Arizona Press, 1995); Jacqueline Orsini Dunnington, *Guadalupe: Our Lady of New Mexico* (Santa Fe: Museum of New Mexico Press, 1999); and Elvira Araiza Velázquez, "La Virgen de Guadalupe de México: Para América," *Boletín Guadalupano* 2.34 (2003): 8–10.

2. Like any great story, the dominant symbols, images, characters, conflict, and resolution of the narrative give rise to manifold interpretations and uses. Juan Diego Cuauhtlatoatzin represents the destitute, doubt-ridden, and affronted devotees who through faith and humility acquire redemption and guidance from their mother—*la Virgen Maria de Guadalupe*. He is, in many respects, the protagonist of the legend. *Guadalupanas/os* appropriate and reinterpret his classic hero journey as the first *peregrinación* [pilgrimage], using it as a model to overcome their own hardships and circumstances. On an institutional level, Fray Juan de Zumárraga—the Spanish missionary who officially accepted the apparition—despite his initial hesitations now epitomizes the benevolence and understanding inherent in the upper echelons of the Catholic Church, particularly clergy members' ability to channel devotees' needs into institutional or formal religion. *La Virgen de Guadalupe's* image, the principal product of the narrative, is both a Roman Catholic icon and a malleable symbol of resistance and strength for devotees across the Americas. Guadalupanas/os from Miguel Hidalgo to Cesar Chávez, from Emiliano Zapata to Alma López have used her iconic image to spark upheaval, foster civil rights and gender equality, strengthen political campaigns, create art, preserve identity, and build communities. These realizations speak to the everyday and extraordinary ways devotees entangle religious belief with cultural and sociopolitical aspirations.

3. "¡Juan Pablo, Hermano, Ya eres Mexicano!," *Católico* 17.9 (September 2002); 13–14.

4. For an in-depth discussion of the numerous labels surrounding migrant communities in the United States, see Frank D. Bean and B. Lindsay Lowell, "Unauthorized Migration," in *The New Americans: A Guide to Immigration Since 1965*, ed. Mary C. Waters and Reed Ueda (Cambridge, Mass.: Harvard University Press, 2007), 70–82.

5. Michel de Certeau, *The Practice of Everyday Life* (Minneapolis: University of Minnesota Press, 1984), 117.

6. See Antonio Pompa y Pompa, *El Gran Acontecimiento Guadalupano* (Mexico City: Editorial Jus, 1967); Ernesto de la Torre Villar and Ramiro Navarro de Anda, eds., *Testimonios Históricos Guadalupanos* (Mexico City: Fondo de Cultura Económica, 1982); Virgil P. Elizondo, *La Morenita: Evangelizer of the Americas* (San Antonio: Mexican American Cultural Center, 1980); Francisco de la Maza, *El guadalupanismo mexicano* (Mexico City: Fondo de Cultura Económica, 1981); Carmen Aguilera and Ismael Arturo Montero García, *Tepeyac Estudios Historicos* (Mexico City: Universidad del Tepeyac, 2000); William B. Taylor, "Mexico's Virgin of Guadalupe in the Seventeenth Century: Hagiography and Beyond," in *Colonial Saints: Discovering the Holy in the Americas*, ed. Allan Greer and Jodi Bilinkoff, 277–98 (New York: Routledge, 2003); Xavier Noguez, *Documentos Guadalupanos, un Estudio Sobre las Fuentes de Información Tempranas en Torno a las Mariofanías en el Tepeyac* (Mexico City: Fondo de Cultural Económica, 1995); Richard Nebel, *Santa María Tonantzin Virgen de Guadalupe, Continuidad y Transformación Religiosa en México* (Mexico City: Fondo de Cultura Económica, 1996); Victor and Edith Turner, *Image and Pilgrimage in Christian Culture: Anthropological Perspectives* (New York: Columbia University Press, 1978); Luis D. León, *La Llorona's Children: Religion, Life, and Death in the U.S.-Mexican Borderlands* (Berkeley: University of California Press, 2004); and Timothy Matovina, *Guadalupe and Her Faithful; Latino Catholics in San Antonio: From Colonial Origins to the Present* (Baltimore: Johns Hopkins University Press. 2005).

7. David A. Brading, *Mexican Phoenix. Our Lady of Guadalupe: Image and Tradition across Five Centuries* (Cambridge: Cambridge University Press, 2001), 6. See also Edmundo O'Gorman, *Destierro de Sombra: Luz en el Origen de la Imagen y Culto de Nuestra Señora de Guadalupe del Tepeyac* (Mexico City: Universidad Nacional Autonoma de México, 1991), 284.

8. Ana Castillo, ed. *Guadalupe: Goddess of the Americas/La Diosa de las Américas; Writings on la Virgen de Guadalupe* (New York: Riverhead, 1996).

9. Jacques Lafayé, *Quetzalcóatl and Guadalupe: The Formation of National Consciousness, 1531–1813*, trans. Benjamin Keene (Chicago: University of Chicago Press, 1974); Stafford Poole, *Our Lady of*

Guadalupe: The Origins and Sources of a National Symbol, 1531–1797 (Tucson: Arizona University Press, 1995); Eric Wolf, "The Virgin of Guadalupe: A Mexican National Symbol," *Journal of American Folklore* 71 (1959): 34–39; Octavio Paz, *The Labyrinth of Solitude and Other Writings*, trans. Lysander Kemp (New York: Grove Press, 1985); Jeanette Rodriguez, *Our Lady of Guadalupe: Faith and Empowerment among Mexican-American Women* (Austin: University of Texas Press, 1994); *Flowers for Guadalupe/Flores Para Guadalupe*, VHS, produced by Judith Gleason with the collaboration of the Colectivo Feminists de Xalapa and Elisa Mereghetti (New York: Filmmakers Library, 1995); Gloria Anzaldúa, *Borderlands/la Frontera: The New Mestiza* (San Francisco: Aunt Lute Books, 1987); and Deidre Sklar, *Dancing with the Virgin: Body and Faith in the Fiesta of Tortugas, New Mexico* (Berkeley: University of California Press, 2001).

10. Timothy Matovina and Gerald E. Poyo, *Presente! U.S. Latino Catholics from Colonial Origins to the Present* (Maryknoll, New York: Orbis, 2000), 147.

11. I would like to thank the editors for inspiring me to articulate this point.

12. Manuel A. Vasquez and Marie. F. Marquardt, *Globalizing the Sacred: Religion Across the Americas* (Piscataway N.J.: Rutgers University Press, 2003), 45.

13. See Rita Arias Jirasek and Carlos Tortolero, *Images of America: Mexican Chicago* (Chicago: Arcadia, 2001), 94; Anita Edgar Jones, "Conditions Surrounding Mexicans in Chicago: A Dissertation" (master's thesis, University of Chicago, 1928), 131–35; and Louise Año Nuevo Kerr, "The Chicano Experience in Chicago, 1920–1970" (PhD diss., University of Illinois at Chicago, 1976), 56, 176.

14. Geoffrey Johnson, "A Common Altar: Chicago's Immigrant Catholics," *Chicago* (September 2005), 79.

15. Pierrette Hondagneu-Sotelo, Genelle Gaudinez, Hector Lara, and Billie C. Ortiz, "There's a Spirit that Transcends the Border: Faith, Ritual, and Postnational Protest at the U.S.-Mexico Border," *Sociological Perspectives* 47.2 (2004): 137.

16. Karen Mary Davalos, "The Real Way of Praying: The Via Crucis: *Mexicano* Sacred Space, and the Architecture of Domination," in *Horizons of the Sacred: Mexican Traditions in U.S. Catholicism*, ed. Timothy Matovina and Gary Riebe-Estrella, 41–68 (Ithaca, N.Y.: Cornell University Press, 1993); and Robert Stark, "Religious Ritual and Class Formation: The Story of Pilsen St. Vitus Parish, and the 1977 Via Crucis" (PhD diss., University of Chicago Divinity School, 1981).

17. Davalos, "The Real Way of Praying," 48.

18. Ibid., 42.

19. Gregory D. Squires and his colleagues address the function and motives of four institutional actors who manipulate neighborhood space—banks and savings and loan institutions, municipal zoning regulators, government agencies, and real estate companies. These players determine who receives and does not receive mortgage money, housing plans in particular metropolitan areas, where racial groups will be "steered," and the enforcement or relaxation of federal guidelines. See Gregory D. Squires, Larry Bennett, Kathleen McCourt, and Phillip Nyden, *Chicago: Race, Class, and the Response to Urban Decline* (Philadelphia: Temple University Press, 1987), 93–94; and Dwight Conquergood, "Life in Big Red: Struggles and Accommodations in a Chicago Polyethnic Tenement," in *Structuring Diversity*, ed. Louise Lamphere, 138–39 (Chicago: University of Chicago Press, 1994).

20. Nicholas De Genova and Ana Ramos-Zayas, *Latino Crossings: Mexicans, Puerto Ricans, and the Politics of Race and Citizenship* (New York: Routledge, 2003), 38.

21. John Betancur, Teresa Córdova, and María de los Angeles Torres, "Economic Restructuring and the Process of Incorporation of Latinos in the Chicago Economy," in *Latinos in a changing U.S. Economy: Comparative Perspectives on Growing Inequality*, ed. Rebecca Morales and Frank Bonilla (Newbury Park, Calif.: Sage, 1993), 124.

22. According to the 2000 census, Illinois' Hispanic population increased by 69.2%, from 625,816 residents to 1,530,262 between 1990 and 2000. This panethnic group now makes up 12.3% of the state's population. This growth has directly affected the city of Chicago's population, which registered its first increase since deindustrialization in the 1950s, as well as her suburbs, which constitute 42% of Illinois' total population. All six Chicagoland counties—Cook, Du Page, Kane, Lake, McHenry, and Will—recorded a significant rise in their Hispanic populations over the past decade.

23. In 2002, Maryville's youth home operation received negative media attention when the state removed 130 wards on charges of negligence and misconduct, specifically in relation to the suicide of a teenage girl and two alleged sexual assaults on campus. Illinois' governor Rod R. Blagojevich publicly denounced the academy, discredited Smyth, and pursued a defunding agenda. Elite members of Chicago's political and social organizations, as well as other public figures, showed their support for

Reverend Smyth during a rally held on the campus in late September 2003. Karl Maurer, "Hundreds Rally to Protest Maryville Closing," http://www.Catholiccitizens.org (accessed October 2003). This high-profile gathering did not reverse the state's decision, nor did it alleviate the academy's or Smyth's tarnished public image. In December 2004, Sister Catherine Ryan, a Franciscan nun, former Maryville board member, and juvenile justice lawyer, replaced Smyth as executive director of the academy. Maureen O'Donnell, "Franciscan Nun to Run Maryville," http://www.Catholiccitizens.org (accessed February 2005).

24. Maria del Carmen Macías, "Un Nuevo Amanecer en Tepeyac de Norteamerica," *Católico* (October 2001), 10.

25. See Francisco Miranda, *Dos Cultos Fundantes: Los Remedios y Guadalupe, 1521–1649; Historia Documental* (Zamora, Michoacán: El Colegio de Michoacán, 1998); Horacio Rodriguez Sentíes, *La Villa de Guadalupe: Crónica Centenaria* (Mexico City: Gobierno del Distrito Federal/Delegación Gustavo A. Madero, 1999); and "Evolución Urbana del Santuario de Nuestra Señora de Guadalupe," in *Tepeyac Estudios Historicos*, ed. Carmen Aguilera and Ismael Arturo Montero García, 195–226 (Mexico City: Universidad del Tepeyac, 2000); Gustavo Watson Marrón, *Los Templos del Tepeyac, Ayer y Hoy* (Mexico City: Archivos Historicos del Arzobispo, 2001); Pedro Ramírez Vázquez, "Basílica de Guadalupe, Santuario de los Mexicanos," in *Tepeyac Estudios Historicos*, ed. Aguilera and Montero García; and Esteban Martinez de la Serna, *Los Santuarios de la Virgen de Guadalupe* (Mexico City: Editora Escalante, 2003).

26. Robert A. Orsi, "Everyday Miracles: The Study of Lived Religion," in *Lived Religion in America: Toward a History of Practice*, ed. David D. Hall, 3–21 (Princeton, N.J.: Princeton University Press, 1997).

27. I would like to thank Curtis Marez for inspiring me to develop this point.

28. See David Harvey, *The Condition of Postmodernity: An Enquiry into the Origins of Cultural Change* (Cambridge, Mass.: Blackwell, 1990).

29. Fieldwork in the Chicago area and central Mexico has shown that devotees proudly sing these lyrics at Tepeyac, on foot to Tepeyac, and at the Second Tepeyac, among other locations. See Elaine Peña, "Making Space Sacred: Devotional Capital, Political Economy, and the Transnational Expansion of the Cult of la Virgen de Guadalupe" (PhD diss., Northwestern University, 2006).

30. de Certeau, *The Practice of Everyday Life*, 117.

31. For a study of the value of sacred relics (bodies or portions of bodies, particles of clothing or objects associated with saints), see Patrick Geary, "Sacred Commodities: The Circulation of Medieval Relics," in *The Social Life of Things*, ed. Arjun Appadurai, 169–91 (Cambridge: Cambridge University Press, 1986).

32. This impassioned speech resonates with the case and cause of Elvira Arellano, an unauthorized Mexican migrant, who has sought sanctuary for over a year in a church in Chicago's Humboldt Park neighborhood to avoid deportation and separation from her son, who is a U.S. citizen. Often likened to Rosa Parks, Arellano has become an international symbol and speaker for comprehensive U.S. immigration reform. Unfortunately, Arellano, who left Chicago to give a speech at an immigration rally in Los Angeles, California, in August 2007, was ultimately deported.

33. *Pastoral Response to Immigration Reform* (Chicago: Maryville Academy Publishing Center, 1997).

34. Katy Gardner, *Global Migrants, Local Lives: Travel and Transformation in Rural Bangladesh* (Oxford: Clarendon, 1995); Thomas Tweed, *Our Lady of the Exile: Diasporic Religion at a Cuban Catholic Shrine in Miami* (New York: Oxford University Press, 1997); Karan McCarthy Brown, *Mama Lola: A Voudou Priestess in Brooklyn* (Berkeley: University of California Press, 1999); Frank J. Korom, *Hosay Trinidad: Muharram Performances in an Indo-Caribbean Diaspora* (Philadelphia: University of Pennsylvania Press, 2003); and Elizabeth McAllister, *Rara! Vodou, Power, and Performance in Haiti and Its Diaspora* (Berkeley: University of California Press, 2002).

35. Matovina and Poyo, *Presente!*, 56.

36. Ibid, 95.

37. I agree with de Genova and Ramos-Zayas when they suggest "the basis for such commonalities must be located in an analysis of the shared historicity of peoples throughout Latin America in relation to the colonial and imperialist projects of the U.S. nation-state, in concert with the concomitant historical as well as contemporary racializations of both Latin America, as a whole, and Latinos in the U.S. in relation to a sociopolitical order of white supremacy." See De Genova and Ramos-Zayas, *Latino Crossings*, 20.

Mexican Nationalisms, Southern Racisms: Mexicans and Mexican Americans in the U.S. South, 1908–1939

Julie M. Weise

These photographs of Hortensia Horcasitas (figure 1) and Robert Canedo (figure 2) should fit comfortably into dominant histories of Mexican immigrant life in the United States during the first half of the twentieth century. The Horcasitas photograph recalls countless others of the "Mexican generation," Mexican immigrants of the 1910s and 1920s who created homeward-looking cultures as bulwarks against a society that had begun to exclude and racialize them as other, different, Mexican. The photograph of Robert Canedo evokes the subsequent "Mexican American generation," for whom service in World War II was an integral component of a new political strategy, and in some cases identity shift, emphasizing U.S. citizenship.[1]

These photos, however, were not taken in Los Angeles or San Antonio, but rather in New Orleans, where they told a different story. There, it was Horcasitas's Mexican cultural politics, not Canedo's Americanism, that best argued for Mexicans' assimilation into the white South. Her generation there successfully engaged Mexico and shaped the image of "Mexicans" to ensure that Mexican immigrants in New Orleans and the rural South, whatever their social class, eventually would claim their place as European-style white immigrants and escape racialization as a distinct group at midcentury.

Their story ends differently than the Southwest's, where the limited success of the Mexican American generation's politics caused their children to adopt a more radical stance. In New Orleans, the "Mexican generation" already lived as whites during the 1920s. Canedo, for example, first acquired his U.S. citizenship during World War II but had enjoyed most of its benefits for decades—benefits not enjoyed by African Americans in New Orleans. While his Mexican immigrant counterparts in the Southwest faced deportation and racial violence, young Robert, in 1930, attended kindergarten with whites. Although his mother was a widow raising a family on the proceeds of her sister's boarding house, Canedo received the same education as other

247

Figure 1.
Hortensia Horcasitas, c. 1925. Courtesy of Carlos Zervigón.

Figure 2.
Robert Canedo, c. 1945.
Courtesy of Hazel Canedo.

working-class whites. By the time he enlisted in the army, he had already fallen in love with his future wife, a U.S.-born white woman named Hazel, to whom the photograph's inscription was addressed.[2] The South's major rural Mexican immigrant community in the interwar years, poor Mexican cotton sharecroppers and wage laborers in the Mississippi Delta, faced significant barriers to achieving social mobility and initially were considered nonwhite.[3] Yet by the 1940s, they too had begun to marry whites and gain acceptance into white society.[4] The Mexican cultural politics represented by Horcasitas's photo largely accounts for both groups' acceptance as whites in the South.

Examining the case of Mexicans and Mexican Americans in the U.S. South from 1908 to 1939, this essay shows how international migration, in this case between the United States and Mexico, can shape the racial ideologies of nations and societies at both ends of migration streams. It traces the arrival of Mexican immigrants to two southern locations, New Orleans and the Mississippi Delta, and discusses their initial experiences of race and class there. It then focuses on the leadership of Mexico's New Orleans consulate, and of its Mexican Honorary Commission in Gunnison, Mississippi, to illuminate the distinctly Mexican strategies which Mexicans of all social classes pursued in their quest to attain and retain white status in the U.S. South. In the early twentieth century U.S. South, there were no Mexican Americans who could call upon U.S. citizenship or claims to be "Caucasian" under the law, nor organizers drawing Mexicans into class-based politics.[5] There, Mexicans' sole cultural and political claims took the form of Mexico-directed activism through which the racial ideologies of both immigrants and Mexican government bureaucrats had a discernible impact upon the Southern color line's shape and foundations. Conversely, it was in the South that Mexican government representatives most directly confronted the black-white eugenic binary of U.S. white supremacy, and did so without the support of U.S.-based institutions or groups. Examining the interaction between Mexican immigrants and bureaucrats in the South, then, helps historians analyze racial politics in postrevolutionary Mexico, where a celebration of race mixing, or *mestizaje*, coexisted with a positivist emphasis on cultural whitening.

Exploring Mexican strategies for negotiating the U.S. color line reveals new dimensions of white supremacy's history in both the South and the Southwest. While the early years of Reconstruction introduced the possibility of blacks' "improvement" through education, social mobility, and political empowerment, by the late 1890s white supremacists had reversed these gains, and had begun to implement the Jim Crow system.[6] The 1920s–1930s marked the height of that system, which used a binary, eugenic definition of race embedded in law and culture to preserve the political interests of wealthy whites.[7] Historians have shown that Jim Crow's ultimate demise was linked to the discrediting of eugenic racism in the wake of World War II, but have not accounted sufficiently for the ways in which some, though not all, of the South's immigrants had spent decades forcing Jim Crow systems to bend, stretch, and adopt definitions of race that looked beyond "blood" and ancestry to include culture, class, and politics.[8]

To the extent that the black-white binary had always ill described the Southwest, historians have shown that Mexican immigrants and Mexican Americans seeking to resist the negative consequences of their racialization there worked for legal inclusion in the "Caucasian" category that Jim Crow had created. Historians have recently paid great attention to this "Caucasian strategy," questioning its origins and intentions as well as its impact on African Americans and on the racial self-identifications of Mexicans and Mexican Americans.[9] Examining the racial politics of the South's isolated "Mexican generation" illuminates an entirely different "Faustian pact" with whiteness, one based not on a "Caucasian strategy," but rather on images and ideologies of Mexican national identity.

These ideologies are themselves the subject of historical debate. By their deliberate abstruseness and claims to national homogeneity, Mexican ideologies of race have proven difficult for scholars to excavate and deconstruct. The post-revolutionary government's promotion of *mestizaje* sought to reconcile Mexico's reality—that of a majority-Indian, caste-divided society—with the ideals of a modern, homogenous nation.[10] This ideology supposedly departed from the overtly whitening, Europhilic, and positivist cultural politics of the Porfirio Díaz dictatorship that had ruled Mexico almost without interruption from 1876 to 1910. The *científicos* at the intellectual center of Porfirismo had emphasized the potential of all Mexicans to whiten through race mixing and European immigration on the one hand, and through education, hygiene, clothing and cosmopolitanism on the other. In this worldview, culture and class could enable urban mestizos to overcome biology.[11] However, historians have shown that "Mestizophilia" and the idea of a Mexican mestizo "cosmic race" had their roots in the late Porfiriato, and contained the promise of whitening Mexico's Indians, promoting their dissolution into a national mestizo identity, and excluding blackness altogether.[12] Thus, one historian has observed that ideologies of *mestizaje* sought to "re-vindicate the race of color through theories designed to legitimate Caucasian groups."[13] Close examination of Mexican workers' and bureaucrats' encounters with U.S. white supremacy offers a critical window into the contradiction between racial mestizophilia and the legacy of Porfirian positivism, and suggests that at least through the 1930s, the latter remained more influential in part because of U.S. white supremacy's power.

The story of Mexicans' and Mexicans Americans' encounter with Jim Crow in New Orleans and Mississippi began in earnest during the twentieth century, but has its roots in the nineteenth. Though the Southeast did not share the Southwest's experience as a part of national-era Mexico, New Orleans' history of Latin American connections was much stronger than most non-Southwestern locales in the United States. Both Mississippi and Louisiana had first been colonized by Spain. While Spanish culture exerted little influence on colonial Mississippi, New Orleans' proximity to Latin America via ship reinforced its ties with Spain's other former colonies in the Western Hemisphere. Since the nineteenth century, the Crescent City had hosted political exiles from Latin America, including Mexican liberals Valentín Gómez Farías and Benito Juárez, even as it served as the prime port for launching filibusters and incursions into Latin America, including the Mexican War.[14]

The Mexican Revolution of 1910–17 created political and economic instability that affected the United States through immigration and the spillover of revolutionary politics itself. North-central Mexico, most affected by the revolution, sent the majority of the era's migrants to the United States. These poor, rural emigrants journeyed to all parts of the United States during the 1920s, from Arizona to Alaska, Michigan to California, and the U.S. South was no exception.[15] Indeed, though Cubans and Hondurans eventually became more numerous in New Orleans, in the 1910s and 1920s Mexicans constituted the city's largest group of Latin American immigrants.[16]

Unlike most of their contemporaries in other parts of the United States, New Orleans' Mexican immigrants had origins in Mexico's Gulf Coast, and as such had escaped the more sustained violence of the revolution.[17] Still, both elite and rural emigration did occur from the region. For these individuals, New Orleans, not Texas, was the closest way into the United States due to its extensive shipping connections with Mexican ports in the states of Tabasco, Veracruz, Campeche, and Yucatán. While 1910–1917 marked the first sustained period of large-scale Mexican immigration to the United States, the Gulf Coast origins of New Orleans' Mexicans meant that Mexican immigration began in earnest there between 1916 and 1920.[18] By 1920, the federal census listed 1,242 Mexican-born whites living in New Orleans—slightly more than were living in Chicago that year.[19] Though white was the favored category for Mexican immigrants on the 1920 U.S. census, it is likely that an additional ten percent lived there as well, classified as negro or mulatto.[20]

Mexicans leaving the Gulf Coast for New Orleans hailed from both urban and rural areas, and from a wide range of economic backgrounds. The upper middle-class Enseñat family ran a successful business manufacturing and servicing machines that crushed and processed Yucatán's most important crop, henequen, which ultimately was used to fabricate rope. Family lore recalls a bullet hitting a windmill in the Enseñats' backyard in 1916, signifying the revolution's threat to their economic status and safety. Originally from Cuba, father Francisco Enseñat moved his family via ship to New Orleans that year, where he purchased the family a car and enrolled his children in Catholic schools. Leaving his wife and children in New Orleans, he continued to commute between the Crescent City and the family home and business in Mérida.[21]

Other immigrants to New Orleans hailed from the Gulf Coast's rural areas. One New Orleans immigrant recalled growing up in rural Veracruz, the son of a farmer. When his father died, the immigrant's mother moved the family to the port city of Veracruz, and from there to New Orleans.[22] Immigrant Peter Nieto was raised in a rural area near Jalapa, Veracruz, where he was literate and managed birth and death records for his town. The feeling of lawlessness in the aftermath of the Mexican Revolution prompted him to take a banana boat to New Orleans in 1924. Within a year he had found work as a watchmaker and married Laura, a woman of Cajun descent from Cutoff, Louisiana.[23]

As the Enseñat and Nieto stories exemplify, most Mexicans of all social classes arrived to New Orleans on the decks of ships, often those owned by fruit companies. Significantly, this "border crossing" bore little resemblance to that of their counterparts in Texas. Historians have observed that while the U.S.-Mexico border, and movement across it, was ill policed and even ill demarcated when the Mexican Revolution began, by the early 1920s the experience of crossing the border became an increasingly humiliating one for Mexicans, and indeed a foundational moment for their racialization as a distinct and undesirable group.[24] Arriving via ship to New Orleans, by contrast, Mexican emigrants of all social classes shared decks with sailors and migrants from around the world, making their arrival experience more akin to that of European immigrants, who were regarded as white or potentially white even if those from Southern and Eastern Europe carried the taint of inferiority.[25]

Mexicans who arrived upriver to the Mississippi Delta, by contrast, hailed from north-central Mexico and had first crossed the border to Texas, where labor recruiters lured them to Mississippi. Since Reconstruction, rural southern elites had fantasized about importing Chinese and Italian immigrants as an alternative to blacks in the rural labor market, and ideas about these potential immigrants remained intimately tied to debates over the fate of blacks.[26] Though the lumber industry in south-central Mississippi recruited Mexican laborers as early as 1908, World War I and the Great Migration of blacks to Northern and Western cities most acutely forced the Delta's white planters to confront the dilemma of their dependence on blacks, and to think seriously about recruiting Mexican workers as an alternative.[27] By the mid-1920s, Mexicans could earn more picking cotton in Arkansas, Louisiana, Alabama, and Mississippi than anywhere else in the country. Farmers there paid Mexicans an average of $4.00 per day for picking cotton, as compared to $1.75 in Texas and $3.25 in California.[28]

The migration to Mississippi reached its peak in 1925. As the cotton picking season arrived that fall, the Catholic priest at Clarksdale claimed that five thousand "Mexicans," as he called them without regard to citizenship, were picking cotton on plantations throughout the region, in Clarksdale,

Greenwood, Greenville, Cleveland, Tunica, and Hollandale. And "more are coming every day."[29] Indeed, by the end of 1925, the priest would pay a visit to every plantation in his Clarksdale parish, finding Mexicans—and presumably, Texas-born Mexican Americans—on all of them.[30]

The profile of these workers mirrored that of the era's Mexican and Tejano migrants overall. Although they had first lived in South Texas locales such as Crystal City, Pearsall, San Antonio, Mercedes and San Benito, $5/6$ of ethnic Mexican household heads, wives, and boarders enumerated by census takers in the Delta's Bolivar County during the 1930 planting season were Mexican born, while $1/6$ were Texas born.[31] A quarter had first crossed the border before the revolution, some as early as the 1880s; half crossed during the Revolution of 1910–17, and a quarter had crossed since the revolution's end.[32]

While most Mexicans and Mexican Americans left the Delta after the last of the cotton crop had been picked in December, many tried to stay in Mississippi. From March to December, they would plant, cultivate, and pick cotton in family groups. Those who remained through the winter bought a few chickens, hogs, and cows, acquiring meager food and eggs.[33] Others, like A. González, left their wives and children in Mississippi and migrated elsewhere for temporary work at the end of the cotton harvest. Living even more precariously than he had in Mississippi, González's tertiary migration ended in tragedy. He was accidentally run over while asleep on the railroad tracks in Middlesboro, Kentucky, in November of 1930.[34]

For Mexican immigrants who considered staying in the South, possibilities for economic advancement were intimately tied to their place relative to the color line. In matters of both education and employment, the Mississippi Delta's blacks had no possibility for social mobility besides leaving the Delta entirely.[35] In New Orleans, Mexican immigrants arrived to an international port city of the Old South, a place more like Caribbean-influenced Tampa than industrial Atlanta. Like Tampa's, New Orleans' racial landscape was in the process of renegotiation.[36] The city in the nineteenth century had included black Creoles who were free and upper class, as well as diverse European immigrants, among them Spanish-speaking immigrants from the Canary Islands.[37] The case named after New Orleans' most famous color line transgressor, Creole of color Homer Plessy, had ruled in 1898 that ancestry and biological race would determine who sat in which train car—who was black and who was white. Still, it took decades for the Jim Crow system to effectively reshape New Orleans. During the 1920s, land development expanded beyond the city's traditional core, and with this expansion, and the legalization of residential segregation, came the struggle to impose Jim Crow's black-white binary on a city where class, culture, and national origin had intersected with skin color to determine social position. As the color line bisected the city's diverse social and cultural groups, European immigrants were afforded the privileges of whites.[38]

Ethnic and immigrant communities in New Orleans and the Mississippi Delta did not respond in uniform or predictable ways to the Jim Crow system, however. A variety of in-between groups—white Creoles, Creoles of color, Chinese, and Italians, to name a few—pursued distinct strategies towards social mobility and status in the South.[39] Italians, for example, freely cohabitated with blacks in the late nineteenth century, advocated labor unionism at a time when the movement flirted with interracialism, and paid the price when eleven Italians died at the hands of a white lynch mob in 1891.[40] As the French-Spanish cultural group known as "Creole" bifurcated along race lines in the wake of emancipation and Reconstruction, some Creoles of color tried to "pass" as white, but others adopted a radical anti-racist ideology inspired by the ideals of French Republicanism; Plessy, who had just one black great-grandparent, emerged from this milieu.[41] White Creoles, meanwhile, created discourses of "purity of blood," actively refuting allegations about their mixed racial ancestry and adopting an emphatically white racial identity that persisted through the twentieth century.[42] In the Mississippi Delta, a Chinese family used the courts to claim, unsuccessfully, that Chinese students should gain admittance to the white elementary school because they were not black.[43] As these divergent paths show, the black-white binary that defined the Mississippi Delta and New Orleans to different degrees by 1930 created both incentives and opportunities for immigrant and ethnic groups to embrace a white racial identity, but did not guarantee that they would do so. Thus, the specific ways the South's elite and working-class Mexicans maneuvered within and around Jim Crow reveals as much about the history of Mexico, as that of the Jim Crow system and the place of in-between groups within it.

Certainly, Mexicans arriving in the South at the close of the Mexican Revolution faced the possibility of becoming racialized as not white nor black, but "Mexican." Historians have argued that over the course of the 1920s, Mexicans elsewhere in the United States were racialized through border-crossing humiliation, social scientists' and reformers' pontifications on the "Mexican problem," "barrio-ization," negative images of the Mexican Revolution, and Mexicans' overwhelming presence in the economic underclass.[44] Though each of these conditions applied in part to Mexicans in rural Mississippi, none would describe 1920s New Orleans.

Compared to Mexicans elsewhere in the United States, those in New Orleans were more middle class. Estimates of the same period in Los Angeles suggest that 70 to 90 percent of Mexicans there were blue-collar workers.[45] In 1920 New Orleans, by contrast, only 37 percent of male Mexican workers had blue-collar positions. A quarter held clerical and office positions, and an additional 15 percent were professionals. Historian George Sánchez's research on Los Angeles, by contrast, found 20 percent of Mexican males who filed for naturalization held "low white collar" positions (including clerical or sales positions) while just 4.4 percent were described as "high white collar."[46] New Orleans' working Mexican women were consigned to much lower positions on the occupational scale. While 19 percent worked in clerical positions, an even greater number worked as domestics—maids, washerwomen, and servants.[47] Since wealthier women did not work at all, those women who did come to New Orleans to work, usually alone, disproportionally occupied low-skilled jobs.

Though Mexicans in many cities, including Los Angeles and Chicago, lived in mixed neighborhoods in this period, New Orleans' Mexicans were spread throughout the city in no discernable residential pattern.[48] The city's geography overall was less racialized than other cities' in this period, since unlike in northern and New South cities, residential segregation there was not yet pronounced.[49] Accordingly, the largest contingent of Mexican households—47 percent—lived in neighborhoods with both native-born whites and native-born blacks. While 39 percent lived in neighborhoods including native-born whites, but no blacks, just 1 percent lived in a neighborhood including blacks, but no native-born whites. Residential patterns also did not suggest an affiliation between Mexicans and not-quite-white immigrants such as Italians or Eastern Europeans. In fact, while 44 percent of Mexicans lived in neighborhoods including at least some Italians, and 14 percent lived among Eastern Europeans, 54 percent lived in neighborhoods including immigrants from Northern and Western Europe. This distribution roughly mirrored the slightly larger number of Northern and Western Europeans in the city, as compared to Italians.[50] While Mexicans in Chicago and East Los Angeles were forced to live among "undesirable" immigrant groups during this period, in New Orleans neither native-born whites nor Western and Northern European immigrants excluded Mexicans from their neighborhoods.[51]

Marriage patterns, however, provide the strongest evidence of Mexicans' freedom to cross into white New Orleans. Since the nineteenth century, Mexican women in the Southwest had been considered eligible marriage partners, while Mexican men were more likely to be seen as a racial threat.[52] These gender-specific racializations persisted, and in interwar Los Angeles 33 percent of Mexican immigrant women married white men, while only 16 percent of Mexican immigrant men married white women.[53] In Chicago during the same period, Mexican men often married European immigrant women.[54] In New Orleans in 1930, Peter Nieto and Robert Canedo were among the 41 percent of Mexican and Mexican American men who had white wives, and of these wives, almost all were native-born white women.[55] The statistic has particular significance in the context of the Jim Crow South, where prohibitions on interracial sex were perhaps the most important ways in which racial boundaries were policed.[56]

Similarly, when a sociologist interviewed Mexican immigrants in New Orleans in the late 1940s, several interviewees who had been in the Crescent City since the 1920s reported that they had never faced discrimination there. "There was too much discrimination in Texas is another reason why I wanted to get away from there," said one interviewee who, representing a small contingent of New Orleans' Mexicans, had arrived in the city via Texas. "I thought New Orleans would be better. I have not found any discrimination in New Orleans so far. See, if I was in Texas I would not be able to be a Mason," he said.[57]

Those who left Texas for the Mississippi Delta did not face such easy acceptance. As in Texas, Mexicans in Mississippi at first were educated in a separate school.[58] Yet, in Mississippi Mexicans did not face clear spatial or sexual taboos. Most Mexicans lived on country roads populated by poor white, black, and Mexican families.[59] In sexual and family relations, too, Mexicans' status was unclear, as they could be found marrying and cohabiting with both whites and blacks. Manuel Sifuéntez and Antonio Martínez, for example, married black women and joined black households.[60] Other black families took in Mexican men for a fee, in one case assigning the nickname "Mexican Sam" to a Mexican-born boarder. The consequences of living with blacks are suggested by the notation of a census enumerator, who in 1930 listed Mexican Sam's race as Negro, rather than Mexican.[61]

Though less common, some Mexican men in the Mississippi Delta married white women as well. Maggie Mackenzie was a Mississippi-born white woman alone in her thirties with six children to support. She married Frank Torres, a Texas-born Mexican American man nine years her junior.[62] While marrying a black man in the 1920s would have been inconceivable and illegal even for an impoverished white woman in the Delta, marrying a Mexican

American man apparently was more acceptable. Having grown up in Texas, Frank Torres knew well the benefits of marrying "up" in the racial hierarchy, which may have motivated him to do so despite Maggie's more advanced age and the financial burden of supporting her six children.

In pursuing strategies to influence the course of their own racialization and social mobility in the South, some Mexicans in the Mississippi Delta acted individually, as Torres had, while others acted collectively. In 1924, for example, Mexicans on the plantation of Richard Neelly near Rolling Fork had their rations cut when Neelly decided they "did not want to work at all." In response, twenty-three of the plantation's thirty Mexican families staged "a small revolution in Camp . . . taking up their belongings and leaving."[63]

Yet even those willing and able to resist stood little chance of effecting change on rural and isolated plantations without the support of political or communal institutions. There was no active tenant organizing in the area, nor did the state typically involve itself in labor matters. Even once the New Deal began, the federal government had no involvement with the Delta's Mexican workers. Catholic priests did visit Mexicans on the plantations, but declined to advocate for them politically.[64] Furthermore, there was no Mexican American middle class in the Delta that might have acted paternalistically on behalf of poorer Mexicans.

New Orleans' Mexican immigrants, facing far fewer barriers to social mobility, made few attempts at collective organization. In 1918, the archbishop of New Orleans had christened Our Lady of Guadalupe parish to serve Mexicans and offer mass in Spanish, but the church attracted only a small percentage of the city's Mexican immigrants. The majority preferred to worship in dispersed parishes throughout the city.[65] Thus, other than Latin American student groups at local universities, the Mexican consulate and its affiliated Honorary Commissions in the rural South provided the only formal structure for collective activity among Mexican immigrants.[66]

For immigrants in both New Orleans and the Mississippi Delta, then, the Mexican government and its New Orleans consulate became critical touchstones. In the rural South, Mexico-oriented organizing took the form of Honorary Commissions, or *Comisiones Honoríficas*, affiliated with the consulate in New Orleans. These commissions, which dotted the Southwest at the time, promoted Mexican culture, organized politically, and offered communal support under the banner of Mexican nationalism.[67] Several groups in the Mississippi Delta, as well as one in Shreveport, Louisiana, formed such *comisiones*. It is likely that their organizers had first experienced them in

Texas, and sought to replicate the model on arrival in the rural South. Poor and isolated on dispersed plantations, and without claims to U.S. citizenship, these immigrants organized not through Mexican American groups in Texas, but rather, the Mexican consulate in New Orleans and the wealthier Mexican community affiliated with it.

As the only institution representing Mexicans in the South, these consular officials and well-connected Mexican families formulated their agendas and cultural programs well aware of both the negative racialization of Mexicans everywhere else in the United States, and the black-white divide of the U.S. South. Since its inception in the 1890s, negative depictions of Jim Crow had found their way into the writings of Latin American intellectuals, including José Martí.[68] Mexico's most well known theorist of racial nationalism, José Vasconcelos, also wrote deliberately against Jim Crow, having studied in Eagle Pass, where he resented the discrimination against Mexicans there.[69] Though consular officials fastidiously avoided mention of Jim Crow or the color line, its presence constantly informed their actions and words.

In responding to the Jim Crow South, these consular officials and upper-class Mexican families could have pursued several different strategies, as diverse as those chosen by Italians, white Creoles, Creoles of color, and Chinese immigrants. They could have emphasized the difference between themselves—whiter, Europeanized, and middle class—and the South's poorer Mexican "peons," protecting their own interests and racialization at the expense of others'. Given that Anglos in the Southwest had made similar distinctions for decades, such a strategy might have been successful.[70] Consular officials could also have pursued a "purity of blood" emphasis as white Creoles had, explicitly distancing themselves from blackness and claiming European heritage. And finally, though it likely would have been a losing strategy, officials could have joined many Latin American intellectuals in their disdain for Jim Crow, made common cause with African Americans, and fought the Jim Crow system itself.

However, the formulation of Mexican racial nationalism constrained these options. The dilemma of how to present Mexicans' racial identities to Jim Crow America engendered discourses that changed perceptibly as the post-revolutionary government consolidated its political rule and cultural program. In 1923, as the Mexican Revolution's competing factions continued to vie for power, the Mexican embassy in Washington had responded to the expulsion of Mexicans and blacks from Johnstown, Pennsylvania, by eugenically distinguishing the two groups. "The percentage of negroes is far lower in Mexico than in the United States, and there is no justification for Mayor Cauffield's act in classifying them with negroes," protested Chargé d'Affairs Manuel Tellez.[71] Blackness would remain the scourge of Mexican racial nationalism, but so too would white supremacy. By 1930, the consolidating government's nationalist project made such eugenic arguments unfashionable and even impractical. Given the increasingly prominent discourse of *mestizaje* coming out of Mexico through cultural production and rhetoric, Mexican elites in New Orleans were unlikely to make or win a eugenic argument for whiteness, and thus preferred to elide rather than address the issue of eugenic race.

As for the idea of challenging Jim Crow itself, not only did the power dynamic within New Orleans make this a losing strategy, but so did the international imbalance of power between Mexico and the United States. Indeed, the New Orleans consulate and the Mexican foreign service in general often cooperated with white supremacist objectives in matters affecting relations between the two countries. Taken together, a series of confusions and rulings on Mexico's relationship to African Americans shows that Mexican bureaucrats were very willing to distinguish between white and black Americans in their day-to-day business. Mexican racial nationalism implicitly excluded blacks from imaginings of white-Indian melding through *mestizaje*, but also rejected overt, U.S.-style racial binaries.[72] Whatever its contradictory ideologies, however, the postrevolutionary government cooperated with white supremacy partly as a matter of survival.

In 1922, Mexican president Alvaro Obregón invited black Americans to settle in Mexico, but between the mid-1920s and the late 1930s Mexican policy changed repeatedly on this count. At various times, blacks were singled out, required to furnish bonds to prove that they would not be an economic burden on Mexico as a condition of entry, or denied admission to Mexico entirely.[73] In the late 1920s, Mexican border agents refused African American boxer Harry Willis entry into Mexico to participate in a scheduled fight. When the director of the Tuskegee Institute asked the Mexican embassy in Washington for a policy clarification, the embassy indicated that in fact there was no official prohibition on African American immigration to Mexico.[74] Still, the border agents' confusion is telling. No Mexican government ever articulated a justification for having separate immigration policies for black and white U.S. Americans. Responding to the policy, Marcus Garvey speculated that Mexico wanted to avoid its historical reputation as a haven for U.S. blacks, lest the United States government have additional pretexts for intervention.[75] Whether or not Garvey's speculation was accurate, Mexican bureaucrats dealing with the United States had, by the 1930s, developed at least a basic sensitivity to the politics of white supremacy, and had established a precedent of willingness to comply with it.

A focus on Armando Amador, vice consul and later consul at New Orleans from 1928-1932, can illuminate the way in which one bureaucrat and intellectual of the newly consolidating revolutionary government, and for a time the most prominent representative of *Mexicanidad* in New Orleans, negotiated the racial landscape of the U.S. South and represented Mexico's history, culture and racial composition to a U.S. audience and to his fellow countrymen. In his representations of race in Mexico, Amador never attempted to assert that Mexicans were biologically European, but he also did not espouse the ideologies of race mixing that by then had become the favored radical rhetoric of Mexico's moderate "Sonoran Dynasty" as it consolidated rule between 1920 and 1935. Amador's own social and racial position exemplified his government's conundrum. A native of Zacatecas, Amador was well educated and multilingual, and worked as a journalist, novelist, and poet before, during, and after his time in the consular service.[76] At the same time, his identity documents defined his race as "trigueño," literally wheat-colored, or "moreno claro," light-dark.[77] Both mestizo and modern, Amador was the quintessential representative of the new Mexican nationalist ideal, but in Louisiana his racial descriptors might have earned him a spot in the black train car alongside another mixed-race intellectual, Homer Plessy.

Hemmed in by an unequal international power dynamic, New Orleans' self-identified upper-class Mexicans understood that they could not successfully challenge white supremacy. Yet, as representatives of a national program celebrating race mixing, and often claiming mestizo identities themselves, they could not claim to be biologically white. For New Orleans' most prominent Mexican citizens, like Horcasitas's father, Andrés, and the Mexican consuls he befriended, the most expedient path was to remain silent about *mestizaje* and race, and draw instead upon Mexico's positivist tradition of whitening through culture and class. They pursued a pact with whiteness in the U.S. South, based not on legal or biological race, but rather, promises of international cooperation, the neutralization of the revolution's political legacy, and the transformation of racial difference into folk culture.

Amador offered speeches throughout the state of Louisiana to educate its populace about Mexico, and also was a leader in the city's Latin American intellectual circles.[78] For example, in 1929 he delivered a lecture in Spanish at Tulane's Latin American Center titled, "The Renaissance of Mexican Art."

Amador's speech celebrated the art of the Maya and the Nahua, yet noted that the dominance of white men over the continent was "unavoidable" from the day Columbus landed in the Americas. "Nonetheless," he said, "the artistic soul of the conquered race was not dead, but rather . . . little by little inserted itself into the new culture, wrapping itself in this new spirit, learning to think and to feel within the new philosophical and ethical norms." In other words, Mexico was "philosophically and ethically" European, but aesthetically influenced by the "ancient" civilizations of the Indians.[79] In Amador's depiction, Mexicans' well-articulated compatibility with southern white culture overshadowed their unmentioned racial background.

At the same time, the accounts of Mexican history that he fashioned for the Louisiana audience eschewed the more radical revolutionary mantle that Mexico's moderate leaders had worked so hard to claim. In a speech to a fraternity at Louisiana State University, Amador asserted that Mexico had had just one "real" revolution—that of moderates Francisco Madero and Venustiano Carranza, not the more radical Pancho Villa and Emiliano Zapata. Just as Mexican government officials began to mythologize Zapata and Villa as heroes of a revolution that, in reality, had defeated them, Amador's account of the revolution to Louisianans ignored these two figures altogether.[80] Once again, though Amador did not affirm Mexicans' biological whiteness, he attempted to neutralize the threat their difference posed in the minds of elite white southerners.

In fact, Amador showed little concern for the defense of Mexicans' eugenic whiteness. In the most striking contrast to white Creoles' insistence on purity of blood, and his own government's eugenically based response to the Johnstown, Pennsylvania, incident seven years before, Amador freely displayed the cultural results of African slavery in Mexico's colonial past. In 1930, he sponsored a gala event at the Jung Hotel in honor of Mexico's Independence Day together with the Mexico Society of New Orleans, a group of white businessmen that promoted business ties with Mexico. Democratic Mayor T. Semmes Walmsley, who as then–city attorney in 1924 had personally created mechanisms to enforce new residential segregation laws, was on the program and offered his personal greetings and congratulations. The event had received its blessing from an ardent segregationist and reactionary.

And then, right in front of Walmsley, Mexican young women performed a "typical" Mexican *jarocho* song and dance. In fact, *jarocho* music was typical to Mexico's Gulf Coast state of Veracruz. Like the U.S. South, Veracruz had a long history of African slavery. Even after its adoption as national "folk" by revolutionary dance artists in the 1920s and 1930s, Mexican audiences would have immediately identified *jarocho* as an African-influenced dance style, in both aesthetics and lyrics.[81] Though he usually described Mexico as being white and Indian, Amador did not have to fear displaying African influences even in front of a segregationist mayor; rather, he simply transformed these influences into a folk dance representing the port that linked Mexican markets to New Orleans. Amador could claim Mexicans' place as politically, culturally, and historically white, without arguing that they were "Caucasian" biologically or legally.

While the consulate's nationalistic lectures and performances helped maintain a Europeanized image of Mexicans in New Orleans, they seemed to resonate little with the city's working-class and middle-class Mexicans. Unlike those in Amador's earlier post of Chicago, New Orleans' Mexican immigrants hailed from the Gulf Coast, where they were likely urbanites or rural migrants recently arrived to the city. These immigrants bypassed Texas, where their Northern Mexican counterparts founded Mexican mutual aid societies and invoked Mexican nationalism as a defense against racism.[82] New Orleans—where hundreds of working-class Mexicans appealed to the consulate for help in economic, criminal, and immigration matters—was likely the first place where Gulf Coast immigrants benefited from the new government's ideology of nationally bounded, cross-class solidarity. Yet, these appeals for Mexican government help did not beget a working-class Mexican nationalism nor foster the creation of a distinct Mexican community life. With white New Orleans giving them little additional reason to consider themselves a distinct group, Mexicans likely felt a weak connection to the new government, its revolutionary promises, or even the reimagined Mexican nation it claimed to represent. In fact, the lack of a visible Mexican community may have been a draw for some immigrants. One immigrant considered migration to both New York and New Orleans, but upon hearing that New York had a "Mexican colony," chose New Orleans instead.[83] Indeed, some Mexican immigrants perceived that in areas where more Mexican immigrants settled, distinct and disparaged racial categories followed.

Mexican leaders in rural Mississippi, who tended to hail from the north-central Mexican states that comprised the core of Mexican revolutionary politics, actively sought communal organization in the face of barriers to their social mobility. Ultimately, though, they too attempted to elide rather than argue about race in their pursuit of the white status that was a prerequisite for even the possibility of social advancement in the Delta. Many Mexican families in

Mississippi sent their children to school in Mississippi, but a 1926 ruling of the Bolivar County Schools Board of Trustees prohibited them from attending the Gunnison Consolidated School along with white children. Instead, the county paid Mexican community leader Manuel Solís to offer instruction at a separate Mexican school on the plantation of J. G. McGehee. By 1928 Solís had left the area, the number of Mexican children had dwindled, and the county was unable to convince a young Tejana woman to assume the role of teacher at the Mexican school.[84] Pupils Hortensia Landrove and her uncle George thus attended the white school for a few weeks during the winter of 1928–1929. The following year, the Robledo children enrolled in the second grade once the cotton was picked. While Telesforo and María Robledo pulled their son Freddo out in February to help seed the next crop, their daughter Jubertina finished out the school year, struggling with English but otherwise earning As and Bs. She was promoted to the third grade at the end of the year, even as many of her peers were left behind.[85] She became the first Mexican to complete the academic year in the white elementary school of Gunnison, Mississippi.

In early 1930, however, school officials decided to enforce the 1926 school board ruling, and told the Mexican families their children could not attend the white school.[86] On its surface, the case evokes contemporary "Mexican school" cases in California and Texas, as well as the "Caucasian strategy" deployed to resolve them. Yet, while Mexican consulates assisted in educational desegregation cases in the Southwest, in Mississippi they were the sole institutional agents of change, acting without the cooperation of Mexican American organizations or allied liberal lawyers.[87] Because there were no political partners in the South who could make claims on U.S. citizenship, Mexicans' racial politics in the South were just that—Mexican.

A group of Mexicans in Gunnison, Mississippi that would thereafter seek to found its Mexican Honorary Commission took the lead in fighting the school board's decision. Their leader was Rafael J. Landrove. Like nearly all Mexicans and Mexican Americans in the Delta, Landrove had spent time in Texas prior to living in Mississippi.[88] He was born in Northern Mexico, probably Nuevo Leon or Coahuila, in 1893.[89] In an area dominated by ranching and agriculture, the Landrove siblings were small-town urbanites, members of the aspiring middle classes that had emerged under the Porfiriato. The climate of economic prosperity in the North led to greater social mobility there than elsewhere, making it "the land of the self-made man" as a small middle class began to develop in its towns and cities.[90]

As the Landroves moved from town to town in Mexico's North, they employed entrepreneurial strategies in their attempts to become "self-made"—attempts that never quite succeeded, at least in Mexico. Rafael's brother Constancio made his living between Lampazos de Naranjo, Nuevo Leon, and San Antonio, Texas, where he moved and married in 1913. Constancio worked as a blacksmith, and owned a home by 1930.[91] Brothers Melchor and José worked as musicians.[92] Sisters Margarita and María owned a restaurant in Lampazos, but did not find the economic stability of marriage. Both gave birth to children out of wedlock and supported them on their own; in Maria's case, that meant moving a few hundred miles north to Laredo, Texas, where she worked as a cook and servant for a middle-class Tejano family, the Saenzes.[93] Margarita, too, eventually moved to the United States, settling in Oklahoma.[94]

Like his sister Margarita and countless other Mexicans and Mexican Americans, Rafael Landrove's journey north began in Texas but did not end there. While the date of his first crossing into the United States is unknown, by the mid-1920s Landrove was in Texas, where he married a Tejana, Martha Perry (or possibly Pérez).[95] The marriage was not his first, as his daughter Hortensia had been born around 1917.[96] Though his brother Constancio had found a measure of economic stability in San Antonio, Rafael's failure to do so parallels the declining fortunes of most Mexicans in South Texas during the 1920s. The uprising of Tejano violence in the 1910s had prompted brutal repression that had all but eliminated the last vestiges of political power Tejanos held.[97] Then, as both immigration from Mexico and the capitalization of Texas agriculture increased, Texas planters tried to create a permanent Mexican underclass, relegating children to inadequate Mexican schools, suppressing wages, and policing the movement of Mexicans and Mexican Americans in the region.[98]

Like many of his north-central Mexican compatriots who had reached Mississippi via Texas, Landrove had borne witness to historic transitions in Mexico. He was about seventeen years old in 1910 when his generation of middling northern Mexicans rebelled against the late Porfiriato's stifled social mobility, though not necessarily against its positivist emphasis on the whitening of Mexicans. Examining Landrove's self representation alongside New Deal era representations of Mexican immigrants in Mississippi highlights the stark differences between the Mexican racial politics of Landrove and his compatriots in Mississippi, and that of the U.S. liberal tradition into which the Southwest's Mexican American activists typically fell. Historians have shown that Mexican school desegregation cases in the Southwest were spearheaded by organizations like the League of United Latin American Citizens, which drew their politics from the U.S. liberal traditions of Progressivism and later the New Deal.[99] In Mississippi, however, Landrove's strategy for racial and economic "progress" drew upon understandings of race and class that emerged from his social position in Mexico.

Though U.S. American liberal institutions scarcely engaged with the Delta's Mexicans, the photographs of Farm Security Administration photographer Marion Post Wolcott represent their ideological perspective (figures 3 and 4). Wolcott shot her photographs in 1939, the same year John Steinbeck's *Grapes of Wrath* drew white middle-class readers into the struggles of poor white migrant workers. More race-conscious than many of her fellow FSA photographers, Wolcott's images sought to inscribe Mexicans, and indeed all the South's poor migrant workers, into the narrative of U.S. migrant poverty that previously had been reserved for whites. In so doing, she and other FSA photographers hoped to convince the American public that the FSA's migrant shelter camps should be extended beyond California to the South, where they would aid the region's black migrant workers.[100] Of Wolcott's thirty-five photographs of Mexican migrant workers in Mississippi, only seven focus closely enough on workers' faces to reveal their skin color.[101] These images of cotton workers, marked as Mexican only by the images' captions, invited a more inclusive vision of who should count as a poor U.S. American worthy of government support. Notably, however, there was no U.S.-based labor, Mexican American, or New Deal initiative that ever achieved any social or economic benefits for Mississippi's Mexicans.

Nearly a decade earlier, however, Rafael and Martha Landrove, the Delta's Mexicans, and their New Orleans Mexican consulate allies engaged Mexican ideas of race, and did win some white privileges for Mexicans, thereby opening the possibility of finding social mobility in the Delta for those Mexican families who wanted to settle there. A photograph of the Landroves (figure 5) shows Rafael's skin to be very dark; too dark to claim European parentage. He thus told the census enumerator in 1930 that while he was born in Mexico, his parents were Cuban.[102] Records in Lampazos, some of which describe Rafael's mother Petra Jayme as a native of the town, reveal that his claim on the census was a clever lie, designed to escape the negative racialization associated with his Mexicans origins.[103]

The Landrove family portrait also reveals their engagement with Mexican ideas of race and progress. Posed family photographs had emerged in the Porfirian positivist tradition as symbols of Mexico's emerging modernity.[104]

Figure 3.
"Mexican children carrying water to old railroad station where many Mexican families live during cotton picking season on Knowlton Plantation, Perthshire, Mississippi Delta, Mississippi." Marion Post Wolcott, FSA photography project, 1939. Library of Congress, Prints & Photographs Division, FSA-OWI Collection, LC-USF33-030539-M4 DLC.

Figure 4.
"Mexican seasonal labor contracted for by planters, picking cotton on Knowlton Plantation, Perthshire, Mississippi Delta, Mississippi." Marion Post Wolcott, FSA photography project, 1939. Library of Congress, Prints & Photographs Division, FSA-OWI Collection, LC-USF33-030539-M3 DLC.

Figure 5.
Landrove family photograph, Mississippi Delta, c. 1930. Courtesy of Nick Enriquez and family.

Though Landrove was a cotton laborer who could very well have been among the migrants in Wolcott's faceless representations of poverty, he represented himself as culturally middle class. The pen in his pocket implied that he was a professional, which he was not; Marta's fur coat and pearl necklace suggested a wealth the couple did not possess. The bench on which they sat certainly did not belong in their sharecroppers' cabins. By the time this photograph was taken, the Landroves may have conformed nominally to the type represented; Rafael Landrove was indeed literate, the couple's more formal clothing suggests at least a modicum of economic progress, and like half of Mexican families in the Delta they claimed Martha did not work.[105] Yet the image nonetheless exaggerates these qualities, depicting an aspiration more than a reality.

Self-representation, social choices, and even legal whiteness, however, would not allow the Delta's Mexicans to access white privileges if local officials made them black under Jim Crow. Indeed, their counterparts in Texas and California were forced to mount legal challenges in order to enforce their rights as Caucasians, but ultimately failed to prevent Mexicans' eventual segregation into inferior schools. In Mississippi, Mexicans could appeal to no middle class of U.S. citizens to pursue a "Caucasian strategy" on their behalf, nor labor organizing to help them win rights as workers. Rather, Landrove and dozens of other poor Mexicans in the Delta sought help from the consulate in New Orleans. In so doing, they drew upon the social and political status which New Orleans' Mexican bureaucrats like Amador and upper-class families like the Horcasitases had amassed through their cultural representations of Mexican-ness to white New Orleans. Though his original correspondence on the matter has escaped the record, Landrove's subsequent communications with the consulate, some of which request help acquiring flags and other symbols to celebrate Mexican Independence Day in rural Mississippi, suggest that the discourse of his petition probably proclaimed a desire to further the goals of Mexican nationalism.[106]

The Mexican government's paternalistic concept of *proteccion*, protection of emigrants, obligated it to respond to the appeal of a poor, dark-skinned Mexican like Landrove, but its articulated ideology of race mixing made claims of biological whiteness unrealistic. The comparable court cases that year in Del Rio, Texas, and Lemon Grove, California, backed by consulates or Mexican American groups and argued by lawyers, claimed that U.S. law did not permit discrimination against Mexicans because they were entitled to all the rights of other Caucasian citizens. In Mississippi, however, the consul did not appeal to U.S. law or to ideas about Mexicans' racial categorization. Rather, he wrote to Mississippi's governor, Theodore Bilbo, asking for Mexicans' admission to the white school based on a presumed mutual "desire to strengthen the cordial relations that fortunately now exist between" the United States and Mexico.[107]

By April, the governor's intervention had resolved the matter in Landrove's favor, and the following school year Hortensia Landrove, her uncle George Pérez and Telesforo Robledo's son Trinidad once again enrolled in the white school after the cotton was picked. All three finished out the academic year and were passed on to the next grade.[108] Rafael Landrove had gained his children's admission to the white school by pursuing whiteness and social status solely under the banner of Mexican nationalism. Nowhere in any correspondence did he or his consulate use the word *Caucasian*, nor appeal to liberal ideas of U.S. citizenship. Rather, Landrove drew the Mexican consulate into his struggle by appealing to an inclusive, modernizing Mexican nationalism. In turn, the consulate utilized the political capital generated through its advantageous position in New Orleans, putting it to use for poor Mexicans in Mississippi, in the service of the Mexican government's post-revolutionary ideal of national homogeneity and equality.

Though most Mexican immigrants left the Mississippi Delta before its limited recovery from the Depression, the strategy of eliding the question of biological race and focusing instead on cultural whitening, shared by the Mexican consulate and Mississippi's local Mexican leadership, ultimately helped prevent the emergence of a separate "Mexican" racial category in local understandings. This international political strategy brought material rewards to the few Mexican Americans who survived the Depression in the Delta. These families—the Enriquezes, Vargases, Palacios, and others—initially worked as sharecroppers and wage laborers. Many maintained a distinctly Mexican communal life in private, staying friends with each other and with newer Mexican arrivals, socializing at country dances with Mexican bands, and often speaking Spanish at home. But since the 1930s they also sent their children to white schools, and since the 1940s they married whites or Mexicans.[109] Ultimately, Mexicans joined the Delta's white middle class, just as their counterparts in New Orleans had begun to do a decade before.

The story of Mexicans in the South during the era of Jim Crow shows how migration became just one form of international influence on the development of both U.S. American white supremacy and Mexico's racial and cultural ideologies of national belonging. Unlike most of the South's other "in-between" groups, and indeed unlike Mexican Americans in the Southwest, the South's Mexicans ignored the question of biological or legal categories of race and instead worked with a publicly upper-class segment of the Mexican community to argue for all Mexicans' cultural compatibility with whiteness. Their choices show that while Mexican nationalists' celebration of race-mixing may have been unpalatable to U.S. sensibilities, their parallel emphasis on cultural, political, and economic whitening—the Porfiriato's legacy—could serve as a wedge into the winning side of U.S.-style white supremacy. That both Mexican government representatives and individual Mexican immigrants so readily dispensed with *mestizaje* reveals the thin penetration of "cosmic race" nationalism a decade after the revolution's close, as well as the influence of U.S. white supremacy on the development of Mexican racial ideologies. Furthermore, it shows that the Jim Crow system incorporated cultural understandings of race into its ostensibly eugenic system decades before segregation's demise forced a shift to more veiled forms of cultural racism. By pushing Jim Crow's architects and policemen into admitting dark-skinned Mexicans to the privileges of whiteness at the height of Jim Crow, Mexican immigrants and their government demonstrated immigration's power to force transnational influences upon a seemingly provincial system of race. So too did the architects and policemen of Mexican nationalism bend as they tried to consolidate a nation in the shadow of another to their north—a place to which the exodus of Mexican citizens had only just begun.

Notes

This research was possible thanks to support from the Yale University Graduate School of Arts and Sciences, the Mexico-North Research Network, the Fox International Fellowship, Yale Agrarian Studies, and the Howard Lamar Center for the Study of Frontiers and Borders. I thank the following for their comments throughout the writing process: Esquina Latina graduate reading group at Yale, Southern Historians of New England, Latino Studies graduate student working group of Yale and Brown Universities, Glenda Gilmore, Gil Joseph, Patricia Pessar, Steve Pitti, Seth Fein and his seminar in fall 2004, Al Camarillo, José Alamillo, Gabriela Arredondo, Carlos Blanton, Matt García, Gerry Cadava, Lisa Pinley Covert, Jerry González, Gustavo Licón, Gerardo Licón, April Merleaux, Chris Myers, Angela Stuesse, Jason Ward, and Karen Weise. In New Orleans and the Mississippi Delta, thanks to Lindsay Stradley, Ellen Steeby, Donna and Richard Enriquez, Michelle Johansen, and Chris Powell. Richard Enriquez, a trained historian and fourth-generation Mexican American Mississippian, shared insight, encouragement, and family along Route 61.

1. Mario T. García, *Mexican Americans: Leadership, Ideology, and Identity, 1930–1960,* (New Haven: Yale University Press, 1989); Douglas Monroy, *Rebirth: Mexican Los Angeles from the Great Migration to the Great Depression* (Berkeley: University of California Press, 1999); George J. Sánchez, *Becoming Mexican American: Ethnicity, Culture, and Identity in Chicano Los Angeles, 1900–1945* (New York: Oxford University Press, 1993).

2. Hazel Canedo, interview with author, New Orleans, May 3, 2007.

3. Another significant rural Mexican community worked in Louisiana's sugar parishes during the late 1910s and early 1920s, but is not discussed here. Paul Wooton, "Mexican Labor May Aid Sugar Planters Here—Serious Situation Can Be Met by Importation of Cane Laborers," *Times-Picayune,* June 21, 1918.

4. Joe Enriquez, interview with author, Cleveland, Mississippi, January 12, 2006.

5. This is unlike in the Southwest. Carlos K. Blanton, "George I. Sánchez, Ideology, and Whiteness in the Making of the Mexican American Civil Rights Movement, 1930–1960," *The Journal of Southern History* 72.3 (2006); Neil Foley, "Becoming Hispanic: Mexican Americans and the Faustian Pact with Whiteness," in *Reflexiones 1997: New Directions in Mexican American Studies,* ed. Neil Foley (Austin: University of Texas Press, 1998); Neil Foley, "Partly Colored or Other White: Mexican Americans and Their Problem with the Color Line," in *Beyond Black and White: Race, Ethnicity, and Gender in the U.S. South and Southwest,* ed. Stephanie Cole and Allison Parker (College Station: Texas A&M University Press, 2004); Neil Foley, *The White Scourge: Mexicans, Blacks, and Poor Whites in Texas Cotton Culture* (Berkeley: University of California Press, 1997); Thomas A. Guglielmo, "Fighting for Caucasian Rights: Mexicans, Mexican Americans, and the Transnational Struggle for Civil Rights in World War I Texas," *Journal of American History* 94.4 (2006); Devra Weber, *Dark Sweat, White Gold: California Farm Workers, Cotton, and the New Deal* (Berkeley: University of California Press, 1994).

6. Glenda Elizabeth Gilmore, *Gender and Jim Crow: Women and the Politics of White Supremacy in North Carolina, 1896–1920* (Chapel Hill: University of North Carolina Press, 1996); Stephen David Kantrowitz, *Ben Tillman and the Reconstruction of White Supremacy* (Chapel Hill: University of North Carolina Press, 2000); C. Vann Woodward, *The Strange Career of Jim Crow,* 3rd ed. (New York: Oxford University Press, 1974).

7. Joel Williamson, *A Rage for Order: Black/White Relations in the American South since Emancipation* (New York: Oxford University Press, 1986), 259; Woodward, *The Strange Career of Jim Crow.*

8. George M. Fredrickson, *Racism: A Short History* (Princeton, N.J.: Princeton University Press, 2002).

9. Blanton, "George I. Sánchez, Ideology, and Whiteness"; Foley, "Becoming Hispanic"; Foley, "Partly Colored or Other White"; Guglielmo, "Fighting for Caucasian Rights."

10. Alan Knight, "Racism, Revolution, and *Indigenismo*: Mexico, 1910–1940," in *The Idea of Race in Latin America, 1870–1940*, ed. Richard Graham (Austin: University of Texas Press, 1990).

11. Ibid.

12. Ibid.

13. Agustín Basave Benítez, *México Mestizo: Análisis Del Nacionalismo Mexicano En Torno a La Mestizophilia De Andrés Molina Enríquez* (Mexico City: Fondo de Cultura Económica, 1992), 92.

14. Kirsten Silva Gruesz, "Delta *Desterrados*: Antebellum New Orleans and New World Print Culture," in *Look Away! The U.S. South in New World Studies*, ed. Jon Smith and Deborah N. Cohn (Durham: Duke University Press, 2004), 55.

15. Because this is a study of Mexicans' insertion into black-white racial systems, my references to "the South" do not include Texas.

16. William C. Hunt, *Fourteenth Census of the United States Taken in the Year 1920*, vol. 3 (Washington, D.C.: U.S. Government Printing Office, 1922), 402; Leon E. Truesdell, *Fifteenth Census of the United States: 1930*, vol. 3, part 1 (Washington, D.C.: U.S. Government Printing Office, 1932), 992–3.

17. Romana Falcón and Soledad García, *La Semilla En El Surco: Adelberto Tejeda Y El Radicalismo En Veracruz, 1883–1860* (Mexico City: El Colegio de México, 1986); Gilbert M. Joseph, *Revolution from Without: Yucatan, Mexico, and the United States, 1880–1924* (Cambridge: Cambridge University Press, 1982).

18. This information comes from samples of households listed on the U.S. Manuscript Censuses for 1920 and 1930 and identified through searches on Ancestry.com, Library Edition. The 1920 analysis results from a sample of one-half of the dwellings in Orleans Parish, Louisiana, that contained at least one resident who was Mexican born. Since there was no race category for "Mexican" in 1920, there was no good way to capture Tejanos, but given how few were in New Orleans even by 1930, it is likely that their number in 1920 was negligible. Mexican-born people, whatever their race listed, were included in the pool, though individuals born to two non-Mexican parents in Mexico, who were not listed as speaking Spanish, were excluded. From the overall pool of dwellings, 226 were randomly selected utilizing an online random number generator. The sample's 226 dwellings together included 591 of the 1,242 Mexicans listed on the census that year. Analysis of neighborhood composition took into account the census page of the dwelling, in addition to the previous and subsequent pages. The 1930 analysis results from a sample of one-half of the dwellings in Orleans Parish that contained at least one resident who was Mexican or Mexican American. Mexicans and Mexican Americans were defined as those listed with the race "Mexican," and born in either Mexico or Texas (a few Central Americans listed as race "Mexican" were excluded), or listed with any other race and born in Mexico (individuals born to two non-Mexican parents in Mexico, who were not listed as speaking Spanish, were excluded). Also, 216 dwellings were randomly selected for inclusion in the sample, utilizing an online random number generator to select dwellings from the overall pool of households. These dwellings together included 572 of the 1,184 Mexican race or Mexican-born white individuals enumerated in the 1930 census in Orleans Parish. Together, 44% of these households had most members listed as "white," which roughly reflects the U.S. Census figures, in which 45% of Mexicans and Mexican Americans were listed as white. Analysis of neighborhood composition took into account the census page of the dwelling, in addition to the previous and subsequent pages. Myron Gutmann, Jan Rieff, and Albert Camarillo provided guidance regarding historical sampling methodology and analysis of manuscript census data. I additionally consulted Roger Schofield, "Sampling in Historical Research," in *Nineteenth Century Society: Essays in the Use of Quantitative Methods for the Study of Social Data*, ed. E. A. Wrigley (Cambridge : Cambridge University Press, 1972). My research assistant Christine Hill did all of the data entry from the manuscript census pages.

19. Hunt, *Fourteenth Census of the United States*, 247, 391.

20. See note 18.

21. Michael Nelken (grandson of Francisco Enseñat), interview with author, New Haven, Connecticut, August 5, 2007.

22. Norman Wellington Painter, "The Assimilation of Latin Americans in New Orleans, Louisiana" (master's thesis, Tulane University, 1949).

23. Kenneth Nieto (Peter's grandson), interview with author, New Orleans, May 2, 2007; Peter Nieto family entry, 1930 manuscript census, New Orleans, accessed via Ancestry.com, Library Edition.

24. Sánchez, *Becoming Mexican American*, 59; Alexandra Minna Stern, "Buildings, Boundaries, and Blood: Medicalization and Nation-Building on the U.S.-Mexico Border, 1910–1930," *Hispanic American Historical Review* 79.1 (1999).

25. Thomas A. Gugliemo, *White on Arrival: Italians, Race, Color, and Power in Chicago, 1890–1945* (New York: Oxford University Press, 2003).

26. Rowland T. Berthoff, "Southern Attitudes toward Immigration, 1865–1914," *Journal of Southern History* 17.3 (1951); Robert L. Brandfon, "The End of Immigration to the Cotton Fields," *The Mississippi Valley Historical Review* 50.4 (1964); Moon-Ho Jung, *Coolies and Cane: Race, Labor, and Sugar in the Age of Emancipation* (Baltimore: Johns Hopkins University Press, 2006).

27. Bishop Gunnis to Rev. Father Jeamard, September 23, 1908. Archives of the Catholic Diocese of Jackson (ACDJ), Bishop Gunnis correspondence, File 9. Another mention of Mexicans in Mississippi in 1908 is in Carey McWilliams, *Ill Fares the Land* (Boston: Little Press, 1942), 249.

28. Manuel Gamio, *Mexican Immigration to the United States: A Study of Human Migration and Adjustment* (New York: Dover, 1971), 39.

29. Nelius Downing to Rev. R. O. Gerow, October 15, 1925. ACDJ, File 11, Folder "Downing, Rev. Nelius 1925." Throughout this paper, I mimic the convention of contemporary observers who used "Mexican" to indicate both immigrants and Mexican Americans. However, my writing distinguishes between these two citizenship groups when it is relevant to the argument.

30. Report of St. Elizabeth's Parish, Clarksdale, 1925. ACDJ, "Reports—Parishes." My analysis shows that approximately 1/6 of ethnic Mexican adults in the Delta in 1930 were Texas born. See note 32.

31. For some birthplaces of Mexican American children, see Sacramental Records, Our Lady of Victories Catholic Church, Cleveland, MS (OLV). Throughout this section, my most careful analysis has focused on Bolivar County, the Mississippi county that enumerated more Mexicans and Mexican Americans than any other in the 1930 Census.

32. This analysis consists of a sample of every third Mexican or Mexican American household in Bolivar County, Mississippi, on the 1930 Manuscript Census, identified through Ancestry.com, Library Edition. These households were defined as those with the race "Mexican," or who were listed as any race but born in Mexico. The total sample included 41 households consisting of 147 individuals.

33. Joe Enriquez, telephone interview by author, June 6, 2005.

34. Report of Protection Activities, 1930, Archivo Histórica de la Secretaría de Relaciones Exteriores (AHSRE), Mexico City IV–69–44.

35. James C. Cobb, *The Most Southern Place on Earth: The Mississippi Delta and the Roots of Regional Identity* (New York: Oxford University Press, 1992), 177–83.

36. Nancy A. Hewitt, *Southern Discomfort: Women's Activism in Tampa, Florida, 1880s–1920s* (Urbana: University of Illinois Press, 2001).

37. Carl A. Brasseaux, ed., *A Refuge for All Ages: Immigration in Louisiana History* (Lafayette: Center for Louisiana Studies, University of Southwestern Louisiana, 1996).

38. Arnold R. Hirsch and Joseph Lodgson, "Franco-Africans and African-Americans: Introduction," in *Creole New Orleans: Race and Americanization*, ed. Arnold R. Hirsch and Joseph Lodgson (Baton Rouge: Louisiana State University Press, 1992).

39. I use these terms though the distinction between white Creoles and Creoles of color is itself, like all racial demarcations, a historically specific construction. See Virginia R. Dominguez, *White by Definition: Social Classification in Creole Louisiana* (New Brunswick, N.J.: Rutgers University Press, 1986).

40. Eric Arnesen, *Waterfront Workers of New Orleans: Race, Class, and Politics, 1863–1923* (New York: Oxford University Press, 1991); Claire Nee Nelson, "Redeeming Whiteness in New Orleans: Politics and Race in the 1891 Lynchings" (paper presented at the Southern Historical Association, Atlanta, 2005).

41. Joseph Lodgson and Caryn Cossé Bell, "The Americanization of Black New Orleans, 1850–1900," in *Creole New Orleans*, ed. Hirsch and Lodgson, 253–57.

42. Dominguez, *White by Definition*, 141–48.

43. James W. Loewen, *The Mississippi Chinese: Between Black and White* (Cambridge: Harvard University Press, 1971).

44. Gabriela Arredondo, *Mexican Chicago: Race, Identity and Nation 1916–39* (Urbana: University of Illinois Press, 2008); Sarah Deutsch, *No Separate Refuge: Culture, Class, and Gender on an Anglo-Hispanic Frontier in the American Southwest, 1880–1940* (New York: Oxford University Press, 1987); Edward J. Escobar, *Race, Police, and the Making of a Political Identity: Mexican Americans and the Los Angeles Police Department, 1900–1945* (Berkeley: University of California Press, 1999); Matt García, *A World*

of Its Own: Race, Labor, and Citrus in the Making of Greater Los Angeles, 1900–1970 (Chapel Hill: University of North Carolina Press, 2001); David Montejano, *Anglos and Mexicans in the Making of Texas, 1836–1986* (Austin: University of Texas Press, 1987); Stephen J. Pitti, *The Devil in Silicon Valley: Northern California, Race, and Mexican Americans* (Princeton, N.J.: Princeton University Press, 2003); Sánchez, *Becoming Mexican American*; Stern, "Buildings, Boundaries, and Blood."

45. Sánchez, *Becoming Mexican American*, 192.
46. Ibid.
47. See note 18.
48. Arredondo, *Mexican Chicago*, 39–58; Sánchez, *Becoming Mexican American*, 77.
49. Arnold R. Hirsch, "Simply a Matter of Black and White: The Transformation of Race and Politics in Twentieth-Century New Orleans," in *Creole New Orleans*, ed. Hirsch and Lodgson, 268.
50. Hunt, *Fourteenth Census of the United States*, 402.
51. Arredondo, *Mexican Chicago*; Sánchez, *Becoming Mexican American*.
52. Montejano, *Anglos and Mexicans*, 37.
53. Sánchez, *Becoming Mexican American*, 138–39.
54. Arredondo, *Mexican Chicago*, 125–29.
55. See note 18.
56. Williamson, *A Rage for Order*.
57. Painter, "The Assimilation of Latin Americans," 55.
58. Superintendent Eckles to Gov. Theodore Bilbo, February 22, 1930. Governor Theodore Bilbo papers, University of Southern Mississippi (USM), Hattiesburg, Box 71, Folder 20.
59. See note 32.
60. Kit Mason household, Antonio Martinez household, 1930 United States Federal Census, Bolivar County, Mississippi, accessed via Ancestry.com, Library Edition.
61. Ocie Jones household, 1930 United States Federal Census, Carroll County, Mississippi, accessed via Ancestry.com, Library Edition.
62. Frank Torres household, 1930 United States Federal Census, Bolivar County, Mississippi, accessed via Ancestry.com, Library Edition.
63. Excerpt of Report of Department of Justice, Concerning Alleged Persecution of Mexican Citizens at Mayersville, Mississippi, Archivo de la Embajada de México en los Estados Unidos (AEMEUA), housed at AHSRE, file 1541/8.
64. "To the Mexican Workers/Para los Trabajadores Mexicanos" from Rev. Father Nelius Downing, Catholic Priest, September 25, 1925, ACDJ, File 11, Folder "Downing"—"Downing, Rev. Nelius 1925."
65. "Visitation Report for the Parish of St. Louis Cathedral," 1939, Archives of the Archdiocese of New Orleans (AANO) parish files, Our Lady of Guadalupe.
66. Interviews with descendants of New Orleans' Mexican immigrants revealed no memories of communal organizations. Painter had a similar finding for Latin Americans in general. Painter, "The Assimilation of Latin Americans."
67. Sánchez, *Becoming Mexican American*.
68. Laurence E. Prescott, "Journeying through Jim Crow: Spanish American Travelers in the United States During the Age of Segregation," *Latin American Research Review* 42.1 (2007): 10–11.
69. Basave Benítez, *México Mestizo*, 130.
70. Deutsch, *No Separate Refuge*; Montejano, *Anglos and Mexicans*.
71. "Diplomat Protests Ban on Mexicans," September 19, 1923, newspaper article from unknown source. Clipped in AEMEUA 1451/1.
72. Basave Benítez, *México Mestizo*.
73. Irwin Gellman, *Good Neighbor Diplomacy: U.S. Policies in Latin America, 1933–1945* (Baltimore: Johns Hopkins University, 1979), 30; Gerald Horne, *Black and Brown: African Americans and the Mexican Revolution, 1910–1920* (New York: New York University Press, 2005), 182–83.
74. Embassy of Mexico to SRE, November 15, 1929. AHSRE IV-122–24.
75. Horne, *Black and Brown*, 182–83.
76. "Expediente personal de Armando Cuitlahuac Amador Sandoval," AHSRE 14-29-4.
77. Ibid.
78. Ibid.

79. "El Renacimiento del Arte Mexicano," lecture by Armando Amador, February 16, 1929, Tulane University, New Orleans, AHSRE IV-263-58.

80. "Says Mexico Had but One Real Revolution," *Morning Advocate*, May 7 1930. Clipped in AHSRE IV-263-62.

81. Anita González, *Jarocho's Soul: Cultural Identity and Afro-Mexican Dance* (Lanham, Md.: University Press of America, 2004).

82. On Amador in Chicago, see Arredondo, *Mexican Chicago*, 80.

83. Painter, "The Assimilation of Latin Americans" 118n16.

84. Eckles to Bilbo, February 22, 1930, Gov. Theodore Bilbo papers, USM.

85. Gunnison Consolidated School Records 1928–1929, 2nd grade. Race: white. Teacher: Mrs. E. M. Pease; 1929–30, 2nd grade. Teacher: Mrs. Edwina M. Delta State University archives, Cleveland, Mississippi (DSU).

86. Eckles to Bilbo, February 22, 1930.

87. Robert R. Alvarez Jr., "The Lemon Grove Incident: The Nation's First Successful Desegregation Court Case," *Journal of San Diego History* 32.2 (1986).

88. Landrove married a Tejana, and the couple's first daughter was born in late 1927 in Mississippi, as were subsequent children Rafael Jr. and Beatriz. Rafael Landrove household, 1930 United States Federal Census, Bolivar County, Mississippi, accessed via Ancestry.com, Library Edition.

89. Rafael Landrove and Petra Jayme, marriage record, 1879. San Juan Bautista parish, Lampazos de Naranjo, Nuevo Leon, Mexico, International Genealogical Index, Church of Jesus Christ of Latter-day Saints, www.familysearch.org; interview, Tomás González Landrove (great-nephew of Mississippi's Rafael J. Landrove), Monterrey, Mexico, July 9, 2006.

90. Alan Knight, *The Mexican Revolution*, vol. 1, *Porfirians, Liberals, and Peasants* (Cambridge: Cambridge University Press, 1986), 11, 43–44.

91. Constancio Landrove household, 1930, United States Federal Census, San Antonio, Bexar County, Texas, accessed via Ancestry.com, Library Edition.

92 Tomás González Landrove, interview with author.

93. Acta #99, *Nacimientos 1921*, Civil Registry of Lampazos de Naranjo, Acta # 171, and Acta #306, *Nacimientos 1908, Lampazos de Naranjo*, Archivo General del Estado de Nuevo Leon (AGENL), Monterrey, Mexico, Acta # 8 and Acta #71, *Nacimientos 1911, Lampazos de Naranjo*, AGENL; Manuel Saenz household, 1910 United States Federal Census, Laredo, Webb County, Texas, accessed via Ancestry.com, Library Edition.

94. Tomás González Landrove, interview with author.

95. Census and school records identify her brother as Perry, while baptismal records identify her as Pérez.

96. Rafael Landrove household, 1930 United States Federal Census.

97. Benjamin Heber Johnson, *Revolution in Texas: How a Forgotten Rebellion and Its Bloody Suppression Turned Mexicans into Americans* (New Haven: Yale University Press, 2003).

98 Montejano, *Anglos and Mexicans*.

99. Blanton, "George I. Sánchez, Ideology, and Whiteness"; Johnson, *Revolution in Texas*.

100. Nicholas Natanson, *The Black Image in the New Deal: The Politics of FSA Photography* (Knoxville: University of Tennessee Press, 1992), 78, 188–9.

101. Marion Post Wolcott photographs, FSA/OWI collection, www.americanmemory.org.

102. Rafael Landrove household, 1930 United States Federal Census.

103. Acta #113, *Nacimientos 1922*, Civil Registry of Lampazos de Naranjo. Great-nephew Tomás González Landrove also was aware of no familial connection to Cuba. Interview by author 2006.

104. Robert M. Levine, *Images of History: Nineteenth and Early Twentieth Century Latin American Photographs as Documents* (Durham, N.C.: Duke University Press, 1989), 62.

105. See note 32.

106. R. J. Landrove to Mexican consulate, August 31, 1931. AHSRE IV-188-16.

107. Castro to Bilbo, February 12, 1931, USM Box 71, Folder 11.

108. Gunnison Consolidated School Record Books, DSU.

109. Joe Enriquez interview by author, January 12, 2006.

Unskilled Labor Migration and the Illegality Spiral: Chinese, European, and Mexican Indocumentados in the United States, 1882–2007

Claudia Sadowski-Smith

The focus of contemporary debates about undocumented immigration to the United States is almost always on Mexican border crossers who enter the country without legal documents. While statistics are generally unreliable, undocumented immigration is estimated to have grown from about 3.2 million in 1986 to 12 million in 2007. In fact, since the mid-1990s, annual arrivals of unauthorized migrants have exceeded those who come under legal categories.[1] So far, these increases have largely been discussed in terms borrowed from discourses of the early 1990s, which blamed Mexican immigrants for California's economic recession and resulted in the passage of state laws declaring unauthorized migrants ineligible for social services. Today's debates similarly center on proposals to curb Mexican immigration by reinforcing the Mexico-U.S. border and by further criminalizing unauthorized immigrants. A federal bill containing such provisions failed to pass Congress in summer 2007 because it also outlined a guest worker program and a path toward legalization.

The overall tendency to equate undocumented immigration with Mexican nationals makes sense in terms of their absolute numbers. Since the 1910s and 1920s when they first became subject to regulation, Mexican immigrants have been the largest group to have arrived undocumented in the United States. But while Mexican nationals represented more than 90 percent of the unauthorized population until the early 1970s, by 2002 they made up only about *half* of this population.[2] The next largest percentage of immigrants comes from Latin, Central, and South America (about 24 percent), and smaller, yet significant groups arrive from every other part of the globe, including Asia, Europe, and Africa.[3] That some of today's undocumented migrants hail from Ireland, Poland, and Russia—areas with long immigration histories to the United States—complicates widespread assumptions that contrast contemporary "illegals" from Mexico with earlier European immigrants who supposedly all came to the United States legally. And that undocumented migrants arrive from various parts of Asia also rarely enters public debates. Alongside other forms of migration from this region, Chinese immigration has a particularly long history. An emerging body of scholarship on Chinese responses to nineteenth century exclusion has highlighted the centrality of this population for any theories of immigrant illegality in the United States.[4]

This essay draws on such scholarship to examine European and Chinese migratory movements as precursors to and contemporaries of Mexican undocumented immigration. Such a comparative approach highlights the structurally similar conditions under which immigrant illegality has been produced in the United States as a set of distinct yet interrelated racial projects. The linkage of nineteenth century Chinese and European non-elite migration to racialized notions of involuntary passage and coerced labor enabled the passage of restrictive immigration legislation. The enforcement of these laws then transformed non-elite arrivals into improperly documented or undocumented immigrants. Undocumented movement, in turn, led to the further tightening of immigration law and enforcement, which added further layers of illegality to assisted migration networks and to the workplace. Set in motion by the nineteenth century legislation of Chinese and European immigration, this "spiral of illegality" later transformed twentieth century Mexican laborers into quintessential *indocumentados* and continues to shape the conditions under which twenty-first century immigrants arrive and live in the United States.

Because they could not otherwise afford the high overseas transportation cost, a large portion of nineteenth-century Chinese and European immigrants came with the help of assisted migration networks. Organized by profit-driven intermediaries, these operations transported different types of immigrants—pioneers, members of family chain migration or recruited labor—to the United States, and often helped them find work in mostly unskilled occupations that were plentiful during the country's industrialization. As immigrants' manner of arrival to work in unskilled occupations became associated with notions of slavery, particularly with unfree movement and coerced labor, this linkage contributed to the passage of 1880s exclusions of Chinese and European (contract) laborers. Newly emerging notions of difference that drew upon earlier forms of immigrant racialization influenced the institution of quotas against eastern and southern Europeans in the 1920s. As restrictionist laws became associated with requirements for immigrant identification, they *created* unauthorized or improperly documented immigrants from China and Europe. Immigrants began to arrive in the United States at less well controlled entry points without the required documents, often with the help of—now illicit—forms of assisted migration and cross border passage. Such unauthorized or improperly documented movements, in turn, spurred the increased enforcement of federal restrictions and the criminalization of assisted migration and border crossings.

While discussions surrounding the passage of nineteenth century restrictionist legislations had similarly racialized the assisted migration of unskilled Chinese and European newcomers by comparing it to slavery, each immigrant group was differently inserted on either end of the dominant black-white race spectrum put in place when slavery became identified with African chattel labor. This difference effected widely divergent racialized constructions of immigrant illegality. Because Chinese newcomers were almost completely excluded as a group and declared racially ineligible for citizenship, they became wholesale associated with illegal entry.[5] In contrast, immigration legislation targeting Europeans focused only on select classes or nationalities, primarily those racialized through association with notions of coerced labor or with pseudoscientific beliefs in inherent differences among different nationalities. Even those Europeans who arrived without proper documentation remained theoretically eligible for naturalization. Although the number of Europeans who came as undocumented immigrants far surpassed that of Chinese newcomers, European entry thus never became completely associated with illegality, and the history of European illegality could be quickly forgotten.

When Mexican immigrants arrived in larger numbers in the 1910s and 1920s to fill unskilled jobs left open by dwindling numbers of Asian and European immigrants, they suffered conditions that had been put in place by the regulation of Chinese and European newcomers. As existing immigration law was now administratively enforced with Mexican nationals, it also became linked to requirements for documentation. The institution of medical inspections along the Mexico-U.S. boundary, the imposition of a head tax, the introduction of border crossing cards, and the implementation of visa requirements created improperly documented Mexican nationals. When they entered a segregated Southwest as virtually nonwhite persons, Mexican migrants' cross-border passage and their insertion into the U.S. economy as unskilled labor also became linked to notions of illegality, thus anticipating the later, wholesale equation of Mexican nationals with undocumented entry and residence in the United States.

New versions of the illegality spiral continue to shape conditions of entry and insertion into the U.S. economy for today's undocumented immigrants who simultaneously arrive from everywhere in the globe, including Asia and Europe. Following a lull in immigration from these two areas, transformations in the U.S. economy since the 1960s and 1980s have again attracted immigrants from China and from regions in Europe with nineteenth century immigrant activity, such as Ireland, Poland, and Russia. While current U.S. immigration legislation no longer allows exclusion on racial or national grounds or specifically targets unskilled workers, it has retained its class-based bias, containing few legal options for those willing to work in the unskilled occupations that dominate today's postindustrial U.S. economy.

Thus, migrants from China, Mexico, and European countries enter the United States surreptitiously as they did at the turn of the twentieth century. Many immigrants come with the help of assisted migration networks that revive aspects of similar nineteenth century operations, and they are inserted into unregulated jobs in small-scale manufacturing, construction, hospitality, and other service industries that resemble nineteenth century unskilled occupations. Contemporary assisted migration networks are also increasingly involved in managing the arrival of those who come with legal documents and overstay their provisions. As in the past, the discursive association of immigrants with informal labor and with illegal transnational organizations that supervise their surreptitious entry has spurred increased U.S. border enforcement and the criminalization of *indocumentados* in federal and state law.

Since their inception in the nineteenth century, U.S. boundary regulations, then, have created ever new layers of racially distinct yet structurally similar forms of illegality, which have shaped the conditions under which immigrants arrive and eventually live in the United States. Recognition of these intersections provides a corrective to currently dominant notions of *indocumentados* as nationals of one particular country. Intersectional accounts of immigration also have much to contribute to ongoing struggles for immigrant rights in the United States. Such accounts can usefully complement fledging *cross-ethnic* forms of immigrant organizing and public protest that have brought together a wide spectrum of immigrants.[6]

Assisted Migration, Unskilled Labor, and the Nineteenth Century Illegality Spiral

The origins of the illegality spiral can be traced back to the first federal piece of immigration legislation, the 1819 Steerage Act. The act limited the number of passengers incoming ships could carry in an attempt to restrict the influx of impoverished European immigrants. Since the seventeenth century, a majority of newcomers from the British Isles, Germany, and Scandinavia had arrived on assisted migration networks, primarily to work as unskilled labor on farms or as domestic servants. The Steerage Act encouraged the decline of immigrants' prevoyage indenture contracts with sea captains, and it likely also contributed to the sudden collapse of the redemptioner system which enabled immigrants to sign a contract with a purchaser upon embarkation.[7] The two systems of indenture came under criticism through their association with slavery at a time when Africans were becoming the labor of choice. Particularly the practice of placing some redemptioners up for sale resulted in references to German redemptioners as "Dutch slaves" and fueled increasing hostility to all forms of bondage for immigrants from Europe.[8]

Even though it only indirectly regulated European assisted immigration, the Steerage Act highlighted the deepening association of assisted unskilled labor migration with slavery. The linkage provided an important context for the implementation of the first exclusionary U.S. immigration law. The 1875 Page Law banned "involuntarily traveling orientals" from admission to the United States. This legislation focused on immigrant pioneers from China who, in order to offset the high cost of overseas travel, had likely come on assisted migration networks that revived aspects of the European indentured and redemptioner systems. The construction of Chinese movement as a form of forced passage drew on the rhetoric of emancipation that equated *all* migration from China since the mid-1800s with the so-called coolie trade to the Americas, particularly the Caribbean. Despite significant differences in Chinese movement to the United States, the term *coolie*, tinged with its association with slave labor, came to be applied to all forms of manual labor performed by Chinese immigrants to the Americas.

When U.S. railroad companies asked entrepreneurs to help them recruit unskilled labor from China in the mid-1870s, the resulting credit-ticket system became even more closely linked to notions of unfree (slave) labor. As principal agents of assisted migration, a collection of Chinese merchant associations, called the Chinese Consolidated Benevolent Associations (the Chinese Six Companies), took on the immigrants' passage debt, helped immigrants find work in the United States, negotiated their terms of labor, and ensured the repayment of their debt. Coupled with the confinement of immigrants to remote worksites where they labored apart from non-Chinese workers, the practice of debt peonage, which involved intermediaries for the Six Companies collecting the laborers' pay and garnishing debt installments, further enabled comparisons to outlawed black slavery in the United States. This linkage became an important source of campaigns for the exclusion of Chinese workers in the context of an economic recession brought on by the completion of the railroads.

The 1882 Chinese Exclusion Act was the first federal legislation to create significant undocumented immigrant movement. The act barred the entry of Chinese unskilled laborers for a period of ten years while exempting merchants, clergy, diplomats, teachers, students, travelers, and Chinese laborers already in the Unites States. Despite its class-based bias toward Chinese immigrants willing to perform the kind of unskilled labor no longer needed after the completion of the railroads, the act also prohibited *all* Chinese immigrants from becoming naturalized, even those exempt from exclusion. At the time, citizenship was granted only to free whites, descendants of black slaves, and immigrants "of African nativity and descent."

Subsequent Chinese Exclusion Acts instituted the requirement that immigrants of ethnic Chinese origin prove their exemption from exclusion through certificates of return, residency, or identity.[9] When some continued to come without these documents or with falsified certificates, they did so as unauthorized or improperly documented immigrants. They entered the United States at official U.S. ports with fraudulent identification falsely claiming exempt status or traveled directly to Canada and then traversed the then unsupervised border into the United States. Local guides transported Chinese immigrants across rivers or lakes in rowboats or guided them across native reservations straddling the border, sometimes disguising Chinese immigrants as indigenous people.[10] Other immigrants used established opium smuggling routes through British Columbia, probably with the assistance of labor contractors who had ties to opium syndicates based on Vancouver Island.[11] Unlike the United States, which completely excluded Chinese unskilled laborers, Canada had imposed a head tax on Chinese, which made entry into Canada more difficult but not illegal. In fact, Canada's 1885 Chinese Immigration Act allowed Chinese immigrants destined for the United States to remain in the Dominion for ninety days without paying the head tax. Between the 1880s and the early 1900s at least a few thousand Chinese entered the country every year via the Canada-U.S. boundary as improperly documented or undocumented immigrants.[12]

The border route had already been employed by immigrants from Europe throughout the nineteenth century. Scandinavians, Russians, and other Northern Europeans arrived in Canada by steamship and entered the United States via the northern land border.[13] A substantial number of mostly poor, Irish

Catholic immigrants, many of whom were subsidized by Irish landlords or the British government, had also used the cheaper overseas route from Britain to Canada, and then traversed the largely unguarded northern boundary.[14]

In the 1880s and 1890s, the Canada-U.S. border became a popular route for even larger numbers of Europeans wanting to avoid increasing restrictions at U.S. ports of entry.[15] Mostly poor immigrants from Italy, Russia, the Baltic States, and Austro-Hungary, with smaller numbers from Portugal, Spain, and Greece, had been arriving in the United States since the 1870s as new sources of unskilled labor when more convenient and affordable transatlantic steamship and European railway systems became available. Poles, many of whom were displaced peasant farmers, unskilled workers, and domestic servants, arrived in large numbers, but were generally counted among Russians, Austrians, or Germans, since Poland had been partitioned among these countries. While many immigrants continued to come within the traditional European pattern of familial relocation and settlement, a stream of single men also arrived. They planned to maximize their earnings in the shortest possible time and then return home.

When some U.S. companies asked intermediaries to recruit eastern and southern European immigrants directly in their regions of origin in the mid-1870s, assisted migration schemes with similarities to the Chinese credit-ticket system emerged.[16] Between 1874 and 1925, migration networks organized by labor contractors oversaw large out-migration, especially from Italy, Greece, Turkey, Hungary, and Bulgaria.[17] Even though they did not always work for U.S. companies, the contractors recruited immigrants, most often of the same national origin, frequently advanced their transportation cost, and found them jobs. Sometimes called *padrones*, the contractors also provided a range of other services, such as sending remittances home or ensuring the availability of legal assistance. These services were at first delivered in return for simple fees and, later, deducted directly from the immigrants' wages in a form of debt peonage reminiscent of the Chinese credit-ticket system.[18] Independently of their contracted status, the new European immigrants worked in unskilled occupations that required little education, training, or language ability, such as the construction of city infrastructures, coal mining, slaughterhouses, farming, and in industries where changes in the production process were creating deskilled jobs.[19]

But the new immigrants were arriving into a context of increasing restrictions. Passed three months after the Chinese Exclusion Act, the Immigration Act of 1882 was directed at Europeans, since Chinese immigrants were already excluded. The act targeted destitute and ill immigrants while also instituting a head tax on all newcomers entering the United States via seaport, yet excepting those arriving via U.S. borders. Concerns that the newest European immigrants were recruited by U.S. companies into conditions of wage slavery spurred the passage of the 1885 Foran Act. These concerns were expressed through the rhetoric of slavery that had already shaped the exclusion of Chinese laborers. Officially called the Anti-Alien Contract Labor Law, the Foran Act barred all immigrants from entering the country if they were under contract or agreement to perform labor in the United States. The rhetoric surrounding the passage of the act compared Europeans to Chinese immigrants because they arrived as single men on similar assisted migration schemes and worked in similar, unskilled jobs.[20] When the Foran Act began to be enforced in combination with provisions of the 1882 Immigration Act, it imposed new barriers to immigration from eastern and southern Europe. Newcomers were required to demonstrate the impossible—that they could support themselves once in the United States, while also denying that they had a job waiting for them.[21]

Discussions of further immigration restrictions in the context of the 1890 recession signaled a shift from a view of race as a biologically determined essence reflected in moral behavior, cultural preferences, and physiological traits toward fledgling, pseudoscientific notions of genetic inferiority. These notions allowed the racialization of certain Europeans on the basis of their national origin. In the 1890s, Congress nearly passed legislation containing a quota for eastern and southern European immigration; literacy requirements that targeted these immigrants had been proposed since the 1880s.[22] The formation of the Office of the Superintendent of Immigration to enforce immigration law, the protection of U.S. seaports, and the creation of Ellis Island in 1892 also signaled a renewed focus on European entry. At Ellis Island, interrogations and medical inspections geared toward excluding immigrants with diseases, those likely to become public charges, and contract laborers excepted first class passengers, thus indicating the importance of manner of arrival for expectations about the future job and class status of immigrants once in the United States.

As with Chinese immigration, these new enforcement tactics spurred the growth of border crossings and assisted migration. Rather than ending the practice of contract labor, the European *padrone* system peaked between 1890 and 1900.[23] Middlemen coached European immigrants on how to circumvent the contract labor law and also provided "show money" to prevent immigrants' exclusion as potential public charges at official ports of entry. In the 1890s, a growing number of Europeans also used the Canada-U.S. border as a back-door into the United States to evade entry inspections at U.S. ports. A special congressional committee report in 1891 estimated that 50,000 Europeans were crossing the border in the second half of 1890. This number equaled approximately 22 percent of all total immigrants admitted to the United States.[24] In contrast to Chinese immigrants, who were required to document admissibility through exemption from exclusion, however, Europeans were generally considered admissible unless excluded at ports of entry.

Reactions to the surge in European border crossings led to another manifestation of the illegality spiral—the requirement that all immigrants entering the United States via Canada be documented, with the exception of Canadians, who also extensively crossed the border at the time to seek work in U.S. border areas. The 1894 "Canadian Agreement" with Canadian transportation companies enabled U.S. officers to be stationed at Canadian seaports, where they issued certificates of admission that immigrants had to present when entering the United States. Those who could not produce these certificates were refused entry and handed over to Canadian railways, which were bound by agreement to return immigrants to as remote a point from the Canada-U.S. border as possible.[25] Immigrants who continued to come to the United States via Canada without these certificates now did so as improperly documented immigrants. Thus was created the European undocumented border crosser.

In addition to supporting the Canadian Agreement, Canada passed its own version of the Foran Act, the Alien Labour Act, in 1897, and also, for the first time, instituted border inspections. When immigrants began to cross the Canada-U.S. border at locales further and further west to avoid these inspections, more entry ports were created until border coverage was deemed complete in 1908.[26] While the Canadian Agreement affected all immigrants who were in transit to the United States, Chinese immigrants were treated especially harshly. In 1910, for example, the United States closed all northern land border ports to Chinese immigrants and routed them via Halifax to Boston, where they had to apply for admission to the United States.[27] In 1923, Canada passed its own version of the Chinese Exclusion Act.

The closure of the Canada-U.S. border through binational enforcement shifted attention to unauthorized immigration across the largely unguarded border with Mexico. Estimates of Mexico-U.S. border crossings by Chinese immigrants range from several hundred each year to between 7,000 and 21,000 between 1910 and 1920 alone.[28] Unlike authorities in Canada, however, Mexico's government was not interested in supporting U.S. enforcement of Chinese exclusion, citing the unconstitutionality of U.S. requests to station

U.S. officers on Mexican territory. The official position was that, because the Mexican constitution allowed free admission into and travel through the country, it was impossible to prevent Chinese immigrants' entry into Mexico or their crossing of the border with the United States. Mexico was more interested in promoting Chinese immigration into Mexico, as manifested in the 1899 treaty with China, and wanted to avoid damaging U.S. economic investments in northern Mexico that, to an extent, also relied on Chinese labor.

Because the Mexico-U.S. border could not be controlled through binational agreement or through Mexican immigration policies, the United States concentrated on the implementation of various enforcement strategies. The Chinese Exclusion Act had created the Chinese Division inside the Immigration Service, which, in the late 1800s, took over the enforcement of exclusion from customs officers at official entry points along seaboards and U.S. land borders. The Bureau of Immigration was transferred to the newly created Department of Commerce and Labor in 1903. This change showed that the purpose of immigration controls was no longer seen as the leveraging of fees on cross-border movement by customs collectors but as a way of protecting U.S. workers from "unfair" Chinese competition. The so-called Chinese Inspectors and mounted guards (later known as customs patrol inspectors) focused on Chinese immigrants who circumvented official ports of entry. Other nationals, including Mexican residents who were exempt from immigration legislation, however, were not required to show proof of citizenship when entering the United States. Nationality even trumped ethnicity: whenever Chinese border crossers were able to claim Mexican citizenship, they were allowed to enter the United States freely.[29]

In a resurgence of the illegality spiral, the enforcement of the Mexico-U.S. border increased immigrants' need for assisted migration networks. Aside from local companies operating in Mexico, the Chinese Six Companies also drew on their expertise as former recruitment agents for U.S. companies to oversee the surreptitious entry of Chinese immigrants from China into the United States. Employees of the Six Companies helped immigrants cross the Mexico-U.S. border and find work in both Mexico and the United States. The Six Companies also used their office in Havana, Cuba, to oversee the movements of Chinese from the Caribbean into the United States, which required surreptitious crossings via the Mexico-U.S. border. A third scheme abused provisions of an 1894 treaty with China, which allowed Chinese transit through the United States on their way to China or to other destinations in bonded freight cars. The Six Companies substituted legal U.S. or Canadian residents for bond travelers or for Chinese immigrants who were about to be deported back to China.[30]

In reaction to such substitution schemes, Chinese immigrant certificates were required to be accompanied by photographs, which set the precedent for subsequent immigrant documentation and border crossing cards for residents of the hemisphere.[31] In 1910, Angel Island was created near San Francisco. While passengers arriving on first or second class tickets and most Europeans were processed onboard their ships, particularly Chinese immigrants were ferried to Angel Island for medical exams and interrogations by immigrant inspectors to ascertain the legality of their documents. Those whose documents were in doubt were detained, sometimes up to several years.

In the context of another recession that lasted from 1920 to 1922, the quota law that was first proposed in 1890 passed in a more restrictive version as the 1921 Emergency Quota Act. Subsequent Quota Acts of 1924 and 1929 further delimited European immigration. In contrast to the Chinese Exclusion Acts, which excluded immigrants because of their supposed racial ineligibility to naturalization, quotas only selectively restricted immigration from eastern and southern Europe on the basis of pseudoscientific theories claiming innate and ineradicable inequalities among various national groups. While the national origins category racialized some Europeans, it reaffirmed their common whiteness. In naturalization applications, European immigrants were expected to fill in their "color" as "white," while indicating their national origin as their "race." Even though the quota laws thus racialized some Europeans on the basis of their "national origins," Europeans were never completely barred from admission and citizenship rights were theoretically accorded even to those who may have arrived in the United States as improperly documented or unauthorized entrants.

Creating another layer of illegality, the quota acts spurned the resurgence and growth of European undocumented immigration via the Canada-U.S. border. Immigrants also enlisted in agricultural labor programs in Canada's west and then entered the United States immediately after their arrival in Canada. Other immigrants went to Canada and, after five years of residence, were admitted as nonquota residents of the hemisphere.[32] In addition to the Canada-U.S. border, Europeans also crossed the southern U.S. border in large numbers. Estimates of unauthorized European entry in the years following the passage of quota laws run from 40,000 to 175,000 a year.[33] The rise in European undocumented immigration displaced attention to Chinese border crossers as the primary problem at the southern boundary. Greek and Italian assisted migration networks, in particular, facilitated the surreptitious entry of Europeans, who were sometimes also disguised as Mexican nonquota immigrants.[34] Other schemes of assisted migration resembled earlier forms of Chinese entry. European immigrants traveled to Mexico City, boarded passenger trains heading north, and then hired local guides to take them to safe houses on the U.S. side. If the immigrants did not have sufficient funds, border crossing guides sometimes made arrangements to collect the money from their friends or relatives in the United States.[35] Overstaying easily obtainable visitor visas was another path to unauthorized European immigration.

In the context of growing undocumented European immigration created by quota legislation, an independent Border Patrol was established as part of the second Quota Act of 1924. Its existence, combined with more rigorously enforced immigration legislation, the interruption of transnational passenger service, and the onset of the Great Depression, slowed immigration from Asia and Europe to a trickle in the late 1920s and 1930s. The unskilled labor vacancies left open by declining Chinese and European immigration were, among others, filled by Mexican nationals and by Canadians, the latter of whom made up 20 percent of all immigrants in the early 1920s.[36] Following the increase of Mexican migration after upheavals accompanying the Mexican Revolution, Mexican movement, which had so far been exempt from legislation, became regulated.

Unlike Chinese newcomers, Mexican immigrants were not declared ineligible to naturalization. U.S. citizenship had already been conferred on some Mexican nationals in what became the Southwest after the 1848 conflict with Mexico, and Mexicans' racial status was deemed to be mixed. Instead, Mexican movement became regulated through a combination of existing immigration legislation and border controls with racial segregation in the U.S. Southwest. At U.S. embassies in Mexico and at border crossings, immigration legislation originally directed at European immigrants to exclude suspected contract labor and ill and impoverished immigrants was now administratively enforced against Mexican nationals.[37] Passed to curtail immigration from eastern and southern Europe, the Immigration Act of 1917 placed a head tax of eight dollars on each immigrant and required immigrants to pass a literacy test. The act also applied to Mexicans and Canadians, who had so far been exempt from the head tax established in the 1882 Immigration Act. In the 1910s, inspection procedures that had been used at Ellis Island and Angel Island, such as medical examinations and interrogations, were instituted at Mexico-U.S. border crossings. Similar to procedures at Ellis Island and Angel Island, which distinguished among immigrants according to their manner of arrival, Mexican nationals who arrived at the Mexico-U.S. land border on first-class rail lines were exempted from medical inspection and vaccination, while those coming on foot were not.[38]

Immigrants who wanted to avoid medical examinations and the enforcement of legislation began to cross along other parts of the border, setting a precedent for the immanent surge in the numbers of unauthorized Mexican border crossings. When border crossing cards were first introduced for Mexican border residents during World War I to be accompanied by photographs in 1928, this requirement created larger numbers of improperly documented Mexican nationals. In another version of the illegality spiral, the regulation of Mexican immigration spurred the growth of the Mexican labor contract system just as the European *padrone* system declined. Single men and families from Mexico continued to migrate each work season, but they now came with the help of Mexican labor contractors, who particularly flourished in sectors of the agricultural industry that remained impervious to labor-saving innovations.[39]

Mexican nationals, like Chinese and southern/eastern European immigrants before them, faced low wages, residential segregation, and little political representation upon arrival in the United States. Yet, unlike European immigrants, Mexican newcomers were associated with an already existing ethnicized group—Mexican Americans—who had been suffering from widespread racialized violence and the application of Jim Crow laws that excluded them from public accommodations in the U.S. Southwest and thus declared them de facto nonwhite. Following the quota laws' equation of national origins with race, the 1930 census even instituted a "Mexican" category outside that of "white" Europeans.[40]

By World War II, however, the various forms of racialization applied to individual immigrant groups had changed. The recognition of national divisions among Europeans at work in the quota laws was replaced by homogeneous categories such as "white" or "European" which glossed entirely over the histories of European illegality.[41] The 1943 repeal of the Chinese Exclusion Act enabled Chinese immigrants to become naturalized. The U.S. census system had already changed in 1936 and 1939 to classify Mexican nationals and Mexican Americans as "white."

Only when they became the single most important source of unskilled labor during World War II did Mexican nationals became transformed into quintessential *indocumentados*. This transformation of Mexican immigration into large-scale illegal movement was sponsored by the U.S. state when it took over the tasks of labor agents and assisted migration networks in organizing the unskilled labor market in the 1940s. Rather than ending quotas against southern and eastern European immigrants or provisions against contract labor, the U.S. government directly recruited workers in Mexico to unskilled occupations in the United States. From 1942 to 1964, the state supervised the large-scale importation of Mexican "bracero" workers into industrial and agricultural work sites. Because many migrants found themselves excluded from the program, it was accompanied by a substantial rise in undocumented immigration. In contrast to the turn of the century, the Mexican government now supported *binational* policies of shared border enforcement because it was interested in keeping its workers at home to participate in the industrialization of Mexico's agriculture. Starting in 1945, U.S. Border Patrol agents delivered unauthorized immigrants who resided in Mexico's interior into the custody of Mexican officials, who forcibly relocated immigrants to points south of the border, particularly to areas experiencing labor shortages. At times when the Bracero Agreement was put on hold, such as in 1949 and 1953, the Mexican government even stationed military along the Mexico-U.S. border to prevent the emigration of its citizens and, in some instances, to force detained migrants to work for Mexican agribusiness.[42]

But unlike nineteenth century cooperation among Canada and the United States along the Canada-U.S. boundary, Mexico's support of U.S. immigration laws did not prevent the further militarization of the Mexico-U.S. border and the transformation of Mexican immigrants into quintessential *indocumentados*. By the 1940s, U.S. policy-making had shifted almost exclusively to Mexican unauthorized immigration along the Mexico-U.S. border, which became viewed as the single most important transit point for illegal movement. In 1943, more Border Patrol agents were stationed along the southern rather than the northern U.S. land border. Among all apprehended immigrants, the percentage of Mexican nationals increased from an average of 17 to 56 percent between 1924 and 1940 to a steady average of 90 percent between 1943 and 1954.[43] As the illegality spiral transformed non-elite Mexican migration to unskilled labor into undocumented movement, immigrants reacted to restrictions by shifting their entry points to more dangerous areas of desert, mountains, and waterways.[44]

The Growth and Diversity of Undocumented Populations, and the Twenty-first Century Illegality Spiral

In the context of global economic restructuring, immigration from China and Europe has resurged to accompany ongoing transnational movements from Mexico. The termination of the Bracero Accord in 1964 in the context of unionist organizing and civil rights struggles formalized a policy of passive labor acceptance in the form of more massive undocumented entry from Mexico. Rapid population growth and a declining Mexico economy in the 1970s and 1980s coincided with the imposition of new restrictions on Mexican migration in 1976, when Western Hemisphere nations became subject to the same annual quota limits of twenty thousand already faced by other nations. The result was a growth in undocumented immigration by agricultural and unskilled workers, those taking service jobs, and a small percentage of skilled workers.[45]

At the same time, the opening of the former socialist countries China, Poland, and later Russia and of other parts of Eastern Europe to immigration, as well as the lack of jobs in Ireland in the 1980s, produced the necessary conditions for large-scale out-migration which took both documented and undocumented forms. The changes that these regions in Europe and China have undergone since the nineteenth century make it difficult to speak about nation- or culture-specific histories of U.S. undocumented immigration. Russia and Poland, for example, did not exist in their current forms in the nineteenth century, and today's immigrants from China tend to come from different regions than they did at the time.

While revisions to the immigration and naturalization laws since the 1940s have eliminated exclusions based on race or prohibitions against unskilled labor, contemporary U.S. immigration law provides very limited options for legal entry under family unification, political asylum, investment, or skilled-based criteria. The majority of Asian immigrants (often ethnically Chinese members of professional and elite backgrounds from Taiwan, Singapore, and Hong Kong) enter the United States legally on employment-based criteria.[46] Others arrive as family members of those who have immigrated since the 1960s. Citizens of China can also seek asylum if they claim persecution under China's one-child policy. Members of the former socialist East Bloc have become the most important sending countries for skilled professionals, alongside those from Asia, and some Eastern Europeans have also received asylum, either under definitions that considered immigrants from socialist countries refugees or as escapees from civil wars. While Soviet Jewish asylum seekers arrived in the 1970s, larger numbers of immigrants, not all of them refugees, came between 1980 and 1989 from Poland, Russia, and the Ukraine. More recent arrivals hail from Bosnia, Herzegovina, Moldova, and Albania. Despite their rising numbers, these populations have remained understudied in scholarship on U.S. immigration.[47]

In direct contrast to the elite transnationalism of high-tech professionals and entrepreneurs from Asia and Eastern Europe who, upon entering the United States, often move directly into the upper reaches of U.S. society, non-elite immigrants from the same regions have had the smallest number of options for legal entry available to them.[48] In fact, alternatives to undocumented entry for those willing to perform unskilled labor have become even more restricted since the income threshold required to sponsor relatives has repeatedly been raised and eligibility for political asylum has been tightened. The overall reduction of employment-based visas and an immense backlog in applications for family unification have created further obstacles to legal forms of immigration.

Even though it contains no explicit exclusions, contemporary U.S. legislation thus achieves effects similar to nineteenth-century immigration law, whose provisions targeted the non-elite segment of each new immigrant group through differential forms of racialization. Through its exclusivity, contemporary U.S. immigration legislation encourages the resurgence of the illegality spiral, which transforms non-elite immigrants into undocumented populations, who then encounter ever stricter immigration law and enforcement, which leads to further forms of illegality. But in contrast to the nineteenth and twentieth centuries, undocumented immigrants now come from everywhere in the world and arrive simultaneously rather than successively.[49]

Chinese immigrants constitute the largest group of *indocumentados* from Asia. And while outflows from the former Soviet Union and Eastern European countries such as Poland have dominated arrivals from Europe, the Irish still register as the single significant group of undocumented immigrants from Western Europe. Similar to the majority of nineteenth century immigrants, today's undocumented immigrants usually arrive with the help of assisted migration networks and are inserted into the bottom of the U.S. economy. They enter the United States as undocumented border crossers or overstay nonimmigrant visas that allow them to visit or reside in the United States for a limited amount of time.

Escaping high unemployment, Irish immigrants left their country in large numbers in the 1980s and early 1990s. While the greatest percentage crossed the border into Great Britain, some also emigrated to the United States. Because Irish immigration had come to a halt by the 1930s, few persons in Ireland had relatives in the United States who could qualify them for family unification slots, and the reduction in the number of work visas precluded the possibility of employment-based entry. Many Irish have thus come as undocumented immigrants. They usually fly to U.S. airports and overstay their visas. According to estimates of the Irish Bishops Commission on Emigration, about 136,000 undocumented Irish lived in the United States in the late 1980s.[50] Many resided in cities with historical Irish populations, such as New York, Boston, and Chicago, where they could make use of existing ethnic networks, religious support, and welfare organizations. When the Irish economy improved, many Irish immigrants moved home from all over the world so that in 1996 the number returning to Ireland surpassed the number leaving.[51] Today, the number of undocumented Irish in the United States has dwindled to perhaps 25,000 or 50,000.[52]

Contemporary Irish immigration coincides with movements from China after the country opened itself to international trade and to the corresponding influx of foreign capital. In contrast to nineteenth century immigrants, who largely arrived from the province of Guangdong, however, today's undocumented immigrants, perhaps up to 100,000 a year, predominantly hail from the Fuzhou area in the northeast coast of Fujian Province.[53] They arrive on assisted migration networks that revive aspects of the nineteenth-century Chinese credit-ticket system and the European *padrone* networks. In most cases immigrants are not directly recruited by U.S. companies, but come on a kinship network of chain migration, their passage being sponsored by relatives, friends, and acquaintances. Immigrants sign contracts with recruiters that stipulate a nonrefundable down payment at the start of the journey and the remainder paid upon arrival by sponsors, who often take out loans from underground associations or Chinese business networks. Arriving in the U.S. with huge "transportation" debts, immigrants are forced to work for years in a state of virtual indentured servitude, often under ethnic subcontractor systems.[54]

Attempts at curbing the influence of assisted migration have enveloped these operations in further layers of illegality. After the capture of several Chinese ships by U.S. authorities in the early 1990s, Chinese cartels began to re-employ the nineteenth-century Caribbean route that requires surreptitious travel across the Mexico-U.S. border. The crossing is contracted out to local guides so that the Mexico-U.S. border has, once again, become one of the major transit points for Chinese immigration. That fewer Chinese crossers are caught by U.S. authorities (and register in official apprehension figures) as compared to immigrants from Mexico, Latin, Central, and South America may, in part, also be the result of much higher smuggling fees and the highly sophisticated networks that, in the words of one journalist, "buy better odds."[55]

The discovery in the year 2000 of the "largest global alien smuggling ring" between the United States and Canada revealed that the northern border with Canada had become another major transit corridor linking China to the United States.[56] As in the nineteenth century, many undocumented immigrants enter the United States across indigenous territory where the international boundary is generally not enforced by immigration or custom controls. Other routes have opened up through Eastern European countries with no visa requirements, which have become major staging points of westward migration.[57]

Like Irish movement to the United States, contemporary Polish immigration peaked in the 1980s after the country liberalized its emigration policies. While most Poles went to other parts of Europe, the United States accounted for about 12.3 percent of the permanent emigration.[58] The new immigrants settled mostly in cities marked by histories of Polish immigration, such as Chicago and New York, with some recent arrivals moving to urban areas with virtually no Polish populations prior to 1980s, such as Dallas, Washington, D.C., and Atlanta.[59] In 2004, this population was nearly 139,000 and approached the historical high of 156,000 in 1930. Approximately half of today's Polish-born arrived after 1990.[60] The Polish Welfare Association in Chicago (PWA) estimates that, in the 1990s, Polish immigrants constituted the second largest undocumented group in Chicago after Mexican nationals.

As Poland became a market economy during the 1990s, Polish immigrants became ineligible for political asylum in the United States, and emigration from Poland decreased sharply to fewer than 50,000 a year. Undocumented immigration from Poland has also declined by more than 25 percent since 1988.[61] However, some immigrants continue to come in order to escape a lack of high-paying jobs as well as corruption in the Polish government. Polish immigrants fly to Cuba, where they obtain visas to visit Mexico or they get visas to Mexico directly, and then cross the Mexico-U.S. border surreptitiously.[62] Like unauthorized migrants from other regions, some also enter across the U.S. northern border, sometimes through reservation land that straddles this boundary.[63] Another version of the undocumented worker is the *wakcjusze* or vacationer, who overstays a visitor or student visa, and violates its provisions against employment.

Polish immigrants are increasingly counted among newcomers from the former socialist East Bloc, some of whom arrive as undocumented immigrants with the help of networks that revive illicit forms of nineteenth-century unskilled labor recruitment migration. A federal investigation, Operation Pisces, found that, between 1995 and 2002, labor contractors provided farms, dairies, and factories in the Midwest and southeastern United States with more than 500 unauthorized workers from Poland and Slovakia who had entered the United States on tourist visas. Three Polish-born residents of the United States residing in Florida were convicted of conspiracy to transport, house, and encourage undocumented immigrants to remain in the United States in what the U.S. attorney in charge of the case called an "illegal employee leasing scheme."[64] Similarly, in a 2003 series of raids on Wal-Mart stores across the country, around 250 undocumented immigrants from Mexico and Eastern Europe were arrested. They worked for various subcontractors that provided cleaning services to Wal-Mart. One of those companies, National Floor Management, employed immigrants from Georgia, Russia, Hungary, the Ukraine, Poland, Lithuania, Mongolia, and the Czech Republic. The convicted labor contractor admitted that he had obtained these workers from middlemen in Russia.[65] In 2007, Operation Return to Sender, directed by the Immigration and Customs Enforcement (ICE), led to the arrest of at least 750 undocumented immigrants from diverse nations, including Eastern European countries.[66]

These contemporary systems of assisted migration have emerged in response to federal legislation, such as the 1986 Immigration Reform and Control Act (IRCA), which fines U.S. businesses for hiring undocumented workers. To circumvent the provisions of this and similar laws, companies hire workers through subcontractors or other middlemen. These intermediaries contact immigrants in their countries of origin, pay for their transport, and, once in the United States, hire them out to U.S. businesses as employees of a subcontracting company, sometimes even agreeing to pay payroll and workers' compensation. Just as unauthorized Chinese immigrants find themselves working in ethnic subcontracting systems, undocumented European workers who are brought on recruitment migration networks are not officially employed by the U.S. businesses that need their labor. The subcontractor thus assumes the risk of hiring undocumented laborers, including potentially incurring fines and criminal charges, while businesses benefit from bargain-basement labor prices without officially breaking the law. These practices are reminiscent of the nineteenth century. The Chinese credit-ticket system enabled U.S. railroad companies to entrust the procurement and subsequent enforcement of work discipline to others, and the reliance of U.S. businesses on *padrones* allowed U.S. firms to circumvent the 1885 Foran Act by hiring unskilled labor through intermediaries.

Mexican undocumented immigrants are subject to the same or similar subcontracting schemes. Mexican immigrants also increasingly employ assisted border crossing systems in response to enhanced enforcement along the Mexico-U.S. boundary. Virtually all of those attempting unauthorized entry across the border today hire a guide or use more extensive assisted networks that transport immigrants to safe houses in U.S. border towns and then to destinations in the United States. Other immigrants abuse the provisions of easily obtainable border crossing cards that allow travel for three days within twenty-five miles of the border. In a new version of the illegality spiral, the increasing linkage of Mexican unauthorized immigration to assisted forms of border crossing has led to calls for further border militarization and increased punitive immigration legislation. Such calls then translate into the hyper-criminalization of immigrants. For example, in 2006 a county attorney in Arizona, where most unauthorized border crossings have taken place since the mid-1990s, indicted forty-eight immigrants on felony conspiracy charges under an "anti-coyote law." The indictment claimed that since these immigrants paid "coyotes" to transport them across the border they were complicit in their own smuggling.[67]

Conclusion

While contemporary immigrants arrive into a postindustrial economy, marked by legal quota preferences and post-civil rights notions of race and ethnicity, much historical continuity exits in the transformation of non-elite immigrants into undocumented populations. The notion of the illegality spiral, which links conditions under which immigrants arrive and are inserted into the U.S. economy with variously racialized discourses of illegality, can be helpful to highlight such structural similarities in non-elite movement to the United States. While the racialization of individual immigrant groups has changed over time—from an equation of culture with race to "national origins" quota to segregationist practices, and, most recently, to post–civil rights realities—the association of non-elite immigration with illegality seems to have remained constant. Recognition of this linkage needs to inform any theory and practice of struggles for contemporary immigrant rights.

Today's undocumented immigrants continue to be racialized differently through insertion into U.S.-specific notions of race and ethnicity. Irish immigrants are usually not subject to ethnic discrimination and enjoy advantages because of their English language skills. Irish construction workers occupy relatively privileged positions in the informal economy, and many Irish have even succeeded in penetrating the formal sector by using their connections in construction unions. In addition, Irish undocumented workers in the hospitality industries occupy the highest paid positions as waiters/waitresses and bartenders, while undocumented Latino immigrants tend to hold kitchen and janitorial jobs.[68] Despite linguistic and cultural differences, Polish and other Eastern European immigrants are also not treated as ethnic others in a context where distinctions among Europeans no longer matter and their histories of illegality have been all but forgotten. And Chinese populations are generally associated with the model minority myth, which overlooks non-elite Asian immigrants, including Chinese undocumented immigrants who come surreptitiously on unauthorized assisted passage systems that leave them with large amounts of "transportation" debt. Viewed as the perpetual "illegal foreigners," Mexican nationals, in contrast, now constitute the main target of immigration debates, punitive regulation, and increased enforcement.

Despite different forms of racialization, however, all *indocumentados* bear the brunt of the ongoing restructuring of the U.S. economy and the erosion of the welfare state that brought modest prosperity and security to an earlier immigrant working class and its children. Contemporary undocumented immigrants work in disproportionate numbers in unregulated low-wage labor markets, where they are generally remunerated below minimum wage, do not receive benefits, or are employed by subcontractors who further exploit them. Even higher levels of education, improved language skills, or longer stays in the United States usually do not translate into higher wages for undocumented populations, so that their upward mobility is severely restricted.[69]

Undocumented immigrants are also increasingly criminalized within punitive local, regional, and national legislation that further exacerbates vulnerability to exploitation. Since the 1990s, undocumented immigrants have had to face enhanced Mexico-U.S. border militarization, such as the implementation of highly visible enforcement operations, the replacement of fences with wall-like structures, the institution of new technologies of control, and the beefing-up of Border Patrol personnel along the Mexico-U.S. border. The Canada-U.S. border has also been enforced by the tripling of the number of U.S. border agents, the installation of new surveillance and satellite tracking systems, and the erection of some fences. These changes along land borders and other official ports of U.S. entry have turned large numbers of those who would otherwise be temporary sojourners into more permanent undocumented migrants, who do not even dare take short trips home to see relatives or friends.[70] Especially the militarization of popular Mexico-U.S. border crossing points has led immigrants to move to remote and arid stretches of the national boundary, which has increased the number of border crossing deaths.[71] In addition, legislative changes since 9/11 have enabled the more stringent enforcement of immigration law, such as widespread immigrant raids and deportations, which often result in the separation of families when U.S.-born children are left behind.

Recognition of these intersections among undocumented immigrants is becoming increasingly central to immigration rights movements.[72] Recent mass rallies for immigration reform in many U.S. cities exemplify such fledgling cross-ethnic coalitions. Hunger strikes and candlelight vigils in 2006 in the San Francisco Bay Area, for example, brought together immigrants from Ireland, Mexico, China, and other areas of the world. At the 2007 Chicago immigration rally, the largest in the country that year, undocumented immigrants from Ireland, Poland, Russia, and various nations in Asia and Africa walked alongside those from Mexico and multiple Latin American countries. Latina/o and Irish immigrants in the San Francisco Bay Area also joined forces to call for immigration reform.[73]

Some umbrella organizations such as the Bay Area Immigrant Rights Coalition (BAIRC) have emerged to more formally unite diverse immigrant advocacy groups. Created in 2000, BAIRC seeks to build a cross-ethnic and strategically linked movement across several immigrant advocacy groups in northern California. The coalition supports the passage of comprehensive immigration reform addressing the growing backlog of immigrant applications, the surge in detentions and deportations, and an increased number of border-crossing-related deaths at the Mexico-U.S. border. Created in 2004, the Coalition for Comprehensive Immigration Reform (CCIR) similarly campaigns for comprehensive immigration reform that promotes a path to citizenship, the easier reunification of families, and possibilities for immigrants' civic participation. The CCIR comprises organizations such as the National Immigration Forum and the Illinois Coalition for Immigrant and Refugee Rights (ICIRR) as well as the Irish Lobby for Immigration Reform (ILIR).

Formed in 2005, ILIR has lobbied for ethnically specific immigration reform under the slogan "Legalize the Irish," but it has also joined the CCIR to support a more comprehensive immigration agenda. In his 2007 testimony before the House Subcommittee on Immigration, the chairman of ILIR, Niall O'Dowd, supported legal provisions that primarily affect other immigrant groups, such as measures for easier family unification and temporary worker visas.[74] In a recent interview, O'Dowd poignantly stated that "when politicians see that even the Irish can be undocumented, then they realize that there's something wrong with the immigration system."[75] The historical and contemporary diversity of undocumented immigration I have sketched out in this essay questions prevalent discourses and public policy-making that have primarily served to criminalize Mexican immigration. Recognition of the racially distinct yet structurally similar conditions that have historically transformed non-elite immigrants into unauthorized populations highlights problems in U.S. immigration legislation and its vexed historical relationship to the needs of the U.S. economy, which affect diverse immigrants, and ultimately, everyone in the United States.

Notes

I would like to thank Erika Lee, Monica Varsanyi, Elizabeth Horan, Marta Sánchez, Isis McElroy, Roger Daniels, David Gutiérrez, Pierrette Hondagneu-Sotelo, and Curtis Marez for their invaluable help in strengthening the argument of this essay.

1. Jeffrey S. Passel, "Unauthorized Migrants: Numbers and Characteristics," June 14, 2005, http://uscis. gov/graphics/shared/aboutus/statistics/Ill_Report_1211.pdf+Estimates+of+the+Unauthorized+Imm igrant+Population+Residing+in+the+United+States:+1990+to+2000&hl=en&gl=us&ct=clnk&cd=1 (accessed May 24, 2007), 6. Numbers in circulation for the size and makeup of undocumented immigrants are generally based on demographic *estimates* for the size of the unauthorized population, which deduct from U.S. Census statistics on the foreign-born admissions by legal permanent immigrants, legalized immigrants, and refugees.
2. Pierre Hauser, *Illegal Aliens* (New York: Chelsea House, 1990), 109.
3. Passel, "Unauthorized Migrants," 4.
4. See, for example, Erika Lee, *At America's Gates: Chinese Immigration during the Exclusion Era, 1882–1943* (Chapel Hill: University of North Carolina Press, 2005); Emily Ryo, "Through the Back Door: Applying Theories of Legal Compliance to Illegal Immigration during the Chinese Exclusion Era," *Law and Social Inquiry* 31.2 (January 2006): 109–46; Lawrence Douglas Taylor Hansen, "The Chinese Six Companies of San Francisco and the Smuggling of Chinese Immigrants across the U.S.-Mexico Border, 1882–1930," *Journal of the Southwest* 48.1 (Spring 2006): 37–61; and Robert Chao Romero, "Transnational Chinese Immigrant Smuggling to the United States via Mexico and Cuba," *Amerasia Journal* 30.3 (2004): 3–36.
5. Anna Pegler-Gordon, "Chinese Exclusion, Photography, and the Development of U.S. Immigration Policy," *American Quarterly* 58.1 (March 2006): 57.
6. For other recent approaches to immigrant organizing, see Pierrette Hondagneu-Sotelo, *Religion and Social Justice for Immigrants* (New Brunswick, N.J.: Rutgers University Press, 2007); and Jennifer Gordon, *Suburban Sweatshops: The Fight for Immigrant Rights* (Cambridge, Mass.: Harvard University Press, 2005).
7. Aristide R. Zolberg, *A Nation by Design: Immigration Policy in the Fashioning of America* (Cambridge, Mass.: Harvard University Press, 2006), 113.
8. Ibid., 111.
9. An amendment to the 1884 Exclusion Act mandated the introduction of return certificates for Chinese laborers who had been in the United States and were, per the 1882 Exclusion Act, permitted to return if they had family, property, or debt in the United States. Customs collectors at ports of departure were to collect identifying information on all Chinese leaving the United States and to provide them with reentry certificates. For those Chinese immigrants exempt from exclusion, the Exclusion Acts mandated identity ("section 6") certificates issued by the Chinese government and countersigned by

a U.S. consular official, specifying financial status, occupation, and other particulars. Laborers and exempt classes in transit across the United States were required to possess identification certificates and evidence of their transit intentions. The 1888 Scott Act prohibited the reentry of Chinese laborers, regardless of whether they possessed return certificates. The 1892 Geary Act required Chinese to obtain certificates of residence, which had to be carried at all times. By 1909 virtually all people of Chinese descent, including U.S. citizens, needed identity certificates, accompanied by photographs, upon entering the United States. See Kennett Cott, "Mexican Diplomacy and the Chinese Issue, 1876–1910," *Hispanic American Historical Review* 67.1 (1987): 72; Pegler-Gordon, "Chinese Exclusion," 55–56; and Kitty Calavita, "The Paradoxes of Race, Class, Identity, and 'Passing': Enforcing the Chinese Exclusion Acts, 1882–1920," *Law and Social Inquiry* 25.1 (Winter 2001): 5, 31.

10. Lee, *At America's Gates*, 151, 196–97.

11. Patrick Ettinger, "'We sometimes wonder what they will spring on us next': Immigrants and Border Enforcement in the American West, 1882–1930," *Western Historical Quarterly* 37 (Summer 2006): 164.

12. Lee, *At America's Gates*, 153. See also Ettinger, "We sometimes wonder," 164. Lawrence Douglas Taylor Hansen argues, however, that no more than 300 Chinese per year crossed the Canada-U.S. border (48).

13. Marian L. Smith, "The Immigration and Naturalization Service (INS) at the U.S.-Canada Border, 1893–1993: An Overview of Issues and Topics," *Michigan Historical Review* 26 (Fall 2000): 129.

14. Roger Daniels, *Guarding the Golden Door: American Immigration Policy since 1882* (New York: Hill and Wang, 2004), 9.

15. Smith, "INS," 129.

16. Michael C. LeMay, *Guarding the Gates: Immigration and National Security* (Westport, Conn.: Praeger Security International, 2006), 62.

17. Sea captains hired agents to recruit immigrants, who were lent money at extraordinarily high interest rates. See Gunther Peck, *Reinventing Free Labor: Padrones and Immigrant Workers in the North American West, 1880–1930* (Cambridge: Cambridge University Press, 2000), 89, 22–23.

18. Ibid., 2.

19. Semiskilled operatives and unskilled workers, supervised by foremen, replaced skilled workers on the shop floor. See Yda Schreuder, "Labor Segmentation, Ethnic Division of Labor, and Residential Segregation in American Cities in the Early Twentieth Century," *Professional Geographer* 41.2 (1989): 133.

20. T. V. Powderly, founder of the national labor movement and future chief of the Immigration Bureau, stated, for example, that the competition for jobs from the new European migrants was "fast becoming as bad as the competition of the Chinese in the West" (quoted in Zolberg, *Nation by Design*, 196). That the Foran Act targeted unskilled workers is also manifested in its exemption of skilled workers as well as professional actors, lecturers, and singers from definitions as contract labor.

21. Between 1892 and 1907, about a thousand persons a year were refused admission as contract laborers. See Daniels, *Guarding the Golden Door*, 29.

22. Claudia Goldin, "The Political Economy of Immigration Restriction in the United States, 1890 to 1921," in *The Regulated Economy: A Historical Approach to Political Economy*, ed. Claudia Goldin and Gary D. Libecap (Chicago: University of Chicago Press, 1994), 224.

23. LeMay, *Guarding the Gates*, 77.

24. Bruno Ramirez, *Crossing the 49th Parallel: Migration from Canada to the United States, 1900–1930* (Ithaca, N.Y.: Cornell University Press, 2001), 41–42.

25. Ibid., 42–43.

26. Smith, "INS," 130.

27. Ibid., 146.

28. Lee, *At America's Gates*, 158; Ryo, "Through the Back Door," 110. Because direct steamship travel between China and Mexico did not commence until 1902, Chinese immigrants traveled to the United States, sailed to Mexico, and then crossed the border. Some were disguised as African Americans or came with fraudulent Mexican citizenship papers. After the discovery of these ships, smuggling networks took more circuitous routes directly to Mexican cities. See Hauser, *Illegal Aliens*, 34; Lee, *At America's Gates*, 161; Ryo, "Through the Back Door," 122.

29. Grace Peña-Delgado, "At Exclusion's Southern Gate: Changing Categories of Race and Class among Chinese *Fronterizos*, 1992–1904," in *Continental Crossroads: Remapping U.S.-Mexico Borderlands History*, ed. Samuel Truett and Elliott Young (Durham, N.C.: Duke University Press, 2004), 188.
30. Chao Romero, "Transnational Chinese Immigrant Smuggling," 3, 4-5, 10.
31. Pegler-Gordon, "Chinese Exclusion," 53; Smith, "INS," 133.
32. Smith, "INS," 132.
33. Hauser, *Illegal Aliens*, 45; Zolberg, *Nation by Design*, 266.
34. Alexandra Minna Stern, "Buildings, Boundaries, and Blood: Medicalization and Nation-Building on the U.S.-Mexico Border, 1910–1930," *Hispanic American Historical Review* 79.1 (1999): 65.
35. Clifford Alan Perkins, *Border Patrol: With the Immigration Service on the Mexican Boundary 1910–54* (El Paso: Texas Western Press, 1978), 79.
36. Ramirez, *Crossing the 49th Parallel*, 50.
37. Mae M. Ngai, *Impossible Subjects: Illegal Aliens and the Making of Modern America* (Princeton, N.J.: Princeton University Press, 2004), 55; Daniels, *Guarding the Golden Door*, 61.
38. Ngai, *Impossible Subjects*, 68.
39. Peck, *Reinventing*, 231.
40. See Stern, "Buildings, Boundaries, and Blood," 52. Diminished work opportunities and campaigns for repatriation and deportation during the Great Depression also led to a decrease in Mexican immigration. See, for example, Francisco E. Balderrama and Raymond Rodriguez, *Decade of Betrayal: Mexican Repatriation in the 1930s* (Albuquerque: University of New Mexico Press, 2006).
41. Naturalization applications no longer asked immigrants to provide both race and color with the expectation of different answers for each. See Nancy Foner, *In a New Land: A Comparative View of Immigration* (New York: New York University Press, 2005), 37.
42. Kelly Lytle Hernández, "The Crimes and Consequences of Illegal Immigration: A Cross-Border Examination of Operation Wetback, 1943 to 1954," *Western Historical Quarterly* 37 (Winter 2006): 435.
43. Ibid., 427, 429.
44. Ibid., 438–39.
45. Michael B. Katz, Mark J. Stern, and Jamie J. Fader, "The Mexican Immigration Debate: The View from History," *Social Science History* 31.2 (Summer 2007): 166.
46. Paul J. Smith, *Human Smuggling: Chinese Migrant Trafficking and the Challenge to America's Immigration Tradition* (Washington, D.C.: Center for Strategic and International Studies, 1997), x.
47. For exceptions, see Nancy Foner, *From Ellis Island to JFK: New York's Two Great Waves of Immigration* (New Haven, Conn.: Yale University Press, 2000); and Gerald Gilbert Govorchin, *From Russia to America with Love: A Study of the Russian Immigrants in the United States* (Pittsburgh: Dorrance, 1993).
48. On Asian immigration, see Aihwa Ong, *Flexible Citizenship: The Cultural Logics of Transnationality* (Durham, N.C.: Duke University Press, 1999), 174.
49. This diversity is perhaps more visible in New York City, where Dominican, Chinese, and Jamaican immigrants make up fewer than 30 percent of all arrivals. No other country accounts for more than 5 percent. See Foner, *From Ellis Island*, 10–11.
50. Elzbieta M. Gozdziak, "Illegal Europeans: Transients Between Two Societies," in *Illegal Immigration in America: A Reference Handbook*, ed. David W. Haines and Karen E. Rosenblum (Westport, Conn.: Greenwood, 1999), 264.
51. Ibid., 265, 268.
52. Daniela Gerson, "Irish Illegal Aliens Win Clinton as Ally of Immigration Law Change," *The Sun*, March 9, 2006.
53. Smith, *Human Smuggling*, x.
54. Peter Kwong, *Forbidden Workers: Illegal Chinese Immigration and American Labor* (New York: New Press, 1997), 159.
55. Sebastian Rotella, *Twilight on the Line* (New York: W. W. Norton, 1998), 72.
56. "Huge Alien-Smuggling Ring Used Canada's Refugee System," *Globe and Mail*, December 11, 1998.
57. Kwong, *Forbidden Workers*, 70.
58. Gozdziak, "Illegal Europeans," 255.

59. Ibid., 258.
60. "Chicago Metro Area Home to Nearly One Third of Polish Immigrants in the U.S.," October 25, 2004, http://polish.org/?load=news&story=2 (accessed May 24, 2007).
61. Gozdziak, "Illegal Europeans," 255; Roger Warren, "Estimates of the Undocumented Immigrant Population Residing in the United States: October 1996," August 13, 1997, http:// uscis.gov/graphics/shared/statistics/archives/illegal.pdf (accessed May 24, 2007).
62. Gozdziak, "Illegal Europeans," 259; "Undocumented Immigrants Gain Sympathy from Poles," May 25, 2006, http://cbs2chicago.com/medillnewsservice/local_story_145100210.html (accessed May 26, 2007).
63. Gozdziak, "Illegal Europeans," 259; Kwong, *Forbidden Workers*, 235.
64. Jim Kouri, "Nationwide Illegal Alien Worker Leasing Conspiracy Uncovered," *American Chronicle*, September 13, 2006.
65. Peter Shinkle, "Details Emerge on Nationwide Scheme to Hire Undocumented Immigrants and Undercut Wages of Janitors," *St. Louis Post-Dispatch*, July 16, 2006.
66. "Illegal Immigrant Raids Include Polish Community," June 20, 2006, http://news.newamericamedia.org/news/view_article.html?article_id=4bcb38b7b883f520fae199499d0a7e5b (accessed May 24, 2007).
67. John Turner Gilliland, "Arizona Prosecutor Has New Twist on Prosecuting Illegal Aliens," *The Nation*, March 15, 2006.
68. Mary P. Corcoran, *Irish Illegals: Transients between Two Societies* (Westport, Conn.: Greenwood Press, 1993), 185.
69. Jeffrey S. Passel, "Modes of Entry for the Unauthorized Migrant Population," Pew Hispanic Center, June 14, 2005, http://pewhispanic.org/files/factsheets/19.pdf, 42 (accessed May 22, 2006).
70. On this point, see, for example, Douglas Massey, Jorge Durand, and Nolan Malone, *Beyond Smoke and Mirrors: Mexican Immigration in an Age of Economic Integration* (New York: Russell Sage Foundation, 2002).
71. For discussions of contemporary border militarization, see Peter Andreas, *Border Games: Policing the U.S.-Mexico Divide* (Ithaca, N.Y.: Cornell University Press, 2000); Joseph Nevins, *Operation Gatekeeper: The Rise of the "Illegal Alien" and the Making of the U.S.-Mexico Boundary* (New York: Routledge, 2002); and Karl Eschbach, Jacqueline Hagan, and Nestor Rodriguez, "Deaths during Undocumented Migration: Trends and Policy Implications in the New Era of Homeland Security," *Defense of the Alien* 26 (2003): 37–52.
72. These include the Immigrant Solidarity Network for Immigrant Rights, the National Network for Immigrant and Refugee Rights, the National Immigrant Solidarity Network, the Illinois Coalition for Immigrant and Refugee Rights, and the Coalition for Humane Immigrant Rights of Los Angeles.
73. Tyche Hendricks, "Irish Join Battle over Illegal Immigration: St. Patrick's Day Vehicle for Activists Seeking Reform," *San Francisco Chronicle*, March 15, 2006; "Chicago Rally Country's Largest But Doesn't Top Last Year," May 2, 2007, http://www.nbc5.com/politics/13227598/detail.html; Jill Tucker, "Irish, Latino Catholics March for Immigrant Rights," *San Francisco Chronicle*, June 10, 2007.
74. The ILIR follows in the footsteps of the Irish Immigration Reform Movement (IIRM), formed in 1987. IIRM originally set out to secure amnesty for undocumented Irish immigrants in the United States, but achieved a more influential position by coalescing with other initiatives to help immigrants from all countries disadvantaged by the 1965 Immigration Act.
75. Gregory Rodriguez, "Illegal? Better If You're Irish," *Los Angeles Times*, April 8, 2007.

"World-Menace": National Reproduction and Public Health in Katherine Mayo's *Mother India*

Asha Nadkarni

"Whenever India's real condition becomes known," said an American Public Health expert now in international service, "all the civilized countries of the world will turn to the League of Nations and demand protection against her."

—Katherine Mayo, *Mother India*

Wildly popular and widely reviled, Katherine Mayo's *Mother India* was a major cultural event when it was published in 1927; as John Rotter has recently argued, "no single book about India written for adult Americans had more influence."[1] An imperialist polemic against Indian self-rule thinly disguised as a journalistic exposé, *Mother India* claimed to reveal "the truth about the sex life, child marriages, hygiene, cruelty, religious customs, of one-sixth of the world's population."[2] *Mother India*'s lurid subject matter led, in part, to its immense popularity. Going into nine reprints within its first year of publication and forty-two reprints by 1937, the book was the basis of a Broadway musical (Madame Nazimova's *India*) and there was even an attempt to make it into a Hollywood film.[3] As controversial as it was popular, *Mother India* generated a flurry of responses. Conferences were arranged to discuss its allegations and protests staged to refute them: all in all, more than fifty books and pamphlets were published in reaction to Mayo's claims.[4] Official British and U.S. public opinion was largely positive (there is even evidence that Mayo was enlisted by the British imperial propaganda machine, if unwittingly), while for Indian nationalists rallying against *Mother India* became a galvanizing cause.[5]

Despite *Mother India*'s international political reach, Mayo's stated purpose in writing it was domestic. She opens chapter 1 by proclaiming she is "neither an idle busybody nor a political agent, but merely an ordinary American citizen seeking test facts to lay before [her] own people" (13). Why, however, would India be a matter of U.S. concern? As Mayo sees it, India is a site of dangerous cultural practices that in her vision not only inhabit India, but could also potentially travel to and infect the rest of the world. Rewriting the Indian nationalist icon "Mother India" as the pathologized figure of a diseased body politic, Mayo articulates the United States' international role as one of protecting women at home and abroad. What makes her polemic so persuasive, however, are the insistent connections she draws between public health concerns and sexual habits. The crux of her argument is that Indians are unfit for self-rule because primitive and debased Hindu sexual practices destroy the bodies of India's women and deplete the bodies of India's men. In making this argument Mayo naturalizes all of India as Hindu, a tactic not only in keeping with U.S. nomenclature of the time, but also exploitative of Hindu-Muslim communal tension. She latches on to the explosive issue of child marriage to paint Indians as "broken-nerved, low-spirited, petulant ancients" whose "hands are too weak, too fluttering, to seize or to hold the reins of government" (32). While the text overflows with multiple images of disease and contagion, these are always connected to sexual practices through a chain of associations that link biology and culture. Understanding the circulation of culture through a model of contagious disease, Mayo advocates an imperial strategy of containing the foreign both domestically and globally. She accordingly figures India as a "world-menace"—a public health problem that should elicit more fear than sympathy.

The terms in which she frames the problem of India, moreover, have immediate consequences for her U.S. audience. Just as her evocation of the figure Mother India (a figure that intimates both nationalist aspirations and the material problems of national reproduction) exceeds the spatial boundaries of India and becomes a problem of U.S. concern, so too does the larger question of national reproduction. Specifically, her obsessive attention to Indian reproductive practices reveals her larger preoccupation with national reproduction *in general.* Because Mayo's argument against Indian self-rule rests on what she perceives as India's inability to reproduce itself, she ties national reproduction to sovereignty. By putting reproduction at the center of the question of sovereignty, however, Mayo troubles reproductive practices at home as well as in India; the sexual and cultural promiscuity of the U.S. "new woman" renders her particularly susceptible to India's threat. For Mayo, this danger emanates both from Indian immigration (even though, as I discuss below, it is negligible at this point) and the so-called Hindu craze—U.S. popular attraction to Hindu spirituality and culture. Mayo's argument against Indian sovereignty, therefore, also rebounds upon U.S. women who do not fulfill their proper reproductive roles.

I thus argue that Mayo maps the domestic issue of immigration onto the international terrain of imperialism—in this case British imperialism in India—to solidify a nativist nationalism.[6] I look at Mayo's many writings on India to trace how she attempts to resolve a fundamental paradox of U.S. imperialism: how can the nation's anti-imperial beginnings and political values be reconciled with its expansionist desires? For Mayo, the solution is a racialized discourse of British and U.S. solidarity that forecloses any analogies between U.S. and Indian nationalist struggles.[7] Insisting instead on the racial and cultural difference between Anglo-Americans and Indians (and by extension arguing for their unfitness for nationhood or U.S. citizenship), Mayo adopts a language of global modernity to expose the United States and India as dangerously inhabiting the same time and space. Her imperialism, however, is riven with intense anxiety; even as her project is meant to strengthen both British imperial and U.S. commercial interests in India, her writings reveal a deep uneasiness with global markets and their ability to bring distant peoples and cultures into contact. That is, for Mayo imperialism is all about preserving the health of the imperial nation, a metaphor she materializes through the discourse of public health. Imagining India as embodying a sexual threat that must be kept in check, she thus fashions a peculiarly U.S. version of imperial containment to segregate populations and police behaviors.[8] This containment strategy is as applicable at home as it is abroad: not only must the Indian threat be neutralized and U.S. borders policed; U.S. women's sexuality must be controlled and channeled into reproductive work for the nation.

"Hinduism Invades America"

Part of Mayo's aim in writing *Mother India* was to combat what Wendell Thomas's 1930 book names an "invasion" of Hindu beliefs and practices onto U.S. soil.[9] While U.S. interest in Hindu spirituality can be traced back at least to Emerson, Thoreau, and Whitman, following Swami Vivekananda's address at the 1893 World Parliament of Religion fascination with mystical India became widespread.[10] This late nineteenth and early twentieth century "Hindu craze" encompassed Hindu religious movements (such as Vivekananda's Vedanta Society and Yogananda's Yogada Sat-sanga Society of America), popular lecture tours by Rabindranath Tagore and Lala Lajpat Rai, and Hindu-influenced religious movements such as Theosophy.[11] This surge of interest in Hinduism can be read as a version of modernist Orientalism (for instance, T. S. Eliot's use of the Upanishads in *The Waste Land*), as well as part of a larger preoccupation with the meaning of U.S. culture in the face of immigration and industrialization.[12]

For some U.S. citizens, India's struggle against British imperialism was another reason to make common cause. Indeed, while the United States government officially supported British imperialism, many prominent Americans were against continued British rule of India, among them Andrew Carnegie and William Jennings Bryan.[13] This pro-India movement was, in part, an offshoot of the Anti-Imperialist League's opposition to the U.S. acquisition of the Philippines. In addition to these U.S.-based anti-imperial efforts, Indian nationalists in the United States actively sought assistance for their cause. In 1914, Indian nationalist Lala Lajpat Rai traveled to the United States to enlist help in establishing Indian self-rule, and in 1917 he founded the Indian Home Rule League of America.[14] The Friends for the Freedom of India was launched just two years later in 1919, and counted Taraknath Das, Sailendranath Ghosh, Robert Mores Lovett and Oswald Garrison Villard among its prominent members.[15] Alongside these more genteel movements, the revolutionary Hindustan Ghadar party was formed in San Francisco in 1913, and was a force until the Hindu-German conspiracy scandal of 1917–18.[16] In short, U.S. fascination with Hindu spirituality often translated into support for Indian nationalism even if (as I will discuss below) it was accompanied by exclusionary immigration and naturalization laws for diasporic Indians living and working in the United States.

Mayo disrupts the idea that India and the United States have a shared anti-imperial mission by insisting on the racial divide between Indians and Anglo-Saxon Americans. One of the most effective ways she does this is by exploiting the gendered nature of the pro-India movement and the Hindu craze. Many pro-Indian anti-imperialists (Agnes Smedley and Margaret Sanger to name just two) united their domestic feminist concerns with their fight against British imperialism. In taking on women's issues in India, however, Mayo attempted to discredit precisely this kind of support by revealing it as hypocritical. Concentrating on Indian women as victims, Mayo challenged the idea that Indian men were oppressed, saying, "if you are looking on from an immense distance . . . you cannot see which is the top-dog and which is the under-dog, and the dog which you stroke when it runs up whining after the fight may be the top-dog. In India woman is the under-dog."[17] Mayo's focus on Indian women's suffering thus reveals (male) Indian nationalists as patriarchal tyrants who disingenuously claim the category of "under-dog." This rhetorical move makes the containment of male nationalism the precondition for saving Indian women, thus exposing feminist support for Indian nationalism as aligned with patriarchy.[18] Finally,

Mayo's focus on issues such as child marriage utterly obscured the work of Indian reformers; in fact, the passage of the 1929 Child Marriage Act in India was widely and incorrectly credited to Mayo's book.[19]

In focusing on the scandalous and sensational, Mayo returned to the stock themes of her earlier work. Although stylistically her writing can be situated within the muckraking tradition of the late nineteenth and early twentieth centuries, thematically it bolstered the very institutions the muckrakers attacked. Her first three books addressed the issue of state police reform, valorizing the Philadelphia police force and ignoring altogether the brutality with which employers had used that force to break strikes.[20] Not only does Mayo reveal her conservative views about labor in these works, but she also articulates her race and gender politics, populating her narratives with "raving mobs" of immigrants, murderous and licentious African American men, and defenseless white women.[21] Mayo's books before *Mother India* established her imperialist credentials as well. Her 1924 *The Isles of Fear: the Truth about the Philippines* attacked the Wilsonian policy of Filipinization and strenuously argued against Filipino independence. As in *Mother India*, Mayo uses *The Isles of Fear* to paint a picture of irredeemably atavistic natives in need of the civilizing influence of the West. One of Mayo's particular targets in *The Isles of Fear* was the 1916 Jones Act, which was a first step toward Filipino governmental autonomy. Indeed, her indictment of this act was effective enough to attract the attention of the British government. A British edition of *The Isles of Fear* was also published in 1925, with an introduction by government official and imperial spokesman Lionel Curtis. In his introduction, Curtis cautions readers that it "cannot be wise for us to ignore the examples and warning afforded in their [the Americans'] more daring experiments."[22] Not coincidentally, Curtis was also one of the architects of the Government of India Act of 1919, which was similarly a step closer to native participation in India's governance.[23] As both Manoranjan Jha and Mrinalini Sinha's archival research has revealed, Mayo's work on the Philippines led British officials to believe she might be useful in enlisting U.S. public opinion in favor of their imperial project in India. Concerned about the growing tide of U.S. support for Indian nationalism, the British propaganda machine encouraged Mayo to do with India what she had done with the Philippines.

A Democracy of Disease

Mayo responded to the "Hindu craze" by rewriting the terms of the debate along scientific lines. She repeatedly insists that in *Mother India* she "[leaves] untouched the realms of religion . . . politics . . . and the arts . . . [and confines her] inquiry to such workaday ground as public health and its contributing factor" (12). Mayo thus counters U.S. fascination with Hindu spirituality and culture by focusing on what she believes to be the material conditions of everyday life in India. Her emphasis on "brass tacks" instead of "poetic theory" allows her to arrive at the conclusion that " 'Spiritual' Hinduism, disentangled from words and worked out in common life, is materialism in the grossest and most suicidal form."[24] By exposing the hygienic horrors of life as it is lived in India, Mayo hopes to disrupt the idea that Hindu philosophy could trump U.S. modernity. For Mayo, the problem is not U.S. materialism, but rather a Hindu materialism named spirituality. She remaps the coordinates of the spiritual and the material by arguing that in India religiously mandated material practices lead to public health problems. Similarly, U.S. modernity, with its emphasis on hygiene and public health, is actually more spiritual in its ability to foster and support life. Her focus on public health thus allows her to argue that far from being a spiritual utopia, India is a democracy of disease.

In a chapter titled "World Menace" she explicitly takes on these concerns, speculating that cholera and malaria in India are caused by the custom of the "village tank"—a stagnant pool that serves the water needs of the village. For Mayo, the tank leads to the "democratization of any new germs introduced to the village, and its mosquitoes spread malaria with an impartial beak—though not without some aid" (366). This "aid" comes in the form of Hindu religious practices that can exacerbate, or even cause, a public health crisis. Specifically, the problem is mothers placing their children at water's edge because if they "protect [their] babies the gods will be jealous and bring [them] bad luck" (366). As Mayo expresses it, this is a perennial problem in many colonial sites. Even though the British are building proper wells,

> exactly as in the Philippines, the people [in India] have a strong hankering for the ancestral type, and, where they can, will usually leave the new and protected water-source for their old accustomed squatting- and gossiping-ground where they all innocently poison each other (369).

Typically, the problem is presented as "ancestral" religious habits retarding the advances of modern science and hygiene. The true crisis, however, is not that these habits prevail but that they coexist with modern science—thus the "democratization" of germs, not populations.

If democracy is signified by the spread of germs, not the spread of the abstract rights of citizenship, then modernity's global circulation of goods, bodies, and practices makes India's condition worthy of global interest and perhaps even intervention. In a telling passage, Mayo shows the universality of this problem by transplanting it to Europe:

> In ordinary circumstances, in places where the public water supply is good and under scientific control, cholera is not to be feared. But the great and radical changes of modern times bring about rapid reverses of conditions; such, for example, as the sudden pouring in the year 1920 of hundreds of thousands of disease-sodden refugees out of Russia into Western Europe. (370)

The movement of refugees from Eastern to Western Europe (a movement that extends even further west to the United States) illustrates the vulnerability of all "healthy" populations from "diseased" ones; the central implication of this passage is that populations must be manipulated in order to prevent disease. Thus "scientific control" alone is never enough—the real problem of modernity is the speed at which bodies can move and public health situations "reverse." This is precisely why immigration is important in a globalizing world. Even as India would seem to be a British problem of little importance to the "average American," Mayo addresses *Mother India* to her fellow U.S. citizens in an attempt to rewrite contagious disease in India as a global problem of local concern (11).

In both *The Isles of Fear* and *Mother India*, public health is a crucial component of Mayo's imperial politics. This focus reflects her investment in a U.S. imperialism that (even more than British imperialism) articulated its mission in terms of public health and hygiene. The science of public health was thus one of the forms the U.S. civilizing mission took, with the related purposes of creating healthy workers and establishing markets for its goods; as David Arnold has argued, "the value of medicine as an aid to economic imperialism was most fully recognized by the emissaries of North American capitalism."[25] In this sense, as Mrinalini Sinha demonstrates in *Specters of Mother India*, Mayo's explicit desire to support British imperialism in India backfires. While she intended to prove that Indians, based on their adherence to Hindu religious practices, were unworthy agents of modernity who desperately needed British intervention, her critique ultimately implicates the negligence of the British colonial state. One result of this was that it implicitly recommended the United States as the more effective imperial modernizing power, which was certainly not the British government's intent in getting Mayo involved. In particular, the Rockefeller Foundation (which was at the forefront of public health projects in the United States and abroad) was one of the most important agents of U.S. expansionist interests. Mayo used the connections she had forged with the Rockefeller Foundation in her work in the Philippines to assist her in her India project. She traveled to India with letters of introduction from the foundation, and her intended focus on cholera in India was suggested to her by them.[26]

Mayo's spotlight on public health thus uniquely married her domestic and imperial concerns. As Nayan Shah argues in his study of public health, immigration, and the racialization of the Chinese in San Francisco, public health was a form of "imperial domesticity" that sought "to manage and reform the 'foreign' within the nation" as well as "to civilize the 'lower races' within the United States and abroad in China and India and, later, in the U.S. imperial territories of the Philippines and Puerto Rico."[27] The notion of public health therefore performs a kind of spatial metonymy whereby all "unhealthy" spaces require the same treatment regardless of their global location.[28] Characterizing India as a public health problem allows Mayo to paint a global modernity that is terrifying in its ability to flatten out geographical distance and difference. While Indian sanitary habits might be dangerous to them, her true concern is that such habits will infect the United States through Indian immigration. Mayo thus employs what Alan Kraut has dubbed "medicalized nativism" to link Indian immigration to contagious disease, redefining in medical terms what nativists viewed as immigrants' racial or cultural unfitness for national membership.[29] She thereby codes the cultural contagion she sees in the Hindu craze as literally an issue of disease, relying upon contemporaneous sociological theories that understand cultural transmission through metaphors of infection. As Priscilla Wald argues in her recent book, *Contagious*, the idea of "social contagion" pioneered by Robert E. Park expressed "the material of culture [as] transmissible and transformative."[30] While this could be a positive process of assimilation and social cohesion, it also "named the danger as well as the power of transformation."[31] By figuring cultural communication in terms of contagion, Mayo launches a plausible excuse for regulation; if culture is catching, then national boundaries need to be strictly policed.

A Tale of Two Cities

While U.S. readers might imagine India as too remote to pose a threat, Mayo undoes this assumption by repeatedly painting India as startlingly near. Her opening description of Calcutta illustrates this danger. While in most of *Mother India* Mayo uses the rational medical language of public health to qualify her assertions as purely scientific, she begins her narrative with a largely impressionistic rendering of Calcutta that reads more like a typical travel narrative. Titled "The Bus to Mandalay," Mayo's introduction describes the city in one mastering, imperialist sweep.

> Calcutta, second largest city in the British Empire, spread along the Ganges called Houghly, at the top of the Bay of Bengal. Calcutta, big, western, modern, with public buildings, monuments, parks, gardens, hospitals, museums, University, courts of law, hotels, offices, shops, all of which might belong to a prosperous American city; and all backed by an Indian town of temples, mosques, bazaars and intricate courtyards and alleys that has somehow created itself despite the rectangular lines shown on the map. In the courts and alleys and bazaars many little bookstalls, where narrow-chested, near-sighted, anaemic young Bengali students, in native dress, brood over piles of fly-blown Russian pamphlets. (3)

Mayo's panoramic and subjectless vision of Calcutta begins with objective, knowable facts and then telescopes inward, finally coming to rest on the depleted and potentially subversive bodies of Calcutta's young men. The deliberately narrowing gaze suggests that everything available to vision is equally knowable—from Calcutta's status as the second largest city in the British Empire to observations about "young Bengali students." By privileging information over experience and by presenting observation as fact, Mayo follows one of the major conventions of travel writing from the late nineteenth century on.[32] But whereas in mid-nineteenth century travel writing observers survey the landscape as a site of future growth (what Mary Louise Pratt calls "the development mode"), Mayo sees degeneration that needs to be kept in check. This eye to containment instead of development is not the only way that Mayo departs from conventional representations of India. While the East is normally constructed as geographically peripheral and exotic, as occupying not only a different space but a different time, Mayo's Calcutta is notable for its resemblance to a U.S. city.[33] In contrast to allochronistic, Orientalist visions of India as representing some kind of "pre-history" of the modern world, Mayo places India firmly within modernity.

For Mayo, just as for a certain brand of conservative anti-globalization critique, the problem is that different cultures refuse to stay distant, occupying instead the same spaces and temporalities.[34] While the journey to India is usually described as a journey through time as well as through space, Mayo organizes her vision in terms of the recognizable public spaces of the city—"Western" and "Indian" spaces that are hierarchically organized but nonetheless occupy the same temporal and spatial plane. Rather than immediately evoke the exotic, Mayo describes a city that is at first glance entirely recognizable to her U.S. audience: Calcutta is "big, western, modern," with the kinds of buildings and institutions that "might belong to a prosperous American city." Her first rhetorical move, then, is to situate the United States and India within the same temporal moment defined by modernity and a knowable geography. Significantly, the "Indian town" that "backs" the "American city" does not predate it—it has "somehow created itself despite the rectangular lines shown on the map." If this is the case, then its creation is predicated on the existence of the city's linear mapping of space. By insisting that the "American city" and the "Indian town" occupy the same space, Mayo suggests that Calcutta's seedy underbelly could potentially exist in the United States as well. While a narrator writing in the "development mode" judges the landscape with a modernizing eye, here Mayo sees not potential development of the Indian other but potential decay of the western self—a decay necessarily linked to the modern façade of the western city with which we are first presented.

In the second paragraph of this opening section, Mayo takes the reader on a bus journey to Kali Ghat. From the antiseptic city of hospitals and garden parties, we are suddenly face-to-face with a goddess dripping blood. After a sensational account of a goat sacrifice, Mayo describes the ensuing chaos:

> A woman who waited behind the killers of the goat has rushed forward and fallen on all fours to lap up the blood with her tongue—"in the hope of having a child." And now a second woman, stooping, sops at the blood with a cloth, and thrusts the cloth into her bosom, while half a dozen sick, sore dogs, horribly misshapen by nameless diseases, stick their hungry muzzles into the lengthening pool of gore. (6)

In this scene, animal sacrifice, unhealthy religious practices associated with childbearing, and disease-carrying dogs are all gathered under the rubric of Kali as Mother India. The animalistic description of the woman who rushes in after the sacrifice, "on all fours," "lap[ping] up the blood with her tongue," connects her to the goats that have just been sacrificed, a description that foreshadows Mayo's signal depiction of Indian women in the text. Mayo also links this woman to the "sick, sore dogs, horribly misshapen by nameless diseases," not only by the similarity of their actions and postures, but also by the "nameless diseases" that we can imagine her catching from them. If this city "backs" the "modern, Western one"—if it exists, as Mayo pointedly demonstrates, in the same space and time—then it is clear such unsanitary practices pose an immediate threat to the West. After all, if Calcutta has all the trappings of "a prosperous American city," what does that say about what an actual U.S. city can contain?

"When Asia Knocks at the Door"

By establishing a connection between Indian and U.S. modernities, Mayo sets the rhetorical stage for chapter 1, "The Argument," which opens with the statement: "Bombay is but three weeks' journey from New York" (11). Her portrait of Calcutta clarifies the significance of such a short journey. Calcutta is not simply a dangerous hybrid of U.S. modernity and Indian tradition; it is a harbinger of how the close relationship between the United States and India threatens U.S. cities. If, as Mayo's depiction of Calcutta suggests, western modernity is made vulnerable by its proximity to other cultures, then U.S. ties with India must be tightly controlled. This is why she ultimately advocates an imperial strategy of containment that relies upon a two-pronged approach of rooting out dangerous practices abroad while also making sure they don't travel home.

In part, Mayo is concerned with increased economic activity between the United States and India. As she explains in a 1928 article, India is "a large, potentially a huge, market for American goods. American and British ships are continually plying between Indian and American ports. Indians are increasingly coming amongst us."[35] The danger, as the rhetoric of this quotation suggests, is that economic ties between the countries will dissolve all distinctions between them. Mayo's description moves seamlessly from India as a "market for American goods" to "Indians . . . increasingly coming amongst us" to demonstrate the dangerous consequences of U.S. expansionist interests. Accordingly, Mayo most often describes U.S.-Indian economic connections in terms of a potentially dangerous and unfettered circulation, labeling Calcutta "wide-open to the traffic of the world and India, traffic of bullion, of jute, of cotton—of all that India and the world want out of each other's hands" (3). As her description of Calcutta equally suggests, however, Calcutta may similarly contain all that the world does *not* want out of India's hands—that is, India's diseased bodies and perverse cultural practices. Precisely because Calcutta is so "wide-open," U.S. borders need to remain tightly shut.

While, as both Sinha and Jha show, part of Mayo's explicit purpose in writing *Mother India* was to support U.S. commercial interests in India, I read in the above rhetoric a deep ambivalence about that agenda. At its base, Mayo's alarm at the situation in India reveals a fear of global markets. While the United States needs the "potentially huge" market that India represents, such a market also means potentially polluting "Indians . . . coming amongst us." This is one of the paradoxes of globalization and expansion—the need for a free exchange of goods and capital, but not of peoples, cultures, and potentially dangerous cultural practices. There are thus two consequences to her argument. The first is the predictably nativist view that the United States needs to tightly control all immigration. To this, however, she adds a decidedly imperialist twist. After all, Mayo's book is expressly intended to strengthen the British imperial project in India and to promote Anglo-U.S. imperialist ties. While classical theories of imperialism understand it as primarily serving the expansion, exportation, and penetration of capital, Mayo advocates imperialism as a mode of containment, as a way of solidifying imperial national boundaries.[36] Just as cold war policies of containment were equally concerned with rooting out the communist threat overseas and at home, Mayo links immigration and imperialism to, in her reckoning, keep the Anglo-Saxon world safe.[37]

Regulating citizenship is a crucial part of this strategy, and Mayo's argument in *Mother India* was designed to intervene in contemporaneous debates surrounding Indian eligibility for U.S. citizenship. In 1917, Asian Indians were barred from immigrating to the United States, and in 1923, the B. S. Thind case upheld the denaturalization of U.S. citizens of Indian origin on the basis of their not appearing recognizably white to the "common man." In 1926, the Hindu Citizenship Bill unsuccessfully attempted to challenge this by arguing that Indians, as Aryans, are racially Caucasian, a "solution" to the problem of Indian citizenship that relied on the same racist logic as the Asian Exclusion Acts.[38] Mayo was a staunch opponent of this bill, and even reportedly wrote *Mother India* because of it. While she later denies this, there can be no doubt that she was a steadfast critic of Indian immigration in general and the Hindu Citizenship Bill in particular.[39]

In fact, Mayo expressly promotes *Mother India* as a "unique opportunity to throw light on immigration problems that hitherto have received no public attention."[40] In a 1927 article titled "When Asia Knocks at the Door," she points to domestic "racial and political unrest" and "movements of trade and emigration" as evidence that Asia and the United States are connected in surprising and disturbing ways. Asia is, to Mayo, an unwanted and uninvited houseguest: "the Far East even now knocks at our door, demanding full rights of American citizenship." She uses the language of the home to suggest a threat that strikes at the heart of the U.S. family, a family not only defined by citizenship but also constituted by race. She raises the specter of "the British East Indian" being "as eligible as the Swede or the Swiss or the Scotchman to a citizen's share in our government," and she warns of "entrust[ing] him with co-guardianship" of "our own heritage." Citing "the safety of our homes . . . the preservation of our standards . . . [and] the unborn children of America, of India and of the world," Mayo describes an implicitly white U.S. family relinquishing control to an invader—a threat to the reproduction of the individual family understood as a threat to the nation as a whole.

As we would expect, Mayo disavows the overtly racist and nativist sentiments of "When Asia Knocks on the Door" by insisting that her interest in India is only clinical; her concern is not race, culture or religion, it is hygiene. Her inquiry into "what sort of American citizen . . . the British Indian [would] make" thus circulates around "social habits . . . in the sense of sanitation, respect for women and children and certain physical-moral laws." While it is easy to see how the categories of race, culture, religion, and hygiene all bleed into each other here, Mayo asserts that these matters are not "abstractions" but of the "practical field." She makes similar claims in *Mother India*, stating that

> John Smith of 23 Main Street may care little enough about the ancestry of Peter Jones, and still less about his religion, his philosophy, or his views on art. But if Peter cultivates a habit of living and ways of thinking that make him a physical menace not only to himself and his family, but to all the rest of the block, then practical John will want details (14–15).

Although it is clear from the rest of the book that Mayo believes "religion," "philosophy," and "views on art" dictate the "habits of living and ways of thinking" that she considers menacing, she rhetorically positions herself as arguing against U.S. fascination with such aspects of Hindu life. In fact, Mayo declares, such preoccupations are dangerous distractions from the issue at hand—the public health threat Indians pose. Just as the need to control immigration on the national level is about protecting the national body, Mayo takes this narrative "global" by marrying nativist concerns about immigration to imperialist concerns about native self-rule. Here, the imperial project gets rewritten not as one of conquest and riches, nor even the "white man's burden," but rather as one of protection from the global circulation of bodies.

Maternal Contagions

But why is the maternal figure in particular so fraught for Mayo? In the first place, Mayo targets "Mother India" to adopt and pervert the terms of Indian nationalist debates. While maternal iconography has a long religious and cultural history in India, the forging of the Mother India symbol as an animating force for Indian nationalism is generally credited to Bankim Chandra

Chatterjee's 1882 novel *Anandamath*, with its slogan "Vande Mataram" ("Victory to the Mother").[41] In this vein, Indian nationalist evocations of Mother India trope the colonized nation as a noble but wronged mother petitioning for freedom for her children.[42] In contrast to this elevated ideal, Mayo's focus on pathologized maternal bodies refigures Mother India as a sick and diseased mother incapable of giving birth to a healthy child, let alone a nation. Mayo's insistent attention to actual maternal bodies thus disrupts Indian nationalism's symbolic use of women to signify Indian cultural purity and distinctness.[43]

Mayo sets up her ironic invocation of Mother India in the chapter "Slave Mentality," noting how "from every political platform" nationalists "stream flaming protests of devotion to the death to Mother India." Here she references the importance of the maternal ideal in Indian nationalism, but distorts it by rewriting Mother India as a "sick—ignorant and helpless" mother (19). She points out what is to her the signal paradox of Indian nationalism: even as Indian nationalists say Mother India is an ideal worth dying for, Mayo claims that *actual* Indian mothers are dying. To this pathetic portrait of India's mothers, Mayo adds an unflattering commentary on India's sons. She describes them in the most unmanly terms, arguing that they "spend their time in quarrels together or else lie idly weeping over their own futility" (19). According to Mayo, with such men as protectors it is no wonder India has ever been "the flaccid subject of a foreign rule" (21). She thus represents all of India as the combination of a compromised masculinity and an uncomplaining and passive femininity. In total, as Mayo puts it in one of her more excessive descriptions, Mother India is "shabby, threadbare, sick and poor . . . victim and slave of all recorded time" (288).

This easy metaphorization is troubled in the eponymous chapter, however, wherein Mother India comes to signify not only the "victim and slave of all recorded time" but also her torturer; the title of the chapter refers both to the Indian mother feebly reproducing the nation and the indigenous midwife, or *dai*, ineptly assisting her. Mayo's metaphorical use of Mother India as the pathological body politic is thereby disrupted by a metonymic movement wherein Mother India comes to represent a threat as well as a victim.[44] She suggests this metonymic relationship in her description of the *dai*, writing that because parturient women are considered to be "ceremonially unclean . . . only those become *dhais* who are themselves of the unclean, 'untouchable' class, the class whose filthy habits will be adduced by the orthodox Hindu as his good and sufficient reason for barring them from contact with himself" (91). And yet the *dai* is the only sanctioned contact that the pregnant woman can have—and this contact turns the birthing chamber into a chamber of horrors:

> [The *dai*] kneads the patient with her fists; stands her against the wall and butts her with her head; props her upright on the bare ground, seizes her hands and shoves against her thighs with gruesome bare feet, until, so the doctors state, the patient's flesh is often torn to ribbons by the *dhai*'s long, ragged toe-nails. Or, she lays the woman flat and walks up and down her body, like one treading grapes. (95)

Utterly unrelated to the tasks a midwife is supposed to perform, the practices portrayed here read like a description of torture. While the *dai* is an active agent, the birthing mother is a passive puppet who does not seem to have even the ability to stand up or to lie down—rather the *dai* "props her upright" or "lays [her] flat." Because *both* of these figures are metonymically linked to the Mother India to which the chapter title refers, Mother India is at once the "ragged toe-nails" and the "flesh [being] torn."

By transforming Mother India from a nationalist symbol of rebirth into a degraded symbol of pathological maternity, Mayo critiques Indian nationalism by calling into question India's ability to reproduce itself. She splits the sign Mother India into the dismembered and diseased maternal body and the "Witch of Endor"–like (94) figure of the *dai* to signify maternity as something that needs to be protected precisely because it simultaneously signifies such a threat. From this perspective, Mayo's argument for British imperialism is an attempt to police national boundaries both globally and domestically. As her description of Calcutta suggests, however, these attempts at management do not always yield the most reassuring results. The real problem is one of proximity between different cultures and bodies, and thus Mayo's obsessive concern with Indian reproduction reveals her larger anxieties about national reproductive processes in general. The problem of indigenous midwifery in India is not just a "family problem," so to speak. By engaging discourses concerning reproduction and the national body, Mayo turns Indian birthing practices into a concern for the "family of nations."

Seducing America's Mothers

Mayo's refiguration of Mother India as the pathological mother emanates not only from her interest in British imperial politics, then, but also from her concern about Indian penetration of the United States. I use the sexually charged language of penetration deliberately because, for Mayo, India represents a sexual threat to which white, bourgeois, U.S. women are peculiarly vulnerable. A 1928 article titled "India" encapsulates the problem of Hinduism's sinister appeal. In it, Mayo describes attending a lecture by an unnamed "East Indian . . .

a slim, handsome, graceful, well dressed young man, [who] spoke with an easy eloquence that seemed to exert upon his audience a sort of spell."[45] The main topic of this young man's speech "implied the spiritual, mental and moral inferiority of America and her need of guidance from the wisdom of the East."[46] Mayo paints a picture of seductive Eastern spirituality to argue that enthrallment with such superficial spirituality represents a symptom of a cultural crisis rather than its solution. Moreover, an interest in Hinduism inevitably raises the specter of miscegenation. Mayo's strongest warning in her article is thus directed at

> Mrs. John J. Smith of Smithville, U.S.A. . . . *Keep away, Mrs. John, from the swamis, the yogis, the traveling teaching men* . . . In your innocence, in your good faith, in your eager-minded receptivity of high-sounding doctrine, in your hunger for color, romance, glamour, and dreams come true, you expose yourself, all unsuspecting, to things that, if you knew them, would kill you dead with unmerited shame.[47]

Mayo paints an evocative picture of "innocent" white women "exposing" themselves to a potentially lethal "shame." Yet even as she says that this "exposure" is "unsuspecting," there is also an element of reprimand. While the main fault lies with "the swamis, the yogis, the traveling teaching men," the women have left themselves open to seduction: although Mayo is putatively addressing a fascination with Hindu spirituality, the phrase "hunger for color, romance, glamour, and dreams come true" seems to suggest that these women are seeking more than a spiritual awakening.

The picture of degraded Indian womanhood Mayo paints in *Mother India* gives weight to her warning here. Contrasting the "high-sounding doctrine" of "the traveling teaching men" with the reproductive practices she describes in her exposé, Mayo argues that U.S. women could, through their own carelessness and sexual hunger, be subjected to the same reproductive practices as their Indian counterparts. They too could become ciphers for an alternatively threatening and abject maternity, and in doing so betray their reproductive duty to their nation. In an essay titled "To the Women of Hindu India" Mayo explicitly addresses this concern. Attached to Mayo's collection of short stories, *Slaves of the Gods* (1929), the essay compares Indian and U.S. women in terms of their ability to reproduce the nation, not to "offer our Western performance as a model for [them] to copy," but rather to praise Indian women for their greater "discipline."[48] While U.S. women "have liberty . . . as great as [Indian women's] thraldom some neglect the privilege, and some selfishly, thoughtlessly and flagrantly abuse it."[49] Indian women are praiseworthy in their devotion to the maternal ideal (though, as Mayo strenuously argues throughout *Mother India* and her other writings, this ideal has been twisted), but U.S. women are in danger of abandoning it altogether. They thus represent opposite ends of the spectrum: Indian women have "discipline" but no "liberty"; U.S. women have "liberty" but lack "discipline." In both cases the results are potentially disastrous—by comparing the subjugated Indian woman to the selfish and thoughtless U.S. one, Mayo calls into question the ability of either nation to adequately reproduce itself.

Mayo further elaborates these concerns in a 1928 article for the *Liberty* magazine titled "Companionate 'Marriage'—and Marriage: A Message to Girls." Though Mayo was herself unmarried (she spent most of her adult life living and traveling with Moyca Newell, an heiress who financed many of her research trips), she nonetheless felt entitled to speak of proper conduct within marriage. In the article, she attacks companionate marriage on the grounds that it twists the higher, procreative purpose of marriage and debases women by reducing them to sexual objects. She opens by describing the marital woes of Roger and Anne. Roger, it seems, is having an affair, and all of Anne's friends and family urge her to leave him. To their surprise and dismay, she does nothing of the kind, insisting that when she married Roger "nothing was said about 'sickness and health' referring to the body only. If Roger had scarlet fever, would you expect me to desert him? My Roger is sick from another fever now, from which, in due course, he will quite recover."[50]

Here we have a familiar equation of sexual perversion and disease. Just as Mayo consistently links practices and morals to disease in *Mother India*, in "Companionate 'Marriage'" she deems Roger's infidelity a "fever" from which he will eventually recover. As the conclusion of the tale attests, this is exactly what happens; Roger and Anne "lived out a happy half century together, and Roger, in all human likelihood, never guessed that his wife knew [of his affair]."[51] This resolution implies that infidelity is cause for little concern or comment, but the thrust of Mayo's warning is aimed not at Roger but at women in Anne's position. Throughout the article Mayo equates women's desire for "self-expression"[52] and "rights" with Roger's fever, saying just "because Roger caught a fever should [Anne] demand a 'right' to rush out and catch one too?"[53] While Roger seems to have contracted a fever through no fault of his own, if Anne were to seek the same infection (that is, if *she* were to go out and have an affair) the consequences would be very different.

Mayo's use of the fever metaphor is consistent with her focus on disease in her other works; in each case she deems deviant behavior contagious. In this particular instance, she uses the metaphor of fever to describe a drive towards self-fulfillment over good citizenship—the problem is placing one's own needs over the needs of society at large. Roger's affair selfishly interferes with his role as husband, but as long as Anne stays by his side it need not have fatal consequences. Relying on an ideology of separate spheres, Mayo argues that it doesn't matter that Roger has temporarily shirked his domestic duties; because women are the guardians of the home, their marital behavior carries more weight. *As mothers* (or even as potential mothers) women are responsible not just for their own well-being, but for society's at large. This grave responsibility is more important than any individual woman's wants and desires. As Mayo warns U.S. women, "when you feel the phrase 'self-expression' forming in your minds, take warning as you would of the flagman's signal at a level crossing. For a death dealer is headed down your track."[54] Mayo's "message to girls" is for them to sublimate their needs in order to remain true to their real "gift"—"the Quality of Motherhood."[55] To ignore this gift is to strike a death blow not only to the individual "girl" but to the nation.

Mayo reminds her readers that "no nation . . . can rise higher than the level of its womankind."[56] Unsurprisingly, she turns to the Indian example to prove this point. While she again lauds Hindu society for "[perceiving] that motherhood is the meaning of womanhood," in the same breath she condemns it, arguing that it "has so debased and soiled and ruined the idea [of motherhood], taking the physical for master, that both men and women tend to become merely a function with a human frame behind it."[57] This emphasis on the "physical" unites Hindu marriage with companionate marriage, which Mayo similarly deems "a public blessing on the delivery of your body to sexual use for no nobler reason than the indulgence of your sexual craving."[58] In both companionate marriage in the United States and Hindu marriage in India, the sexual trumps the maternal to catastrophic ends. By placing Indian and U.S. women on a continuum of motherhood, Mayo describes it as a slippery slope down which the U.S. girl, "the mainspring of America's true progress," could easily fall.[59] If progress is so easily and thoughtlessly vulnerable to reversal, then here again is one of the dangers of the flow of bodies and practices between the United States and India. By framing the issue of U.S. marriage in the language of disease, and by once again mobilizing the plight of Indian women as an object-lesson, Mayo reveals that her concern with Indian reproduction is also a means for policing U.S. womanhood.

Mayo's concerns are thus domestic in both senses of the word. In a logic that recalls what Amy Kaplan has theorized as "manifest domesticity," Mayo's focus on the private sphere of the home allows her to envision U.S. women as crusaders in the world at large.[60] As she declares, "the American girl is the most potential force for good on earth today."[61] The problem is that these "girls" are falling down on the job. While Kaplan's argument describes the palliative role an ideology of domesticity played in a moment of nationalist expansion, the moment Mayo is writing in is quite different. Instead of expansion, this is a time of nativist consolidation of U.S. identity in which the question of empire was vexed at best. Even as Mayo advocates imperialism, her descriptions of the United States and India as coeval reveal the real anxiety she feels about the United States' role on the global stage. And these imperial anxieties find expression in Mayo's critique of U.S. women's sexual and cultural looseness. If they are so open, of course they could catch the fever Mayo describes. For her, the consequences of women embracing the ideals of companionate marriage and "self-expression" are dire: "Drop your standards, girls, and the national standard must trail in the mud. You are the keepers of the race. Our men are what you make them."[62] Mayo's model of imperial containment thus forms an interlocking strategy wherein ideas about proper U.S. gender roles are used to police Indian women, and representations of Indian female sexuality are used to police U.S. women. In this sense, Mayo compares female sexuality in India and the United States to promote gender containment in both sites.

Indeed, the responses to *Mother India* exploit the implications of Mayo's logic for U.S. women. While some (such as Lala Lajpat Rai's *Unhappy India* and Dhan Gopal Mukerji's *A Son of Mother India Answers*) refute Mayo on the basis of facts, many *tu quoque* responses employ her methods to expose U.S. evils.[63] One of the most popular of these, K. L. Gauba's *Uncle Sham: Being the Strange Tale of a Civilization Run Amok*, devotes no less than seven of eighteen chapters to sex problems in the United States, arguing "if girls and boys go the way of fornication and adultery, if marriage becomes a fraud, then civilisation must go the way of Sodom and Gomorrah."[64] What's most revealing, however, is how closely Gauba's assessment of companionate marriage resembles Mayo's. Gauba similarly finds equal rights for women suspect, arguing that "equal rights [imply] equal [sexual] liberties."[65] Just as Mayo contrasted Anne's "right" to have an affair with her "duties" to her family, Gauba claims that "with companionate marriage the home goes by the board and the whole idea of the family with it."[66]

Mayo's indictment of Indian reproductive practices thus also travels, ultimately reflecting back upon the United States. In reading *Mother India* in its U.S. as well as Indian context, I suggest that Mayo advocates a strong arm overseas as a means of policing the boundaries of the nation at home. Not only do unfit Indian reproductive practices make them unworthy for nationhood, so too could cultural and sexual promiscuity in the United States undo the U.S. national project. Mayo uses the trope of infectious disease to make this threat literal. Insisting that the United States and India occupy the same spatial and temporal plane, Mayo presents unsanitary Hindu sex practices as a "world-menace." Accordingly, she maintains that if the United States is to continue to advance in a new era of international circulation of goods and bodies, then it must tighten its borders. So, too, Mayo writes, must U.S. women strengthen their moral resolve to withstand the seductions of Indian spirituality on the one hand and the ideology of the "new woman" on the other. She thus recasts the problem of global markets in terms of sexual contamination in order to argue for an imperial policy of containment both at home and abroad. Ultimately, her focus on national reproduction argues that a woman's place is in the home. The world's women must simply stay in their *own* homes, rather than spreading their unsanitary (indeed, unpatriotic) reproductive practices to "ours."

Notes

I would like to thank that following people for their insightful comments on various versions of this essay: Maria Josefina Saldaña-Portillo, Daniel Kim, Rey Chow, Christopher Lee, Jason Moralee, Nerissa Balce, Timothy Bewes, Jane Degenhardt, Kirstie Dorr, Sara Clarke Kaplan, Matthew Pursell, and Cathy Schlund-Vials. I also thank David G. Gutiérrez, Pierrette Hondagneu-Sotelo, and the editors of *American Quarterly* for their extremely productive feedback. I have presented sections of this work at the American Studies Institute (Dartmouth College, 2003), the 19th Annual South Asia Conference at UC Berkeley (2004), and the American Studies Association (2007). Earlier formulations of some of the arguments presented here appeared in "Eugenic Feminism: Asian Reproduction in the U.S. National Imaginary," *NOVEL: A Forum on Fiction* 39.2 (Spring 2006): 221–44.

1. Andrew Jon Rotter, *Comrades at Odds: The United States and India, 1947–1964* (Ithaca, N.Y.: Cornell University Press, 2000), 1.

2. This is the quote on the book jacket of the 1943 edition of *Mother India*. Katherine Mayo, *Mother India* (New York: Harcourt Brace, 1927). Further references will be cited parenthetically.

3. Kumari Jayawardena, *The White Woman's Other Burden: Western Women and South Asia During British Colonial Rule* (New York: Routledge, 1995), 95. Mrinalini Sinha, "Introduction," in *Mother India: Selections from the Controversial 1927 Text*, ed. Mrinalini Sinha (Ann Arbor: University of Michigan Press, 2000), 2. My discussion of the historical background of *Mother India* and of the controversy that *Mother India* generated is indebted to Sinha, *Specters of Mother India: The Global Restructuring of an Empire* (Durham, N.C.: Duke University Press, 2006); "Refashioning Mother India: Feminism and Nationalism in Late-Colonial India," *Feminist Studies* 26.3 (Fall 2000): 623–44; "Reading Mother India: Empire, Nation, and the Female Voice," *Journal of Women's History* 6.2 (Summer 1994): 6–44; and Manorajan Jha, *Katherine Mayo and India* (New Delhi: People's Publishing House, 1971).

4.   To name just two events, on November 21, 1927, there was a conference hosted by Eleanor Rathbone in London. There was also a meeting of mass protest against *Mother India* in San Francisco on March 22, 1928. *Katherine Mayo Papers*, Folder 206, Box 37, Manuscript and Archives Division, Sterling Memorial Library, Yale University, New Haven, Connecticut. Sinha, "Introduction," 2.

5.   See Jha, "'Mother India' and the British" (61–65) and "'Mother India' and the Americans" (74–79).

6.   See the special issue of *The Journal of Colonialism and Colonial History* 2.1 (Spring 2001) on "Pairing Empires: Britain and the United States, 1857–1947" for an in-depth discussion of the relationship between British and U.S. empires.

7.   See Paul Teed, "Race Against Memory: Katherine Mayo, Jabez Sunderland, and Indian Independence," *American Studies* 44.1–2 (Spring-Summer 2003): 35–57.

8.   For more on the erotics of U.S. imperialism, see Nerissa S. Balce, "The Filipina's Breast: Savagery, Docility, and the Erotics of American Empire," *Social Text* 24.2 (Summer 2006): 89–110.

9.   I take this section title from a 1930 book by Wendell Thomas, *Hinduism Invades America* (New York: Beacon Press, 1930).

10.   See Malini Johar Schueller, *U.S. Orientalisms: Race, Nation, and Gender in Literature, 1790–1890* (Ann Arbor: University of Michigan Press, 1998); and Vijay Prashad, "Of the Mysterious East," *The Karma of Brown Folk* (Minneapolis: University of Minnesota Press, 2000): 11–20.

11.   See Andrew Jon Rotter, "Gender Relations, Foreign Relations: The United States and South Asia", in *The Journal of American History* 81.2 (September 1994): 518–42; Rotter, *Comrades at Odds*; Sinha, "Introduction"; Prashad, *The Karma of Brown Folk*; and Joy Dixon, "Ancient Wisdom, Modern Motherhood: Theosophy and the Colonial Syncretic," in *Gender, Sexuality and Colonial Modernities*, ed. Antoinette Burton, 193–206 (London: Routledge, 1999).

12.   Prashad, *The Karma of Brown Folk*, 18.

13.   Jha, "Mother India," 2; Alan Raucher, "American Anti-Imperialists and the Pro-India Movement, 1900–1932," *The Pacific Historical Review* 43.1 (February 1974): 83–110.

14   See Prashad, especially "Of Authentic Cultural Lives," 109–32; Raucher, "American Anti-Imperialists," 94.

15.   See Jha, "Mother India," 8.

16.   The Hindu-German Conspiracy involved links between Indian revolutionaries and the German government, and included (among other things) an attempt to smuggle arms into India. See Maia Ramnath, "Two Revolutions: The Ghadar Party and India's Radical Diaspora, 1913–1918," *Radical History Review* 92 (Spring 2005): 7–30.

17.   Interview, *Katherine Mayo Papers*, Folder 45, Box 6.

18.   Despite Mayo's dubious relationship to the feminism of her time, *Mother India* has been championed as a feminist text, most notably by Mary Daly in *Gyn/Ecology, the Metaethics of Radical Feminism* (Boston: Beacon Press, 1978). For a similar (if somewhat more measured) feminist recuperation, see Elisabeth Bumiller, *May You Be the Mother of a Hundred Sons: A Journey among the Women of India* (New York: Random House, 1990). Such recuperations have been heavily critiqued, most notably by Audre Lorde, "An Open Letter to Mary Daly," *Sister Outsider: Essays and Speeches* (Trumansburg, N.Y.: Crossing Press, 1984); and Uma Narayan, *Dislocating Cultures: Identities, Traditions and Third-World Feminism* (New York: Routledge, 1997). There has also been a good deal of critical work done on *Mother India* and its relationship to imperialist feminism, including Kumari Jayawardena, *The White Woman's Other Burden: Western Women and South Asia During British Colonial Rule* (New York: Routledge, 1995); Liz Wilson, "Who Is Authorized to Speak? Katherine Mayo and the Politics of Imperial Feminism in British India," *Journal of Indian Philosophy* 25 (1997): 139–51; Joanna Liddle and Shirin Rai, "Feminism, Imperialism and Orientalism: The Challenge of the 'Indian Woman,'" *Women's History Review* 7.4 (1998): 495–520; and Catherine Candy, "The Inscrutable Irish-Indian Feminist Management of Anglo-American Hegemony, 1917–1947," *Journal of Colonialism and Colonial History* 2.1 (2001), http://muse.jhu.edu.silk.library.umass.edu:2048/journals/cch/v002/2.1candy (accessed June 4, 2007). Sandhya Shetty is one of the few feminist literary scholars to consider *Mother India*. See her "(Dis)figuring the Nation: Mother, Metaphor, Metonymy," *Differences* 7.3 (1995): 50–78.

19.   See Sinha, "The Lineage of the 'Indian' Modern: Rhetoric, Agency and the Sarda Act in Late Colonial India," in *Gender, Sexuality and Colonial Modernities*, ed. Burton, 207–21.

20. See Katherine Mayo, *Justice to All: The Story of the Pennsylvania State Police*, 5th rev. ed. (Boston: Houghton Mifflin, 1920), *Mounted Justice: True Stories of the Pennsylvania State Police* (Boston: Houghton Mifflin, 1922), and *The Standard-Bearers: True Stories of Heroes of Law and Order* (Boston: Houghton Mifflin, 1930).

21. Mayo, *Justice to All*, 153.

22. Quoted in Jha, "Mother India," 210.

23. The Government of India Act of 1919 instituted "dyarchy," a form of government in which responsibility for certain areas (such as agriculture, health, education, and local self-government) was transferred to Indian ministers.

24. Mayo, "India," 36.

25. David Arnold, "Introduction: Disease, Medicine and Empire," *Imperial Medicine and Indigenous Societies*, ed. David Arnold, 1–26 (Delhi: Oxford University Press, 1988), 15.

26. Jha, "Mother India," 66–68; Sinha, *Specters of Mother India*, 74. Letter from the Rockefeller Foundation, signed by Major Greenwood, Esq., Ministry of Health, Whitehall, S.W. 1, London, England. *Katherine Mayo Papers*, Folder 32, Box 5. Despite this letter of introduction, Mayo claimed not to have any institutional affiliations in the United States or Britain.

27. Nayan Shah, *Contagious Divides: Epidemics and Race in San Francisco's Chinatown* (Berkeley: University of California Press, 2001), 106. See also E. Richard Brown, *Rockefeller Medicine Men: Medicine and Capitalism in America* (Berkeley: University of California Press, 1979); and John Ettling, *The Germ of Laziness: Rockefeller Philanthropy and Public Health in the New South* (Cambridge, Mass.: Harvard University Press, 1981). Thanks to Jean Kim for help with this research.

28. Thanks to Christopher Lee for this point.

29. Alan Kraut, *Silent Travelers: Germ, Genes, and the "Immigrant Menace"* (Baltimore: John Hopkins University Press, 1995).

30. Priscilla Wald, *Contagious: Cultures, Carriers, and the Outbreak Narrative* (Durham, N.C.: Duke University Press, 2008), 117.

31. Ibid., 134.

32. Mary Louise Pratt, "Travel Narrative and Imperialist Vision," *Understanding Narrative*, ed. James Phelan and Peter J. Rabinowitz, 199–221 (Columbus: Ohio State University Press, 1994). See also Mary Louise Pratt, *Imperial Eyes* (New York: Routledge, 1992).

33. In *Time and the Other: How Anthropology Makes Its Object* (New York: Columbia University Press, 1983), Johannes Fabian deems this tendency to read other cultures as occupying earlier temporalities "a denial of coevalness" (31). Ronald Inden calls the "primordialization of . . . Asia . . . the most spectacular instance of this temporal distancing." *Imagining India* (Bloomington: Indiana University Press, 1990), 53.

34. For an influential example of this point of view, see Samuel P. Huntington's "clash of civilizations" thesis, *The Clash of Civilizations and the Remaking of World Order* (New York: Simon and Schuster, 1996), 20–21.

35. Mayo, "India," *Liberty*, January 14, 1928, 36. *Katherine Mayo Papers*, Box 21, Folder 147a.

36. See J. A. Hobson, *Imperialism: A Study* (New York: J. Pott, 1902); Rudolf Hilferding, *Finance Capital: A Study of the Latest Phase of Capitalist Development* (London: Routledge, 1981); Rosa Luxemburg, *The Accumulation of Capital* (New York: Routledge, 2003); Nikolai Bukharin, *Imperialism and World Economy* (New York: Monthly Review Press, 1973); and Vladimir Lenin, *Imperialism, the Highest Stage of Capitalism: A Popular Outline* (New York: International Publishers, 1983).

37. See Christina Klein, *Cold War Orientalism: Asia in the Middlebrow Imagination* (Berkeley: University of California Press, 2003). See also Priscilla Wald, "Viral Cultures," *Contagious*.

38. Sucheta Mazumdar, "Racist Responses to Racism: The Aryan Myth and South Asians in the United States," *South Asia Bulletin* 9.1 (1989): 47–55, and "The Politics of Religion and National Origin: Rediscovering Hindu Indian Identity in the United States," in *Antimonies of Modernity: Essays on Race, Orient, Nation*, ed. Vasant Kaiwar and Sucheta Mazumdar, 223–60 (Durham, N.C.: Duke University Press, 2003).

39. Sinha, *Specters of Mother India*, 95.

40. Mayo, "When Asia Knocks at the Door," *Brookline Standard Union*, June 7, 1927, 14. *Katherine Mayo Papers*, Folder 147a, Box 21.

41. Bankim Chandra Chatterjee, *Anandamath* (New Delhi: Vision Books, 1992).

42. See Sandhya Shetty, "(Dis)Figuring the Nation," 53–54; Nalini Natarajan, "Woman, Nation, Narration in *Midnight's Children*," *Scattered Hegemonies: Postmodernity and Transnational Feminist Practices*, ed. Inderpal Grewal and Caren Kaplen (Minneapolis: University of Minnesota Press, 1994), 84; Tanika Sarkar, "Nationalist Iconography: The Image of Women in 19th Century Bengali Literature," *Economic and Political Weekly* 2.47 (November 21, 1987): 2011–15.
43. See Partha Chatterjee, *The Nation and Its Fragments: Colonial and Postcolonial Histories* (Princeton, N.J.: Princeton University Press, 1993).
44. For more on the relationship between metaphor and metonymy in *Mother India*, see Shetty, "(Dis)figuring the Nation." Shetty argues that the metonymic movement from suffering mother to torturing *dai* "breaks the back of the nationalist-patriarchal allegory" (53). Contrary to Shetty's argument, however, I suggest that in order for Mayo to mobilize Mother India as an allegorical figure, it is essential for her to split it into both victim and threat.
45. Mayo, "India," 36.
46. Ibid.
47. Ibid., 39. Emphasis in original.
48. Mayo, "To the Women of Hindu India," in *Slaves of the Gods* (New York: Harcourt, Brace, 1929), 238.
49. Ibid.
50. Mayo, "Companionate 'Marriage'—and Marriage: A Message to Girls," *Liberty*, May 26,1928, 1924. *Katherine Mayo Papers*, Folder 147a, Box 21.
51. Ibid., 19.
52. Ibid., 20.
53. Ibid., 19.
54. Ibid., 20.
55. Ibid., 20.
56. Ibid., 24.
57. Ibid., 24.
58. Ibid., 24.
59. Ibid., 20.
60. Amy Kaplan, "Manifest Domesticity," *American Literature* 70.3 (September 1998): 581–607. See also Amy Kaplan, *The Anarchy of Empire in the Making of U.S. Culture* (Cambridge, Mass.: Harvard University Press, 2002).
61. Mayo, "Companionate 'Marriage'," 20.
62. Ibid., 20.
63. Lala Lajpat Rai, *Unhappy India* (Calcutta: Banna Publisher, 1928); Dhan Gopal Mukerji, *A Son of Mother India Answers* (New York: E. P. Dutton, 1928).
64. K. L. Gauba, *Uncle Sham: Being the Strange Tale of a Civilization Run Amok* (Lahore, India: The Time Publishing, 1929), 12.
65. Ibid., 83.
66. Ibid., 82.

Re-Producing a Nationalist Literature in the Age of Globalization: Reading (Im) migration in Julia Alvarez's *How the García Girls Lost Their Accents*

Sarika Chandra

H ow should critics respond to the imperative to globalize the field of American literature?[1] Wai Chee Dimock and Lawrence Buell's edited volume *Shades of the Planet: American Literature as World Literature* is a useful contemporary example of how this is being attempted. It begins by taking up a by now familiar question, what is American literature in a global context?[2] The editors suggest de-linking the word *American* from its national and geographical boundaries. This question of de-linking has become especially important in a context of increasing U.S. military and economic aggression. But it is a difficult task indeed for a field with the name *American* in it.[3] *Shades of the Planet* is, in fact, one of a number of Americanist projects that have attempted to displace and decenter the field—projects that have helped to reinvigorate the discipline.[4] In their introduction, Dimock and Buell suggest treating American literature as a subset of, and a "taxonomically useful entity" within, the field of global literature (4). This invocation of the planetary allows them to "modularize the world into smaller entities able to stand provisionally and do analytical work, but not self-contained, not sovereign" (4). That is, the entity of American literature is not displaced entirely but is repositioned within the space of the "planet"—although Dimock and Buell are careful to argue that this "should not lure us into thinking that this entity is natural" (4).

Survival of Nationalist Paradigms

Each of the essays in *Shades of the Planet* proposes its own particular way of decentering American literature, ranging from including literatures written in languages other than English to reimagining the spatial coordinates of America as beyond national boundaries. But I want to take a brief look at Jonathan

Arac's essay, "Global and Babel: Language and Planet," since it serves as an especially good example of the difficulties encountered by scholars of American literature as they attempt to deal with issues of globalization.[5] The essay proposes a dyad: the "global," defined as "a movement of expansion that one imagines may homogenize the world," and "Babel," defined as a "movement of influx that diversifies our land, as in multiculturalism" (24). Parts of the essay make a case for displacing the English language from American literature by having graduate students learn three languages and also by helping students to learn the "value of imperfect speech" and "the capacity to speak on the street" (24). A major part of the essay deals with the reading of literary texts in a manner that unhooks them from national borders. Some of the authors whose work exemplifies the "global Babel" here are Emerson, Thoreau, Whitman, Henry Roth, and Ralph Ellison. Consider Arac's reading of Thoreau's *Walden*, which he cites as follows: "observe the forms which thawing sand and clay assume in flowing down the sides of a steep cut on the railroad" (25–26). Here Thoreau, says Arac, "feels as if he is in the 'laboratory of the Artist who made the world,' and 'nearer to the vitals of the global,'" which "'continually transcends and translates itself and becomes winged in its orbit'" (Arac's citations from *Walden*, 26). Arac interprets this for us, stating that "Thoreau's globalism at home provides the most morally reassuring babble" (26), and finds in Thoreau a guide for American literary critics to think globally. But here the focus is largely on language and the terminology of globalization and not on the sociohistorical conditions that might help us better understand the global context of Thoreau's work. Arac reads Ellison's *Invisible Man* in a similar way, citing the famous passage in which the narrator, looking at yams being sold in the streets of Harlem, proclaims: "I Yam what I am." The essay presents this as an example of heteroglossia, that is, Babel, as it "sets against each other radically different social registers of language," observing that the "root and its name aren't simply southern [that is, American] but also African" (27). Such connections indeed lead us to a broader interpretation of the text and Arac is careful to note what he calls the imperialist *thinking* of the authors in question. For example, while invoking the global dimension of Whitman, he also draws upon Edward Said, whose work, he says, "enables us to think openly, rather than defensively, about the imperialism that inescapably grids the planetary reach of Whitman's democratic idealism" (27). Arac cites Whitman's poem *A Broadway Pageant* as an example of this: "'Comrade Americanos!, to us then at last the Orient comes . . . Lithe and Silent the Hindoo appears, the Asiatic continent itself appears the past, the dead'" (27). The problematic aspect of this language, from the standpoint of the essay, is the imperialism of Whitman's "vision." However, globalization here remains primarily an issue of language, a linguistic globalism, as practiced by authors who already have a secure place in the American literary canon. In arguing for this kind of globalism, Arac thus allows the history of the U.S. imperialist economic and military policies to slide out of consideration.

It is true that the works of Melville, Emerson, and Whitman remain crucial for students of globalization today even as they must be critiqued as implicit apologies for imperialism. But it is notable here that despite the inclusion of Ralph Ellison, whose notion of America is often positioned against that of Thoreau or Whitman, the centrality of a traditional canon is left intact. In the very attempt to decenter American literature, there is a simultaneous move to shore up the canon to which such decentered works belong. In this respect "Global and Babel" has much in common with other moves in literary and cultural studies to "globalize" the field in such a way that the older curricular paradigms continue to exist unaffected and unthreatened.[6] I argue that this is a *rhetorical strategy* that critics employ to produce a larger transnational context for categories such as American literature—categories whose partial displacement is advocated only so as to resolidify the *nationalist* basis of the category per se. I would also insist on distinguishing between this rhetorical strategy and the historical processes of globalization themselves, processes that cannot be reduced to the former.

But, while critics such as Arac attempt to decenter nationalist paradigms and American literature itself by linking the established writer's work directly to the global in ways that nonetheless reinforce the national, other critics—especially those working in the field of immigrant/ethnic literary studies—have attempted to decenter American literature in what may appear to be a diametrically opposed move by displacing canonical works themselves so as to make room for other, less sanctioned writers within American literature. In this essay, I examine how the concepts of immigration and immigrant literatures—in ways subtly analogous to the rhetorical strategy described above—also assist American literary studies in reconstructing a nationalist paradigm even while attempting to "globalize" or update disciplinary practices. While the idea of immigration has long helped the United States to produce a national imaginary, the concept is now shifted in order to serve the same purpose in the "new era."

(Im)migration and Globalization

U.S. writers in the eighteenth and nineteenth centuries, including Benjamin Franklin and Ralph Waldo Emerson, took on the task of defining the "American" as the self-reliant and the self-sufficient. Their writings drew upon the notion of the "foreign" to define American-ness and positioned the United States as a nation of nations—an idea employed even today in chronicling the accomplishments of immigrants.[7] The image of immigrants who have nothing and yet are able to pull themselves up by the bootstraps has been fundamental for the way it suggests the rebirth of the immigrant upon reaching the United States, repositioning the "foreignness" of the immigrants within domestic borders. This repositioning then provides the immigrants with their particular identities in relationship to the United States as a nation. In *The Next American Nation*, Michael Lind describes this phenomenon in a more contemporary context.[8] He suggests that many of the differences between groups of people that make up the population living within a nation are mitigated once they immigrate to the United States and are asked to join already existing, homogenized ethnic categories: "Mexicans and Cubans join Hispanic America; Chinese, Indians, and Filipinos join Asian and Pacific Islander America, and so on. Moreover each race, in addition to preserving its cultural unity and distinctness, is expected to act as a monolithic political bloc" (98). In effect, immigrants become localized ethnics in the United States. The term *immigrant* nevertheless continues to designate those who are different or "other" in some way. Unity is sought in diversity, but for such unity to exist, something, or someone, has to remain on the outside. A "unity" cannot simply be the sum of its parts. It must have an "other" as well.

Recent theories of globalization, moreover, have questioned the notion of stable and localized ethnic identities positioned as insider/outsider. In "Patriotism and Its Futures," Arjun Appadurai suggests that the "U.S. is not so much a nation of nations or immigrants but one node in a postnational network of diasporas."[9] While he may be a bit too quick to conclude that immigration has been supplanted by "migration," he appropriately suggests that the positioning of immigrants outside the dominant U.S. experience has become extremely complex. Though a significant number of earlier immigrant narratives such as Anzia Yezierska's *Bread Givers* (1925)[10] and Abraham Cahan's *The Rise of David Levinsky* (1917)[11] portrayed immigrants as negotiating their ethnicity and their status within this bounded space of the United States, more contemporary narratives such as Esmeralda Santiago's *América's Dream* (1997)[12] and Julia Alvarez's *How the García Girls Lost Their Accents* (1991)[13] present immigrants who conduct similar negotiations but in a much more interconnected world. I examine Alvarez's novel below in some detail.

As literary critics undergo pressures to globalize their fields, they must do so in ways that prevent the complete dissolution of the discipline itself.

In the contemporary, "globalized" context, critics present immigrant/ethnic literatures as cultural texts able to mediate current discussions of globalization because such literature has always produced an imaginary of displacement and made possible a connection between the United States and the rest of the world. Yet, might not the interest of critics in this broadening of literary scholarship be to *continue*, here in the name of the immigrant as marginal, the work that has always defined the field of American literature? In what follows, I will demonstrate how the figure of the marginal—here in the guise of the immigrant—is taken up in literary studies not simply out of an ethical opposition to the marginalizing of certain groups of people, but also to valorize this figure itself; not only for being outside the dominant, but also for the less obvious way in which it leaves what is inside the dominant intact. The figure of the immigrant comes to occupy the position of an "outsider" that helps make the "inside" seem more secure.

My critique takes aim at a domestic form of multiculturalism and politics of identity. I want it to be clear, however, that I am differentiating between identity as a politics of recognition and other ways of thinking and analyzing questions of identity that link culture to history, economics, and politics. By linking ethnic identity to a politics of recognition, decontextualized perspectives often position immigrants as necessarily in opposition to dominant groups. Such a notion of identity has been significant to immigrant/ethnic literatures. But analysis of identity need not remain within such a framework. A wide range of scholars, among them Anthony Appiah, Linda Alcoff, and E. San Juan Jr. have weighed in on the essentializing and liberal tendencies of identity politics and multiculturalism. Still others have noted that there has been a significant shift in what counts as politics both in and out of the university. Critics such as Jon Cruz, Paul Smith, Avery Gordon, Wahneema Lubiano, and Lisa Lowe have provided models for a scholarship that analyzes the dominant production and appropriation of identity categories within capitalist relations.[14] As Jodi Melamed has written:

> Race continues to permeate capitalism's economic and social processes, organizing the hyperextraction of surplus value from racialized bodies and naturalizing a system of capital accumulation that grossly favors the global North over the global South. Yet multiculturalism portrays neoliberal policy as the key to a postracist world of freedom and opportunity.[15]

Melamed argues that since the "1990s multiculturalism has become a policy rubric for business, government and education."[16] For instance, reading the 2002 Bush administration *National Security Strategy*, she notes its reference to the "opening" of "world markets" as a "multicultural imperative . . . opening societies to the diversity of the world."[17] In another example, Melamed reminds us that Bush has consistently used language of multiculturalism to justify the indefinite incarceration of Arab and Muslim prisoners at Guantánamo. His much publicized idea that the prisoners are given Korans and time to pray is supposed to work as a marker of racial sensitivity. This new racism uses the language of multiculturalism to at once change older racial binaries, such as Arab versus white, and also to obscure their continuation.[18] Questions of racial identity become in some ways even more salient in the global context outlined by Melamed. Analyses of identity that look at the uneven co-optation of groups of people in a globally structured economy must be distinguished from studies of identity as a politics of recognition and representation. Analytical frameworks that consider identity in its sociohistorical context are able to show how race, ethnicity, and gender-identity paradigms are part of the structural makeup of society.[19] Consider, for example, Lisa Lowe's argument in *Immigrant Acts* that the production of multiculturalism with a fetishized focus on identity as a positive force " 'forgets' history, and in this forgetting exacerbates a contradiction between the concentration of capital within a dominant class group, and the unattended conditions of a working class increasingly made up of heterogeneous immigrant, racial and ethnic group."[20] These kinds of identity analyses have shown the problems that arise when positioning the categories of identity—easily appropriated by capital—as though they were themselves outside and critical of the dominant social relations. Multiculturalism then presupposes a politics of representation and recognition within a national frame that overlooks and even obscures the supranational power relations represented by international financial organizations such as the World Bank and the World Trade Organization (WTO). Even though there is disagreement in critical circles about whether the wars on Iraq, Afghanistan, and Lebanon are indications of the impending demise of the nation-state, there is a pervasive sense that politics and scholarship based on what are by some accounts the parochial domestic paradigms of multiculturalism and identity as a politics of recognition are inadequate or even out of date. In this context of pressure to move beyond previously accepted paradigms within immigrant/ethnic literary studies, there arises a countervailing pressure within the field to find new ways to consolidate the older paradigms. And, since immigration is often imagined as the movement from one nation into another—meaning that these paradigms are themselves predicated on the nation—we have in the process a consolidation of the nation and nationalist paradigms as well.

Identity politics' most prized notions—"multiculturalism," "diversity," and the generalized figure of the dominated "other"—are easily employed to move toward a global paradigm even while securing a nationalist one. As an argument for inclusion, identity politics has played an important and positive role in recent history. The question is, "inclusion" within *what*? I will show that identity politics and multiculturalism have sought to incorporate the figure of the immigrant into their own project of universality, and that this project remains, fundamentally, a nationalist one.

Globalizing Practices in Literary Criticism: Reading *How the García Girls Lost Their Accents*

I will examine the move to "globalize" and at the same time renationalize practices in literary studies by focusing on the critical work produced in response to Julia Alvarez's novel *How the García Girls Lost Their Accents* (1991). Through an assessment of this critical material, I show how the curricular locus of immigrant/ethnic fiction, counterposed to dominant literary categories, helps critics "globalize" while reproducing a nationalist imaginary within a domestic paradigm of race and gender politics. I have chosen to focus on this novel for several reasons. The scholarly reception of this text, which is widely taught in university classrooms, reflects how literary practitioners have produced a canon of immigrant/ethnic literatures with a heavy concentration of women writers, in part because women writers and their female protagonists allow for simultaneous conversations about race and gender. Moreover, since its publication in 1991, *The García Girls* has generated a significant amount of scholarship, work that reveals some of the changes that have been occurring within the field of literary studies in relationship to theories of globalization. For the remainder of this essay, I will show that, although Alvarez's text is in conversation with historical processes that complicate issues of localized immigrant identities, many critics have attempted to reappropriate those aspects of the novel, producing criticism in which "identity-thinking" is reintroduced, globalizing even while preserving the discipline of American literary study itself. Here, I emphasize the distinction between practices that at once displace and shore up the discipline of American literary study, and theories that scrutinize the United States as a historical entity with policies/practices that play a role in producing (im)migration.

The novel tells the story of the flight of the García family—father Carlos, wife Laura, and their four daughters, Yolanda, Sandi, Sophia, and Carla—from the Dominican Republic to the United States. In Santo Domingo they were a wealthy and prominent family, able to employ maids and servants. Carlos is implicated in a failed CIA plot to kill the dictator Trujillo and must flee with his family or face certain and violent retribution. The narrative itself begins in the 1980s and chronicles the life of the family as the García girls grow up in New York City. The circumstances leading to the family's emigration from Santo Domingo are not related until the end of the novel, in a flashback to the 1950s. It is important to note, however, that these circumstances include the already widespread Americanizing influences on the island and that even after their emigration to New York—and the death of Trujillo in 1961—the family frequently returns to the Dominican Republic.[21] Critical scholarship on the novel for the most part consists of readings that focus on the negotiation of identity as part of the process the Garcías undergo as immigrants creating a space for themselves in the United States. In such critical work the identity of the Garcías is seen as dual or bicultural.[22] Other critical work attempts to place the novel in the context of conversations about globalization.[23] Such scholarship, attempting to displace identity-based readings, argues against dual/bicultural identity of the characters in favor of a transnational or global one. For example, Pauline Newton in *Transcultural Women* states:

> I do not wish to create a false binary relationship between the writers' new U.S. American culture and their old cultural differences or to delve into comparisons of various migrant generations or cultures, so instead I recognize their transcultural evolution within and outside of and across their cultural regions (2).

However, this change, for the most part, remains one of terminology, because "transcultural evolution" keeps the emphasis on identity rather than the changed contexts of identity negotiation.

This strategy is common, but I will focus here on "From Third World Politics to First World Practices" by Maribel Otriz-Márquez, since it is a good example of the impetus to globalize/consolidate nationalist paradigms. The essay is part of a volume of critical feminist scholarship titled *Interventions: Feminist Dialogues on Third World Women's Literature and Film*, edited by Bishnupriya Ghosh and Brinda Bose (with a foreword by Chandra Talpade Mohanty). *Interventions*, according to Mohanty, is the first in a series called "Gender, Culture, and Global Politics," whose premise is based on the "the need for feminist engagement with global as well as local/situational, ideological, economic, and political process." Ortiz-Márquez's essay is an attempt to engage with such a global/local "political process." She speaks to issues of nationalism and displacement by asking:

How could one successfully write about Latino/Latina writers in the United States without problematizing the categories which are at the core of our own definition of national literature? How could one engage in a discussion of the 'politics of displacement' and cultural dislocation without, at least, questioning the notion of the Third World and those narratives?"

And she employs key words in the vocabulary of globalization studies: "dislocation," and "displacement." These are, according to the essay, notions that must be urgently considered if we are to understand current Latino/a literary production. Yet this exhortation to displacement further consolidates the very categories that she contends need to be displaced. Her questions are symptomatic of the way in which Latino/Latina narratives are employed to shore up the categories of American literature itself.

As I suggested earlier, immigrant fiction provides a ready narrative for resituating the study of American literature. For example, in thinking about *The García Girls*, Ortiz-Márquez certainly gives due attention to the ways in which travel between homelands and the United States is important to the construction of identities, but this is considered only in the context of how immigrants' cultural practices affect their position in the United States. It is only at one point that she gestures toward what she calls the "social reality" of the political turmoil that "lies at the margins of the text"—namely the escape from the Trujillo dictatorship (236). But apart from a cursory mention, hardly any attention is given to the ways in which historical processes of Americanization have influenced immigrants even before leaving the Dominican Republic. Ortiz-Márquez's essay is thus a good example of how, given "globalization," one now needs an "international" dimension within which to relocate the "national." Immigrant subjects are thus privileged in American literary studies because they serve as unique sites for that combination of the local and the global now required to reproduce the dominant imaginary of the United States itself as an "identity."

In addition to looking at Alvarez's writing, Ortiz-Márquez's essay also analyzes the work of Esmeralda Santiago and Christina Garcia. "Belonging," she says, "is the privileged feeling in all three narratives. It expresses the need to be somewhere where the boundaries of 'here' and 'there' can be easily defined, where the sense of estrangement can be easily defined" (233). Although she argues against easy definitions, Ortiz-Márquez casts the "negotiation" of belonging-ness for these characters in terms of gendered identities, concentrating on how female characters negotiate their place in the United States through their bodies. If, then, such gendered identities appear vexed, this is precisely because of issues of assimilation. Ortiz-Márquez thus states that "differences between male and female reproductive organs . . . translate . . . to differences in the way boys and girls are to behave once they enter puberty. The meaning of those differences is tied, in the novel, to Yolanda's understanding of language and language acquisition *in the United States*" (233; my emphasis). That is, the essay claims that assimilation in the form of language acquisition in the United States is "related to the configuration of sexual and gender identities" (233).

Analyzing gender politics is indeed crucial, but Ortiz-Márquez's reading, resting on a binary opposition between the two countries, implies that the United States is, a priori, less sexist than the Dominican Republic. This becomes clear if we consider how she reads the opening scene of the novel, in which Yolanda arrives on the island on one of her trips from the United States—the first of several chapters that cover (in reverse order) the time period stretching from 1989 back to 1972. Here is the description of Yolanda's entry, narrated from her own vantage point:

> The old aunts lounge in the white wicker armchairs, flipping open their fans, snapping them shut . . . [T]he aunts seem little changed since five years ago when Yolanda was last on the Island. Sitting amongst the aunts in less comfortable dining chairs, the cousins are flashes of color in turquoise jumpsuits and tight jersey dresses . . . Before anyone has turned to greet her in the entryway, Yolanda sees herself as they will, shabby in a black cotton skirt and jersey top, sandals on her feet, her wild black hair held back with a hairband. Like a missionary, her cousins will say, like one of those Peace Corps girls who have let themselves go so as to do dubious good in the world. (3–4)

While not citing this passage, Ortiz-Márquez writes about it as follows: "the opening scene is marked by Yolanda's subtle struggle to reject the norms established by her maternal family as proper 'woman's' behavior and her 'foreign' approach to issues such as clothes, makeup, traveling, and friends" (236). She interprets Yolanda's struggle as a challenge to the gender norms in the Dominican Republic and goes on to say that the "relative freedom she enjoys in the U.S. is clearly intertwined with the comfort she experiences in the familiarity of the surroundings in the Dominican Republic" (236). Though Ortiz-Márquez argues for reading this intertwining as a blurring of boundaries, she positions the familiar, comfortable, but, in matters of gender politics, less than ideal Dominican Republic against the unfamiliar, uncomfortable, but relatively free United States. This combining of experiences gestures at first toward blurring the boundaries, but only so as to redraw them in the end. And it is this blurring and preserving of boundaries that is read most pointedly through women's practices.

Here a politics of nationalism and displacement, inflected by issues of assimilation and dislocation, is equated with identity. *The García Girls* is read almost exclusively so as to reproduce arguments about race and gender identity negotiation and to bear the burden of representation that comes with such discussions. Although she wants to question what she calls the "ethnic reading" of these texts and even suggests that a "Latino" ethnicity is imposed on Alvarez's characters as a result of migration, Ortiz-Márquez nevertheless produces a reading of the novel that is in keeping with the U.S. rhetoric of individual identity as one that must be negotiated alone. She suggests that Alvarez's characters have taken on a fractured identity through mobility—which suggests in turn that somehow those not required to be "mobile" can have unfractured identities. Though the essay acknowledges that Latinas must struggle both in the United States and in their homelands, in the case of the García girls this struggle is also precisely what *gives* them identity. And there is an implicit argument here in *favor* of preserving this struggle indefinitely so as not to risk *losing* that identity. In fact, this narrative of displacement alongside "struggle" is not necessarily a narrative of dispossession and can just as well be understood as a narrative of cosmopolitanism in which the characters are presented as possessing a desirable perspective that *could only come* from being displaced. Displacement in such analyses is removed from the material realities in the lives of immigrants and becomes a kind of ethical privilege.

Other critical work on the *The García Girls*, such as Joan M. Hoffman's "She Wants to be Called Yolanda Now," concentrates, like many other readings of Latina texts, exclusively on how immigrants, in this case the Garcías, manage their lives in the United States.[24] Hoffman says:

> All of these girls—Carla, Sandra, Yolanda and Sofía—do come to some trouble in the New World. . . . As the title of the novel suggests, not only words, but also the manner of speech is significant to the story of the García girls' coming-of-age in America. The struggle to master a second language is a constant reminder to these girls of their weakened position as strangers in a new land (21–22).

On the one hand, Hoffman acknowledges that the girls suffer from a weakened position as a result of being immigrants; yet on the other hand, she champions that same identity. The article ends with the following remark about Yolanda:

> As troubled as it may be—by memory or failed love or fragmented identity or that precarious tightrope that is the immigrant's life—Yolanda still has spirit in her, she still has her art, her writing, her refuge. With that she will always be able to invent what she needs to survive (26).

Hoffman makes a case for reading the novel almost exclusively along the lines of the U.S. rhetoric of individuality and individual immigrant spirit. She concentrates on what is most typical about immigrant struggles and ends with the suggestion that even though Yolanda is in a precarious position as an immigrant, she has become sufficiently Americanized to realize that she can "invent" her own life. The foregrounding of Yolanda's "identity"—though neither Dominican nor U.S./American per se—serves to keep the novel well within the horizons of a U.S. nationalist paradigm.

This tendency to champion the tough, adaptive spirit of immigrants while defending their identity rights can be traced in sociohistorical scholarship on (im)migration as well. For instance, Mary Chamberlain in her introduction to the edited volume *Caribbean Migration*, a broad and instructive examination of the phenomenon of mobility from and through the Caribbean, states of the project that it "shifts the focus away from the causes of migration toward the nature and meaning of the migration experience, a shift that has radical implications for those concerned with the consequences of migration and its future."[25] It results in a form of analysis that attempts to capture what she calls the "vibrant culture of transnational and circular migration, in the home and the host countries" (10). In this shift, the focus on migrant *culture* can become celebratory—as signaled in the terms "vibrancy of culture." Take here as another example Peggy Levitt's cultural profile of Dominican (im)migrants in her book *The Transnational Villagers*.[26] While the latter places its findings within a global economic and social context, it nevertheless exhibits a tendency to rely on the descriptive language and metaphors of a more cosmopolitan narrative of (im)migration. Emphasizing the continuous contact between the residents of the Dominican city of Miraflores and Boston, Levitt writes:

> Though electricity goes off nightly for weeks at a stretch, nearly every household has a television, VCR, or compact disc player. And although it takes months to get a phone installed in Santo Domingo, the Dominican capital, Mirafloreños can get phone service in their homes almost immediately after they request it (2).

"Because someone is always traveling between Boston and the Island," she goes on to say, "there is a continuous, circular flow of goods, news, and information. As a result when someone is ill, cheating on his or her spouse, or finally granted a visa, the news spreads as quickly in Jamaica Plain as it does on the streets of Miraflores"(3). There are a couple of points here that are especially worth considering. While Levitt does not state this, the mainland-island networks through which flow the goods, news, and information mentioned above are not unlike the financial networks connecting cities such as New York, London, and Beijing—networks that appear to transcend unevenness within and across national boundaries so as to produce a culture of transnational cosmopolitanism. Invoking the gossip that travels faster between Boston and Miraflores than between Miraflores and Santo Domingo feeds into this same cosmopolitan narrative of mobility, even if unintentionally. Emphasis is placed on cosmopolitan interconnectedness rather than, say, on the uneven distribution of electricity.

Nevertheless, such metanarratives of (im)migration are still highly instructive when placed next to the critical neat narratives informing the scholarship on the *García Girls*. The details provided by Levitt show the extent to which the lives of Dominican immigrants in Boston are lived in continuous contact with the lives of those who remain on the island—a reality elided in the fetishized identity-based reading of immigrant culture and in narratives of assimilation within the United States. Chamberlain's edited volume, while tending to foreground the cultural and to celebrate the ways in which women adapt and change in the face of an obligatory mobility, nevertheless opens up new ways to consider the "links between subjectivity and material life" (11).[27] Take, for example, Elizabeth Thomas-Hope's "Globalization and the Development of Caribbean Migration," which situates the Caribbean colonies from the "outset as part of the wider global political economy."[28] Thomas-Hope analyzes the way that mercantilism, the trans-Atlantic slave trade, and the plantation were already signs of globalization. The essays in *Caribbean Migrations*, despite sharing with the identity-based work on U.S. (im)migrant literary fiction a focus on the *culture* of (im)migration, help to bring to light the *connections* between the material and the cultural.

One of the reasons that *The García Girls* has been so readily accepted into the canon of American literary studies can be inferred in the tendency of scholarship to emphasize the novel as a story about girls growing up in New York as "Latinas," trying to assimilate within the United States while still holding on to Dominican cultural practices. This is a real aspect of the novel—resulting perhaps from a need to keep up with a demand from publishers and readers for coming-to-the-U.S. (and finding-liberation) narratives—but their emphasis tends to be encouraged by scholarship that highlights identity-based readings. One can, to be sure, read certain aspects of *The García Girls* as reproducing dominant ideologies. For example, growing up in the United States, the girls rebel against what they see as their old world parents. In an effort to preserve their Dominican cultural practices, the parents send the girls to the Dominican

Republic in the summers during their teenage years. Yet the girls experience their parents as overbearing and overprotective because of these very same cultural practices—a constant source of struggle in the family. The resolution of their scuffles is described as follows: "It was a regular revolution: constant skirmishes. Until the time we took open aim and won, and our summers—if not our lives—became our own" (111). The fact that their skirmishes are described as a "revolution" seems to resonate with the title of Ortiz-Márquez's essay "From Third World Politics to First World Practices." But the "revolution" in the Dominican Republic concerns the political situation that had implicated Carlos García (and by extension his family) in a plot to kill Trujillo, a situation from which they eventually had to flee. The "revolution" in the United States is about the girls being able to stay out late at night and go to school dances. It is precisely these teenage scuffles, presented within the context of an old/new world binary as the García girls try to figure out their place in their new environment, that become the focus of readings that emphasize women's identity formation and self-assertion as though outside the patriarchal old world, but also as though outside a dominant and oppressive *new* world.[29] Of course, one could also read such an episode, conveyed tongue in cheek, as a commentary on a U.S., metropolitan form of life in which the right to stay out could be even thought of as a "revolution."

What is most important here is how the concept of immigration itself allows critics to place *The García Girls* in a position to repudiate old world politics just as immigrants are seen to repudiate their homelands in search of a better life. Yet they are also expected to have the freedom in the United States to preserve those old world cultural practices. Furthermore, it is by staging the "revolution" of teenage rebellion that the urgency of cultural preservation—and women's need to be bearers of this preservation—is conveyed. That is, we have here a "critical" discourse that demands the preservation of Latino culture and yet at the same time is able to argue for the need for women to be outside of it. The revolution to overthrow Trujillo in the Dominican Republic turns into the revolution of keeping one's cultural identity in New York. Moreover, the old/new cultural practices dimension of the novel is best understood when read in connection with the rest of the novel, as well as its sociohistorical milieu; otherwise we can run the risk of decontextualizing the above characteristics.

To summarize, readings of *The García Girls* like the one proposed by Ortiz-Márquez appropriate the narrative's global frame of reference so as to make more credible and politically acceptable a localized situating of the novel as

"U.S./American." Meanwhile, however, these approaches to the novel, in another move of displacement and consolidation, remain within the overarching framework of domestic multicultural identity issues. Either way, *The García Girls* is understood exclusively in the terms of a gendered and racialized identity effectively precluding other possible readings.

The New Context of (Im)migration

Notwithstanding how readily *The García Girls* has been appropriated by a domestic multiculturalism, however, I propose that the book *also* provides a place to examine some of the operative assumptions about (im)migration and how (im)migration as a rhetorical strategy often works to obscure the role of the United States in producing the phenomenon of immigration. That is, there may be ways in which the novel itself, in conversation with the (im)migration experience, refuses easy categorization within accepted U.S. literary paradigms of localized ethnic identity. I analyze some of these aspects of the novel below. I do not wish to produce a comprehensive reading here, but rather to merely point toward some ways in which we can see this recalcitrant aspect of Alvarez's narrative.

Local vs. Global

Insofar as *The García Girls* is ascribed to a "marginal literature" and counterposed to dominant literary categories, its characters are seen—or made—to fit the more U.S.-localized and "resistant" category of a Latina ethnicity. However, the book elides this easy localization of ethnicity at one level simply because the characters move back and forth and their lives are in continuous contact with Dominicans on the island itself. Recall that the girls' grandparents already live in New York because of their grandfather's post at the United Nations. But they also spend a lot of time in the Dominican Republic, bringing presents for the girls and thus prompting them to imagine a world beyond their hometown even before their own emigration. The girls' father, Carlos, also goes to New York often, and return visits to Santo Domingo remain frequent after emigration to the United States.

Moreover, the novel resists any positing of the local as a site of critical opposition—not only because the characters travel back and forth with such regularity, but also because the local itself varies in different contexts. To see what I mean here by the variation of the local, consider the following. Antiglobalization scholarship sometimes posits the nations of the "global South" as localities that can counter the forces of globalization. The Dominican Republic, as depicted in *The García Girls*, can be read on the surface as precisely that kind of locality in relationship to the globality of the United States. Thus, to return to the beginning of the novel, Yolanda's visit to the Dominican Republic becomes the opportunity for various characters to stress the "localism" of Santo Domingo in relationship to the global United States. Her aunts greet her by saying, "Welcome to your little island." The cousins join in a chorus for her, singing, "Here she comes, Miss America." Yolanda, by the mere fact that she has been living in the United States, represents that country to her cousins. Her family encourages her to speak in Spanish, which she describes as her "native" tongue, thus choosing at least for the moment to assume an uncomplicated connection between herself, the Spanish language, and the Dominican Republic. But beneath the surface these easy connections and the sense of an uncomplicated locality rapidly fall apart. Recall the opening scene again:

> The old aunts lounge in the white wicker armchairs, flipping open their fans, snapping them shut . . . [T]he aunts seem little changed since five years ago when Yolanda was last on the Island. Sitting amongst the aunts in less comfortable dining chairs, the cousins are flashes of color in turquoise jumpsuits and tight jersey dresses. . . . Before anyone has turned to greet her in the entryway, Yolanda sees herself as they will, shabby in a black cotton skirt and jersey top, sandals on her feet, her wild black hair held back with a hairband. Like a missionary, her cousins will say, like one of those Peace Corps girls who have let themselves go so as to do dubious good in the world. (3–4)

In addition to raising questions about behavioral norms and Yolanda's appearance, this passage suggests that the precise context in which the United States is seen as "global" is that of U.S. intervention in its various forms, including the Peace Corps. Note here as well that while those in the Dominican Republic come, for the moment, to occupy the "local" position (the aunts who "seem little changed") and Yolanda the global, when she is in the States, Yolanda is also part of a different kind of locality, that of a Hispanic woman or Latina. In addition, if the local can, in some sense, be said to represent accumulated cultural practices in the Dominican Republic, then how to account for Americanizing influences on the island? By the same logic, if we designate the U.S. "Latina" as the site of the local, then how to account for differences of class structure within this category, not to mention the differences of race/gender/language that give people within such categories varied access to the dominant sphere? Since the United States can claim Latino/a cultural practices as, in one sense, within its borders, it can posit itself as both a local and a global nation. The point of view according to which localized cultural practices are always a refuge from the global and in opposition to it thus becomes extremely complicated in relationship to the newer immigrant cultures and literatures. What then do we do with those aspects of the novel that complicate the equation of the local with an ethnically marginal position as construed by some identity-based readings?

Aside from telling the story of how its main characters become good U.S. subjects, complete with phases of teenage rebellion, the novel simultaneously points to the fact that such a negotiation of identity cannot necessarily be summoned to provide critical resistance to dominant cultures. Rather, the novel speaks to a condition in which, due to the U.S. presence in the Dominican Republic, one's identity shifts in relationship to the United States well before any physical act of immigration. We learn that Carlos is working with the U.S. State Department in the Dominican Republic in organizing against the dictator. Victor Hubbard, whom the girls call Tio Vic, a consul at the American embassy who is in fact a CIA agent, helps the family escape. Hubbard is presented as a good man who has followed through on his word to help get the failed anti-Trujillo conspirators out of the country should any problems arise. "It wasn't his fault that the State Department chickened out of the plot they had him organize" (202). His "orders changed midstream from organize the underground and get that SOB out to hold your horses, let's take a second look around and see what's best for us" (211). That is, caught in the turmoil of rapidly changing political events, the García family is sketched against a backdrop of what is already a complex historical account.

But this history is mentioned in much of the scholarship on the novel in a cursory way and often with little or no reference to the history of U.S. intervention. Perhaps inadvertently, this recalls what is often the downplaying of such intervention in much of the historiography produced about the Trujillo period, which, in a reflection of the lurid representations of Trujillo himself as evil incarnate, has tended to represent the actions of the United States (which installed the dictator in the 1930s) as exceptional, a necessary departure from the supposedly more benign parameters of the Good Neighbor Policy or the Alliance for Progress.[30] It is true, of course, that political events—especially the U.S. military invasion of the country in 1965 to overthrow the left-leaning Juan Bosch government and restore military rule—were the impetus for the first large waves of Dominican emigration to the United States.[31] But, although the phenomenon of (im)migration from the Dominican Republic and from the Caribbean in general cannot be truthfully represented without an understanding of this kind of political chronology, limiting oneself to chronological events alone runs the risk of obscuring the larger phenomenon of mobility in the context of the globalization of the region itself. I cannot adequately summarize here the breadth of the historical and economic research into the structural causes of the Dominican exodus to the United States, but work by scholars such James Ferguson, Eric Williams, Tom Barry, Peggy Levitt, Greg Grandin, Sherri Grasmuck, and Patricia Pessar allows us to see how the larger history of (im)migration from the island can be traced to the very socioeconomic conditions that have themselves given rise to the history of U.S. occupation and intervention.[32] A careful study of the history of what has been, since the end of the ironically more nationalist and protectionist regime under Trujillo, the ever more merciless yoking of Dominican society to the needs of international (largely U.S.) capital, whether via IMF austerity programs or the forced conversion of the Dominican Republic into a tourism-based economy that has left the better part of the local population with little choice except to emigrate, helps to correct the limitations of American literary scholarship. This is a picture of suffering and hardship that is the unexceptional equivalent of the "exceptional" torture and brutality inflicted by Trujillo and by U.S. neocolonial aggression—and that Dominicans must contend with whether they leave the island or not.

While in some ways limited, too, by a more dramatic, "political" understanding of the causes of Dominican emigration, Alvarez's novel allows us to see not only the role of the United States in forcing the Garcías to flee the island, but also how their plight is symptomatic of interconnected economic, political, and cultural factors that produce (im)migration to the United States as a general phenomenon, and how these factors also affect those who will never (im)migrate. As James Ferguson has noted in *Far from Paradise*, U.S. popular culture in the form of television, films, and other media already fuels the desire of many Dominicans to reside in the United States. Even before emigration, the García girls are introduced to the world of New York through the gifts that their grandparents and father bring back with them. Given that the Garcías already have the money, the class status, and the family connections required to be quasi-"Americanized" before emigrating, it seems only natural for the family to do the logical thing and emigrate. However, even those who cannot and will probably never emigrate are also formed by this same kind of experience. Thus, for example, the U.S. magazines and television programs available in the Dominican Republic translate into Americanized cultural practices not only for the members of the prominent García family, but also for those who work for them as servants. The latter also contend with ideas of their own identity in relationship to the United States—a relationship that is again not indicative of critical resistance but rather of a desire to be part of the dominant order. Carla, the oldest sister, tells of how her mother, Laura, characterizes Gladys, one of their servants: "[she] was only a country girl who didn't know any better than to sing popular tunes in the house and wear her kinky hair in rollers all week long, then comb it out for Sunday mass in hairdos copied from American magazines my mother had thrown out" (258). Gladys, too, dreams of the metropolis: "'I wonder where I'll be in thirty two-years,' Gladys mused. A glazed look came across her face; she smiled. 'New York,' she said dreamily and began to sing the refrain from the popular New York merengue that was on the radio night and day" (260). She is in some sense already practicing to be in New York before she gets there, and it does not fundamentally matter whether she ever gets there: her desires, too, are formed by the particular environment of transnational migration.

There is little here about fleeing from bad gender politics or poverty to the generous shores of a new country. Instead, the García family's immigration is portrayed in the novel itself as interconnected with the economic and political integration of the United States and the Dominican Republic. By not taking such conditions into account, and reading the novel—and immigration itself—exclusively in terms of a racialized and gendered identity, scholarship places itself in the position of regarding such interconnections, together with the current conditions that determine the experience of (im)migration, as secondary to a multiculturalist/identity politics framework—a framework that does not itself extend much, if at all, beyond U.S. borders. Or if it does, it is subordinated to and divorced from the historical and socioeconomic conditions of (im)migration.

The pressure on critics, readers, and teachers to rethink and update the field of immigrant/ethnic literatures in the face of globalization results in a displacement that is at the same time a reconsolidation of the U.S. nationalist tendencies underlying the field itself. Reading "(im)migration" as primarily a process affecting identity formation produces certain valid insights but leaves many questions unanswered. In the end, such "globalizing" practices, in an effort to resituate and resecure scholars' own disciplinary loci, are unable to address and account for certain aspects of the texts themselves. But the question still remains: what are the implications for disciplinary practices as we engage the theories of globalization? Does the fact that categories such as the immigrant/ethnic have come under critical scrutiny mean that those categories ought to be displaced in favor of new ones? As I have shown, questioning nationalist paradigms, identities, and notions of immigration linked to these ideas does not necessarily mean that we should abandon them. We can certainly ask how it is that texts both produce and are produced by ideas of immigration, identity, nationalism, and globalization. But it is also fruitful to read the texts, especially contemporary narratives of (im)migration, for the ways that they discover contemporary historical and social processes on their own terms. Whatever else they show, newer immigrant/ethnic texts should dispel the notion that a culturalist identity politics can, on its own, become a refuge from and provide critical resistance to the contemporary forces of globalization.

Notes

1.   The use of the term *American* to signify the United States is obviously problematic. My own usage of the term in this manner is restricted to accepted conventional categories of study such as "American literature." In some places, I have used "U.S./American" as a modifier. In addition, I have utilized the term *Americanization* since it has been historically employed to describe the political and economic influence wielded by the United States.
2.   Wai Chi Dimock and Lawrence Buell, *Shades of the Planet: American Literature as World Literature* (Princeton, N.J.: Princeton University Press, 2007).
3.   Janice Radway, in her 1998 presidential address to the American Studies Association, proposed changing the name of the association and possibly dropping the term *American.* "What's in a Name? Presidential Address to the American Studies Association, 20 November 1998," *American Quarterly* 51 no. 1 (March): 1-32.
4   See, for example, Carole Levander and Robert Levine, eds. *American Hemispheric Studies* (New Brunswick, N.J.: Rutgers University Press, 2008); John Carlos Rowe, *The New American Studies* (Minneapolis: University of Minnesota Press, 2002); Donald Pease and Robyn Wiegeman, eds. *The Futures of American Studies* (Durham, N.C.: Duke University Press, 2002).
5.   Jonathan Arac, "Global and Babel: Language and Planet in American Literature," in *Shades of the Planet*, ed. Dimock and Buell (Princeton, N.J.: Princeton University Press, 2007).
6.   This strategy is a broader phenomenon in the field of literary studies. Marjorie Perloff's 2006 MLA presidential address makes a case for a return to aesthetics and the "merely literary," advocating single author studies by positioning Samuel Beckett as a global writer because his work is globally read and celebrated. A further example of the attempt to globalize that consolidates nationalists paradigms can be found in Stephen Greenblatt's essay "Racial Memory and Literary History," published in the January 2001 special issue of the *PMLA* on "Globalizing Literary Studies." Greenblatt makes an argument similar to Perloff's about Shakespeare being a global writer. He argues that "Shakespeare may never have left England, yet his work is already global in its representational range" (59). Arguing that Shakespeare's works are read globally, he leaves the author's centrality in the canon intact.
7.   Benjamin Franklin, *Autobiography*, ed. J. A. Leo Lemay and P. M. Zall (New York: W. W. Norton, 1986); Ralph Waldo Emerson, *Complete Essays and Other Writings* (New York: Modern Library, 1950).
8.   Michael Lind, *The Next American Nation: The New Nationalism and the Fourth American Revolution* (New York: Free Press, 1995).
9.   Arjun Appadurai, "Patriotism and Its Futures," *Public Culture* (Spring 1993): 423.

10. Anzia Yezierska, *Bread Givers* (Garden City, N.Y: Doubleday, Page, 1925).
11. Abraham Cahan, *The Rise of David Levinsky* (New York: Harper, 1966).
12. Esmeralda Santiago, *América's Dream* (New York: Harper Perennial, 1997).
13. Julia Alvarez, *How the García Girls Lost their Accents* (Chapel Hill, N.C.: Algonquin Books, 1991).
14. See the following essays published in Avery Gordon and Christopher Newfield, eds. *Mapping Multiculturalism* (Minneapolis, MN: University of Minnesota Press, 1996): John Cruz, "From Farce to Tragedy: Reflections on the Reification of Race at Century's End," 19-39; Lisa Lowe, "Imagining Los Angeles in the Production of Multiculturalism," 413-23; Wanheema Lubiano, "Like Being Mugged by a Metaphor: Multiculturalism and State Narratives," 64-75; Avery Gordon and Christopher Newfield, Multiculturalism's Unfinished Business," 76-115.
15. Jodi Melamed, "The Spirit of Neoliberalism from Racial Liberalism to Neoliberal Multiculturalism," *Social Text 89*, 24.4 (Winter 2006): 1.
16. Ibid.
17. Ibid.,16.
18. Ibid.
19. See, for example, the work of E. San Juan Jr., Michael Omi, and Howard Winant, and Paul Smith.
20. Lisa Lowe, *Immigrant Acts: On Asian American Cultural Politics* (Durham, N.C.: Duke University Press, 1996), 86.
21. Although the earlier immigrant works also spoke about the way in which the United States encouraged immigration (Cahan's character, David Levinsky, says that in Russia, he was told that U.S. streets were paved with gold), the passage to the United States for these characters was characterized as very clear and definitive.
22. Much critical writing on Julia Alvarez's novel focuses on the aspects that speak to identity construction of the characters as they make adjustments and adapt to lives in the United States. See for example, Ellen Mayock, "The Bicultural Construction of Self in Cisneros, Alvarez, and Santiago," *Bilingual Review/La Revista Bilingue* 23.3 (September-December 1998): 223–29; William Luis, "A Search for Identity in Julia Alvarez's *How the García Girls Lost their Accents*," *Callaloo* 23.3 (Summer, 2000): 839–49; Julie Barak, " 'Turning and Turning in the Widening Gyre': A Second Coming into Language in Julia Alvarez's *How the Garcia Girls Lost Their Accents*," *MELUS* (Spring 1998): 159–76.
23. Lucía M. Suárez, "Julia Alvarez and the Anxiety of Latina Representation," *Meridians: Feminism, Race, Transnationalism* 5.1 (2004): 117–45; Pauline Newton, *Transcultural Women of Late-Twentieth-Century U.S. American Literature* (Burlington, Vt.: Ashgate, 2005); Maribel Ortíz-Márquez, "From Third World Politics to First World Practices: Contemporary Latina Writers in the United States," in *Interventions: Feminist Dialogues on Third World Women's Literature and Film*, ed. Bishnupriya Ghosh and Brinda Bose, 227–44 (New York: Garland, 1999).
24. Joan M. Hoffman, " 'She Wants to Be Called Yolanda Now': Identity, Language, and the Third Sister in *How the García Girls Lost Their Accents*," *Bilingual Review/La Revista Bilingue* (January-April 1998): 21–27.
25. Mary Chamberlain, ed., *Caribbean Migration: Globalized Identities* (New York: Routledge, 1998), 10.
26. Peggy Levitt, *The Transnational Villagers* (Berkeley: University of California Press, 2001).
27. See, for example, Helma Lutz's study of Surinamese mothers and daughters. Helma Lutz, "The Legacy of Migration: Immigrant Mothers and Daughters and the Process of Intergenerational Transmission," in *Caribbean Migration*, ed. Chamberlain, 95–108.
28. Elizabeth Thomas-Hope, "Globalization and the Development of a Caribbean Migration," in *Caribbean Migration*, ed. Chamberlain, 188–99.
29. Generational conflict is a rather old theme in immigrant narratives. For example, Anzia Yezierska's work in the 1920s depicts the parent's "old ways" as clearly a result of their experience in Eastern Europe, which is then placed against what is presented as the newer and more Americanized ways of the children.
30. See for example: Russell Crandell, *Gunboat Democracy U.S. Interventions in the Dominican Republic, Grenada and Panama* (New York: Rowan and Littlefield, 2006).
31. Lucía Suárez for instance cites the U.S. invasion in 1965 and the post-invasion period until 1970 that produced a major wave of emigration from the Dominican Republic (123).

32. Eric Williams, *From Columbus to Castro: The History of the Caribbean 1492–1969* (New York: Vintage, 1984); Sherri Grasmuck and Patricia Pessar, *Between Two Islands: Dominican International Migration* (Berkeley: University of California Press, 1991); Tom Barry and Beth Wood, et al., eds. *The Other Side of Paradise* (New York: Grove Press, 1984); James Ferguson, *Far from Paradise: Introduction to the Caribbean Development* (London: Latin America Bureau, 1990); Greg Grandin, *Empire's Workshop: Latin America, the United States and the Rise of the New Imperialism* (New York: Metropolitan Books, 2006).

Police Riot on the Net: From "Citizen Journalism" to Comunicación Popular

Sasha Costanza-Chock

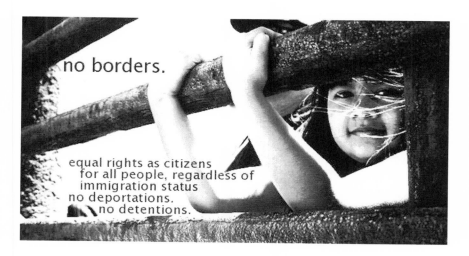

Figure 1.
Graphic from noborderscamp.org.

*A*merican Quarterly readers probably don't need to be reminded that the militarization of borders and the expansion of the state apparatus of surveillance, raids, detentions, and deportations are key control mechanisms for capitalist white supremacist patriarchal power in the United States of America. The consolidation of Immigration and Naturalization Services into the Department of Homeland Security was followed post-9/11 by so-called Special Registration, then a new wave of detentions, deportations, and "rendering" of "suspected terrorists" to Guantánamo and other secret military prisons for indefinite detention and torture without trial. In 2006, Immigration and Customs Enforcement (ICE) increased the number of beds for detainees to 27,500, opened a new 500-bed detention center for families with children in Williamson County, Texas, and set a new agency record of

187,513 "Alien Removals."[1] By the spring of 2006, it became politically feasible for the Republican House of Representatives to pass the infamous HR 4437, the proposed Sensenbrenner bill. Sensenbrenner would have criminalized the state of being an undocumented person and the act of providing shelter or aid to an undocumented person, making felons of millions of undocumented folks, their families and friends, and service workers, including clergy, social service workers, and educators.[2]

The response to Sensenbrenner was the largest wave of mass mobilizations in U.S. history. March, April, and May of 2006 saw major marches in every metropolis as well as in countless smaller cities and towns. Half a million people took to the streets in Chicago, a million in Los Angeles, hundreds of thousands more in New York, Houston, San Diego, Miami, Atlanta—the list could go on for pages. The surging strength of the migrant rights movement was built through the hard work of hundreds of organizations, including those that work to organize the base directly, those that function as regional or national coordinating hubs, those that intervene in policy debates, and the Spanish-language media that support them, including *locutores* [radio hosts], papers, and television channels. The rapid growth of this movement was reflected in the slogan "The sleeping giant is now awake!" and its power briefly caught the political class off guard. The Sensenbrenner bill died, crushed by the *gigante* of popular mobilization.

Quickly reorganizing, the state launched a new wave of ICE raids. Simultaneously there was an explosion of right-wing information warfare stretching from the mass base of talk radio up through the national news networks, spearheaded by racist, anti-immigrant talking heads on Fox News and by Lou Dobbs on CNN. The renewed attack from the Right came to a crescendo by May Day 2007. On the anniversary of the historic 2006 May Day marches, hundreds of thousands of people again took the streets across the country. This time, though, the LAPD prepared to deal what they hoped would be a crushing blow in downtown Los Angeles.

Macarthur Park, only a few city blocks to the west of L.A.'s main business district, was initially built in the 1880s as a white, middle-class vacation destination surrounded by luxury hotels. The area around the park became a working-class African American neighborhood during the 1960s, and once this transition took place, the city withdrew park maintenance resources. By the 1980s the park had gained a media reputation as a dangerous and violent place. In the 1990s the area was again transformed, this time into a working-class Latino neighborhood.[3] It is currently represented in the Anglo press as a danger zone of "gangbangers," drug dealers, sex workers, and general racialized urban chaos, and is especially infamous as an area where fake identification cards can be easily purchased. This portrayal of Macarthur Park persists despite the actual decline of violent crime in the area and the park's present-day heavy use by Latino/a immigrant families, especially by children and teens on the soccer field, picnickers with food and blankets, and young lovers who relax under the park's shade trees. On the afternoon of May Day 2007, Macarthur Park's usual crowd of hundreds was multiplied tenfold as people streamed in for a post-march rally organized by the Multi-Ethnic Immigrant Worker Organizing Network (MIWON), a coalition that included the Garment Worker Center (GWC), Koreatown Immigrant Worker Alliance (KIWA), Pilipino Worker Center (PWC), Institute of Popular Education of Southern California (IDEPSCA), and the Coalition for Humane Immigrant Rights of Los Angeles (CHIRLA).

One moment, white-clad families, including many small children and elderly folks, were relaxing in the park with the bells of ice cream vendors ringing in the air and the smell of bacon-wrapped hot dogs wafting across the soccer field which had been transformed into a dance floor as bands performed from the MIWON sound truck. The next moment, people were screaming and running in a mass panic as around five hundred officers, many in full riot gear, used batons and rubber bullets to attack the peaceful crowd, injuring dozens and hospitalizing several. Members of the media, including Christina Gonzalez of Fox News affiliate KTTV 11, Pedro Sevcec of Telemundo, Patricia Nazario of KPCC, Ernesto Arce from KPFK, and reporters from L.A. Indymedia, were also attacked and injured by police.[4] The official line from LAPD chief William Bratton holds that there was a communication breakdown in the chain of command that led to a ". . . significant use of force while attempting to address the illegal and disruptive actions of 50 to 100 agitators who were not a part of the larger group of thousands of peaceful demonstrators."[5] Longtime observers of the LAPD argue that by the time the riot squad was deployed on the edge of the park, the decision had already been made to clear the crowd by force. Regardless of whether the attack on the peaceful crowd and reporters was a breakdown of communication or a calculated tactic to instill fear, the result was the same: images of the brutal police riot filled TV screens in L.A. for days, sending a clear message that it was time for the *gigante* to sit down, shut up, and get back to work.

The repressive atmosphere continued to escalate nationwide for the rest of the summer of 2007. The spirit of Sensenbrenner was revived, if masked, in

MAY 1ST CELEBRATION

Multi-ethnic Immigrant Workers Organizing Network

Figure 2.
Graphic from MIWON flyer for May Day 2007.

the Secure Borders, Economic Opportunity, and Immigration Reform Act of 2007 (S. 1348). This time, the bill was portrayed as a "compromise" but continued to focus on border militarization and policing: it included funding for 300 miles of vehicle barriers, 105 camera and radar towers, and 20,000 more Border Patrol agents, while simultaneously restructuring visa criterion around "high skill" workers for the so-called knowledge economy.[6] That bill fell apart by June, but at the time of this writing it is clear that border militarization will continue, detentions and deportations increase, and raids intensify, while there is little to no chance for meaningful legalization legislation, let alone amnesty. In July of 2007, three *billion* dollars in new "border security" funding was approved.[7] There has also been a complete, and completely unsurprising, failure of the mass media to discuss either the root causes of migration or the only per-

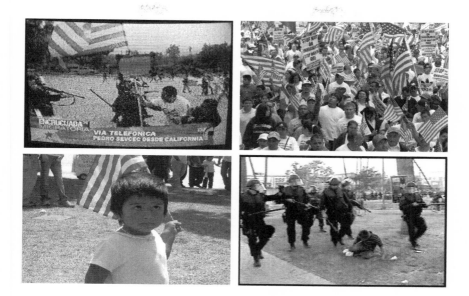

Figure 3.
Macarthur Park May Day images posted
to la.indymedia.org.

manent meaningful solution in an age of unrestricted cross-border capital flows: an open border policy.

English-language news channels (FOX and CNN) play key roles in the information war that swirls around migration and immigrant rights, alongside right-wing talk radio. Of course, Spanish language press, including nationally syndicated networks Telemundo and Univisión, as well as commercial radio stations, provide counterbalancing coverage of the movement. In fact, Spanish language commercial radio has not only covered protests, but played a significant role in announcing them and mobilizing people. This is widely known and reported on in the English-language press[8] and has recently been documented in a study by Carmen Gonzalez, who found in a survey that radio was in fact the key media used to inform people about the marches in Los Angeles (friends and family were the primary source of information, followed by radio).[9] A recent study by Graciela Orozco for the Social Science Research Council also analyzes the important mobilization role played by Radio Bilingue, a more than two decades old nonprofit network of Latino community radio stations with six affiliates in California and satellite distribution to over a hundred communities in the United States, Puerto Rico, and Mexico.[10]

However, in the rest of this review I want to focus not on radio but on the role of popular communication online, especially grassroots video activists, immigrant rights organizers, and everyday people participating in the mobilizations who later post video documentation to the Internet. My discussion of movement video online will be grounded in my own experience as an active videomaker within the Independent Media Center network (www.indymedia.org), a transnational network of grassroots mediamakers that emerged out of the alterglobalization movement during and after the protests against the 1999 World Trade Organization ministerial in Seattle.[11]

Online Video and Popular Communication

As audiences for traditional mass media (TV and newspapers especially) continue to shrink and fragment, the media industry is increasingly turning to new business models that either entirely or partially rely on capturing revenue from the monetization of user generated content and social networking labor.[12] Online video and social networking sites are big business (YouTube was famously acquired by Google for $1.6 billion, kicking off the newest round of venture capital frenzy around online video), and they also replicate the structural inequalities of race, class, and gender present throughout the media industry as a whole, both in representation and employment practices.[13] Movement appropriation of commercial "social media" sites can certainly be an effective visibility strategy, but activists need to clearly understand what else their participation in these sites produces.

As a short aside, I'd like to clarify that "citizen journalism" is dead on arrival as an organizing concept for participatory reporting by noncitizens. Alternative media, grassroots media, community media, or *comunicación popular* are more useful framings for the immigrant rights movement.[14] This is not just a quibble over terminology: mass detentions, deportations, and police riots against peaceful crowds fail to ignite nationwide coverage and protest in part because of a deep lack of connection between "citizen journalists" and the immigrant rights movement. Just imagine the rage and mobilization if in 2006 more than 187,000 white antiwar activists had been detained, disappeared, and held in detention centers for months without trial. In some ways it's simple: just like the "old media," the "new media" is dominated by white, liberal, college-educated males.

Yet this observation doesn't diminish the real importance of the Internet as an organizing tool in the current wave of immigrant rights activism, especially by Latino youth. For example, students in L.A. Unified School District used MySpace and SMS (text messaging) to help communicate and coordinate walkouts that saw 20,000 to 40,000 students take the streets during the week following the March 25, 2006, marches.[15]

As has been widely documented, the Internet, especially the rise of social networking sites like MySpace and YouTube, has opened possibilities for movement appropriation, especially for *autorepresentación* [self-representation] via text, photos, videos, and audio.[16] This is true even as social networking sites are also spaces where users replicate gender, class, and race divisions (for example, see danah boyd on how Indian Orkut users have replicated the caste system and on the class division between MySpace and Facebook).[17] At the same time, in business-speak, "User Generated Content" means free cultural product for monetization and cross-licensing, "participation" means free user data to mine and sell to advertisers, and all user activity is subject to surveillance and censorship.

This latter thread was taken up by Dmytri Kleiner and Brian Wyrick in a recent article for *Mute* magazine titled "Infoenclosure 2.0," in which they describe Web 2.0 as "a venture capitalist's paradise where investors pocket the value produced by unpaid users, ride on the technical innovations of the free software movement, and kill off the decentralising potential of peer-to-peer production."[18] In a similar vein, Andrew Lowenthal dissects the business model of Web 2.0 media darlings such as YouTube and MySpace:

> One of the key business models for these "Web 2.0" start ups has been the basic idea of providing an infrastructure and technology for users and then selling those eyes to advertisers and the contributor community to a larger company—it happened with Flickr, YouTube, MySpace and more. There is a huge rush of companies trying to create the next big site to bring in the people and make their pot of gold. Users need to become far more savvy as to the imbalance in power that is being generated and who they are helping make millionaires.[19]

This is an important and necessary step toward critique and education around the extension of the media and cultural industries into the Internet. However, for many involved in social movement activity, surveillance and censorship are concerns that are at least as significant as (if not more than) the monetization and value extraction realized through content licensing and advertising revenue. For instance, immediately following the May Day police riot, several people quickly posted video clips to YouTube and MySpace, as well as to personal video blogs and to the Los Angeles Independent Media Center (http://la.indymedia.org).

Figure 4.
Walkout Warriors sticker, seen on a
MySpace user's page.

During the first police commission hearing following May Day, LAPD Chief William Bratton publicly mentioned that police were reviewing all the police videos, the surveillance cameras from the park, and all the clips that had been posted to YouTube, in order to understand what took place and also to identify and track down those who resisted police violence.[20] Bratton's comments underscore the need for activists in the immigrant rights movement, as in all movements for social justice, to be aware of what may be done with the video they post online. In the immediate wake of the Macarthur Park police riot, Indymedia activists circulated this message via e-mail and posts to YouTube and MySpace, in English and Spanish:

> Be careful with the video you submit. Several things to keep in mind:
>
> 1. Don't upload ANY video that shows people doing anything illegal. The police are watching all these videos, so don't put evidence in their hands.
>
> 2. If you have to include a clip of someone, say, fighting back against the police, in order to show police brutality, be sure to blur the face of that person.
>
> 3. If you put clips on YouTube, keep this in mind: (a) you are doing free labor for YouTube and allowing them to make money from ads off of your content; (b) YouTube will take your material down as soon as LAPD or the feds ask them to; (c) YouTube will give your IP address to the police, which allows them to track the video to the person who uploaded it (you).

Figure 5.
Fox News coverage of Mayday 2007, reposted to YouTube, from youtube.com/watch?v=v7xO-GKmH2c.

So, YouTube may be a good way to get things seen, but it is NOT a safe or long-term solution for movement media. So what can you do?

Upload to noncommercial sites like archive.org, ourmedia.org, and indymedia.org (including video.indymedia.org). These sites won't make money off of you, and some of them (like Indymedia) won't track your IP address, won't take material down on request of the pigs, and will do everything they can to defend your rights to privacy and free speech if need be.

Don't hate the media—become the media![21]

In other words, social movements need to both appropriate corporate Web 2.0 spaces and use them to circulate their struggles, while educating themselves about corporate appropriation of mediamaking and social networking labor, state surveillance of social network sites, and the ease of corporate or state censorship of material on such sites. At the same time, they need to help build and participate in the already existing autonomous infrastructure of communication. Meanwhile, independent mediamakers, tech activists, bloggers, and other alternative and popular communicators should think about how they can contribute to training and capacity building for community-based organizations that are currently marginalized in both mass media and online spaces. This means doing the hard work of power-sharing (in mediamaking practices, equipment and infrastructure access, funding access, and so on) with grassroots, poor-led, community-based, people of color, youth-led, and queer organizations.

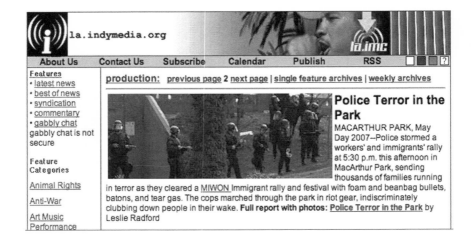

Figure 6.
Screenshot of la.indymedia.org
coverage of Macarthur Park.

Next Steps

This kind of analysis is already present among some movement organizations in the U.S. context, and is slowly gaining visibility. For example, during the U.S. Social Forum (USSF), a meeting of about 10,000 activists and organizers that took place in Atlanta in July of 2007, the Ida B. Wells Media Justice Center was planned with the explicit goals of partnering poor-led antipoverty organizations with media activists to share perspectives and skills, and work together on grassroots coverage.[22]

In terms of self-representation, on the one hand there is a need to continue pushing for better mass media coverage in both the English- and Spanish-language press, as well as to enter and utilize online corporate spaces that allow user-generated content; but there is also a need to develop a deeper critique of corporate media, which includes so-called Web 2.0. In the long run, more immigrant rights movement communication would ideally live on the back of a stronger autonomous communication infrastructure, using Free and Open Source Software (FOSS) in tandem with existing autonomous communication infrastructure, tools, and networks. To help achieve this goal, tech activists are busy enhancing the usability and functionality of FOSS and of activist-focused tools and nonprofit resources. There is a new generation of FOSS focused on the needs of media activists and social movement organizations,

¡**Gigante Despierta!** es una compilación en DVD de videos de las manifestaciones por los derechos de inmigrantes del año 2006. Tiene cortometrajes desde muchos lugares en todo el país.

Giant Awake! is a DVD compilation of compelling short films from all around the country, due to hit the streets in the weeks before Mayday 2007.

Es una memoria colectiva y una herramienta para inspirar la acción para el primero de Mayo de 2007, cuando el Gigante va a levantar la voz de nuevo para decir: ¡Somos un pueblo, sin fronteras! ¡Aqui estamos, y no nos vamos!

It is a collective memory and a tool to inspire action this MayDay 2007, when the Giant will raise its voice again to say: we are one people, without borders. We are here, and we are here to stay!

para pedir copias del DVD:

DVD pre-orders available:

www.gigantedespierta.org

Figure 7.
Gigante Despierta poster, from gigantedespierta.org.

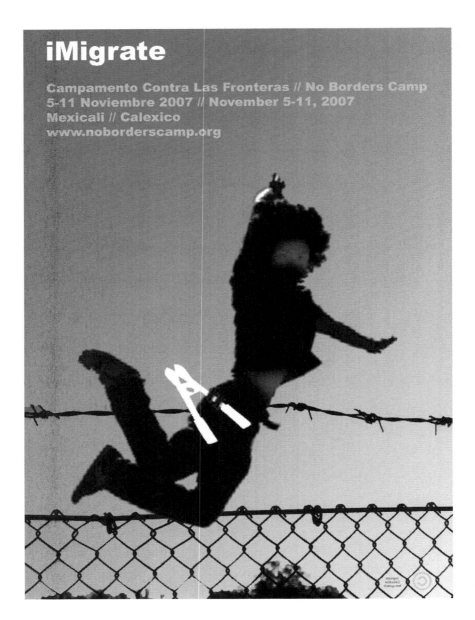

Figure 8.
iMigrate, by Shock, remixed by anonymous MySpace user.

from content management systems such as plumi (http://plumi.org) and filmforge (http://filmforge.koumbit.net), to content hosts such as the Internet Archive (http://www.archive.org), to decentralized content hosting such as indytorrents and v2v (http://www.v2v.cc), to application service providers such as civicspace (http://www.civicspace.org), to software for editing audio and video such as kino and audacity (http://audacity.sourceforge.net), and even entire FOSS operating systems tailored to activists and mediamakers, such as dyne:bolic (http://www.dynebolic.org).

One recent example of the mobilization of autonomous communication infrastructure in support of the immigrant rights movement is the *¡Gigante: Despierta!* project (full disclosure: this author participated in the project). This short film compilation was shot by independent videomakers across the country, gathered together using FOSS social bookmarking tool videobomb. org, coordinated online, cut in San Francisco and New York City, assembled in Los Angeles, and distributed around the country beginning in April 2007:

Pulling together short films from sixteen producers in different locations, the compilation was screened in community centers, universities, and independent cinemas nationwide in the weeks just before and after May Day 2007.

While many immigrant rights organizations have used offline popular communication as part of their organizing, most remain strapped for resources and lack capacity to bring popular communication online through autonomous (noncorporate, nonstate) tools and infrastructure. It is thus the responsibility of better-resourced tech activists, independent media makers, bloggers, and other communication activists to reach out to these organizations. Those tied to the "citizen journalist" label might want to publicly rethink their reasons for conceptually linking the right to speak in new communication spaces to legal membership in the nation-state. For their part, some immigrant rights organizations are already working hard to clarify their analysis of the cultural industries, both the mass media as well as the "new" online corporate spaces, and are developing a long-term strategy that doesn't rely solely on the "free as in beer" offerings of so-called Web 2.0 firms. As these pieces come together, we will all benefit from the mash-up of the rich history, tools, and skills of *comunicación popular* with the autonomous Internet.

Notes

1. ICE, "Fact Sheet: ICE Office of Detention and Removal," November 2, 2006, http://www.ice. gov/pi/news/factsheets/dro110206.htm (accessed August 20, 2007).
2. Immigrant Legal Resource Center, "Dangerous Immigration Legislation Pending in Congress," December 2005, http://www.ilrc.org/resources/hr4437_general.pdf (accessed August 21, 2007).
3. Jason Byrne, personal communication with the author, September 23, 2007.
4. Amy Goodman, "L.A. Immigration Protest: The Police 'Were Relentless. They Were Merciless,'" May 4, 2007, http://www.alternet.org/columnists/story/51454/?comments=view&cID=651184&pID=650213 (accessed August 25, 2007).
5. Bratton, William. May 2, 2007. Media Brief on Macarthur Park Disturbance, May 2, 2007 http://lapdblog.typepad.com/lapd_blog/2007/05/chief_bratton_b.html (accessed July 10, 2008).
6. Nicole Gaouette, "Senate Gets Tougher on the Border," Los Angeles Times, May 24, 2007, A16.
7. S. A. Miller and Stephen Dinan, "Senate OKs $3 Billion to Guard Border," Washington Times, July 27, 2007, http://www.washingtontimes.com/apps/pbcs.dll/article?AID=/20070727/NATION/107270098/1001 (accessed September 1, 2007).
8. Mandalit Del Barco, "Spanish-Language DJ Turns Out the Crowds in LA," National Public Radio, April 12, 2006, http://www.npr.org/templates/story/story.php?storyId=5337941 (accessed September 1, 2007).
9. Carmen Gonzalez, "Latino Mobilization: Emergent Latino Mobilization via Communication Networks" (unpublished seminar paper, Annenberg School for Communication, University of Southern California, Los Angeles, 2006).
10. Graciela Orozco, Understanding the May 1st Immigrant Rights Mobilizations (New York City: Social Science Research Council/Media Hub, 2007), http://mediaresearchhub.ssrc.org/grants/sponsored-projects/preliminary-report-on-qualitative-study-of-immigrant-latino-audiences (accessed July 10, 2007). See also http://www.radiobilingue.org/.
11. For more on Indymedia, see Dorothy Kidd, "Indymedia.org: A New Communications Commons," in Cyberactivism: Online Activism in Theory and Practice, ed. M. Ayers (New York: Routledge, 2003), 47–69.
12. This is not a new process; see Tiziana Terranova, "Free Labor: Producing Culture for the Digital Economy," Social Text 8.2 (2000): 33–58.
13. This is clear even to casual observers of the "new media" industry, but researchers need to better document these inequalities.
14. For example, see the internal debate over the "citizen's summit" parallel to the World Summit on the Information Society at http://lists.ou.edu/cgi-bin/wa?A2=ind0510&L=ourmedia-l&F=PP&S=&P=5372 (accessed September 20, 2007).
15. Amy Goodman and Juan Gonzalez, "Students Protest Anti-Immigrant Bill," WireTap, March 29, 2006, http://www.wiretapmag.org/immigration/34230/ (accessed July 24, 2007). See also Democracy Now transcript, http://www.democracynow.org/article.pl?sid=06/03/29/154212#transcript (accessed September 20, 2007).
16. Sasha Costanza-Chock, "Mapping the Repertoire of Electronic Contention," in Representing Resistance: Media, Civil Disobedience, and the Global Justice Movement, ed. Andrew Opel and Donnalyn Pompper (Westport, Conn.: Greenwood) , 173–91; John Downing, Radical Media: Rebellious Communication and Social Movements (Thousand Oaks, Calif.: Sage Publications, 2001); Dorothy Kidd, "Indymedia.org: A New Communications Commons," in Cyberactivism: Online Activism in Theory and Practice, ed. M. Ayers (New York: Routledge, 2003) , 47–69.
17. danah boyd, "Viewing American Class Divisions through Facebook and MySpace," Apophenia blog essay, June 24, 2007, http://www.danah.org/papers/essays/ClassDivisions.html (accessed September 1, 2007).
18. Dmytri Kleiner and Brian Wyrick, "InfoEnclosure 2.0," Mute Magazine, January 2007, http://www.metamute.org/en/InfoEnclosure-2.0 (accessed August 24, 2007).
19. Andrew Lowenthal, "Free Media vs. Free Beer," March 2007, http://www.transmission.cc/node/86 (accessed May 10, 2007).
20. Bratton, William. 2007. Testimony to Board of Police Commissioners, Regular Meeting, Tuesday, May 8, 2007, Parker Center, LA.
21. Personal communication, Indymedia Video Distribution Network mailing list, May 17, 2007.
22. Unfortunately, this space itself seems to have been pushed to the margins of the USSF. See https://www.ussf2007.org/en/mjc (accessed September 20, 2007).

Contributors

Laura Briggs

Laura Briggs is head of the Department of Women's Studies at the University of Arizona and author of *Reproducing Empire: Race, Sex, Science, and U.S. Imperialism in Puerto Rico*. She is currently writing a history of transnational and transracial adoption and is coediting a volume with Diana Marre on intercountry adoption that draws together scholars from many nations.

Rachel Ida Buff

Rachel Ida Buff teaches in the history department and the Comparative Ethnic Studies Program at the University of Wisconsin–Milwaukee. She is editor of the collection *Immigrant Rights in the Shadows of Citizenship* (New York University Press, 2008).

Sarika Chandra

Sarika Chandra is an assistant professor of English at Wayne State University. She teaches in the areas of globalization studies and contemporary American literary/cultural studies. Currently she is working on a book-length project that examines the convergence of concepts such as Americanization, travel, ethnicity and nationalism with theories of globalization.

Kornel Chang

Kornel Chang is an assistant professor of history and Asian American studies at the University of Connecticut, Storrs, and a postdoctoral fellow and visiting assistant professor of American studies and the Program in Ethnicity, Race, and Migration at Yale University. His current book project is a study of the U.S.-Canadian borderlands in the Pacific world, examining the transnational dynamics that gave rise to a regional world with shifting boundaries in the nineteenth and early twentieth centuries.

Sasha Costanza-Chock

Sasha Costanza-Chock is a media activist and researcher who works on the political economy of communication, tactical media production, and the transnational movement for communication rights. He holds a BA from

Harvard University and an MA from the Annenberg School for Communication at the University of Pennsylvania, and is a PhD candidate at the University of Southern California. He lives in Los Angeles and is working to help grassroots immigrant rights organizations build stronger popular communication strategies.

Fatima El-Tayeb

Fatima El-Tayeb is an assistant professor for African American culture and film in the Department of Literature at UC San Diego. Originally from Germany, she was active in black, migrant, queer, and feminist organizing there and in the Netherlands. She is coauthor of the movie *Everything Will Be Fine* and cofounder of the Black European Studies Project. Her first book, *Schwarze Deutsche*, published in German in 2001, explored the relationship between race and national identity in early-twentieth-century Germany. She has published numerous articles on the interactions of race, gender, sexuality, and nation, and is coediting a special issue on black Europe for *African and Black Diaspora*. She is working on a book on the racialization of migrants and minorities in contemporary Europe and the queering of ethnicity as a minoritarian counterstrategy. She is an Andrew W. Mellon postdoctoral fellow and visiting professor at the University of California, Los Angeles.

Adrián Félix

Adrián Félix is a doctoral candidate in politics and international relations at the University of Southern California. His dissertation research focuses on international migration, immigrant transnationalism, immigrant political mobilization, ethnicity and nationalism, and politics, identity, and culture in rural Mexico. Aside from his research on naturalization, Félix is working on a study of the transnational practice of repatriating the bodies of deceased Mexican migrants from the United States to their hometowns in Mexico.

Graham Finlay

Graham Finlay teaches the history of political thought, human rights, and international justice in the School of Politics and International Relations at University College Dublin.

David G. Gutiérrez

David G. Gutiérrez is a professor of history at the University of California, San Diego, where he has taught since 1990. Educated at the University of

California, Santa Barbara, and Stanford University, he has taught at the University of Utah, Stanford University, and the California Institute of Technology. He is author of *Walls and Mirrors: Mexican Americans, Mexican Immigrants, and the Politics of Ethnicity* (1995), and editor of *Between Two Worlds: Mexican Immigrants in the United States* (1996) and *The Columbia History of Latinos in the United States since 1960* (2004). He is working on a book-length project titled *Antinomies of the Nation: Citizens and Noncitizens in a Transnational Age.*

Pierrette Hondagneu-Sotelo

Pierrette Hondagneu-Sotelo is a professor and the director of graduate studies in the Department of Sociology at the University of Southern California. Her published research has focused on gender and immigration, informal sector work, and religion and the immigrant rights movement. She is the author or editor of seven books, the most recent of which is *God's Heart Has No Borders: How Religious Activists Are Working for Immigrant Rights* (University of California Press, 2008).

Philip Kretsedemas

Philip Kretsedemas is an assistant professor of sociology at the University of Massachusetts, Boston. His research explores the relationship between immigration and the changing discourse on race as well as the impact of social policy and law enforcement on immigrant populations. He is coeditor of *Keeping Out the Other: A Critical Introduction to Immigration Enforcement Today* (Columbia University Press, 2008).

Sunaina Maira

Sunaina Maira is an associate professor of Asian American studies at UC Davis. She is the author of *Desis in the House: Indian American Youth Culture in New York City* (2002). She coedited an anthology, *Contours of the Heart: South Asians Map North America* (1997), which received the American Book Award from the Before Columbus Foundation, and is coeditor of *Youthscapes: The Popular, the National, the Global* (2005). She received a grant from the Russell Sage Foundation for an ethnographic study of South Asian Muslim immigrant youth in the United States and their notions of cultural citizenship after September 11, 2001, which is the basis of her forthcoming book, *Missing: Youth, Citizenship, and Empire After 9/11* (Duke University Press).

J. M. Mancini

J. M. Mancini teaches American and world history at the National University of Ireland, Maynooth. She is vice chair of the Irish Association for American Studies.

Gladys McCormick

Gladys McCormick is completing her PhD in Latin American history at the University of Wisconsin-Madison. Her dissertation compares popular mobilizations in the sugar-growing regions of Morelos, Puebla, in south-central Mexico and the northern state of Tamaulipas. Her research interests include political and economic history, questions of memory and political violence, and the experiences of rural peoples more broadly. Her next project looks at the role of corruption in shaping state-society relations in mid-twentieth-century Mexico. She is a member of the Tepoztlán Institute for Transnational History of the Americas.

Asha Nadkarni

Asha Nadkarni is an assistant professor of English at University of Massachusetts, Amherst, where she teaches courses in postcolonial literature and theory, transnational feminism, and literatures and cultures of the South Asian diaspora. She is working on a book project about feminism, nationalism, and development in the United States and India. This book traces an often overlooked conversation between U.S. and Indian nationalist feminisms, suggesting that both launch their claims to feminist citizenship based on modernist constructions of the reproductive body as the origin of the nation.

Elaine Peña

Elaine Peña received her PhD in performance studies at Northwestern University. She is an assistant professor of American studies at George Washington University and a postdoctoral associate and lecturer at Yale University's MacMillan Center for International and Area Studies. She holds appointments in the Ethnicity, Race, and Migration Program; religious studies; and the American studies department. Among her publications, Peña is most proud of her work with performance artist and cultural critic Guillermo Gómez-Peña. She edited and wrote the introduction for *Ethno-Techno: Writings on Performance, Activism, and Pedagogy* (Routledge, 2005). She is preparing a manuscript that engages the intersections among devotional performances, transnational migration circuits, and the political economy of sacred space production titled *Performing Piety: Building, Walking, and Conquering in Central Mexico and the Midwest.*

Claudia Sadowski-Smith

Claudia Sadowski-Smith is an assistant professor of English at Arizona State University. She is the author of *Border Fictions: Globalization, Empire, and Writing at the Boundaries of the United States* (University of Virginia Press, 2008) and the editor of *Globalization on the Line: Culture, Capital, and Citizenship at U.S. Borders* (Palgrave, 2002). She has published several articles on border theory, literatures of the U.S.-Mexico border, and the internationalization of American studies in such journals as *South Atlantic Quarterly, Comparative American Studies, Arizona Quarterly*, and *Diaspora.*

J. T. Way

J. T. Way received his PhD in history from Yale University in 2006. His forthcoming book, *The Mayan in the Mall: Development, Globalization, and the Making of Modern Guatemala* (a transnational work), explores the processes of "development from above" and "development from below" in Guatemala from 1920 to 2000. It argues that far from being "underdeveloped," Guatemala has participated fully in the development process throughout its modern history. He lives and works in Panajachel, Guatemala, where he founded the Atitlán Multicultural Academy, a progressive international school. He also serves as president of the John T. Way Global Education Foundation, Inc., a nonprofit that exists to promote education in Guatemala, and for two summers he has taught for the University of Arizona Study Abroad program at CIRMA in Antigua, Guatemala.

Julie M. Weise

Julie M. Weise is an assistant professor of international studies at California State University, Long Beach. She received her PhD in history at Yale University in 2009. Her larger research project explores the histories of Mexicans and Mexican Americans in the U.S. South from 1910 to 2010. She has presented her research at conferences for the Latin American Studies Association and the Southern Historical Association, and will be presenting for the American Studies Association and the Organization of American Historians. Her work on Mississippi and Arkansas appeared in *Latino America: State by State* encyclopedia (2008).

Index

Immigration Act of 1924, 75
Immigration Act of 1965, 200
Immigration and Customs Enforcement (ICE), 23–24, 28–29, 34, 38–39, 41, 43–44, 295, 349
Immigration and Nationality Act, 239
Immigration and Naturalization Services (INS), 33, 34, 86, 88, 349
Immigration Customs Enforcement Mutual Agreement between Government and Employers (IMAGE), 43
India and Indian immigrant(s), 303–25, 366; assimilation of, 310; and Australia, 76; and caste system, 355; and citizenship, 314; and economic development, 210; films, 207; Muslims, 200, 211; national history, 12; nationalism, 306–7, 315–17; Non-Resident Indian (NRI) / Person of Indian Origin (PIO), 206; and resistance to imperialism, 14; restaurant(s), 195; state socialism, 128; stores, 197, 211; technomigrants, 212; and the U.S., 134; youth, 200, 205
Indian nations, 21, 23, 43, 171, 225, 262; in British Columbia, 186; Lumbee, 42
indigenous spirituality, 219
Indonesia, 7, 167
inegalitarian ascriptive principles, 87
information war, 350, 353
INS. See Immigration and Naturalization Services
institute for historical and theological worship, 224
Institute of Popular Education of Southern California (IDEPSCA), 351
intellectual movement, 126
internationalism, 30, 92, 123, 125
Internet, 349–63
interracialism, 255
Iraq, 24, 133, 148, 153, 159, 211, 332
Ireland: immigration to, 10; Irish Nationality and Citizenship Act, 73, 78, 92; Irish Citizenship Referendum, 77–82
Italy, 10, 76, 131, 283

Jalisco, 105, 235
Jamaica, 233, 338
Jerusalem, 157, 223
Jim Crow, 13, 23, 250–51, 254–55, 257, 259–60, 268, 270, 289
Johnson, Lyndon B., 73
Judeo-Christianity, 154

Jung, Karl, 263
jus soli, 85–92

Kaplan, Amy, 213, 320, 321
Kennedy, Edward M. (Ted), 38, 64
Kerber, Linda, 86
Kerry, John, 38
Keynesianism, 60
kinship, 135, 139, 185, 204, 214, 293
Korea, 33, 34, 139, 171, 179, 219, 351
Koreatown Immigrant Worker Alliance (KIWA), 351
Ku Klux Klan, 42–43

labor movement, 36
legalization of immigrants: 5, 101, 116, 208, 254, 277, 352
liberalization: of citizenship laws, 75; of U.S. economy, 63
lynching, 21

machismo, 128, 130
mainland-island networks, 338
marginalization of Europeans of color, 159, 162, 164
market-driven logic, 58
massacre(s), 138, 157, 181, 206
materialism, 308
Mayo, Katherine. See *Mother India*
McCarthy, Eugene, 37, 215
McCarthy era, 9
Mckay, Steve, 32
mercantilism, 339
mestizo, 140, 225, 251, 261
metanarratives, 339
Mexico and Mexican immigrant(s): agricultural workers, 6; assimilation of, 100, 104, 116, 120, 247, 336; citizenship and, 4, 113, 221, 221, 286; deportation of, 27–29; nationalism of, 117–19, 259–71; upper class, 259, 261, 269–70; U.S. border with, 26. See also Bracero Program
micropolitics, 199
militarization: of borders 28, 349; of domestic and international life, 33; global, 26; of Mexico-U.S. border, 290, 296, 297, 349, 352; and privatization, 136; against terror, 21; of the Western hemisphere, 39
miscegenation, 318
MIWON. See Multi-Ethnic Immigrant Worker Network

religion(s) and religiosity, 13. *See also* Catholic(s); Judeo-Christianity; Protestant(s); Virgen de Guadalupe
religious movement, 305
revolution, 13, 43, 92, 128, 100, 252, 270, 340
right-wing: state in Portugal, 35, 37; U.S. media, 350, 353
Rivera, Alex, ix–x
Rofel, Lisa, 134
Roosevelt, Eleanor, 91
Roosevelt, Theodore, 179, 181

Sánchez, George, 32, 100, 101, 256
Sargent, Frank (U.S. Commissioner-General of Immigration), 182
Saudi Arabia, 214
Schwarzenegger, Arnold, 29, 99, 100, 119
Scott, Joan, 135, 136, 137, 145
Second Tepeyac, 219–25, 233; development, 234; and Día de la Raza, 239; and diversity, 242; meaning of, 235; organizers, 231; popular appeal, 228; religious sanctuary and, 238
September 11, 2001 (9/11): and the Bush administration, 211; and terrorist "others," 9; and clash of civilizations, 158; climate/context/moment, 12, 102, 198; and detention and deportation, 23–24, 34, 207; and flexible citizenship, 210, 212; and immigrant youth, 199; legislative changes since, 298, 349; and naturalization, 203; personal reflections on, 195, 196; scapegoating of Muslims after, 201; terror threats and, 206, 208; War on Terror, 61, 209; world, 147
Sleep Dealer, The, ix–x
Singapore, 7, 291
Smith Act of 1940, 26
socialism, 126–29
Social Science Research Council (SSRC), 124
social welfare benefits, 83
socioeconomic, 59, 344, 345
sociohistorical, 328, 332, 338, 340
solidarity movement, 128
South African Citizenship Act, 76
South Asian immigrants, 179, 184, 186, 200, 204
spatial segregation, 160
SSRC. *See* Social Science Research Council
Stalinism, 151
state(s): and power, 9, 26; and violence, 118
statelessness, 23, 30, 31, 34, 35
Steerage Act, 280, 281

structural racism, 160
sweatshop(s), 39
Sweden, 75, 92, 233
Swing, Joseph M., 33, 34

Tepoztlán Institute, 124
Third World feminism, 126
Third World, 127: and development, 88, 139; feminism(s), 11, 126; within First World, 130; nationalisms, 125; and publishing, 141
Thoreau, Henry, 305, 328, 329
time-space, 212, 228
totalitarianism, 24
transatlantic: trade systems, 283; Western unity, 148
transborder: labor, 171, 172; mobility of Asian migrants, 178, 190, 191; world, 169
Transcultural Women, 334
transmigrants, 3, 5, 8, 9, 13, 139
transnationalism: anti-imperial, 126; category, 123–26; corporate, 125, 290; European public, 148; geneaolgies, 126–31; and immigration, 196; interventions, 131–35; history, 135–43; migrant response, 201
transnationality, 16
Turkey, 157, 283
Tuskegee Institute, 261

Ukraine, 291, 295
underclass, 159, 160, 162, 256, 266
underdevelopment, 88, 136, 144, 156
undocumented immigrant(s): and children/families, 10, 116; Chinese, 297; from Europe and Asia, 279; as "illegal aliens," 77; and INS, 103; intersections among, 298; Irish, 292–93; and law enforcement, 278; Mexican, 296; movement, 282; and networks, 294; and public services, 103; racialized differently, 296; and Wal-Mart, 295; youth, 203
unions, 30, 36, 83, 137, 295
upper middle class, the, 200
uprising(s), 148, 155, 160, 266
U.S. citizenship, 14, 101, 247, 259; benefits of, 205; and immigrant political engagement; 10, 14; and Indian eligibility, 305, 314; and Mexican nationals, 106, 288; and naturalization, 120; and permanent residency, 201; and race, 87, 250, 264, 269; reasons for, 5; and regulation, 91